Defending Deterrence

* Sample copies available upon request

Defending Deterrence

MANAGING THE ABM TREATY REGIME

INTO THE 21ST CENTURY

EDITED BY

Antonia Handler Chayes

AND

Paul Doty

PRODUCED UNDER THE AUSPICES OF
THE AMERICAN ACADEMY OF ARTS & SCIENCES

 PERGAMON-BRASSEY'S
International Defense Publishers, Inc.

| *Washington* | *New York* | *London* | *Oxford* | *Beijing* |
| *Frankfurt* | *São Paulo* | *Sydney* | *Tokyo* | *Toronto* |

U.S.A. (Editorial)	Pergamon-Brassey's International Defense Publishers, Inc. 8000 Westpark Drive, Fourth Floor, McLean, Virginia 22102, U.S.A.
(Orders)	Pergamon Press Inc., Maxwell House, Fairview Park, Elmsford, New York 10523, U.S.A.
U.K. (EDITORIAL)	Brassey's Defence Publishers Ltd., 24 Gray's Inn Road, London WC1X 8HR, England
(ORDERS)	Brassey's Defence Publishers, Headington Hill Hall, Oxford OX3 OBW, England
PEOPLE'S REPUBLIC OF CHINA	Pergamon Press, Room 4037, Qianmen Hotel, Beijing, People's Republic of China
FEDERAL REPUBLIC OF GERMANY	Pergamon Press GmbH, Hammerweg 6, D-6242 Kronberg, Federal Republic of Germany
BRAZIL	Pergamon Editora Ltda, Rua Eça de Queiros, 346, CEP 04011, Paraiso, São Paulo, Brazil
AUSTRALIA	Pergamon-Brassey's Defence Publishers Ltd., P.O. Box 544, Potts Point, N.S.W. 2011, Australia
JAPAN	Pergamon Press, 5th Floor, Matsuoka Central Building, 1-7-1 Nishishinjuku, Shinjuku-ku, Tokyo 160, Japan
CANADA	Pergamon Press Canada, Suite No. 271, 253 College Street, Toronto, Ontario, Canada M5T 1R5

Pergamon-Brassey's books are available at special discounts for bulk purchases for sales promotions, premiums, fund-raising, or education use through the
Special Sales Director
Macmillan Publishing Company
866 Third Avenue, New York, NY 10022

Library of Congress Cataloging-in-Publication Data
Defending deterrence : managing the ABM treaty into the 21st century / edited by Antonia Handler Chayes & Paul Doty. — 1st ed.
p.   cm.
Includes bibliographies and index.
Contents: Introduction and scope / by Paul Doty & Antonia Handler Chayes — Underlying military objectives / by Ashton B. Carter — The political environment / by Ralph Earle II — The legal environment / by John B. Rhinelander & Sherri Wasserman Goodman — The nature and purpose of ABM research / by John C. Toomay & Robert T. Marsh — Non-ABM technologies with ABM potential / by Richard L. Garwin & Theodore Jarvis — Ground-based ABM systems / by Thomas H. Johnson — Limitations and allowances for space-based weapons / by Ashton B. Carter — Limits on and adaptions for sensors / by John Pike & Barry Fridling — Assessing verification and compliance / by Sidney N. Graybeal & Patricia B. McFate — Living under a treaty regime : compliance, interpretation, and adaption / by Abram Chayes & Antonia Handler Chayes — Managing the ABM treaty regime / by Albert Carnesale.
ISBN 0-08-036744-5 : $24.95
1. Soviet Union. Treaties, etc. United States. 1972 May 26 (ABM) 2. Nuclear arms control—United States. 3. Nuclear arms control—Soviet Union. I. Chayes, Antonia Handler, 1929–0 II. Doty, Paul.
JX1974.7.D425   1989   89-31090
327.1'74—dc19   CIP

British Library Cataloguing in Publication Data
Defending deterrence : managing the ABM treaty into the 21st century.
1. Warfare. Deterrence
I. Chayes, Antonia Handler II. Doty, Paul
355'.0217
ISBN 0-08-036744-5

Designed by Jack Meserole
PRINTED IN THE UNITED STATES OF AMERICA

10   9   8   7   6   5   4   3   2   1

CONTENTS

FOREWORD

On October 6, 1988, the Senate and House Armed Services committees held an unusual joint hearing on the outgoing Reagan administration's major restructuring of the Strategic Defense Initiative (SDI) program. During the hearing, I asked General Robert T. Herres, the vice chairman of the Joint Chiefs of Staff (JCS), what the Joint Chiefs' position was as to the continued value of the 1972 Anti-Ballistic Missile (ABM) Treaty.

Speaking for the Joint Chiefs, General Herres declared: "Our view is that we should continue to abide by the ABM Treaty until it is clear when we should withdraw and for what purpose we should withdraw. . . . A deployment decision for Phase One would be the only reason that we would see on the horizon." When questioned as to when the United States would be in a position to make an informed decision whether to deploy an SDI Phase One defense in contravention of the Treaty, General Herres replied, "I think we are talking about the mid-1990s." General Herres added that actual deployments of SDI Phase One weapon systems that could make a "militarily significant contribution to deterrence" could not occur until "just after the turn of the century."

General Herres's time frame reflected the substantial annual increases in the SDI budget that were forecast by the Reagan administration in its final defense budget request. However, a more realistic assessment is that Congress will hold SDI to a roughly level funding profile, with increases sufficient for covering the cost of inflation and a small, steady growth, thereby further extending the date by which a fundamental deployment decision on Phase One will likely have to be confronted.

In light of these considerations, it is only prudent that we carefully and objectively examine the question of how we keep the ABM Treaty viable for at least the next decade. That is the task that is so admirably addressed in *Defending Deterrence: Managing the ABM Treaty Regime into the 21st Century*, edited by Antonia Chayes and Paul Doty. As Chayes and Doty note in their introduction, "This book is based upon the premise that the United States will continue to rely on deterrence provided by offensive nuclear systems well into the next century and will want to continue the support that the ABM Treaty supplies to that posture."

The book draws together informative and insightful essays by a number of distinguished commentators on the technological, political, legal, and diplomatic dimensions of these critical national security challenges. It concludes with a wide range of possible policy choices for the consideration of decision-makers, including options for making the current ABM regime either more restrictive or more permissive.

As Chayes and Doty emphasize, the book neither attempts to make those choices nor offers any single prescription for the future. However, in illuminating the pros and cons of alternative approaches for managing the ABM Treaty regime, this study performs an extremely valuable service for all those who are concerned about preserving deterrence and strengthening strategic stability through the end of this century and beyond.

Senator Sam Nunn
March 30, 1989

PREFACE AND ACKNOWLEDGMENTS

An ABM Treaty of unlimited duration had to cope with what has always been a dilemma of arms control: Technology moves forward, leaving arms control behind: scientists are forever coming up with weapons, more sophisticated and capable than those that diplomats have in mind as they haggle over treaty language. Scientific breakthroughs—the development of new devices—translate into military breakthroughs—the development of new weapons that upset the strategic stability.[1]

—STROBE TALBOTT

By the end of 1987, the hostility that had marked the superpower relationship since the Soviet invasion of Afghanistan began to ease. New channels of communication were opening between the United States and the Soviet Union. The heads of state of the two nations had met three times between 1985 and 1988 and discussed a wide range of issues affecting mutual security. The INF Treaty banning all intermediate-range nuclear forces had been concluded, and negotiations to reduce strategic offensive forces were well under way. Although the United States remained concerned about Soviet treaty violations, the Soviets had ceased construction on the phased-array radar at Krasnoyarsk, the most nettlesome and least deniable of the alleged violations.

In this changing atmosphere, it seemed important to reexamine the one arms control treaty then in force between the superpowers, the Anti-Ballistic Missile (ABM) Treaty. In that Treaty, the parties agreed to impose stringent limitations on the development, testing, and deployment of defenses against attack from strategic nuclear missiles. These limits allowed each side to feel some confidence in the retaliatory capability of its strategic offensive forces, since neither would be impelled to increase its arsenal to overcome defenses of uncertain effectiveness. That confidence became a cornerstone of mutual deterrence, which is widely believed to be an essential condition for the reduction of strategic nuclear forces.

The notion of mutual deterrence has been widely criticized in recent years. In seeking a less stressful basis for the superpower relationship, some have advocated a freeze on offensive forces, others a declaration of no first use of nuclear forces, and still others the technical pursuit of strategic defenses. By late 1987, however, the challenges to mutual deterrence seemed to have lost their immediacy. The likelihood of replacing deterrence with a full population defense seemed remote, as it became apparent that research was not revealing any practical solutions. Nevertheless, the ABM Treaty was clearly under both technological and political pressure, which could only increase with advancing technologies and continuing dissatisfaction with the strategy of deterrence.

What can be done to safeguard the equilibrium provided by the ABM Treaty? The editors proposed to convene a working group to consider what might be required to assure the durability and adaptability of a treaty regime based on a continuing strategy of deterrence. We emphasized the notion of a "treaty regime" rather than the Treaty itself, because many current and future issues were not, and could not have been, addressed explicitly by the drafters of the ABM Treaty in 1972. An adequate examination of this problem clearly required participants with backgrounds in science and technology, national security, military matters, law, and diplomacy. The premises set forth in chapter 1 governed the choice of participants to some extent, but every attempt was made to seek a wide range of both political views and relevant experience.

Defending Deterrence: Managing the ABM Treaty Regime into the 21st Century represents the fruits of the inquiry carried out by the working group of twenty listed on the following page together with the stimulus of several younger academics specializing in national security matters. The work involved more than fifteen day-long meetings over a year's time, and much additional time in writing, critiquing and editing successive chapter drafts. (One coauthored chapter went through twenty-three drafts.)

Ashton Carter, Abram Chayes, and John Rhinelander served with us as an editorial committee and were unstinting in their willingness to think through the completeness and logic of the organization of the book and its underlying premises and to edit the authors' work. Ashton Carter, Richard Garwin, Daniel Fisher (an outside critic), and Charles Zraket gave invaluable assistance in assuring technical soundness and helping to reconcile differences in technical outlook. The dedication, hard work, patience, persistence, and cooperation of the entire working group made for a process that deepened the thinking and enhanced the product of each author.

The convening powers of the American Academy of Arts and Sciences and its atmosphere, so conducive to productive meetings, were critical to the project. The support and encouragement of its Committee on International Security Studies and its executive director, Jeffrey Boutwell, were also very helpful to our work. But above all it was the prompt and generous support of the Carnegie Corporation, the MacArthur Foundation, and the Rockefeller Family Fund that made this inquiry possible.

We are deeply grateful to Nancy Jackson, our editor, whose insistence on clarity and whose refusal to accept opaque and awkward passages helped make a highly technical subject more accessible to the reader. We also thank our rapporteurs, Captain Joseph Wood and Sarah Chayes, for turning discursive talk into useful summaries. Finally, we express our thanks to our research assistant, Caroline R. Russell, who picked up the project toward its completion and shepherded it through the publication process.

Antonia Handler Chayes
Paul Doty
February 23, 1989

Note

1. Strobe Talbott, *Master of the Game* (New York: Alfred A. Knopf, 1988), p. 129.

WORKING GROUP MEMBERS

Dr. Albert Carnesale
Professor of Public Policy
Academic Dean
Harvard University

Dr. Ashton B. Carter
Professor of Public Policy
Associate Director, CSIA
Harvard University

Abram Chayes
Felix Frankfurter Professor of Law
Harvard University

Antonia Handler Chayes, Esq.
Chairman
Endispute, Inc.
Former Under Secretary of the U.S.
    Air Force

Dr. Paul Doty
Professor of Public Policy
Director Emeritus, CSIA
Harvard University

Ambassador Ralph Earle II
Chairman of the National
    Advisory Board,
The Lawyers Alliance for Nuclear
    Arms Control
Former Director of ACDA
    and chief SALT II negotiator

Dr. Barry E. Fridling
Research Staff
Science & Technology Division
Institute for Defense Analyses

Dr. Richard L. Garwin
IBM Fellow and Science Advisor
Thomas J. Watson Research Center
IBM Corporation

Sherri Wasserman Goodman, Esq.
Staff Member
Senate Armed Services Committee

Ambassador Sidney N. Graybeal
Senior Vice President, Policy and
    Planning
System Planning Corporation
Former Director of the CIA Office of
    Strategic Research and U.S. Com-
    missioner of the Standing Consulta-
    tive Commission (SCC)

Dr. Theodore Jarvis, Jr.
Director, Strategic Studies
The MITRE Corporation

Lieutenant Colonel Thomas H. Johnson
Professor of Applied Physics
Director of the Science Research Lab-
    oratory
U.S. Military Academy

General Robert T. Marsh
U.S. Air Force, Retired

Dr. Patricia Bliss McFate
Senior Scientist
Systems Planning Corporation

Philip O'Neill, Esq.
Edwards & Angell

John E. Pike
Associate Director of Space Policy
Federation of American Scientists

John B. Rhinelander, Esq.
Shaw, Pittman, Potts & Trowbridge
Former legal adviser to the U.S.
   SALT I Delegation

Dr. Jack Ruina
Professor of Electrical Engineering
Director of Defense and Arms Control
   Studies
Massachusetts Institute of Technology

General John C. Toomay
U.S. Air Force, Retired

Charles A. Zraket
President and CEO
The MITRE Corporation

I

INTRODUCTION AND SCOPE OF STUDY

Paul Doty and Antonia Handler Chayes

THIS BOOK seeks to determine whether and how the underlying objectives of the 1972 Treaty Limiting Anti-Ballistic Missile Systems (the ABM Treaty) can be preserved in a rapidly changing technological and political environment. The major premise of the Treaty, as stated in the preamble was "that effective measures to limit anti-ballistic missile systems would be a substantial factor in curbing the race in strategic offensive arms." The Soviet Union and the United States had calculated that despite the enormous power of their thermonuclear forces, defensive deployment by one side could shake the other's confidence in its retaliatory capacity. This in turn would lead to an increase in offensive weaponry to ensure that the retaliatory mission could still be performed effectively. The linkage between defense and offense remains a fact of life.

The book is not about the merits or practicality of the Strategic Defense Initiative (SDI). Most experts agree that no system will be available for the foreseeable future that would support a strategy based upon a defensive shield against nuclear attack.

This book is based upon the premise that the United States will continue to rely on deterrence provided by offensive nuclear systems well into the next century and will want to continue the support that the ABM Treaty supplies to that posture.

It is the product of a year-long study by a group of technical, legal, and military experts with wide-ranging political and policy views. We have come together to explore how the ABM Treaty can best be managed through the 1990s and beyond. We have focused on ensuring that the development of emerging technologies with potential military and civilian applications remains compatible with a treaty regime prohibiting the development, testing, and deployment of nationwide ballistic missile defenses.

This book offers options and a framework for making policy choices among them. It does not attempt to make those choices. It seeks to illuminate the policy implications of some technical issues that were at the center of serious arms control debate for most of the Reagan years but were not readily accessible to even an informed public. Beyond the specific issues posed by the ABM Treaty, the study also bears on the broader need to find ways to adapt any arms control treaty to the inevitable changes in the political and technological environment. It is concerned with both substance and process.

Background

The ABM Treaty and the Interim Agreement on Limitations of Strategic Offensive Weapons, which together make up SALT I, were companion agreements concluded in 1972 between the United States and the Soviet Union. Accepting the logic of an inextricable linkage between offensive and defensive constraints, the ABM Treaty sharply limited defensive systems, and the Interim Agreement put various constraints on offensive systems. The Interim Agreement expired by its terms in 1977. The SALT II Treaty of 1979, planned as the follow-on, was signed by the parties but was withdrawn from the Senate and never ratified. Until 1988, when the Intermediate-Range Nuclear Force (INF) Treaty was ratified, the ABM Treaty remained the only nuclear arms control agreement in full force and effect between the United States and the Soviet Union.

The two superpowers have responded to the inevitable stalemate of the nuclear age primarily by increasing the number, accuracy, and variety of weapons in their nuclear arsenals. They have sought to deter attack by assuring that a sufficient nuclear capability to retaliate would survive. Throughout the 1950s and 1960s, both nations also tried out defensive systems designed to blunt and neutralize a nuclear attack. With the signing of the ABM Treaty, they sharply curtailed this effort. To achieve some measure of stability, they agreed to limit ABM deployments to a token force, with severe constraints on ABM development as well. They struck a balance between offense and defense that overwhelmingly favored offense.[1] In essence, they judged defensive systems to be unequal to the task of true defense and a needless distraction from the inevitable state of mutual deterrence.

For the United States, the ABM Treaty was based on three major premises:

First, that the only insurance against nuclear war for the foreseeable future remained a stable nuclear deterrent based on invulnerable second-strike forces.

Second, that agreed qualitative and quantitative restraints on strategic offensive forces could enhance stability.

Third, in the current state of relatively ineffective defenses against nuclear weapons, development and testing of air- or space-based antiballistic missile systems would reduce each side's confidence in its retaliatory capability, erode stability, and undermine incentives to limit strategic offensive forces. Since there was little reason to believe that rudimentary ABM technology could provide a cost-effective defense, ABM deployment would stimulate additional offensive deployments and countermeasures, thereby accelerating the arms race.

Whether the Soviets accepted these premises is a matter of conjecture. They may well have been motivated by other factors, particularly a fear that the United States could surpass them in a high-technology race. For whatever reason, they decided that the theoretical benefits of ballistic missile defense (BMD) systems were offset by the dangers of an unbridled offensive arms race and intensified competition in military technology. In agreeing to the ABM Treaty, the Soviets appeared to have accepted the American position on offense-defense linkage that, as chapter 3 points out, they had rejected at the Glassboro summit in 1967.

The Underlying Purpose of the ABM Treaty

Unlike the INF Treaty, the ABM Treaty was not intended to eliminate an entire class of weapons systems. Its provisions might have proven simpler and clearer had that been its aim. But President Nixon rejected the idea of total elimination, both for domestic political reasons and because it was felt to be nonnegotiable. As Rhinelander and Goodman state in chapter 4:

> Although [the Treaty] text reflects trade-offs important to the time, its central thrust is to prohibit the United States and Soviet Union from deploying an ABM system that could provide a nationwide defense or even an effective area defense.

Thus, although a token deployment was permitted, the major effort was to create a buffer zone so that neither party could come close enough to a deployment to be worrisome to the other. In chapter 2, Carter derives three principles from the structure of the Treaty that, taken together, describe this buffer zone:

1. It should be impossible for either party to deploy an ABM system that is militarily threatening (i.e., that would substantially interfere with any mission of strategic offensive forces).

2. The parties should be barred from creating a "base" that would enable one side to deploy a system more rapidly than the other could counter offensively or match defensively. Otherwise the parties would have to hedge aggressively against the possibility of such a breakout.

3. Military systems deployed for other, non-ABM purposes should not be capable of a militarily threatening ABM breakout or providing a "base" for a subsequent defensive deployment.

In practice, he says, the buffer is assured by the need for "conspicuous and time-consuming testing, manufacturing, site preparation, construction, satellite launching and other deployment activities" before a party could achieve anything approaching a significant defensive capability. The original ABM Treaty met these criteria. But today, emerging technologies with ABM potential raise the question whether the original language is sufficient to support the underlying Treaty objectives now and into the next century. These issues are examined in detail in chapters 4 and 6 through 9.

The Challenges to the Treaty Regime

The ABM Treaty faces both political and technical challenges. Americans are still largely agreed that, under present technological conditions, a defensive strategy cannot supplant reliance on deterrence. But some want to explore the possibility that new technology will eventually change this situation. They want to know whether the ABM Treaty unduly constrains the exploration of a defensive alternative. This is a legitimate question, and this book attempts to provide some reasoned answers.

THE TECHNOLOGICAL CHALLENGE

Since the Treaty entered into force in 1972, scientific and technological developments have challenged the buffer it provides and will continue to do so in the future. Striking improvements in ground-based ABM systems may be made possible by advances in microelectronics that permit target acquisition, precision tracking, and interception to be performed in large part on board the interceptor rather than from vulnerable ground-based radars. Moreover, improvements in the guidance of interceptor missiles may make it possible to substitute conventional for nuclear interceptor warheads or even to rely on simple direct impact. Advances in technology also benefit the offense, thus complicating any effort to shift the offense-defense balance.

Space-based ABM concepts present technical advantages and disadvantages wholly different from those of the ground-based systems that were the main concern of the 1972 negotiators. If directed-energy or beam weapons in space over enemy territory could be given sufficient power and accuracy, they could destroy attacking missiles in the boost phase. Or, since such weapons could reach targets at the speed of light and shift quickly from target to target, they might be able to destroy warheads in their midcourse trajectory, provided the targets could be distinguished from decoys. The capabilities of sensors, communications, and sophisticated software for managing components have all reached levels that, although foreseen, could not have been systematically addressed in 1972.

Soviet efforts since that time are partly known and partly a matter of conjecture. The Soviet Union has maintained its ground-based system around Moscow, continually improving its capability, in conformity with the provisions of the Treaty. An extensive modernization program was begun in 1978. When it is completed, the system will consist of two layers: silo-based modified Galosh missiles designed to intercept incoming missiles outside the atmosphere; and Gazelle high-acceleration missiles, also silo-based, for interception at shorter ranges within the atmosphere—100 launchers in all. Associated engagement and guidance radars include the new large, four-sided phased-array radar located at Pushkino, north of Moscow, for battle management.

The extent and quality of Soviet efforts in more exotic directions comparable to the U.S. SDI are not described in detail in the unclassified literature and are probably not known to the United States with any confidence.[2] There is a concerted Soviet effort to improve the permitted ground-based defense system around Moscow, development activity associated with traditional ground-based radars and interception systems, and sufficient other ambiguous activity at known military test sites to be consistent with a moderately paced, long-term effort to develop ground-based lasers and to explore a variety of directed-energy space capabilities.

Although the United States has expressed concern about Soviet violations of the Treaty, none of these involves testing and development of space-based systems or systems involving "other physical principles."

In general, the exploitation of space for military uses has accelerated since the Treaty came into effect. Inevitably, some future developments will conflict with the Treaty's restrictions. Any set of legal prescriptions limiting the capabilities of military technology will require interpretation, new rules of application, and possibly even revision if the original goals are to be met. The ABM Treaty is the pioneering example of such a "living treaty," and its resilience and adaptability can provide a useful model for other situations in which the parties want the benefits of both new technologies and arms control restraints.

THE POLITICAL CHALLENGE

For nearly twelve years the parties to the ABM Treaty stayed with the basic bargain they had struck, albeit uneasily, as their political relationship deteriorated in the late 1970s and early 1980s. Then, in 1983, President Reagan's Strategic

Defense Initiative challenged the fundamental technological and strategic premises on which the bargain had been based. The president's proposition, as it began to be developed, asked for a shift from offense to defense dominance on the premise that an ABM system could be devised that would provide reliable, enduring, and cost-effective nationwide defense. The initial speech was followed by other official statements expressing an intent to deploy a nationwide ABM system as soon as it became technically feasible. Such a deployment, as well as the late stages of research and development leading up to it, would end the bargain made in 1972.

The SDI thus reopened the basic question of whether U.S. security is best served by the traditional doctrine of deterrence, with its reliable threat of retaliation, or by pursuit of defensive deployments that, if realizable, might provide greater security as well as an escape from the risks and moral burdens of nuclear deterrence. The political allure of this vision is immense. As Earle notes in chapter 3, American public opinion has displayed a persistent duality: a traditional desire for military strength as a bulwark against foreign enemies is accompanied by a concern that the continuous multiplication of forces on both sides might undermine strategic stability.

The technological feasibility of defensive technology has now been under intense study for nearly six years, at a cost of $17 billion. The overwhelming weight of technical and military judgment is that, for the next decade or more, the United States lacks even a candidate ABM system for a defense that would protect its people and military targets, given the possibilities for Soviet countermeasures. The initial, highly ambitious goals set for the SDI program—to offer a total, nationwide, population defense—have now been stretched far into the future. Moreover, it is now widely thought that the costs of any early attempt at nationwide deployment would be prohibitive, especially given the costs of bolstering U.S. offensive forces to assure a retaliatory capability against unconstrained Soviet defenses.

Recently, interest has revived in more limited, though technologically advanced, space-based defenses that could provide substantial protection to land-based missiles and hardened command, control, and communications sites and would also have some antisatellite capability. There is a major change in emphasis from the original vision of a nationwide defense to protect the population, justified as enhancing deterrence rather than replacing it. Although less likely to enjoy the political appeal of the original vision, some SDI supporters see it as a first phase toward a more ambitious nationwide deployment, when technology, political support, and funding become available. Critics claim that even limited defenses are highly destabilizing, placing a premium on a first strike. Moreover, it seems probable that the cost of defense would exceed the cost to the attacker of overcoming it. Under these circumstances, it is unlikely that the technical and financial wherewithal for even this more limited alternative will be forthcoming in the near term. This study therefore assumes that no defensive system that violates the current ABM Treaty will be deployed in this century. Discussions about protection against accidental launch have been couched within the framework of Treaty compliance.[3]

In an attempt to surmount the prohibitions in the ABM Treaty on space-based development and testing, the Reagan administration advanced a reinterpretation of the Treaty. Under this "broad" interpretation, testing and development of space-based systems and components employing "other physical principles" would not be constrained by the Treaty. (In chapter 4, Rhinelander and Goodman summarize the arguments and evidence from the exhaustive analyses in response to the reinterpretation.) The broad interpretation has been rejected by the Congress, by all but one of the SALT I negotiators, and by the substantial weight of legal opinion. Consequently, the current policy of the executive branch is to keep SDI research and development within the limits of the traditional interpretation. Moreover, Congress has reliably prohibited testing under the broad interpretation since fiscal year 1988. The present study therefore assumes that the traditional interpretation of the ABM Treaty will continue to govern. Political challenge to the Treaty has come from the Soviets as well. The large phased-array radar erected in Krasnoyarsk is a clear breach of Treaty provisions. Despite continuous pressure from the United States at all levels, the Soviets have not dismantled the radar and no satisfactory resolution has been reached.

Yet, despite these challenges to the treaty regime, the overall *objectives* of the ABM Treaty as traditionally understood remain in the U.S. interest and will continue to do so at least for some years to come. In that context, the following chapters address the subtle and difficult challenge of finding ways to ensure that the ABM Treaty can continue to serve its purpose in a much changed, and still changing political, military, and technological environment.

The ABM Treaty

The particular terms in which the ABM Treaty was drafted reflect the political, strategic, and technical conditions of 1972. This study speaks of the *treaty regime:* not just the 1972 language, but its abiding objectives and the processes and practices by which they can be maintained over time. Chapter 4 provides a full analysis of the Treaty provisions. Here a brief overview will suffice.[4]

A ban on deployment alone was considered insufficient protection against breakout (abrogation of the Treaty followed by rapid deployment of a defensive system already developed and tested, with components produced and stockpiled). As noted above, most of the Treaty's provisions are designed to prohibit the activities that would ordinarily precede large-scale deployment, creating a buffer against breakout. The principal provisions to this end are

- A prohibition against creating a "base" from which a nationwide system might be rapidly deployed (Article I). The concept of a base is not further defined in the text of the Treaty.
- A prohibition on development and testing of sea-based, air-based, space-based, or mobile land-based ABM systems or components (Article V).
- A prohibition on giving ABM capability to weapons and systems developed to perform other military missions (Article VI).
- A prohibition against "testing non-ABM systems in an ABM mode" (a phrase that is not further elaborated in the Treaty but is further developed in two classified agreed statements in 1987 and 1985).
- A prohibition on the deployment of large phased-array radars except along the periphery of the national territory and oriented outward (where they would be highly vulnerable and would have only limited value for ABM battle management) (Article VI).

The Treaty permits limited, fixed land-based ABM deployments, yet it maintains the principle of a buffer against breakout. Only two deployment sites (later reduced to one) are allowed. The number and location of the ABM interceptors, launchers, and radars at these sites are also highly circumscribed, thereby restricting defensive capability to a confined area. Testing of fixed land-based systems, including components based upon "exotic" technology (i.e., derived from "other physical principles") is allowed at certain fixed ABM test ranges.

The Treaty, unlimited in duration, recognized that new ABM technology would develop in the future. It defines ABM systems in functional or generic terms: "a system to counter strategic ballistic missiles or their elements in flight trajectory." However, the Treaty negotiators could not foresee the exact form that technological developments would take and how they might affect the buffer. Thus, the Treaty could not provide a ready formula for translating its general restrictions into specific or quantitative measures appropriate nearly two decades later.

For the most part, the Treaty does not deal directly with related military activities known to be relevant to the buffer. It does not expressly address air defense. It does not specifically constrain tactical antiballistic missile (ATBM) systems, i.e., defenses against shorter-range ballistic missiles. It does not regulate, much less ban, antisatellite (ASAT) systems. Each party wished to protect certain non-ABM systems it was developing in 1972 and was willing to narrow the buffer against ABM breakout to permit them. Today such systems employ technology that is increasingly relevant to ABM development, as Garwin and Jarvis show in chapter 6. As mentioned above, the Treaty recognizes the problem of potentially impinging technologies by its prohibition against giving ABM capability to systems that are not ABM systems and against testing them "in an ABM mode." The precise technical meaning of these terms is not fully spelled out, however, which has provided much fodder for dispute since 1972.

The ABM Treaty also provided new ways to deal with the issue of compliance, although they may seem rudimentary by today's standards.

- By providing that compliance would be verified by national technical means of verification (NTM), the Treaty legitimized satellite surveillance, a technology that had developed sufficiently to assure visibility of the systems regulated by the Treaty.
- To enhance the effectiveness of monitoring, the Treaty outlawed deliberate concealment measures and interference with NTM.
- It created a new forum, the Standing Consultative Commission (SCC), for adjusting issues of compliance, differing interpretations, and adaptation to changing circumstances.

Living under the Treaty for more than sixteen years has uncovered many ambiguities; some were recognized in 1972 but could not be resolved; others revealed themselves only later. Some of the compromises made in 1972 have been worn thin by experience. For example, chapter 4 points to the need to refine the term *component* now that technology has moved beyond missiles, launchers, and radars, the three examples listed in Article II of the Treaty.

Research is not mentioned in the Treaty and, consistent with the usual rule that what is not prohibited is permitted, it remains unconstrained. Neither party was interested in limiting research. The United States would not accept limitations that could not be verified and, in addition, wanted to maintain a research program of its own as a hedge against Soviet breakout. The Treaty does not draw a line between permitted research and prohibited development. During the negotiations, American representatives proposed a pragmatic distinction between activities that could not be verified by NTM and those that could, which the Soviets appeared to accept.[5] But the formula does not provide effective guidance for research in new technologies, some of which must be carried on in space.

The ABM Treaty was to be "of unlimited duration." But the negotiators necessarily made compromises and cast specific arrangements in terms of the technology that was known, used, or reasonably foreseeable in 1972. Inevitably the passage of time has created the need for some kind of updating.

Policy Issues Arising from Current Technological Developments

The bulk of this study is devoted to a specific examination of planned and potential uses of emerging technologies and the policy choices they present for adaptation of the treaty regime. The study presents a schematic framework for these choices. It groups the possible levels of constraint in three categories, each consistent with the fundamental objective of the existing treaty regime to prevent nationwide ABM deployments and preparations for rapid deployment:

1. *The ABM Treaty approach:* A level of activity corresponding roughly to that embodied in U.S. policy before March 1983 and in U.S. practice to date.
2. *A more restrictive approach:* New and more extensive restraints on collateral or dual-mission technologies, in order to create a more secure buffer against the development of ABM systems.
3. *A more permissive approach:* Considerable development and testing of ABM-relevant technologies, including space-based components, would be permitted. The risks of such a course might be judged acceptable in view of the long lead time required for deployment of any space-based system.

As the final chapter states, although a coherent approach has much to recommend it, there is no implication that one of these approaches must be adopted across the board. The policymaker might find it better to seek tighter restraints in some areas than others: for example, it might be desirable to relax some constraints on space-based sensors, because of their other military uses and the difficulty of defining and verifying the ABM capability of sensors. But in such a case the reduced buffer to deployment might require other adjustments, such as tougher restrictions on weapons.

The three categories are presented as an organizing framework for the array of detailed choices and policies that affect the treaty regime. Against this background, chapters 5 through 9 consider the technical policy issues.

Generals Toomay and Marsh in chapter 5 identify four potential objectives for an ABM research program:

1. Seeking breakthrough ABM capabilities for the United States;
2. Being prepared to respond to a Soviet breakout;
3. Ensuring against technological surprise; and
4. Developing penetration aids for offensive missile forces.

Even though research is formally unconstrained by the Treaty, a number of these research programs may nevertheless encroach on the buffer. A breakthrough program (like SDI) is technically very demanding. Although its initial stages would not violate the Treaty if conducted prudently and without pressures for early deployment, the subsequent demonstration of promising technologies in a system role to confirm overall feasibility would press against and possibly exceed Treaty constraints.

A research program to provide protection against breakout necessarily develops knowledge that would facilitate deployment and, under certain circumstances, might be seen as approaching a "base" for a nationwide system, in violation of Article I of the Treaty. Work on measures to counter an ABM system could involve designing a highly advanced ABM system against which to test those countermeasures. Garwin and Jarvis in chapter 6, however, do not regard penetration aid testing as a threat to the Treaty.

According to the authors of chapter 5, only a program to ensure against technological surprise, involving technology experiments to increase scientific understanding and explore unknown potential, can be said to raise no Treaty questions and leave the buffer completely intact. Yet it is doubtful that a research program of consistently high quality can be maintained or continue to attract large funds if there is no possibility of development and deployment. Thus, the chapter poses hard policy choices about legitimate research pursuits.

In contrast to chapter 5, which considers research programs expressly directed toward ABMs, chapter 6 deals with research on technology, components, and systems for other missions not directly prohibited by the Treaty that may nonetheless erode the Treaty buffer. Such areas of research include surface-to-air missile (SAM) systems for air defense, ATBM systems, offensive penetration aids, ASAT systems and systems for defense of satellites (DSAT), sensors, and civilian space activity. As to each, they ask three questions:

- Would the deployment of a particular system for one of these other purposes result in a significant ABM capability?
- Would such a deployment create a significant base for rapid breakout from the Treaty?
- Would research and development on advanced versions of these systems erode the buffer?

Garwin and Jarvis agree with Johnson in chapter 7 that current air defense and ATBM systems do not threaten the buffer. However, they find that a deployed ATBM system could be legitimately tested in ways that are closer to ABM performance levels than current air defense. They conclude that the resulting ABM capability would nonetheless be limited and readily overcome.

Some ASAT and DSAT approaches, such as lasers, defensive interceptors on board satellites, and high-speed direct-ascent interceptors would press Treaty limits and erode the buffer. Here "relabeling," that is, carrying out an ABM-relevant program under the guise of a Treaty-permitted activity such as ASAT, could be a serious problem.

On the difficult subject of sensors, Garwin and Jarvis stress that both large, ground-based phased-array radars and satellite-borne infrared sensors perform important non-ABM missions. But such sensors can also discharge the essential ABM functions of surveillance, acquisition, tracking, and fire control. Space-based short-wave length infrared sensors (SWIR) can observe an attack in the boost phase; long-wavelength infrared sensors (LWIR) can pick up reentry vehicles (RVs) in the midcourse phase after they have been discharged from the postboost vehicle. Neither type is sufficiently accurate to bring an interceptor or directed-energy weapon to the point of intercept without additional guidance. But a SWIR sensor could transfer data to a homing interceptor, and both could cue engagement sensors to control the intercept. The actual ABM utility of these devices would depend on the development of other programs as well as on the survivability of the satellite and its sensor. These issues are discussed at length in chapter 9 by Pike and Fridling.

Johnson in chapter 7 considers the policy problems associated with ground-based weapons (defined as systems in which the rockets or lasers that intercept the missiles are on the ground when the attack begins).[6] He concludes that the ABM technology used in the Soviet system around Moscow (as permitted by Article III of the Treaty), even if deployed in numbers and at sites well beyond what is permitted by that article and even if "upgraded" with passive space-based sensors, could easily be penetrated by U.S. countermeasures, increased numbers of offensive missiles, or both. Only an active space-based sensor, able to discriminate warheads from decoys to permit much earlier engagement of the attacking warheads in midcourse, would make this ground-based technology a serious threat. To prevent such a development, Johnson suggests that tests of space-based sensors against decoys should be expressly forbidden.

This chapter also concludes that the development of ground-based ASAT interceptors and radars does not necessarily threaten the ABM buffer since they deal with a much simpler problem. The concerns that have been expressed could be dealt with by requiring ASATs to be tested at agreed test ranges and by modest limits on the number of deployment sites of directed-energy weapon ASATs.

Johnson discusses the many difficulties in giving a significant ABM capability to existing widely deployed ground-based air defense systems. (Much of the discussion is equally applicable to possible ATBM systems.) Any air defense site can perform intercepts only within a fairly limited neighboring area, whereas an ABM role would require much wider coverage. A key to such coverage is an effective search and acquisition capability to pick up the RVs at a great distance and cue the radars at the site. Direct routes to such a capability are forbidden by the Treaty. Johnson suggests, however, that the search and acquisition capability might be provided by sophisticated internetting of air defense radars at many sites. None of the routes to air defense upgrade is very promising. But Johnson concludes that the ABM Treaty buffer could be fully protected against them by an agreement limiting tests of SAM or ATBM interceptors to a burnout velocity of 3 kilometers per second, too low to permit effective intercept of fast-moving intercontinental and submarine-launched ballistic (ICBM and SLBM) missiles and warheads.

Chapter 8, by Carter, deals with space-based weapons: space-based intercepters and directed-energy weapons. He describes the way the ABM Treaty's limits are applied to space weapons today, at least in the United States. He then analyzes limits on testing practices and test weapons that would be necessary to maintain the purposes of the existing treaty regime under the three approaches (status quo; more restrictive; more permissive) described above. Since a key element against breakout for space weapons is the process of deployment, Carter explores the possibility of limiting overall lift capability but concludes that Soviet capability is already approaching the limit that would have to be imposed.

Carter emphasizes the importance of testing practices and modes, as opposed to performance thresholds, as a basis for agreed constraints. He suggests a number of such practices to improve capability for monitoring tests of space-based items. The most novel of these approaches is the conception, under a more permissive regime, of an agreed orbital test range (AOTR), analogous to the agreed ranges for ground-based testing now permitted under the Treaty, in which all space tests of elements relevant to ABM development would be conducted.

The subject of sensors is among the most controversial of those related to Treaty adaptation. Chapter 9, by Pike and Fridling, reviews the functions and types of sensors and their potential for each of the ABM sensor missions. They identify a range of sensor capabilities that, in combination and with defined improvements, could erode the buffer provided by the ABM Treaty. In so doing Pike and Fridling expose the enormous complexity of the policy choices in any decision (which necessarily becomes equally applicable to the Soviets) to permit the development and deployment of a class of satellites that could serve as ABM system components.

The authors identify considerations relevant to the establishment of limits on sensor research, development, and deployment:

- Possible Treaty clarifications to reduce ambiguities
- The type of limits that might be imposed, including limits on
    —Sensor testing in an ABM mode,
    —Sensor capability, and
    —The number of deployed sensor platforms
- The verifiability of any limit by NTM alone and supplemented by potential improvements in verification through cooperative measures
- The existence and capabilities of other sensors and weapons needed to perform the complete ABM function

Then they examine candidate restraints under each of the three approaches to the treaty regime defined above. They conclude that, despite the difficulties of verification, sensor development should not be permitted to run free, while relying on other constraints to ensure the maintenance of a robust buffer. Rather, they argue, there is a need for early, specific, and conscious clarification and perhaps adaptation of the Treaty to govern sensor development, some of which is clearly inevitable.

Verification, Dispute Settlement, Adjustment, and Adaptation

Any permanent treaty regime will have to adapt to new developments, only some of which can be anticipated. Planning for changing circumstances involves creating institutional arrangements for clarifying or adapting treaty provisions. Without such arrangements, the parties will face recurring crises of implementation.

If a treaty "of unlimited duration" is to endure, ways must be found to accommodate change while retaining its central purpose. The ABM Treaty has no court system—no independent arbiter—to resolve issues of interpretation, make adjustments to unanticipated situations, and develop new applications; all found in our domestic legal system and even in some less-sensitive international treaties.

Accommodating change without altering basic premises involves a complex interplay of technology, international law, and diplomacy. This is what we mean by "managing a treaty regime." Although a great deal of attention has been paid to the process of negotiating treaties, little work has been done on the subsequent management of treaty regimes in a changing technological context.

Traditionally, the major concern about behavior under a treaty regime is verification of compliance. Verification issues have been critical to the negotiation of arms control treaties and, in the United States, to the ratification process. Until recently verification has been accomplished unilaterally by each party using national technical means, with only rudimentary cooperation from the other side.

The kinds of agreed constraints discussed in chapters 7, 8, and 9 will go beyond the capabilities of existing NTM and require increasing use of cooperative measures, including forms of on-site inspection. Although the Soviets had generally rejected these forms of verification in the past, they have recently shown surprising receptivity, especially in connection with the INF Treaty. This, in turn, has led the United States to reexamine the problems of on-site inspection, resulting in something less than an unqualified endorsement, in large part because of the security concerns of Soviet intrusion. Yet a situation in which each party judges its own compliance based upon undivulged technical parameters is not satisfactory. These problems and prospects are discussed in chapter 10 by Graybeal and McFate.

In fact, monitoring by NTM has not presented unusually difficult problems under the ABM Treaty or other arms control agreements. The United States has been able to obtain very substantial information about Soviet activity in areas covered by these treaties. The problem has been how to proceed when information indicates a possible violation, particularly when lack of cooperation between the parties makes it difficult to clarify ambiguous data. The treatment of alleged violations remains a conundrum to both parties.

Americans tend to view treaty compliance as a problem of law enforcement: crime and punishment. Yet the experience under arms control treaties has been one of continuous negotiation over this very question—the assurance of compliance. The issues are only very rarely clear-cut, as in the case of the Krasnoyarsk radar. Most problems involve evaluation of inconclusive evidence or controverted interpretations of treaty language. These disputes are not resolved by accusation and confession. They require a process of consultation and ultimately accommodation and agreement.

In chapter 11, Chayes and Chayes accept the reality of ongoing, post-treaty negotiation as a fact of life in arms control treaties. They argue for making a virtue of necessity by using this same process to adjust and adapt treaty provisions to new technological developments. The ABM Treaty refers such activity to the Standing Consultative Commission, but it is by no means the exclusive forum. Issues of treaty adjustment and adaptation form a major part of the bilateral diplomacy between the United States and the Soviet Union, carried on through ordinary diplomatic channels, in the arms control negotiations in Geneva, at the level of foreign ministers, and even at the summit. Some of these changes (in particular some of the proposals in chapters 7, 8, and 9) might require more formal processes of treaty amendment, including approval by the U.S. Senate. Chapter 11 argues for acceptance of this conception of the adjustment process and suggests ways to improve it.

In Chapter 12, Carnesale concludes the study with a systematic and summary examination of the issues, followed by observations, findings, and approaches to guide policy choice. The policymaker will find here a wide range of possible steps that may be appropriate or necessary in the future, depending on emerging technological possibilities and on the course of U.S.-Soviet relations. In the end, a study that might have evolved toward a single prescription for the future has instead become a compendium of interrelated choices.

U.S. policymakers and diplomats will be required to educate themselves on the various options available and the likely consequences that derive from each. Those who have carried out this study know how demanding and difficult it is to keep in perspective all the technological, political, legal, and diplomatic dimensions of this crucial national security problem. It is the goal of this book to provide some help in accomplishing that complex task.

Notes

1. Moreover, the number of ballistic missile launchers remained relatively stationary. Between 1973 and 1987 the number of U.S. launchers increased by 3 percent; Soviet launchers decreased by 7 percent. International Institute for Strategic Studies, *The Military Balance, 1973–4 and 1987–8.* (London).

2. Department of Defense and Department of State, *Soviet Strategic Defense Programs* (Washington, D.C.: U.S. Government Printing Office, 1985). And in "The Near Term Impact of SDI on Soviet Strategic Programs," in Joseph S. Nye, Jr., and James A. Schear, eds., *On the Defensive? The Future of SDI* (Lanham, MD: University Press of America, 1988), Stephen M. Meyer provides a detailed description of the various organizations responsible for Soviet development programs in this area. Long-term scientific research, involving concept studies and proof-of-principle research, is covered by Nauchno-issledovatel'skaya rabota (NIR). Meyer states that the programs remaining in NIR, although they may have begun in the early 1960s, include fixed ground-based laser, space-based laser components, particle-beam components, exoatmospheric ABM weapons, and airborne lasers. Opytno-Konstruktivnaya rabota (OKR) covers the actual development of Soviet weaponry or their programs in line to be fielded in the 1990s. According to Meyer, the strategic programs in OKR are overwhelmingly related to strategic offense, not ballistic missile defense. Also, he states that the Soviet ABM programs at present are all based on traditional ABM technologies, somewhat equivalent to U.S. ABM technologies of the early 1970s. Meyer concludes that, although the Soviets are not prepared in the short-term to respond to SDI, their research is substantial enough to cope with the immediate impact of SDI deployment, should it occur. Furthermore, he states that the "scope and direction of Soviet NIR, along with Gorbachev's grand investment program, suggest a foundation for dealing with the long-term implications of SDI," as well (p. 77).

3. See, in particular, a speech delivered by Senator Sam Nunn at the Arms Control Association on January 19, 1988.

4. The full Treaty text is reproduced in the Appendix.

5. Mason Willrich and John B. Rhinelander, eds., *SALT, The Moscow Agreements & Beyond* (New York: The Free Press, 1974), pp. 139–40, 167–70.

6. Johnson notes that this definition is not a Treaty definition. The Treaty does not define the term. All that the Treaty permits to be deployed are fixed ground-base weapons specified in Article III.

2

UNDERLYING MILITARY
OBJECTIVES

Ashton B. Carter

S O LONG as the United States does not have an ABM system worth deploying, it is in the nation's military interest to preserve the ABM Treaty regime. Legal and political considerations, discussed in subsequent chapters, also contribute to an assessment of the national interest, but military considerations are central. To be militarily worthwhile, an ABM system would have to be able to play some significant role in defending people or military targets, even if the Soviet Union adopted countermeasures of comparable cost. The system's defensive protection would furthermore have to be worth the price of equipping U.S. missiles to penetrate the Soviet ABM system that would almost surely be deployed in response to U.S. deployment.[1] Such a system might become possible in two years, or ten, or perhaps never. In the meantime, an intact ABM Treaty obliges the Soviet Union not to deploy a defense either.

The absence of Soviet defenses makes it easier and cheaper for the United States to plan its future missile forces. For example, the current U.S. Trident 2, MX/Peacekeeper, and Midgetman ballistic missile programs are all moving forward with relatively little effort to incorporate penetration aids, or countermeasures to ABM defenses. The designs of the B-2 Stealth bomber and of U.S. cruise missiles, by contrast, are dominated by the need to penetrate Soviet air defenses, which are not banned by any treaty. Similarly, the United States can agree to reduce its missile forces at the Strategic Arms Reduction Talks (START) with a clearer idea of where reductions will leave U.S. nuclear retaliatory power than if the Soviet Union had ABM defenses.

The key U.S. military objective is therefore to limit Soviet ABM-related activities so that the United States enjoys the full military benefit of the treaty regime. These limitations will be expressed as rules on testing of ABM technology and deployment of ABM-related military systems. As the United States and the Soviet Union adapt these rules to new technologies, whether in the Standing Consultative Commission (SCC), in the formal Defense and Space Talks, or in amendments to the Treaty, the rules that emerge ought foremost to reflect underlying U.S. military considerations. Legal and political objectives may affect the form of the U.S.-Soviet agreement and the process of establishing and maintaining it. The precise rules of conduct for the changed technological circumstances of the 1990s may derive directly from the language of the 1972 ABM Treaty or depart from its precedent in specified ways. Moreover, all the rules that constrain Soviet ABM-related activity will apply symmetrically to U.S. programs like SDI, so a price will be paid for excessive strictness. But, fundamentally, negotiators formulating a U.S. approach to the ABM Treaty regime in the 1990s should be guided by three principles that express the U.S. military interest in having the regime in the first place.

First, it should be impossible for the Soviet Union to deploy a militarily threatening ABM system without breaking the rules. The notion of ''militarily threatening'' is explored more concretely below, but in essence it refers to any Soviet defensive capability that interferes significantly with an offensive task the United States believes it must be able to carry out with its existing strategic missile forces. Rather than prohibit *all* militarily significant ABMs, an alternative regime might permit the Soviet Union a defense system of a specified type in return for a specified U.S. deployment. But this book addresses only regimes akin to the 1972 ABM Treaty, which permits *no* ABM deployments beyond a token 100-interceptor ground-based system.

Second, the Soviet Union should be unable to create a base from which it could quickly deploy a militarily threatening defense after breaking out of the Treaty. The regime should ban technical activity that would position the Soviet Union to deploy an ABM faster than the United States could mount appropriate countermeasures. Otherwise the United States would have to hedge continually against breakout, deploying larger and more sophisticated missile forces incorporating penetration aids. The United States should satisfy itself that a comfortable buffer of conspicuous and time-consuming testing, manufacturing, site preparation, construction, satellite launching, and other deployment activity stands between a breakout decision by Soviet leaders and achievement of a militarily threatening Soviet ABM.

Third, Soviet military systems deployed for other, non-ABM purposes should not be capable of militarily threatening ABM defense or constitute a base for rapid ABM deployment. That is, ABM-capable systems that compromise the first two principles should not be allowed to escape the regime's limits by being relabeled "air defenses," "antisatellites," "space-track sensors," and so on.

Against these principles, discussed at greater length below, must be balanced the U.S. desire to investigate ABM-related technologies thoroughly; U.S. desires for technological advancement and actual deployments in the technologically related areas of missile warning, air defense, and the like; and the U.S. requirement that the Soviet Union be fully bound by the rules that bind the United States—that is, that the rules be verifiable. These balancing factors are discussed in subsequent chapters.

Militarily Threatening Defensive Capability

Given agreement on a set of rules of conduct for the ABM regime, any clear-cut Soviet breach of the rules would be a matter of concern, because it might cast doubt on the seriousness of the Soviet commitment to the regime. But in adapting the regime to new technological circumstances, U.S. negotiators need to think in terms of rules whose violation would pose a genuine *military* problem for the United States. Construction of the Krasnoyarsk radar in the interior of the USSR, for example, clearly contravenes the language of the Treaty restricting all warning radars to the periphery of the USSR. But the Krasnoyarsk radar is not worrisome militarily: it could be easily overwhelmed or destroyed by U.S. forces before it could possibly play a defensive role. Nor does the Krasnoyarsk radar bring the USSR close to the point where it could rapidly deploy a significant ABM.

The Soviet Union will presumably continue to test ABM components and deploy related military hardware for interception of aircraft and satellites, observation of space objects, and other military purposes. Most of this equipment will have, or could be upgraded to have, some ABM capability. At what point would its potential capability constitute a *militarily* serious violation of the regime's underlying principles?

SCALE AND SCOPE OF THE DEFENSE: GUIDANCE FROM THE 1972 TREATY

What did the negotiators of the 1972 ABM Treaty consider to be militarily significant? The Treaty's restrictions on scale and scope of allowed defenses offer some clues to their thinking. First, the Treaty allows the Soviet Union to deploy 100 interceptors and a few radars in the Moscow area, which the Soviets have done. The U.S. negotiators evidently regarded the ability to intercept 100 reentry vehicles (RVs) as militarily *in*significant. In 1972, the U.S. missile arsenal contained about 4,000 RVs, and the strategic arsenal (including the bomber force) mounted a total of 6,000 warheads. Today the United States has a total of 8,000 missile RVs and 12,000 total strategic warheads. The START agreement (still incomplete) would allow each side only 4,900 ballistic missile RVs on intercontinental and submarine-launched ballistic missiles (ICBMs and SLBMs).

Since the capability to intercept 100 RVs is equivalent to the capability to intercept between ten and thirty MIRVed boosters (launching multiple independently targetable reentry vehicles), the 1972 standard could be extended to set a numerical threshold for the level at which boost-phase ABM capabilities might take on military significance. Such boost-phase defense potential might come about, for example, through deployment of space-based antisatellite (ASAT) systems with inherent ABM capability. By this standard, a Soviet deployment of space-based interceptor (SBI) ASATs that could intercept no more than thirty U.S. ICBM and SLBM boosters would be deemed militarily insignificant for ABM. The rules of the 1990s regime could make it clear that such an ASAT deployment would be regarded as compatible with treaty obligations.

The 1972 Treaty also attempts to restrict the geographic scope of defensive capability, limiting deployments to local coverage. Nationwide defenses were viewed as more threatening militarily. The Treaty does not limit the range of the interceptor missiles in the Moscow ABM system, but the radars that control the interceptors are confined to the Moscow area and hence cannot direct defensive engagements that occur over the horizon from Moscow. A comparable emphasis on restricting geographic coverage in the rules of the 1990s ABM regime would severely constrain technical activity related to boost-phase defense, which inherently provides nationwide coverage.

RELATION TO OFFENSIVE MISSIONS

Restrictions on the scale and scope of an ABM system are an indirect way of getting at the essence of military significance: the ability of Soviet missile defenses to interfere with—frustrate physically or just create doubts about—an offensive role the United States wants to be certain its missile forces can accomplish.

The most elemental mission for U.S. strategic forces is to be able to devastate the Soviet Union, but more particularly to paralyze its military machine, even if the Soviet Union strikes first. If the only goal were to preserve this capability, the United States could be very permissive of Soviet ABM-related activity. Since the fully survivable, at-sea U.S. SLBM force numbers some 3,700 RVs,[2] even a Soviet breakout defense capable of intercepting 2,000 RVs would not be worrisome. The remaining 1,700 U.S. RVs could destroy most important fixed military targets in the Soviet Union (even though older, shorter-range models of U.S. SLBMs have certain coverage restrictions). In addition, of course, U.S.

ICBMs and bombers would almost certainly make some contribution to retaliatory damage.

But two factors impel the United States to require stricter limits on Soviet ABM-related activity. First, the United States has enunciated other, lesser goals for its strategic forces besides massive retaliation against the Soviet military. Less extensive Soviet defensive capabilities could threaten fulfillment of these so-called limited nuclear options. Second, the United States demands high and unambiguous confidence that its missiles could penetrate to their targets. Given the many technical unknowns about the performance of offensive and defensive weapons, conservative analysis can impart a threatening character to even marginal Soviet defensive capabilities.

The history of the surface-to-air missile (SAM) upgrade debate in the United States illustrates the strength of U.S. concerns about missile penetration for offensive missions well short of massive retaliation. These concerns imply a historical U.S. preference for a rather strict ABM regime. Although superficially resembling radar-plus-interceptor types of ABM, SAM systems are designed to intercept aircraft and actually have, at most, extremely limited ABM capability. Even if upgraded to incorporate more powerful radars, faster interceptors, and nuclear warheads, SAMs could intercept only older models of strategic missile RVs, and then only in restricted circumstances. Few claim that the basic deterrent U.S. retaliatory punch would be significantly blunted if the Soviets upgraded their many thousands of SAMs in a leakout from the ABM Treaty. Yet SAM upgrade has been a persistent concern, at least among some U.S. analysts, since 1969.

This U.S. concern springs from the potential of upgraded SAMs to give the Soviet Union defensive capabilities: (1) to limit retaliatory damage to the Soviet Union significantly if U.S. retaliation suffered completely unforeseen ("worse than worst case") problems—for example, if command and control collapsed, SLBMs failed to perform properly, and the other two legs of the triad were completely destroyed; (2) to protect a small but supposedly important subset of military targets chosen in advance by the Soviets—a bunker here, an air base there—from comprehensive American retaliation, using the tactic of preferential defense; (3) to interfere with limited (strategic) nuclear options; or (4) to erode the deterrent power of French, British, or Chinese missile forces. A Soviet capability to intercept a few *hundred,* rather than a few *thousand,* RVs would be militarily threatening by these stricter standards. These concerns essentially demand that missile forces be guaranteed unencumbered transit—a so-called free ride—to their Soviet targets.

If the outcomes of hypothetical engagements between offensive missiles and defensive systems could be calculated confidently and precisely, one could establish unambiguously what Soviet ABM-related capabilities would be militarily threatening. In practice, uncertainties about Soviet systems, and about a type of warfare that has never yet taken place, preclude such exact assessment. Thus U.S. analysts are driven to conservative assessments, which focus on the least favorable, rather than the most likely, outcomes of offense-defense engagements. In this context marginal Soviet defensive capabilities look more significant.

In summary, the United States pursues two types of offensive goals, implying two distinct standards for judging when Soviet defensive capability becomes militarily threatening. We shall refer to the two goals loosely as "thorough retaliation" and "free ride." We make the further conservative assumption that a Soviet capability to intercept about 50 percent of the survivable U.S. missile arsenal would violate the thorough retaliation standard and a capability to intercept 10 percent would violate the free-ride standard.

Creating a Base for Rapid Deployment

The treaty regime must keep the Soviets from positioning themselves to attain a militarily threatening ABM capability quickly or covertly. The rules should ensure that breakout from Treaty restrictions would be a time-consuming and conspicuous affair.

Six steps would intervene between conception of a new ABM approach and a breakout deployment:

1. exploration of key principles with experimental devices;
2. creation of production-model prototypes from experimental devices;
3. testing of prototypes;
4. manufacturing of components;
5. deployment of components (almost certainly a long and conspicuous process, involving site preparation and construction for ground-based defenses and the launching of many hundreds of tons of payload for space-based defenses); and
6. integration of defensive weapons with sensors, battle management, and other defensive layers.

The United States must ensure that these steps create a comfortable buffer between permitted technical activity and attainment of a militarily threatening defensive capability.

The buffer period should be long enough that the United States could deploy a first generation of offensive countermeasures to the Soviet breakout defense. The better prepared the United States is to deploy penetration aids quickly, the shorter the buffer period—and the more permissive the regime's rules—can be. It would take the United States several years (say, five) to complete development and testing to deploy, with urgent priority, a comprehensive first array of countermeasures to a widespread Soviet breakout deployment and a short time (say, two years) to mount initial "off-the-shelf" countermeasures to a limited or incomplete Soviet deployment. By implication, the rules of the regime should be defined so as to keep the Soviet Union about five years away from a deployment that would threaten thorough retaliation and about two years away from deployment of a defense that could deny the current U.S. missile arsenals a free ride.

Relabeling

The problem of devising the ABM Treaty regime's rules is complicated by technical kinship between ABMs and other military activity. Technically similar missions include air defense, antitactical and antitheater ballistic missile defense systems (ATBMs), antisatellite systems, advanced offensive weapons used to attack and penetrate ABMs, and sensors for missile warning, space track, and intelligence (see chapter 6). Thus the Soviets have two other ways of attaining a threatening defensive capability besides rapid breakout of illegally developed ABMs. One avenue involves development of ABM components in the guise of developing other legal types of military system, such as ASATs and ATBMs. The second avenue involves upgrading previously deployed ASATs, ATBMs, or other systems to have ABM capability. The rules of the treaty regime should be drafted to preclude leakout by these two paths.

The rules must therefore limit overt deployments of ASAT, air defense, and ATBM systems, as well as development, testing and covert preparation for deployment of ABM technology. Deployments of systems for other legitimate military purposes must be expected. Someday, for example, the Soviets may be manufacturing and continually upgrading space-based ASAT weapons in a large-scale plant, with extensive launch facilities. Overt deployments of this sort are more likely to erode the ABM Treaty buffer than are sporadic tests of experimental advanced ABMs.

Consequences of Offensive Arms Control

If arms control agreements reduce the U.S. missile arsenal significantly, will stricter rules of conduct be required for the ABM regime? The smaller the U.S. missile arsenal that can survive a Soviet first strike, the greater will be U.S. concern about penetration of its strategic RVs—unless U.S. concerns are dominated in the first place by guaranteeing penetration by limited U.S. strategic options and penetration by allied missile forces, which are unrelated to the overall size of the U.S. strategic arsenal. Today's survivable missile force of about 4,000 RVs would probably decline to between 2,400 and 3,000 RVs under the draft START agreement, a reduction of some 25 to 40 percent.[3] This remaining force would be comparable to the survivable missile arsenal in 1972, which numbered about 2,500 RVs,[4] though today's RVs are more difficult to defend against, being on average faster and presenting smaller cross sections to radar detection. Assuming the number of truly important Soviet military targets has not increased greatly since 1972, START reductions would therefore not require stricter rules on ABMs than those envisioned by the drafters of the 1972 Treaty.

Much deeper reductions in the more distant future, however, might necessitate stricter rules for ABMs. Arms control cuts designed to increase first-strike stability would, of course, not reduce survivable missile arsenals as much as they reduced the overall missile arsenals. Moreover, U.S. targeting objectives might be relaxed in accordance with some vision of reduced reliance on nuclear weapons. And greater reliance might be placed on bombers and cruise missiles rather than ballistic missiles. But if the United States maintains a strategic ballistic missile force, it will continue to insist on the force's ability to penetrate to Soviet targets. Beyond a certain point, the survivable missile arsenal could become small enough that even marginal Soviet defensive capabilities, like upgraded SAMs, would be deemed militarily threatening. Fulfilling the ABM Treaty's principles in this world of deep reductions would require strict constraints on ABM-related activity, probably going well beyond the present Treaty.

Consequences of Offensive Modernization

Under the ABM Treaty regime, the United States can be certain of accomplishing its offensive goals without increasing the number of its missiles or equipping them with penetration aids. Thus, any Soviet defense that is effective against today's "unresponsive" U.S. missiles has to be regarded as militarily threatening if the United States is to enjoy the full benefits of the treaty regime. The fact that an upgraded SAM or rapidly deployable ABM system could be defeated by a "responsive" U.S. missile force—that is, one equipped for saturation, decoys, chaff, antisatellite attack, or other ABM countermeasures, qualitative or quantitative—is not relevant to judging Soviet compliance with the ABM Treaty regime unless these countermeasures could very quickly be mounted by the United States. The United States has generally chosen not to position itself for rapid deployment of penetration aids.[5]

By contrast, analyses of whether defensive systems or components are worth deploying focus on their effectiveness against *future responsive* missile offenses. Thus, lasers and other exotic components that could be defeated easily with offensive countermeasures should be judged "not ABM-capable" by the

Strategic Defense Initiative Organization (SDIO), even if they could destroy or interfere with current-generation Soviet ICBMs. The same capabilities in Soviet ABM-related programs, however, should be viewed as "ABM-capable" for purposes of compliance with the treaty regime, since the value of the Treaty is to forestall the need for upgrading the U.S. missile force.

The longer the ABM Treaty regime is in place, the more awkward becomes this mismatch in definitions of ABM effectiveness between those concerned about U.S. penetration and those exploring U.S. ABM concepts. Under the treaty regime, defensive *concepts* continue to evolve while offensive *deployments* change slowly, if at all. Insofar as penetration of ABMs is concerned, for example, the MX/Peacekeeper being deployed today represents only a slight technological improvement over the Minuteman III deployed in 1972. Yet ABMs that could be deployed today would perform better against MX than the Safeguard system of 1972 could perform against Minuteman III. If the treaty regime is successful in obviating the need for new offensive technology and thus in slowing its deployment, the offensive arsenals now in the field will ultimately represent yesterday's technology. These technologically static arsenals will make more and more tempting targets for the advancing defensive technology of tomorrow. Only when tomorrow's defenses are measured against technologically feasible upgrades to the offensive arsenals does the actual offense-defense technological balance become clear.

To illustrate this point with an analogy to airborne delivery of nuclear weapons, imagine that a treaty banning air defenses had been signed in 1955 and that in 1989 the United States was still relying solely on high-altitude bombers for its deterrent. Such bombers make easy targets for today's radar and interceptor technology. But if the Soviets violated the treaty and deployed such defenses, the United States would begin to fly at low altitudes and to deploy electronic countermeasures, stealth, short-range attack missiles (SRAMs), cruise missiles, and ballistic missiles (which were originally viewed as a penetration alternative to the bomber).

This hypothetical air defense treaty regime would be frustrating to Soviet air defense designers, since the rules would restrict testing even of air defense systems that would be effective only against old, high-flying bombers. If the rules were to be changed, however, both superpowers would have to stand ready to deploy countermeasures quickly to the types of defenses the other side might deploy. Analogously, if the United States wishes to relax the ABM Treaty's restrictions on ABM-related activity to permit expanded testing for the SDI, it will need to prepare its offensive missiles to cope with a correspondingly increased threat of Soviet breakout. Yet the United States has generally been unwilling to fund the full development of penetration aids to counter potential Soviet breakout ABMs.

Conclusion

The rules of the ABM Treaty regime should be devised so that the United States can be reasonably confident that it would take the Soviet Union at least

- Several years (say, roughly five years) of visible deployment activity to create a defense that could intercept, under realistic operational conditions, a substantial fraction (say, roughly 50 percent) of the then-current survivable U.S. missile RVs (today, mostly SLBMs) and
- A shorter time (say, roughly two years) to create a defense that could intercept even a small fraction (say, roughly 10 percent) of the then-current survivable missile RVs.

From a military point of view, the United States could accept a more permissive set of rules if it

- Deployed, or stood ready to deploy quickly, countermeasures to plausible Soviet breakout ABMs, or
- Relaxed its criteria for damage to Soviet targets with its offensive missile force, or
- Decided to forgo further arms control reductions in its strategic missile forces.

The precise interception percentages and duration of the buffer period are arguable, but the military guidance given to U.S. negotiators devising rules of conduct for ABMs should assume this general form.

Notes

1. If defenses were introduced by agreement in a cooperative transition to defense dominance, as some imagine, the United States would not attempt to stop the Soviet Union from nullifying U.S. missile forces, and the cost of U.S. penetration aids would not be incurred.

2. Two-thirds of the roughly 5,600-RV SLBM force.

3. Today's survivable arsenal includes the two-thirds of the 5,600-RV SLBM force that is at sea plus a few hundred ICBM RVs. Under START, the United States could have between fifteen and twenty-one Trident submarines (2,880 to 4,032 RVs), two-thirds of them at sea, and 500 survivable mobile ICBM RVs (Midgetman or Rail-mobile MX/Peacekeeper).

4. Only one-half of the 2,200-RV SLBM force was normally at sea. The Minuteman III MIRV program was not yet complete in 1972; its RVs numbered about 1,400.

5. The budget of the U.S. penetration aids development program, for example, is small in relation to the size of the overall offensive missile force budget, the SDI budget, and U.S. estimates of the budget of the Soviet ABM development effort.

3

THE POLITICAL ENVIRONMENT

Ralph Earle II

THE POLITICAL ENVIRONMENT of ballistic missile defense (BMD) has never been a simple one. Almost since the outset of the nuclear age, U.S. thinking has been marked by tension between the traditional desire for security from foreign enemies and a concern for maintaining strategic stability. Military analysts and policymakers struggle to reconcile these goals amid continuing public confusion about both the value and the meaning of strategic defense, and indeed whether we in fact have such a defense. Finally, to compound the uncertainties, our allies in the North Atlantic Treaty Organization (NATO) and the Soviet Union have both fluctuated in their attitudes toward the issue.

The history of the debate in the United States can be roughly divided into three periods: (1) a "pre-ABM" era from the late 1950s until the beginning of the SALT I negotiations in 1969; (2) from SALT I until 1983; and (3) from President Reagan's "Star Wars" speech of March 23, 1983, to the present.

Before the ABM Treaty

Before 1969, when the ABM Treaty negotiations began, the American public generally supported the concept of a defense against nuclear weapons. The Cold War was at its height, and mistrust of the Soviets and fear of nuclear war were widespread. Civil defense was a popular theme, and the armed forces, not without some interservice rivalry, were eager to participate in what they believed to be the beginning of a significant defensive buildup to counter Soviet missiles as well as aircraft; these U.S. efforts included Nike-Zeus and later Nike-X ABM systems, in addition to Nike-Ajax and Nike-Hercules SAM systems and interceptor aircraft and their forward basing (e.g., in Iceland). The Soviets had launched Sputnik in 1957, and their development of the Griffon and Tallin air defense systems seemed to underline the need for U.S. progress. Even more influential on U.S. concerns were U-2 photographs taken in April 1960 of the test site at Sary Shagan, which revealed significant Soviet progress on BMD systems.[1] Public concern was heightened by talk about bomber and missile gaps in the 1960 presidential campaign and by the Cuban missile crisis of 1962.

Soon thereafter, however, skepticism about the wisdom of missile defense began to grow. During the debate over ballistic missile defense and multiple independently targetable reentry vehicles (MIRVs), serious doubts emerged regarding the efficacy of a future missile defense system. Initially, these doubts were expressed by members of the scientific community, such as Herbert York.[2] In his testimony before the Senate Armed Services Committee in April 1969, York stated that "[h]istory [has been] littered with Maginot Lines," and he argued that ABMs were a defense that could not function as originally intended.[3] Gradually the technological problems with ABM development became clearer to the policymakers, and their doubts began to override the continuing strong support from some sectors, especially the U.S. Army. President Lyndon Johnson remained skeptical about the army's claims for Nike-X. At the Glassboro summit in 1967, he and Secretary of Defense Robert McNamara argued to Premier Aleksei Kosygin that ballistic missile defense in the nuclear age was not only impossible but destabilizing—even though Congress had only the year before funded ABM production and polls indicated that the public strongly supported its deployment.

In any event, because of Kosygin's recalcitrance and because of mounting pressure from Congress and the Joint Chiefs of Staff, Johnson continued on the path toward at least partial deployment. In a speech delivered in San Francisco in September 1967, McNamara criticized BMD generally and drew back from the concept of a full-scale territorial defense of the country. To the prevalent "keep ahead of the Soviets" argument, McNamara countered that any present or future ABM system "can rather obviously be defeated by an enemy simply sending more offensive warheads, or dummy warheads, than there are defensive missiles capable of disposing of them."[4] Then, somewhat inconsistently and with a notable lack of enthusiasm, he announced the administration's decision to pursue a limited defense capability.

The Sentinel system, as the Johnson-McNamara ABM system was known, was conceived as a "thin" defense against the emerging but limited Chinese threat. Twenty-five cities around the country were to be protected by fourteen ABM sites. This move was at least partly an attempt to head off Republican charges in the upcoming election campaigns of being weak on defense. In mid-1967 Congress allocated $782.9 million for antiballistic systems in fiscal year 1968; of that amount, $366 million was to be used specifically for the Sentinel system. Later that year the army began acquiring property near Boston, Chicago, and Seattle.[5] In March 1968 President Johnson gave the impression, at least in public, that he believed the Sentinel program to be of the highest national priority.[6]

Almost immediately, however, public and congressional support of the Sentinel system began to evaporate. Opposition came from two sources. First, contrary to the administration's expectations, citizens of the twenty-five cities to be protected objected vociferously to having nuclear-tipped weapons, even defensive ones, in their neighborhoods. Demonstrations and other manifestations of opposition testified to the vitality of antinuclear sentiment.

Second, as McNamara had warned in his San Francisco speech, pressures arose to expand the "thin" defense into a heavy Soviet-oriented ABM system.[7] The approaching presidential election provided critics with the ideal arena in which to campaign for such a move. The Republicans, led in Congress by Melvin Laird, vigorously attacked Johnson's apparent decision against a heavy defensive system that would protect the United States from Soviet attack.

Shortly after the 1969 inauguration, the Nixon administration proposed a new version of an ABM system. Although Safeguard was presented to the public as a completely different system, it merely reversed Sentinel's priorities. Whereas Sentinel was to address first the Chinese, then the Soviet threat, Safeguard would initially protect U.S. ICBM silos and would later be expanded to include a nationwide defense against a "light" Chinese attack. The major political difference between the projects was that the Safeguard antimissile sites would be located away from heavily populated areas.

In a March 1969 message to Congress, President Richard Nixon articulated his ABM program—initially a limited defense of U.S. ICBM sites to be followed by a territorial defense comprised of twelve sites around the country. He hoped that this compromise would defuse congressional and public opposition to ABMs. Nixon's request for funds to proceed with the first phase brought the issue to a head, however, and questions of cost and technical effectiveness soon began to take hold. In August of the same year, Vice President Spiro Agnew had to cast the decisive vote to break a 50-50 deadlock in the Senate on the ABM authorization bill.[8] Although the Nixon administration had escaped with a "victory," the August vote served as warning that the number of legislators who opposed ABMs was increasing rapidly. Nixon's compromise had failed to win additional support.

Facing mounting opposition and a torrent of questions from Congress concerning Safeguard's feasibility, the president changed tactics. He began to solicit support for Safeguard because of its merits as a bargaining chip, to be used to gain Soviet agreement to limit ABM systems. National security adviser Henry Kissinger maintained that Sentinel had piqued Soviet interest in arms limitation talks initially and that it would take Safeguard to keep the Soviets at the table.

"Phase two," the territorial defense, was no longer mentioned. Administration efforts were geared toward obtaining the necessary funding for the previously approved sites at Grand Forks, North Dakota, and Malmstrom Air Force Base, Montana, and for two additional sites, also to be located near Minuteman bases.[9]

This change in strategy seemed to provide some leverage in the continuing debate with Congress. In the next round of defense appropriation votes in the Senate, Nixon's Safeguard was again able to scrape by, this time by a vote of 52 to 47. Several key votes, however, came from senators who admittedly voted for a bargaining chip to be traded away; their votes were clearly not an endorsement of an ABM program to be funded indefinitely.[10]

SALT I negotiations had begun in November 1969, and in May 1971 the sides agreed to concentrate on the limitation of defensive systems. In effect, both sides were acquiescing in the prevalent view that strategic offensive weapons and strategic defensive systems are inextricably linked. As Secretary McNamara had set forth in his September 1967 San Francisco speech, if the United States were to deploy an anti-Soviet ABM system, the Soviets would respond by increasing their offensive capability. This action-reaction relationship, said McNamara, would "be foolish and reckless because [it would] trigger a senseless spiral upward of nuclear arms [that] in the end would provide neither the Soviets nor us with any greater relative nuclear capability."[11] Although occasionally ignored and sometimes attacked, this idea of linkage has survived. When General Secretary Gorbachev was asked, following the June 1988 Moscow summit, whether SDI was an obstacle to START, he replied that it would not "meet normal logic" to reduce Soviet strategic forces if the United States seriously planned to deploy an antimissile system.[12]

Given public opposition to further deployment, increasing doubt about the long-term technological outlook, and a desire to prevent the spiral McNamara described, the United States became more willing to negotiate ABM technology away in return for an agreement from the Soviets. In this context Kissinger bypassed the Geneva negotiations, and in May 1971, accepted an earlier Soviet proposal to negotiate an ABM treaty separately from the talks on strategic offensive arms. Concrete progress was made when, in April 1972, both sides agreed to limit deployment to two ABM sites. In the following month Nixon and Brezhnev signed the ABM Treaty; it was ratified and took effect in October of that year.

1972 to 1983

The ABM Treaty—a pact of "unlimited duration"—set official ABM policy for the foreseeable future. In 1974 a protocol added to the Treaty reduced the number of permitted sites on each side from two to one. It was understood in the

United States that modest funding for research would be regularly appropriated, but until 1983, neither Republican nor Democratic administrations suggested that anything beyond modest research and development was needed.

Advocates of missile defense remained active on the periphery, however, and their cause was indirectly supported in the later 1970s by growing concern about the vulnerability of U.S. retaliatory systems as the number of deployed Soviet MIRVed missiles and warheads steadily increased. Moreover, the public had not lost its basic desire for effective protection from the Soviet Union or its concern about nuclear weapons. The optimism that followed SALT I was wearing thin as a result of events throughout the world (such as Soviet support of communist regimes in Cuba and Angola). The SALT II Treaty, signed in June 1979, was attacked as a symbol of excessive accommodation of Soviet activity. Then the Soviet brigade was "discovered" in Cuba, the Soviets invaded Afghanistan, President Jimmy Carter withdrew the SALT II Treaty from Senate consideration, and Ronald Reagan was elected president (running on a Republican platform that charged the Democrats with weakness in defense and urged "vigorous research and development [R&D] of an effective ABM system").[13]

In the first three years of the Reagan presidency, public opinion reflected a mixture of fear, anger, insecurity, and indifference. On the one hand, antinuclear sentiment was becoming strong and vocal. As a result of Reagan's increasingly strident anti-Soviet stance (e.g., his description of the USSR as an "evil empire"), the rise in U.S. military spending (38 percent in real terms over 1980 levels by 1983),[14] and the lack of serious attempts at arms control, the freeze movement prospered. At the same time, however, Reagan's hawkish stance inspired conservative followers. Polls show that the country had been shifting to the right politically since the Iranian taking of American hostages in 1979, a shift partly responsible for Reagan's victory over the incumbent President Carter. Even though the antinuclear movement was on the rise, public desire for a strong military posture was still stronger. In short, the mood of the early Reagan years was relatively conservative and generally supportive of increased defense expenditures across the board.

1983 to 1988: SDI and Arms Control

Although the ABM Treaty is of unlimited duration, was signed by a conservative Republican, and was approved overwhelmingly (88-2) by a bipartisan Senate, the change in political climate made it possible for Reagan to champion building an effective missile defense of the nation. His "Star Wars" speech of March 23, 1983, announced a proposal to develop an antimissile defense system so comprehensive that it would render "nuclear weapons impotent and obsolete."

Reactions to the president's SDI proposal ranged widely; some condemned it as impossible and destabilizing, while others saw it as the potential savior of the nation. Within the bureaucracy, support for SDI became a litmus test of loyalty. Senior officials supported the proposal, in large part because it represented a clear personal commitment on the part of the commander in chief. From the outset, however, some senior defense officials expressed doubts. Even Richard DeLauer, Pentagon chief of research and development, stated flatly that "[t]here's no way an enemy can't overwhelm your defenses if he wants to badly enough."[16] There was also concern within the Department of Defense that the program would divert funds from more pressing needs.

Support for SDI reflected various motivations. Robert McFarlane, deputy national security adviser, seemed to see SDI as a bargaining chip that could be used to secure an agreement from the Soviets to decrease the size of their strategic arsenal. Secretary of Defense Caspar Weinberger and his assistant Richard Perle, on the other hand, became outspoken advocates for SDI, apparently in the hope of stalling the START negotiations and continuing the U.S. strategic buildup. The reaction in Congress, at least at the outset, was split but generally supportive—President Reagan's influence was then at its height.[17]

The public reaction to Reagan's speech was uncertain or ambivalent. On the one hand, SDI represented a classic American prescription, dollars and technology, to solve a difficult and unpleasant problem; it would be consistent with citizens' traditional desire for defense from foreign enemies; and it addressed a moral issue raised by the Roman Catholic bishops and others: the propriety of deterrence or mutually assured destruction (MAD). On the other hand, the specter of another arms race, this time in space, and the prospect of large expenditures dampened enthusiasm.

As time passed, most of the initial enthusiastic endorsements were diluted. Assessing the technological feasibility of an SDI, the scientific community expressed views ranging from skepticism through analytical pessimism to outright outrage. The criticism may be best summed up by the American Physical Society's report on one of SDI's principal components. In this April 1987 document the society estimated "that even in the best of circumstances, a decade or more of intensive research would be required to provide the technical knowledge needed for an informed decision about the potential effectiveness and survivability of directed energy weapon systems."[18] Similar questions were raised in June 1988 by the congressional Office of Technology Assessment, which warned that because of the difficulty of testing the elaborate SDI computer systems under realistic conditions, there would be "a significant probability that the first (and presumably only) time the BMD system were used in a real war, it would suffer a catastrophic failure."[19] As such studies accumulated, it became clear that the SDI Organization's (SDIO)'s assessment of SDI's feasibility was not widely shared.

In addition, growing deficits reduced congressional and public support for committing the huge sums requested by the administration for SDI. Suspicion and mistrust of the Soviets began to diminish at the end of the Reagan administration, in part because of the president's own apparent change of heart and goals. Opposition to SDI increased as it began to appear that the plan was undermining strategic offensive arms control efforts and therefore promoting an arms race.

THE ALLIES

Although their role has not been a major one, the NATO allies have been affected by the change of U.S. attitudes toward a ballistic missile defense. The allies welcomed the ABM Treaty in 1972, both as a step toward superpower cooperation and as a pact that codified and justified the French and British nuclear forces. Now they believe the two superpowers may be moving away from those achievements and entering into a new phase of competition that, incidentally, may reduce the importance of NATO nuclear forces. Moreover, the deployment of defenses against strategic ballistic missiles would undermine a fundamental NATO doctrine: extended deterrence. Despite lip service paid to SDI, it does not appear that the granting by the United States of a small number of research contracts to European companies has reassured the allies on the vital question of U.S. intentions.

In the late 1970s, the Soviets began modernizing their intermediate- and short-range ballistic missiles and testing an air defense system that was judged capable of defending the Warsaw Pact against NATO's theater weapons. Under political and military pressures to answer the threat posed by these developments, some Western Europeans saw antitactical ballistic missiles (ATBMs) as an attractive option. The general notion, as articulated by the German Defense Minister Manfred Woerner and the Supreme Allied Commander in Europe, General Bernard Rogers, was that having an antimissile defense was preferable to redefining NATO's defensive doctrine into an offensive one that included plans to use Pershing IIs and ground-launched cruise missiles for deep strikes into Warsaw Pact territory. The Europeans also felt pressure to keep up with the superpowers in ABM technology. In 1985, consequently, Woerner and others endorsed ATBMs as a viable option.[20]

Subsequently strategic and economic questions have arisen, similar to those that undermined support for SDI in the United States. One leading query is whether it would be to NATO's strategic disadvantage to be faced by Warsaw Pact ATBMs, as the Pact would most surely follow suit if NATO constructed an ATBM defense. Perhaps the most damaging questions have concerned the impact of ATBM development on the future of the ABM Treaty. ATBM testing and deployment would provide a substantial R&D base with which the Soviets could develop new technologies based on "other physical principles," something the ABM Treaty expressly restrains. This, in turn would make it significantly easier for one or both sides to break out of the ABM Treaty. Moreover, the signing of the INF Treaty undercut to some extent the argument for ATBMs, since it removed all ballistic missiles with ranges between 500 and 5,500 kilometers. At the same time, however, so long as missiles with a range of less than 500 kilometers remain deployed, particularly if the United States pursues plans to upgrade the 120-kilometer range Lance missile, there will continue to be advocacy for ATBMs in Europe.[21]

In the Middle East, interest in ATBMs has increased as ballistic missile acquisition by both Arab states and Israel has grown alarmingly. Israel has the Lance and Jericho missiles, with ranges of 120 and 480 kilometers respectively. At the same time, Syria, Egypt, Libya, and Iraq have acquired numerous missiles, ranging from the Soviet-made Frog 7 with a range of 70 kilometers to the SS-12 with a range of 900 kilometers. In addition, Saudia Arabia recently purchased from China the CSS2 ballistic missile with a range of 2,600 kilometers.[22]

Also in June 1988, the United States agreed to fund, out of its SDIO budget, 80 percent of a new Israeli missile program (Arrow) that will be able to destroy incoming missiles at up to 1,000 kilometers.[23] If this program is pursued, some believe that Israel could have its own ATBMs in as little as five years. Some observers argue that ATBMs could bring stability to the region by encouraging a more secure Israel to cooperate with its Arab neighbors. Others, however, recognize that such an approach could at least as easily invite preemptive attack and would most certainly lead to an invigorated offensive-defensive arms race on both sides.[24]

At present, the ATBM issue in both regions seems to be on hold. Western Europe, however, remains threatened by Soviet short-range missiles, and NATO's existing ballistic missile force, a key element of its deterrent, could be rendered nearly meaningless by a dense Soviet ATBM defense. Similarly, tensions in the Middle East continue to be exacerbated by the flow of ballistic missiles to both sides. Such realities cannot be ignored. As with ABMs, pressure for ATBM deployment is likely to build again in the future unless successfully addressed through arms control.

THE SOVIET UNION

Throughout the periods of U.S. fluctuation, the Soviets appear to have steered a more consistent course. Undoubtedly motivated in part by a history of relative Russian indefensibility, the Soviets for years maintained a pro-defense attitude that led to large expenditures for air and missile defenses; these began with Griffon around Leningrad, continued with Tallin in the northern Soviet Union, and culminated, as of 1972, with Galosh around Moscow. However, whether for reasons of economy or as a genuine strategic policy change, the Soviets effectively abandoned the possibility of a territorial defense when they signed the ABM Treaty.[25] In making this reversal, they maintained the linkage between offensive and defensive limitations, a position that has continued throughout the current START and Defense and Space negotiations.

The Reagan SDI proposal of 1983 met with strong Soviet criticism, which intensified when the U.S. administration announced a reinterpretation of the ABM Treaty that would permit weapons based on "other physical principles" to be developed and tested in space (see chapter 4). Indeed, it appeared that the U.S. position might destroy the political will to reach an agreement that would reduce strategic offensive weapons and might thereby prevent a START Treaty.

ARMS CONTROL EFFORTS SINCE 1983

The years since 1980 have seen drastic fluctuations in U.S.-Soviet nuclear arms control negotiations, particularly with respect to the relationship of offense and defense. Talks reached a complete standstill in 1984, yet three years later the signing of the INF agreement generated optimism that even a START agreement might be possible. Space-based antimissile systems have been a key influence on the START negotiating pace since President Reagan first outlined his "Star Wars" dream.

In late 1983 the Soviets walked out of the negotiations in Geneva to protest the installation of U.S. intermediate-range missiles in Europe. In early January 1985 Secretary of State George Shultz and Soviet Foreign Minister Andrei Gromyko agreed that the U.S.-Soviet nuclear arms negotiations would resume in three areas: intermediate- and shorter-range missiles, offensive strategic weapons, and space.

Before he left for Geneva in early 1985 Shultz noted privately that he was willing to negotiate on SDI if the Soviets were willing to admit to and bargain with their superiority in ICBMs.[26] While making it clear that it would not bargain with SDI until the Soviet Union set numerical limits on strategic missiles, the United States expressed the hope that, if this approach failed, the negotiating teams could concentrate instead on START alone.

Denouncing SDI as an "offensive system," the Soviets saw it as an anticipatory breach of the ABM Treaty and charged the United States with attempting to upset the balance achieved in the 1970s. They also maintained that SDI was an attempt to price the Soviet Union out of an arms race in space. Accordingly, their response combined an assurance that they would pursue their own system if the United States did the same and a commitment to link space talks with the strategic weapons talks. Since 1985 the Soviets have maintained that they would accept no strategic reductions without a compromise on the ABM/SDI issue.

In November 1985 President Reagan and General Secretary Gorbachev met for the first time in Geneva. SDI was a major source of contention, in part because the Reagan administration had recently announced its reinterpretation of the ABM Treaty. Reagan attempted to convince Gorbachev that SDI offered them an opportunity to free the world from the "uncivilized doctrine" of mutually assured destruction. Gorbachev countered that "what you call research" on SDI could very well produce "offensive nuclear weapons circling the earth." As he put it, the United States was "plotting to use SDI to reestablish a 'one-sided advantage' over the Soviet Union."[27]

Gorbachev also noted that although Reagan claimed the guidelines he presented at Geneva would assure adherence to the ABM Treaty, they allowed each side to investigate and pursue, if feasible, strategic defense systems. Reagan concurred and stated that U.S. SDI plans "must continue."[28] The summit ended on this impasse.

The delegations resumed negotiations in Geneva with neither side willing to compromise on the SDI issue. In May 1986, however, the Soviets moved a bit. For the first time they retreated from their insistence on an immediate and comprehensive ban on all "space-strike arms." Instead they proposed interim measures, including a ban on antisatellite weapons, a ban on "space-to-earth weapons," and a "strengthening of the ABM Treaty." They suggested the addition of a new protocol that would prohibit either side from withdrawing from the ABM Treaty for fifteen to twenty years, except for purposes of a supreme national interest.[29] In June 1986, they officially altered their definition of strategic weapons, thereby removing what Paul Nitze, Reagan's chief arms control adviser, believed to be a principal sticking point to START. No longer would the Soviets count American forward-based INF missiles and bombers under START ceilings.[30] Gorbachev's critics could no longer write off his pronouncements as merely another turn in the "perennial [Soviet] peace offensive."[31] Even so, the START negotiations continued at a painfully slow pace. An attempt to break the impasse was made at Reykjavík in October 1986.

History may well judge the Icelandic summit to have been a failure, because Reagan was not willing to compromise on SDI. Several significant steps were taken toward a START agreement, even though no formal agreement was reached. Gorbachev agreed for the first time to allow Soviet heavy ICBMs to be counted in the 50 percent reduction figures. Both sides agreed formally on ceilings of 6,000 "nuclear charges" and 1,600 launchers, and the Soviets accepted in principle that in some areas, such as ICBMs, they would have to cut more than would the United States. With respect to the ABM Treaty, the sides discussed a possible nonwithdrawal period.

Although the Geneva negotiations resumed in December 1986, no significant progress was achieved until April 1987, when the Soviets proposed that the two sides agree on which space-based ABM tests would be permissible under the ABM Treaty and which would not. It is still not clear why the Soviets became willing to modify their earlier objections to all space-based testing. Perhaps, after conducting their own analysis, they had concluded that SDI was not technologically feasible. Perhaps their own progress toward a successful antimissile defense or, conversely, visions of overwhelming Soviet offensive deployments gave them the cushion they thought they needed. And perhaps, as Reagan's SDI encountered increasing opposition at home, particularly on Capitol Hill, the Soviets hoped it might die on its own. As one adviser reportedly told Gorbachev, "There is no need for us to ask for more than reasonable and influential members of the Congress are insisting on."[32]

In April Gorbachev acknowledged the possibility that an SDI might someday be deployed. With this concession, however, came the promise that if one side undertook the "practical establishment of an ABM system," the other side would immediately be released from its obligation to reduce its offensive weaponry. Again linking offensive and defensive arms control, the Soviets proposed adherence to the ABM Treaty as a prerequisite for START implementation. Although the United States rejected that proposal, the Soviets held steadfastly to the need to link offensive and defensive arms control efforts.[33]

In December 1987 Gorbachev and Reagan, with much fanfare, signed the INF Treaty. At the same time, regarding START, they both agreed to a subceiling of 4,900 on ICBM and SLBM warheads, only 100 more than the United States had proposed originally. As for SDI, Gorbachev seemed comfortable papering over their differences for the time being. According to the joint communiqué, both sides agreed to commit to the ABM Treaty "as signed in 1972, while conducting their research, development, and testing [of antimissile defenses] as required."[34]

Claiming that this statement resolved the SDI conflict, Reagan announced that the greatest threat to SDI came not from the Soviets, but from Congress, which was adhering to a strict interpretation of the ABM Treaty. According to the president, the United States and the Soviet Union had agreed to "[go] forward with whatever is necessary in the research and development [of SDI] without regard to an interpretation" of the ABM Treaty.[35] In due course, however, even the participants concluded that the communiqué simply represented an agreement to disagree. The Soviets had not accepted the "broad" interpretation of the ABM Treaty, nor were they ready to dissociate strategic reductions from SDI. After the Moscow summit, as noted, Gorbachev argued that it would not "meet normal logic" to consider a reduction of Soviet strategic forces when faced with even the possibility of a U.S. strategic defensive shield (see note 12). Although two minor agreements were signed in Moscow and some headway was made on a few verification questions, START remained unfinished, stalled in large part by SDI.

Since the Moscow summit, support for SDI has been eroded by technological questions, budgetary constraints, and the perception that the program is a key obstacle to a START Treaty. Yet it is probable that SDI—whether defined as a system to protect against an accidental launch (ALPS), astrodome defense, or simply research, has acquired a life of its own. A significant sum has always been available for research (approximately $500 million annually at the end of the Carter years, roughly doubled by March 1983), and the current level (about $4 billion a year) will probably not be dramatically cut, at least at the outset by the Bush administration. The SDIO has created a contractual base for itself, and the private sector has acquired a vested interest (important in political and economic terms) in the continuation of the program. In addition, since the Soviets have had a substantial program for a number of years, it would be politically unacceptable for the United States to withdraw unilaterally to previous funding levels. The public, astonished to learn that the United States has no defense against even one stray missile, believes that vigorous research and development should be continued. Its support was solidified by the initial Soviet objections to the Reagan initiative—"if the Russians don't like it, it must be all right."

It remains to be seen, however, whether massive expenditures for deployment will be supported. Since none of the military services has yet requested SDI funds of its own, the program lacks a Pentagon patron—a virtual necessity if it is to be viable over the long term.

Conclusion

SDI represents the latest attempt to reconcile the U.S. desire for defense against nuclear destruction with the concern for strategic stability. As we have seen, this debate has a long history and is likely to continue as politicians struggle to satisfy both these seemingly opposed views.

The political environment of antimissile defense has been volatile. When fear of the enemy and fear of the destructive force of nuclear weapons have converged ABMs have seemed the ideal solution to many politicians. In the early 1970s, however, other factors, such as the desire for strategic stability, intervened to produce the 1972 ABM Treaty, which prohibits the testing and deployment of more than one fixed ground-based antimissile complex. It is up to the new administration to decide what the future of the ABM Treaty will be and to resolve the many pressures it faces. Essentially President Bush must determine what the long-standing ABM Treaty is worth and whether it should be abandoned, amended, or observed. Even if he reaffirms his commitment to the Treaty, he will have to contend with the negative pressures it faces.

Currently, several factors are working against the Treaty, most of which involve increased pressure to deploy SDI. As in 1968, ABMs became an 1988 election issue with SDI a litmus test for a candidate's support of a strong defense. Second, the increased funding for SDI research and development in the past several years has led to public and congressional pressure to produce some sort of tangible outcome; that pressure is likely to grow if the current expenditures are maintained. Third, if START remains stalled, the need for a defensive shield will seem greater, at least to some observers. Finally, additional pressure is placed on the Treaty by compromises that are not ABM-compliant, such as an ALPS that would defend the continental United States and the report issued by the Defense Science Board that recommends considering fixed land-based defensive systems as an alternative to the space-based SDI. Adoption of any of these alternatives will mandate a breakout or a revision of the Treaty as it currently stands.

On the other hand, the adhesive that binds the ABM Treaty regime together has a good chance of maintaining its hold. To take the unprecedented step of abrogating a treaty with the Soviet Union now, just as relations are settling into their first thaw in over a decade, would prove diplomatically and domestically destructive. Moreover, few officials seem interested in even discussing amendments to the Treaty, lest such deliberations give the Treaty's opponents an opportunity to do away with its finer constraints. Congressional and public support as a whole favors adherence to the Treaty. The Senate approved the INF Treaty for ratification with the understanding that future administrations would be prevented from the sort of reinterpretation President Reagan applied to the ABM Treaty. Polls show that although most citizens favor SDI development, they do not favor it over adherence to the ABM Treaty.[36]

Many observers fear that continued support of SDI will harm future arms control efforts. Their fear has effectively decreased SDI's appeal as a bargaining chip. Ironically, Weinberger, who reportedly supported SDI because he believed it could be used to disrupt the arms control process, appears to have been the most prescient. Although many difficult issues, such as ceilings on the number of certain missiles and verification, have been largely resolved by the negotiating teams, the SDI issue has persisted through four summits as the principal obstacle to a START agreement. Finally it appears that financial and technological realities are beginning to play a large role in diminishing support for SDI. If that is the case, so long as the START negotiations remain incomplete, SDI may have substantially exhausted its support.

Nothing regarding BMD, however, is certain. For example, although cost could be a deterrent to SDI, the system's recent funding history is already increasing pressure for deployment. Similarly, although ongoing START negotiations could ease the pressure for protection against offensive nuclear weapons, a stalled START could just as easily increase the demand for defense.

The unilateral statement to the 1972 ABM Treaty delivered by chief SALT negotiator Gerard Smith was prophetic in predicting that the Treaty's future would hinge on continued reductions of each side's strategic arsenals. In that statement, the United States made it clear that if an agreement limiting strategic arms were not signed, "U.S. supreme interests could be jeopardized," which "would constitute a basis for withdrawal from the ABM Treaty. . . . It is because we wish to prevent such a situation," it concluded, "that we emphasize the importance the U.S. Government attaches to achievement of more complete limitations on strategic offensive arms."[37]

Tensions created by support for SDI may have eroded both sides' attitude toward the politico-military buffer provided by the ABM Treaty. On the other hand, if the new administration significantly reduces its commitment to SDI deployment, enabling the two sides to reach a reasonable compromise on ABM-SDI issues, it will constitute success for those who see strategic defenses as undesirable and destabilizing.

The only certainty is that the debate over ABMs will continue. SDI is the current measuring stick. Other threats to the buffer established by the ABM Treaty are sure to follow. It is therefore imperative that President Bush, whatever his position on SDI, first recognize and contend with the existence of the ABM Treaty before he takes further action. The decision to abandon, amend, or observe the treaty regime is his alone and must be made before the next round of the ABM debate can be addressed.

Notes

1. Laurence Freedman, *U.S. Intelligence and the Soviet Strategic Threat,* 2d ed. (Boulder, CO: Westview Press, 1977), p. 87.

2. For further information, see Herbert York, *Race to Oblivion* (New York: Simon and Schuster, 1970) and York, "Military Technology and National Security," *Scientific American,* August 1969.

3. Abram Chayes and Jerome B. Wiesner, eds., *ABM, An Evaluation of the Decision to Deploy an Antiballistic Missile System* (New York: Harper and Row, 1969) p. 2.

4. Walter Stutzle, Jasani Bhupendra, and Regina Cowen, eds., *The ABM Treaty, to Defend or Not to Defend?* (New York: Oxford University Press, 1987), p. 32.

5. York, *Race to Oblivion, p.* 195.

6. Center for the Study of Democratic Institutions, *Anti-Ballistic Missile: Yes or No?* (New York: Hill and Wang, 1968), p. 116.

7. Chayes, *ABM,* p. 242. From MacNamara's September 18, 1967, San Francisco speech to UPI editors and publishers.

8. Gerard Smith, *Doubletalk* (New York: Doubleday and Co., Inc., 1980), p. 30.

9. John Newhouse, *Cold Dawn* (New York: Holt, Rinehart and Winston, 1973; McLean, VA: Pergamon-Brassey's, 1989), p. 187.

10. Gerard Clarfield and William Wieeck, *Nuclear America* (New York: Harper and Row, 1984), p. 332.

11. Chayes, *ABM*, pp. 239–40. From MacNamara's 1967 San Francisco speech.

12. From Gorbachev press conference, June 1, 1988.

13. Republican platform, 1980.

14. The Defense Budget Project, 1988. Figures adjusted for inflation.

15. Phone interview with Thomas W. Graham, Center for International Studies, Massachusetts Institute of Technology, July 11, 1988.

16. The Arms Control Association, *Star Wars Quotes*, July 1986, p. 34. Quoting DeLauer from an interview in *Government Executive*, July-August 1983.

17. Strobe Talbott, "Inside Moves," *Time*, May 30, 1988, p. 34. In May 1988, McFarlane testified before the House Armed Services Committee and explained his motives for supporting SDI in the fall of 1982. According to that testimony (taken six years after the fact), one of the primary factors that influenced his decision was a belief that the Soviets would be forced to question the efficacy of their political-economic system when faced with an "extended American investment in high technology." Reassuringly, McFarlane concluded that, in regard to its effect on Soviet policy, SDI has been a success as it convinced the Soviets that they could not compete with the United States given their economic woes, and therefore it served as a major impetus for Gorbachev's *perestroika*. Robert McFarlane, testimony before the U.S. House Armed Services Committee hearing on U.S. Strategic Forces and START, May 17, 1988.

18. American Physical Society Study Group, *Science and Technology of Directed Energy Weapons*, April 1987, introduction, p. 2.

19. Office of Technology Assessment, *SDI Technology Survivability and Software* (Washington, D.C.: U.S. Government Printing Office, May 1988), pp. 4–5.

20. Donald L. Hafner and John Roper, eds., *ATBMs and Western Security* (Cambridge, MA: Ballinger Publishing Co., 1988), pp. xiii–xviii, especially chapters by J. Eberle and A. Baer; D. Gormley; and C. Kelleher.

21. Hafner, *ATBMs*, pp. xv–xvi.

22. Hafner, *ATBMs*, p. 263, and David Ottaway, "U.S., Israel to Develop New Missile," *Washington Post*, June 29, 1988.

23. Ottaway, *Washington Post*.

24. See Hafner, *ATBMs*, especially chapter by S. Chubin.

25. Although the Soviets have upgraded these defensive systems, they remain largely inadequate.

26. Talbott, *Time*, p. 31.

27. Talbott, *Time*, p. 34.

28. Ibid.

29. Strobe Talbott, *Master of the Game* (New York: Alfred A. Knopf, 1988), pp. 300–301.

30. Talbott, *Master of the Game*, p. 302.

31. B. Nahaylo, "Mr. Gorbachev: The Kremlin's Latest Fighter for Peace," *Radio Liberty*, 108/85, p. 1.

32. Talbott, *Time*, p. 35.

33. This interrelationship was most recently articulated by Victor Karpov, a senior Soviet arms control adviser. Facing a possible U.S. breakout from the ABM Treaty over the Soviet radar near Krasnoyarsk, Karpov warned in September 1988 that if the United States withdrew from or violated the Treaty, the Soviets would not continue the START negotiations. Karpov emphasized the Soviet position, first articulated by Gorbachev in June 1988, that "an organic relationship" exists between the ABM Treaty and a negotiated reduction in strategic arms.

34. Washington summit, Joint Communiqué, December 1987.

35. Lou Cannon, "Reagan Says SDI Intact after Summit," *Washington Post*, December 12, 1987. Reagan quoted from his postsummit press conference.

36. *Americans Talk Security,* Martilla & Kiley, Inc. November 1987. When asked if they supported the development of SDI, 54 percent of those surveyed responded yes, 34 percent responded no. However, when the question read "If the U.S. had to choose between continuing its development of Star Wars or continuing to live by the ABM Treaty," 47 percent wanted to keep the Treaty, 37 percent wanted to develop SDI.

37. "United States's Unilateral Statement to the Treaty Between the United States of America and the Union of Soviet Socialist Republics on the Limitation of Anti-Ballistic Missile Systems," delivered by Gerard Smith, May 1972.

4

THE LEGAL ENVIRONMENT

*John B. Rhinelander and Sherri Wasserman Goodman**

U.S. POLICYMAKERS attempting to manage both U.S.-Soviet relations and progress in strategic defense and related technologies need to appreciate the legal environment in which they act. The ABM Treaty severely limits the pursuit of strategic defenses. On that foundation can be based a more complex set of rules to allow either tighter or looser restraint of activities that press against the Treaty's limits.

This chapter describes the most important provisions of the ABM Treaty, the major problems that have arisen to date, including attempts at "reinterpretation,-" and issues that must be addressed in the future as technology evolves. The legal framework provides the basis for understanding the interaction of the Treaty and the technical issues discussed in chapters 5 through 9 and in chapter 10 on verification. We conclude with a discussion of treaty ratification, interpretation, and amendment, topics explored at greater length in chapter 11.

A short document signed by President Nixon at the Moscow summit in May 1972, the ABM Treaty consists of a preamble and sixteen articles. It is supplemented by seven agreed statements initialed by the heads of the United States and Soviet delegations. Five common understandings, which were not formally documented but culled from the negotiating record by the United States without prior discussion with the Soviets, were transmitted to the Senate for its advice and consent, as were several noteworthy unilateral statements.[1] The

* We wish to thank the individuals who were generous in their comments on this chapter. The views in this chapter are those of the authors and do not necessarily represent the views of the Senate Armed Services Committee or its members.

43

Senate approved the ABM Treaty by a vote of 88 to 2 in August 1972 without condition or amendment. It entered into force on October 3, 1972.

A protocol signed at the Moscow summit in 1974 amended the Treaty by reducing the number of authorized ABM deployment areas in the United States and USSR from two to one. That protocol received the advice and consent of the Senate by vote of 63 to 15 in November 1975 and entered into force on May 24, 1976.[2]

Four interpretive documents, labeled protocols, or agreed statements, have been agreed upon since 1972, but their texts remain classified. Two protocols (1974 and 1976) cover procedures for replacing and dismantling ABM systems. Two agreed statements (1978 and 1985) define ABM test ranges and the term "tested in an ABM mode" and include criteria related to permitted and prohibited air defense activities at ABM test ranges. These four documents became effective on execution. Although they were submitted to congressional committees for information, they were not subject to approval.

Compared with the very lengthy and highly specific texts and supplementary documentation of the SALT II Treaty of 1979 and the INF Treaty of 1987, the ABM Treaty looks simple. Appearances, however, are deceptive, particularly because the ABM Treaty reflects different rules for ABM systems depending on basing mode and type of technology. For fixed land-based ABM systems not based on "other physical principles," the Treaty allows full development and testing and limited deployment. But only research and limited development, and neither testing nor deployment, are permitted for sea-based, air-based, space-based, and mobile land-based ABM systems and components, whatever the technology. Further, two terms critical to understanding the ABM regime—*fixed land-based* and *research*—are never used in the Treaty's text.

The United States considered "zero" ABM deployments even for fixed land-based systems during SALT I but eventually rejected that possibility in favor of the ABM Treaty's approach, which permitted two fixed land-based sites on each side. President Nixon indicated in a 1971 letter to Gerard Smith, the head of the U.S. SALT delegation, that the United States would reconsider zero ABMs at SALT II,[3] but the issue was not pursued then and has not been raised subsequently between the superpowers.

Consistent with the ABM Treaty, the United States deployed one fixed land-based ABM system to defend Minutemen ICBM silos and dismantled a partially completed second such system. The deployed site at Grand Forks was deactivated in 1975 because it was not considered cost effective, although an ABM radar there is used for early warning. The United States now has no active deployed ABM site. The Soviet Union has continued to deploy, and has upgraded within the Treaty's limits, a fixed land-based ABM system around Moscow with 100 permitted ABM launchers for 100 nuclear-armed ABM interceptor missiles, together with associated ABM engagement radars.

The Structure of the Treaty

The ABM Treaty, a U.S. initiative, was hailed as a triumph of American diplomacy in 1972. Although its text reflects trade-offs important to the time, its central thrust is to prohibit the United States and the Soviet Union from deploying an ABM system that could provide a nationwide defense or even an effective area defense. The preamble to the Treaty asserts the premise that the limitations on ABM systems would contribute to limitations on strategic offensive systems. Moreover, in a unilateral statement made at the conclusion of SALT I the United States noted that the failure to achieve more extensive offensive arms limitations could jeopardize U.S. interests and would be a basis for withdrawal from the Treaty.

Before analyzing the major problems that have arisen to date and the issues that must be addressed in the future, we will summarize the Treaty's key provisions.[4]

THE BASIC PURPOSES (ARTICLE I)

The basic purposes of the Treaty are to prohibit deployment of either an ABM system for "the defense of the territory" of the United States or Soviet Union or a "base for such a defense." The former includes a nationwide defense, whether on land or sea or in air or space, and the latter encompasses items such as powerful, large phased-array radars, which are the long-lead-time items of a deployed land-based ABM system.

THE KEY DEFINITIONS (ARTICLE II)

An ABM system is defined, for Treaty purposes, in functional terms as a system "to counter strategic ballistic missiles or their elements in flight trajectory." An ABM system is then described as "currently consisting of" three components—ABM launchers, ABM interceptor missiles, and ABM radars. When tested or deployed, these components can readily be monitored by satellites and other forms of national technical means (NTM) of verification.

Two key modifiers used in the definition are particularly noteworthy. First, the word *strategic* was included to preserve the option to deploy antitactical ballistic missiles (ATBMs). Second, the word *currently* was included to make clear that the Treaty encompassed all ABM systems, whether based on current or future technology; the 1972-era components listed in the Treaty were illustrative only. At the time, the ABM systems of both the United States and Soviet Union used nuclear-armed interceptors, but the Treaty also applies to weapons based on kinetic or directed energy, whether considered current or future technology.[5]

ABM components are defined in Article II as either "constructed and deployed for an ABM role" or of "a type tested in an ABM mode." These definitions dovetail with provisions in Article VI(a) prohibiting the "testing in an ABM mode" of non-ABM systems, such as surface-to-air antiaircraft missile systems (SAMs). The ability to monitor by NTM various tests on ABM and non-ABM systems at Soviet test ranges made feasible this approach, which is central to the scope of the ABM Treaty.

For purposes of the Treaty, "deployment" includes an ABM component, such as an ABM radar that is under construction, and not just those that are in operation. This provision is one of the buffers intended to provide significant lead times in the event of violation or termination of the Treaty.

During the negotiations, both sides agreed that certain auxiliary equipment, described as "adjuncts" to an ABM component, was not limited by the Treaty. The one example given by the United States during the negotiations was an optical telescope used in conjunction with an ABM radar. An "adjunct" was understood to be a device that supplements, but does not substitute for, an ABM component. There has been no mutual attempt to develop further the distinction between "components" and "adjuncts."

AUTHORIZED FIXED LAND-BASED DEPLOYMENTS (ARTICLES III AND V[2])

Since the 1974 amendment to Article III, the Treaty permits only one ABM deployment area in the United States and one in the Soviet Union. An authorized deployment area, with a radius of 150 kilometers, must be centered either on the national capital area or on ICBM silos. Although not clear, the 1974 Protocol does not appear to have rescinded the requirement that the latter (i.e., silo defense) must be at least 1,300 kilometers from the national capital area. The ABM components must be located within the deployment area and must be fixed land-based. Further limitations include a ceiling of 100 ABM launchers and 100 ABM missiles "at launch sites" in the ABM deployment area.

The radar constraints differ for each type of deployment area. The ABM radars in a national capital deployment area must be located within six small circular areas, but there are no limits on the number of radars or the power (potential) of any radar within those areas. The ABM radars used for defense of ICBM silos are differentiated by levels of power; two large and eighteen smaller ABM radars may be located in each such deployment area. Because the earth's curvature limits the coverage of fixed land-based ABM radars located at the original authorized sites 1,300 kilometers apart, the Treaty effectively prevented a broad area defense.[6]

Article V(2) prohibits certain features on fixed land-based components, such as automatic, semiautomatic, or rapid reload ABM launchers and launchers that could launch more than one ABM interceptor missile at a time. Agreed Statement E extends the prohibitions in Article V(2) to ABM interceptors with multiple independently targetable reentry vehicles (MIRVs). The prohibitions on rapid reload and MIRVed interceptors, when coupled with the limit of 100 launchers at an authorized ABM deployment area, preclude an effective defense against a sophisticated threat.

ABM TEST RANGES (ARTICLE IV)

The provision for ABM test ranges prohibits, among other things, ABM deployments in various locations around the country under the guise of test facilities. The numerical limitation of fifteen launchers at an ABM test range reinforces this purpose.

The United States has two ABM test ranges—one at White Sands, New Mexico, and the other on Kwajalein Island in the Pacific—from which fixed land-based ABM components may be tested. During SALT I the United States recognized a single Soviet ABM test range at Sary Shagan. The Soviets refused to discuss their test ranges but later claimed, and the United States accepted, the existence of a second ABM test range on the Kamchatka Peninsula.

SPACE AND OTHER PROHIBITED ENVIRONMENTS (ARTICLE V[1])

The prohibitions in Article V(1) apply to space-based, air-based, sea-based, and mobile land-based ABM systems and components. This article applies to a space-based ABM component, such as an interceptor missile, that is part of an otherwise fixed land-based ABM system. The U.S. delegation insisted on revising the draft Treaty text to make clear that only fixed land-based ABM components may be developed, tested, or deployed.

The ban in Article V(1) covers development and testing as well as deployment. The United States originally proposed that the constraints include production, but not development. The Soviets suggested testing and deployment bans only. The United States then proposed, and the Soviets accepted, dropping the ban on production but prohibiting development. This latter approach was based on the theory, espoused by U.S. delegate Harold Brown and others, that the constraint should be moved back as far in the research and development cycle as could be monitored by NTM.

During the SALT I negotiations, the United States insisted that Article V place no restraints on research or on those aspects of exploratory and advanced development that precede field testing. As explained during the 1972 Senate ratification hearings, the dividing line, determined by the verification limits of NTM, is drawn at the point at which field testing is initiated on a prototype or a "breadboard" model.[7] The Soviets apparently accepted this U.S. approach, but no attempt has since been made to define further the line between permitted research and prohibited development and testing.

SDI activities are now beginning to push against this ill-defined dividing line.

Further, the Soviets could not verify by NTM alone whether some SDI experiments comply with the treaty. (See chapter 8.)

(See chapter 8.)

FUTURE OR EXOTIC SYSTEMS (ARTICLES II, III, AND V, AND AGREED STATEMENT D)

At SALT I the United States introduced and the Soviets accepted a two-part proposal on the control of future or exotic systems, such as lasers. The negotiators amplified the basic Treaty approach, which is built on Articles II, III, and V, by introducing the concept of "other physical principles." This phrase was intended to make clear that this U.S. initiative was not directed at the Soviet SAM network, but at new technologies (which the U.S. negotiators were not initially authorized to identify). Equally important, Agreed Statement D speaks of components "capable of substituting for" conventional ABM components. Agreed Statement D explicitly refers to Article III, which covers fixed land-based components, but the concepts of "other physical principles" and components "capable of substituting for" conventional ABM components apply equally to the limitations in Article V(1).

Accordingly, with respect to space-based and other ABM components limited by Article V(1), the prohibitions on future or exotic devices capable of substituting for an ABM component, such as a space-based laser, include development and testing as well as deployment. However, the U.S. negotiators at SALT I did not explore the threshold capabilities at which the ban on development in Article V(1) would begin to apply to a particular type of device in order to differentiate, for instance, an ABM-capable laser from a laser for permitted purposes. The technologies were not sufficiently advanced to make such judgments in 1972.

Under Articles III and IV and Agreed Statement D, different rules apply to fixed land-based components based on future systems, such as an ABM laser to destroy ICBM warheads. They can be developed and tested at an ABM test range but cannot be deployed.[8] In other words, more stringent *deployment* constraints were applied to fixed land-based ABM systems based on future technology than to those using 1972-era technology. However, this ban on deployment of a fixed land-based killer laser under Article III is consistent with the ban under Article V on deploying rapid reload or MIRVed ABM launchers, which applies to fixed land-based 1972-era technology.

DUAL-CAPABLE SYSTEMS (ARTICLE VI[A])

The constraints in Article VI(a) seek to differentiate ABM systems from non-ABM systems, which are not explicitly covered by the Treaty. The approach used is to prohibit non-ABM systems, such as SAMs for antiaircraft purposes, from having "capabilities to counter strategic ballistic missiles" or from being "tested in an ABM mode."

During the SALT I negotiations, the United States spent considerable time and attention on dual-capable technologies, particularly SAMs. The Soviet Union had, and has maintained, an extensive SAM network with over 10,000 SAM interceptor missiles at 1,200 sites. Concerned that the Soviets might upgrade those systems to have a nationwide "ABM capability," the United States tried to limit testing. It sought, but failed to get, detailed agreement on what SAM activities were prohibited by the formula "tested in an ABM mode." The United States has not sought to quantify the meaning of "ABM capabilities" as used in Article VI(a).

The U.S. negotiators made a detailed proposal on "tested an ABM mode" in 1972, which was published as Unilateral Statement B. During the Senate ratification hearings, several additional quantitative parameters were suggested as consistent with the U.S. approach, such as a maximum permissible altitude of a target vehicle for testing of a SAM. The United States and the Soviet Union finally reached agreement in this area in 1978. This agreement apparently does not include all details of the 1972 U.S. position, such as altitude limits for target vehicles, in part because the United States had changed its position.[9]

LARGE PHASED-ARRAY RADARS (ARTICLES III, IV, VI[B], AND AGREED STATEMENT F) AND SPACE-BASED SENSORS

During SALT I, the United States determined it could not rely solely on technical parameters to differentiate ABM engagement radars, which were to be tightly constrained, from early-warning radars for ballistic missiles. The fundamental problem was that the newest technology—phased-array radars—could be used for many purposes, including battle management and early warning. Some key technical features, such as operating frequencies, could not be distinguished by NTM during the construction phase and before operation of the radar.[10]

SALT I took a primarily geographic approach to ground-based radars combined with quantitative limits on phased-array technologies. ABM radars were confined to authorized ABM deployment areas or ABM test ranges; early-warning radars constructed in the future were to be located on "the periphery of the country" and "oriented outward." The periphery requirement assumed that a radar so located was vulnerable to military attack and therefore not strategically effective. The outward orientation was intended to prohibit the over-the-shoulder coverage necessary for an effective ABM radar providing coverage of incoming ballistic missiles within territorial boundaries. The two explicit exceptions to these rules, stated in Agreed Statement F, are radars for space tracking or for NTM, which are not limited in terms of power, location, orientation, or other factors.

Agreed Statements B and F include the only quantitative threshold agreed upon in 1972 governing phased-array radars. A phased-array radar with a "potential" (defined as the product of "mean emitted power" in watts and "antenna area" in square meters) of more than 3 million is constrained by the Treaty.

Space-based sensors and phased-array radars raise many similar issues, since both can perform many different functions. The U.S. negotiators understood that some space-based sensors were akin to early-warning or NTM radars and that their deployment in space was fully consistent with the purpose and letter of the Treaty. For instance, a space-based infrared sensor available in 1972 could detect the launch of a missile but had almost no tracking capability. On the other hand, although not then available, space-based sensors capable of substituting for ABM radars are banned by Article V(1).

The task of differentiating permitted and prohibited space-based sensors was not discussed between the United States and the Soviet Union at SALT I and was left to the future. That challenge is rapidly approaching and is complicated by the fact that current space-based sensors designed to perform important NTM and related functions could have considerable ABM capabilities, thereby raising difficult policy choices. Further, the capabilities of various passive and active space-based sensors that may be deployed in the future probably cannot be fully monitored by NTM. (See chapters 6, 7, and 9.)

NONTRANSFER (ARTICLE IX)

The Treaty prohibits the transfer by the United States or Soviet Union of "ABM systems or their components limited by this Treaty" to other countries. This provision applies to transfers from (not to) the United States or Soviet Union at the point that Article V becomes applicable (i.e., at development stage) and applies equally to all ABM systems and components regardless of basing mode. The article does not apply to SAM, ATBM, or antisatellite (ASAT) systems that are not "ABM capable" and have not been "tested in an ABM mode."

Agreed Statement G prohibits providing "to other States technical descriptions or blueprints" for ABM systems or components. Consistent with the Treaty as a whole, this provision does not apply to the research stage and other activities not covered by Article V.

VERIFICATION (ARTICLE XII)

The ABM Treaty explicitly states that verification is by "national technical means," a phrase denoting satellites and other collection systems located outside a nation's borders. The acceptance of NTM, the corollary provision on noninterference with NTM, and the prohibition of deliberate concealment methods reflect technical and political achievements of the SALT process. In the early 1970s, on-site inspection (OSI) was unacceptable to the Soviet Union.

The ability to monitor Treaty constraints with NTM was an important U.S. concern at SALT I. If a more restrictive treaty regime is agreed on in the future, cooperative measures including OSI may be necessary.

STANDING CONSULTATIVE COMMISSION (ARTICLE XIII)

The ABM Treaty established the Standing Consultative Commission (SCC) as a forum to address compliance issues and ongoing problems and challenges. The SCC is not a third-party neutral forum but a mechanism for the authorized agents of the United States and Soviet Union to discuss sensitive matters in confidence. Under the terms of the Treaty, the SCC could consider not only compliance issues but also proposals for agreed interpretations and amendments. The SCC has been a successful, if underused, bilateral U.S.-USSR forum under the Ford and Carter administrations but was severely criticized as ineffective by the Reagan administration.

DURATION, WITHDRAWAL, AND REVIEW (ARTICLES XV AND XVI)

The Treaty has an unlimited duration. Like other major post–World War II arms control treaties, however, it includes a ''supreme interests'' withdrawal clause that can be unilaterally exercised with only minimal notice, six months in the case of the ABM Treaty. The United States understood in 1972 that under international law it had the right to suspend, in whole or in part, or terminate its performance under the ABM Treaty if the Soviets committed a ''material breach.'' This right was understood to be independent of the ''supreme interests'' withdrawal clause.

The ABM Treaty calls for a formal review every five years. The 1977 and 1982 reviews were not controversial, but the review that took place in August 1988 involved an exchange of noncompliance charges with no apparent progress in resolving or clarifying any outstanding issue. In its unilateral statement at the end of the conference, the United States charged that the Krasnoyarsk radar was a ''significant'' violation of the Treaty, and that unless the radar was dismantled ''without conditions,'' the United States would have to consider declaring it a ''material breach.'' The United States reserved the right to take ''appropriate and proportionate'' responses in the future and declared that the continued existence of the Krasnoyarsk radar made it impossible to conclude a START Treaty.[11] The Soviet unilateral statement denied Krasnoyarsk was a violation, offered to dismantle the equipment there if the United States agreed to observe the ABM Treaty ''as signed'' (i.e., the traditional interpretation), and charged that the U.S. early-warning radars at Thule and Fylingdales Moor were violations. The

United States rejected the Soviet proposal to trade the Krasnoyarsk violation for the traditional interpretation of the ABM Treaty.

Threats to the ABM Treaty Regime

Seven basic problems could threaten the integrity of the treaty regime in the future. The following discussion is not based on any ranking of the seven.

One problem is the declared intent of the United States to deploy strategic defenses as soon as practicable and to pursue a research and development program toward this end. However, policymakers have not agreed on the objectives of the SDI program, and recent descriptions seem less immediately threatening to the Treaty.[12] Congress has never fully funded the president's annual SDI budget requests. Should the United States decide to pursue aggressively, and Congress agree to fund, SDI activities prohibited by the Treaty, the United States may have to withdraw from the Treaty over the next five to ten years unless the Soviets agree to various amendments.

Soviet violation of the Treaty by construction of the Krasnoyarsk radar is another threat to the Treaty. Presidential findings and votes in both houses of Congress[13] have judged the radar to be a deliberate violation of Article VI(b) of the Treaty.[14] Although the military significance of the radar has been questioned, the fact that it is a violation is undisputed. The Soviets appear to recognize that their justification, that the radar is for permitted space-track purposes, is not persuasive. In the fall of 1987, they took the unprecedented step in inviting a congressional delegation to visit and photograph the site and stopped construction the following month. During 1988, the Soviets made a number of proposals concerning the radar, but the United States required complete dismantlement and refused to link that radar with any other Treaty issue.

The replacement of the U.S. radars in Thule, Greenland, and Fylingdales Moor, England, raises questions about Treaty compliance. The United States's position is that it is simply modernizing existing radars as implicitly permitted under the reasoning of Article VII of the Treaty (which permits the modernization of Treaty-compliant ABM radars that are more capable than early-warning radars). The Soviets claim the radars are phased-array radars, whose deployment on foreign territory is prohibited by Agreed Statement F.

A third threat to the Treaty is the unilateral reinterpretation put forth by the Reagan administration. This view would permit the development and testing of all "future" ABM systems and components regardless of basing modes. Such activity would erode a key buffer of the Treaty and would reduce the long lead time to breakout. The origins of the reinterpretation are explored further below.

A fourth problem is the failure to achieve U.S.-Soviet agreement reducing strategic offensive weapons. The ABM Treaty's preamble declares that a fundamental premise is the more complete limitation of strategic offensive forces. Although the SALT I Interim Agreement and the unratified SALT II Treaty constrained U.S. and Soviet programs from 1972 until 1987, both sides were allowed to increase the number of deployed strategic ballistic warheads. Some observers believe that the failure to reach agreement on strategic reductions in a START Treaty could undermine the basic premise of the ABM Treaty.

A fifth problem relates to SAMs. The United States has deactivated its network of Nike-Ajax and Nike-Hercules antiaircraft sites, which were in place in the 1960s, but the Soviets have maintained and improved their extensive SAM network. The most recent Soviet weapon, the SA-12, has been tested against short-range tactical ballistic missiles (as has the U.S. Patriot SAM system). The Soviet SAM systems have an inherent dual nature, or residual ABM capability, and radars for Soviet SAMs and ABM systems were previously tested at the same time at the test range at Sary Shagan. The 1978 and 1985 agreed statement and common understanding were intended to address the principal U.S. concerns. So far, however, agreement has been confined to "tested in an ABM mode" and has not dealt with the parallel provision in Article VI(a) on "ABM capability." Further, very difficult issues under the Treaty are raised by the renewed U.S. interest in ATBMs and the possibility that a mobile land-based SAM network might be coupled in the future with space-based sensors with significant ABM capability. (See chapters 7 and 9.)

A sixth problem is the failure to clarify ambiguities in the Treaty. The U.S.-Soviet roles of 1972 were reversed in important respects during the Reagan presidency. Since April 1987 the Soviets have sought, through reinforcements of the existing text or new understandings, agreements on limits stated in greater detail, although they have done so while seeking to protect their own ABM programs. The United States resisted formal discussion in areas that might impinge on SDI until October 1988, when it began to fill gaps in its negotiating position.[15]

Seventh, technological developments in strategic defenses and related areas, particularly space-based sensors, will continue to prompt activity whose Treaty compliance is ambiguous. Because of technological advances, much future activity will be conducted within the Treaty's buffer zones. Without agreement clarifying some of the ambiguities discussed in this chapter, the programs of both the United States and Soviet Union will press against the Treaty's limits.

The Controversy over Reinterpretation of the Treaty

In 1985, the Reagan administration announced a new interpretation of the ABM Treaty that appeared to open the door to unrestrained development and testing of the components of a space-based strategic defense system using future or exotic technology. The reinterpretation would apply the same rules for development and testing of fixed land-based systems to those that are space-based. Shortly after the announcement, amid sharp protests from members of Congress and NATO allies, Secretary of State Shultz explained that the new interpretation reflected U.S. legal rights, but that the United States would not change its policy.[16]

During 1986 and 1987, however, the Reagan administration told the Senate that the executive is not bound by its own testimony on the meaning of a treaty since only the negotiations between the treaty parties count. State Department legal adviser Abraham Sofaer said, "When [the Senate] gives its advice and consent to a treaty, it is to the treaty that was made, irrespective of the explanations it is provided."[17] This so-called Sofaer Doctrine became the doctrinal justification for the reinterpretation of the ABM Treaty.

The most effective opponent of the reinterpretation was Congress, in particular the Senate. The lead role of challenging, and eventually defeating, the reinterpretation was undertaken by Senator Sam Nunn of Georgia, chairman of the Senate Armed Services Committee since January 1987. Senator Nunn's review of the ratification record found that the Nixon administration presented the Senate with the traditional interpretation of the Treaty's limits on space-based and other mobile types of exotics, and the Senate clearly understood this interpretation when it gave its advice and consent to the ratification of the Treaty.[18]

The immediate result of congressional review was to block the administration's switch to the "broad" interpretation. In both the fiscal year 1988 and 1989 defense authorization acts, Congress enacted provisions requiring that SDI funds be spent on activities consistent with the traditional interpretation.[19] The long-term result was the rejection of the Sofaer Doctrine during the 1988 debate on the INF Treaty. By then, former President Nixon, who had signed the ABM Treaty at the summit in 1972, had stated publicly his unequivocal support for the traditional interpretation.[20]

Ironically for the proponents of the reinterpretation, the effect of the debate was to place greater constraints on SDI activities than had it never occurred. A spring 1988 Pentagon review of the SDI program, which is considered to be the first turning point in scaling back the near-term goals of the program, concluded that "the present testing program is in a straitjacket. This has come about in large part because in the course of debate on 'narrow' vs. 'broad' interpretations of the Treaty, the 'narrow' interpretation of the Treaty itself was so squeezed by both the opponents and proponents of SDI that it lost all reasonableness."[21] At the very least, the reinterpretation has made compliance of SDI activities subject to much greater public scrutiny.

Treaty Issues Raised by Emerging Technology

The reinterpretation debate obscured the fact that emerging technology raises many unresolved issues even under the traditional interpretation of the Treaty. The following issues are among those that must be addressed.

DEPLOYMENT OF A BASE FOR A NATIONWIDE ABM SYSTEM

Article I(2) prohibits deploying a nationwide defense and providing a "base" for such a defense. Is that prohibition limited to those activities specifically prohibited by other articles of the Treaty, or are certain activities, not specifically constrained by the Treaty's terms, prohibited because they could constitute a territorial defense or a base for a territorial defense?

During the SALT I negotiations the Soviets argued that because Article I(2) prohibited a base for a nationwide system, Agreed Statement D limiting future systems was necessary. The United States accepted the base concept but also insisted on a specific provision (Agreed Statement D) to deal with futures and an explicit Soviet agreement to the U.S. view that Article II, which defines ABM components, included future technology such as lasers.

The United States viewed the base concept as reinforcing the prohibitions on ABM components and ABM-capable systems in the more specific Articles III, IV, V, and VI of the Treaty. For instance, U.S. negotiators indicated that the prohibition on a deployment base would reinforce the ban on constructing long-lead-time components, such as large phased-array radars, in different parts of the country. Soviet construction of the phased-array radar near Krasnoyarsk is the kind of activity the United States sought to preclude by this approach. The Reagan administration noncompliance reports came very close to declaring Soviet ballistic missile defense (BMD) activities a base that violates the Treaty.[22]

Another issue is whether certain activities, not otherwise specifically limited by the Treaty, could constitute a prohibited "territorial defense." The proposal to study the feasibility of developing an Accidental Launch Protection System (ALPS), first made by Senator Sam Nunn in January 1988, raises questions about the type of fixed land-based system prohibited as a territorial defense. One issue is whether an ALPS consistent with the Treaty's other provisions, such as those governing location and the limitation of 100 ABM interceptor missiles, would violate Article I if its interceptors could intercept targets over either coast from a single deployment area in North Dakota. Since the Treaty does not specifically limit the size, range, velocity, or internal guidance systems of interceptors, such features would not appear to determine what constitutes a prohibited territorial defense.

COMPONENT VERSUS ADJUNCT

When is a device an "ABM component" whose development, testing, and deployment are prohibited by Article V(1) of the Treaty, and when is it merely an "adjunct" not subject to the Treaty's limitations?

The Treaty limits ABM systems and components but makes no reference to subcomponents and adjuncts. Thus, subcomponents or adjuncts are exempt from the Treaty's constraints. Guidance from SALT I indicates that an optical telescope was considered to be an adjunct that supplements, but does not substitute for, an ABM radar. The parties have not subsequently agreed on any classification of prohibited ABM components or permitted subcomponents and adjuncts.

The distinction between "supplement" and "substitute" is raised by the Airborne Optical Adjunct (AOA), a long-wavelength infrared (LWIR) radar that, when tested, will operate aboard a modified Boeing 767. (See chapter 9.) The flight test of the AOA, which could occur as early as 1989, is expected to validate the capability to detect and track incoming ballistic targets, discriminate real warheads from decoys, and transfer data to the ground-based radar to allow for the interception and destruction of warheads.

The term *adjunct* indicates that the airborne sensor will operate in conjunction with a ground-based radar specifically designed for tracking and discriminating reentry vehicles from decoys. The AOA was originally designed as an adjunct to the fixed ground-based radar that was included in the Low-Altitude Defense System (LoADS) for defense of MX missile silos. In this configuration it would have performed fewer functions than are now being considered by SDI officials. However, a laser that was being considered for target ranging and designation is not now included in the AOA experiment. The laser ranger was thought to provide a capability that would enable the AOA to substitute for an ABM radar.

In the absence of agreement, U.S. and Soviet officials must continue to make independent judgments about the appropriate dividing line between an adjunct and a component in particular cases. Each side has the opportunity, and incentives, to press against the Treaty's limits in its program and to challenge the compliance of the other side.

SENSORS FOR ABM PURPOSES VERSUS SENSORS FOR EARLY WARNING, NTM, OR SPACE TRACKING

When is a space-based sensor subject to the Treaty's limitations because it is "capable of substituting" for an ABM radar, and when is it Treaty-compliant as an early-warning, space-tracking, or verification sensor?

The ABM Treaty explicitly allows radars for the tasks of early warning, space tracking, and verification but places a threshold limit on the power of phased-array radars that could be used for ABM purposes. Many non-ABM radars, even some deployed in 1972, had some ABM capability. The functions of permitted and prohibited radars and sensors overlap and will increasingly do so. The situation is made more complex today by the likelihood that a single sensor need not perform all the functions of a phased-array ABM radar but could operate in conjunction with other sensors or radars to enable the system to perform the full range of functions required for ballistic missile defense (BMD). Thus, no one sensor may by itself be "capable of substituting for" an ABM radar. (In the 1960s, an earlier U.S. ABM system used four different types of ABM radars, and the ABM system actually deployed at Grand Forks, North Dakota, had two ABM radars, the perimeter acquisition radar [PAR] and the missile site radar [MSR].) One possibility, which was explored but not resolved by the Reagan administration, is whether a space-based sensor that can perform most, but not all the functions of an ABM radar can be developed, tested, and deployed within the Treaty's limits.

Advanced sensor technology will soon allow sensors designed for non-ABM purposes to perform some significant ABM functions. Chapters 7 and 9 examine four functions a BMD sensor must perform: surveillance, tracking discrimination, and fire control. Sensors for non-ABM purposes, such as air defense, need to perform all four functions, but at less challenging levels. The exact level of capability may depend as much on testing and operating practices as on the inherent features of the device itself.

These sensor distinctions will soon be tested by the Boost Surveillance and Tracking System (BSTS), which is scheduled to begin full-scale engineering development in fiscal year 1991. The issue will be whether the BSTS is simply an improved version of the current Defense Support Program (DSP) missile-warning satellites, or whether it will possess the capability to substitute for an ABM radar. The answer will likely depend on how much missile-tracking capability is required to be considered "capable of substituting for" an ABM battle management radar. This determination is complicated by the 1988 revision to SDI's Phase I architecture, which relies more heavily on the tracking satellites for battle management than did the previous architecture.

An approach examined in chapters 7 and 9 is the development of threshold limits for sensors similar to those the Treaty imposes on phased-array radars. An issue discussed in chapter 9 is whether such limits alone could provide an effective, verifiable dividing line between permitted and prohibited capabilities. Threshold limits could strengthen one of the Treaty's important buffer zones but might impede NTM and early-warning capabilities. Policymakers will have to weigh the importance of preserving the NTM and early-warning capabilities of future sensors against the need to maintain limitations on radars and sensors with ABM capabilities. The distinction chosen in 1972 to differentiate ground-based ABM radars from ground-based early-warning radars—the requirement that the latter be on the periphery and oriented outward—is not available for space-based sensors.

THE MEANING OF "SPACE-BASED"

What does "space-based" mean for purposes of applying the Article V(1) limits on development and testing and the Article VI(a) limits on "tested in an ABM mode"?

Since the ABM Treaty prohibits space-based development and testing (under the traditional interpretation) but permits such activities for fixed ground-based devices at agreed ABM test ranges, the parties may want to develop and test as much of their own ABM technology as possible in a ground-based configuration. Several types of issues will challenge the distinction between "space-based" and "land-based."

Are space-based devices only those that are tested in stable orbit, or do they also include those lofted into space for a few minutes on a suborbital trajectory? As explained in chapter 8, the United States's lofted testing of the infrared probe in the 1970s set a precedent for the interpretation that this type of testing is not considered space-based for purposes of the Treaty. The probe is an infrared sensor mounted on a small ground-launched rocket, which would operate in a suborbital trajectory to acquire and track reentry vehicles. The United States has considered such lofted tests to be Treaty-compliant ground-based tests when conducted from an ABM test range.

Devices such as the space-based interceptor (SBI), which would ultimately be deployed in space, could be tested from the ground in a lofted mode. Should such testing from an ABM test range be considered a Treaty-compliant ground-based test? This type of issue was not discussed by the Treaty's negotiators during SALT I. Subsequent practice suggests that some lofted tests may be Treaty-compliant, ground-based tests if conducted from an ABM test range. The parties could agree either to confirm the legality of lofted tests or to ban them.

THE MEANING OF "MOBILE LAND-BASED"

What is the distinction between a "mobile land-based" ABM system or component, which is subject to the limits of Article V(1), and a "fixed land-based" ABM system or component, which can be developed and tested at an ABM test range?

Common Understanding C reflects the position that the ban on development, testing, and deployment of mobile land-based ABM systems or components prohibits all but "permanent fixed types." However, this distinction itself raises many questions.

In the last several years the issue has come to the fore because some Soviet radars may be rapidly deployable, movable, or transportable. The Reagan administration's noncompliance reports found Soviet actions with respect to ABM component mobility to be "ambiguous."[23] The United States was concerned about the engagement and guidance radars, designated "Flat Twin" and "Pawn Shop." The Flat Twin radar can reportedly be disassembled, transported, and reassembled in a period of several months, but extensive advance preparation of the deployment site is required. The Pawn Shop radar is smaller and possibly easier to transport, although its container is not thought to be a transporter. Such modular construction techniques, which will have more widespread application in the future, can significantly reduce the lead time to deployment of an ABM system, perhaps to months, which could seriously erode one of the Treaty's buffers.

Although modular ABM radars may not generally be considered "permanent fixed types," they cannot be moved in a matter of hours. An agreed interpretation could seek to define more precisely the meaning of the term *mobile*. In any case, the shorter lead times to deployment made possible by modular construction will probably erode the buffer against a prohibited base.

"OTHER PHYSICAL PRINCIPLES"

What systems are based on "other physical principles" and thus cannot be deployed even in a fixed land-based mode?

According to Article III and Agreed Statement D, a device based on "other physical principles" cannot be deployed, even in a fixed land-based mode, without agreement amending the Treaty. Thus, the Treaty is more restrictive with respect to exotic systems based on "other physical principles" than it is for nonexotic technology, which can be deployed in a fixed land-based mode. The United States and Soviet Union have not agreed on a definition of "other physical principles." In fact, the United States itself has no official definition for use in the government's own internal compliance review.[24] The issue is whether only technologies that were unknown in 1972 should be considered to be "based on other physical principles" or whether the phrase should be applied to all technologies that were not incorporated in the ABM systems that existed at the time the Treaty was signed.

One example of how this issue may arise concerns an infrared homing device being considered in conjunction with the Exoatmospheric Reentry Vehicle Interceptor System (ERIS) as part of an ALPS. Placing an infrared sensor aboard a land-based missile raises several issues. Two questions—whether the device is land-based or space-based and whether it is "capable of substituting for" an ABM radar—have already been discussed. The third is whether such a device is based on "other physical principles," which is one of the most pressing issues under the Treaty. If such devices are not considered to be based on "other physical principles," deployment in a fixed land-based mode would be permitted, but development, testing, and deployment in a *space-based mode* would be prohibited, even under the reinterpretation.

"TESTED IN AN ABM MODE"

If an interceptor missile does not destroy its strategic ballistic missile target, has it been "tested in an ABM mode"? What about an interceptor that attempts to intercept a nonstrategic ballistic missile or a radar or sensor that tracks and guides a non-ABM interceptor missile?

Many such questions will arise in designing tests of ABM and related technologies. The most precise guidance to date is the classified 1978 agreed statement that has been excerpted in recent unclassified reports to Congress. (See "Threats to the ABM Treaty Regime," above.) Clearly, attempting to intercept a *strategic* ballistic missile or its elements in flight trajectory is considered testing in an ABM mode. Moreover, as chapter 8 discusses further, if a test target has the "flight trajectory characteristics of strategic ballistic missile or its elements over the portions of the flight trajectory involved in testing," the device should be considered to have been "tested in an ABM mode."

More complicated is the question of what constitutes an "attempt to intercept (successfully or not)" a strategic ballistic missile. One example, discussed in chapter 8, is a space-based laser that illuminates an ascending strategic booster but does not destroy it, either because the laser is operated at low power or because the test target is specially hardened. Without an agreed definition of the term *intercept*, more than one interpretation might be considered consistent with the Treaty. For example, one could argue that the interceptor must at least attempt to destroy the target to qualify as "tested in an ABM mode." Or, drawing on the common understanding of the term *weapon-delivery vehicle* agreed between the United States and Soviet Union during the Senate's consideration of the INF Treaty, one could argue that an attempt to "damage or destroy" counts as testing.[25] Moreover, since tests of nuclear-armed ABM interceptors have been conducted without actual detonation of a nuclear ABM warhead, one could argue that the defensive interceptor need not operate at full power to qualify as "tested in an ABM mode." The verifiability of any approach is, of course, an important related issue.

As for radars or sensors, can they track and guide non-ABM interceptor missiles, such as antitactical ballistic missiles, without being subject to the limits of the Treaty? The answer is yes, provided that none of the components have been constructed or deployed for an ABM role and none have been tested in an ABM mode (as defined above).

ABM CAPABILITIES

When do non-ABM systems, such as ASATs, ATBMs, and SAMs, acquire ABM capabilities that are prohibited by the Treaty?

ASATs were not discussed at SALT I, where the Article VI(a) focus was primarily on SAMs. Distinguishing an ABM system from an ASAT will become a pressing issue. The latter category is not covered by the Treaty unless a particular ASAT has ABM "capabilities" or is "tested in an ABM mode." Other ASATs can be tested and deployed anywhere. This will inevitably become an issue with respect to some SDI experiments. In addition, newspaper articles and photographs from the French commercial Satellite Pour l'Observation de la Terre (SPOT) satellite raise questions about a Soviet facility under construction at Dushanbe near the Afghanistan border.[26]

Testing ASATs against orbiting satellite targets could demonstrate some capability against strategic ballistic missiles, depending on such parameters as speed, timeliness, sensitivity to decoys, proximity to target, and extent of damage to target. The question is what level of capability would be prohibited by the Treaty. The parties could decide to define such thresholds, as suggested in chapter 8.

Various issues involving ABMs and ASATs will arise whether or not a separate treaty on ASATs is negotiated. If an ASAT treaty is sought on its own merits, the parties will have to consider whether to ban testing as well as deployment of fixed land-based exoatmospheric (i.e., outside the atmosphere) ABM interceptor missiles. Such a ban might be appropriate to prevent circumvention of an ASAT treaty by an authorized ABM system. It would severely curtail SDI tests that may be technologically feasible in the next decade but would also limit the current Soviet ABM system around Moscow.

The development and testing of ATBMs and SAMs raise a common issue: what are the flight characteristics of a strategic ballistic missile that determine whether ATBMs or SAMs have a Treaty-prohibited capability to counter strategic ballistic missiles? This problem was originally part of the SAM upgrade issue. In 1972 the United States wanted to preserve the option to deploy its SAM-D (now Patriot) system. It also feared that the Soviets might give their widely deployed, antiaircraft SAM forces an ABM capability, putting the United States at a strategic disadvantage and enabling the Soviet Union to break out from the Treaty.

The United States and the Soviets may now be exploiting this legal loophole with their Patriot and SA-12 systems, which can counter tactical ballistic missiles. (See chapter 6.) They probably have some residual capability against ICBMs and submarine-launched ballistic missiles (SLBMs). Although U.S. interest in ATBMs to counter tactical ballistic missiles with ranges greater than 500 kilometers may have declined as a result of the INF Treaty, which eliminated all such missiles from U.S. and Soviet arsenals, both NATO and Israel have expressed interest in ATBM systems to counter the threat posed by short-range tactical ballistic missiles. The proliferation of conventionally or chemically armed ballistic missiles in the Middle East may be the greatest incentive to development of ATBMs.

Within the current treaty regime, thresholds could be specified to define more precisely the prohibited ABM capabilities of non-ABM systems. Chapter 7 suggests thresholds for the velocities of defensive interceptors. Thresholds could also be defined for characteristics of the target vehicle.[27]

Steps Toward Treaty Adaptation

Together, the ABM Treaty reinterpretation dispute, the Sofaer Doctrine, and the INF Treaty hearings and debate may have changed the U.S. political climate in which future arms control agreements will be reviewed. In general, the process will probably become more complex and more formal, at least between the executive branch and the Senate. A major undercurrent of the Byrd-Biden amendment to the INF Treaty was clarification of the proper roles of the Senate and the executive in the treaty-making process.

The legal process offers a number of ways to adapt the ABM Treaty to the changing technological environment. With minor exceptions such moves will involve only the political branches of the government—the executive and Congress—and not the courts.

APPROVAL OF TREATIES

The Constitution requires that a treaty be approved by two-thirds of the senators present and voting but does not require that all international agreements be treaties. Article 33 of the legislation establishing the Arms Control and Disarmament Agency requires that an international agreement limiting arms be subject to approval as a treaty or by joint resolution of Congress.[28] The U.S. practice of an international agreement approved by a joint resolution adopted by simple majority of the House and Senate was used with the Interim Offensive Agreement of 1972, which was signed at the same time as the ABM Treaty. Although it does not qualify for the label *treaty* under U.S. Constitutional practice, such an agreement can accomplish the same substantive end. However, only the treaty process has an explicit constitutional foundation, which gives the Senate leverage to insist that a particular agreement be submitted to it as a treaty.

Ratification of the INF Treaty led to developments in the treaty-approval process that may become standard for arms control treaties in the future. After holding separate hearings, the Armed Services and Intelligence committees formally reported to the Foreign Relations Committee, which reported out the treaty with a favorable recommendation.[29] This process led to approval by a final vote of 93 to 5. It was the first ratification of a nuclear arms control treaty between the United States and the Soviet Union since 1972.

INTERPRETATION OF TREATIES

The executive has traditionally exercised the power to interpret the text of a treaty. As part of the ratification of the INF Treaty in the spring of 1988, the Senate attached the Byrd-Biden amendment to the resolution of ratification by a vote of 72 to 27. The amendment provides that the United States shall interpret the Treaty in accordance with the common understanding of the Treaty shared by the president and the Senate when the Senate gave its advice and consent to ratification. Moreover, the United States shall not agree to adopt an interpretation different from that common understanding except pursuant to Senate advice and consent to a subsequent treaty or the enactment of a statute.[30]

Under U.S. and international law the general principle is that a treaty is to be interpreted in good faith in accordance with the ordinary meaning to be given its terms in light of their context and in light of the treaty's object and purpose. In the absence of adjudication, the president is responsible for interpreting treaties, and interpretation by the executive branch is given great weight in U.S. law.

In practice, treaty interpretation is an ongoing process. In the SALT context, it may be carried out by the United States and the Soviet Union in various forums, including the SCC. The result may be an agreed statement or common understanding, such as the agreements on "tested in an ABM mode" that were reached in 1978 and 1985. An interpretation that clarifies but does not change the meaning of a treaty and is not inconsistent with the Senate's understanding during ratification, such as agreement on laser brightness as a threshold for Article V(1), should not be an amendment requiring prior congressional approval. However, an agreement that banned ATBMs or space nuclear power sources, or added on-site inspection requirements, would clearly require prior Senate advice and consent.

Within the U.S. government, interpretations are reflected in the annual arms control impact statements and other reports to Congress, such as the annual report on the SDI and compliance reports. The compliance of U.S. programs with the ABM Treaty is handled through separate channels from those dealing with Soviet compliance, and coordination has not always been required. Further, in implementing the ABM Treaty since 1972, the Department of Defense has had to devise ad hoc quantitative thresholds for many Treaty constraints stated only in general terms.[31] These thresholds and limits remain unpublished and classified, are not coordinated with compliance decisions on Soviet programs, and are made on a case-by-case basis. The existence of these Defense Department limits suggests that quantitative approaches in certain areas applicable to both sides have become a practical necessity for translating legal concepts into rules usable by engineers and program managers.

Executive reports, congressional hearings, congressional reports, and occasional legislative enactments create mechanisms through which the executive and Congress manage a treaty regime. This process may lead to negotiations with the Soviets on particular issues. The Soviets must, of course, agree to be bound to an interpretation if it is to have more than unilateral application.

International courts and international arbitration have not had, and almost assuredly will not have, any direct role in interpreting arms control obligations of the United States. The U.S. Supreme Court and the lesser federal courts have the authority to interpret treaty obligations of the United States, but in practice they are unlikely to interpret arms control treaties, given the "political question" and other special legal doctrines.[32]

Congress influences treaty interpretation most effectively by wielding the power of the purse. For example, it has prohibited the expenditure of funds for SDI activities inconsistent with the traditional interpretation of the ABM Treaty.

WITHDRAWAL, TERMINATION, OR SUSPENSION

Under general principles of international law a party has a right to withdraw from a treaty according to its terms. A party may also terminate or suspend its performance in whole or in part in the event of a "material breach" by the other party. The rights of the executive and Congress under the Constitution are not as clear.

The Supreme Court has not resolved the question of the president's right to withdraw from, terminate, or suspend a treaty without involvement of the Senate or Congress. The president acting alone probably can exercise those rights, unless there is a contrary provision in a treaty or a legislative condition.[33] No such express condition exists that would block a president from unilaterally withdrawing from, terminating, or suspending U.S. adherence to the ABM Treaty.

A political and legal debate on this general issue occurred when President Carter unilaterally terminated the 1954 Mutual Defense Treaty with Taiwan in 1978. An attempt by some members of Congress to force judicial resolution of this action was thwarted by the Supreme Court's decision in *Goldwater v. Carter*,[34] which, in dismissing the complaint, vitiated any precedential value of the earlier rulings in that case and left the termination issue basically unresolved.

In the case of a material breach, a party is entitled to terminate the treaty or suspend its operation in whole or in part. If a treaty is suspended in part, the question arises whether a "proportionate response" is required and, if so, what constitutes such a response. Could the United States, for example, implement the broad interpretation of the ABM Treaty if the Krasnoyarsk radar is declared a material breach? Since neither international practice nor constitutional doctrine provides much guidance on this matter, the range of choices of a proportionate response could be broad, and any decision would be largely political and not reviewable by the federal courts.

CLARIFICATION OR MODIFICATION BY AGREEMENT

The United States and the Soviet Union can clarify or modify the ABM Treaty by written agreement. The label attached by the parties to such an agreement (e.g., a protocol) does not control the domestic processes and requirements under U.S. law. An agreement changing a treaty's meaning or effect, such as the 1974 protocol to the ABM Treaty, which reduced the authorized ABM sites from two to one, is an amendment that requires congressional approval before entry into force. In practice, the amendment process is tantamount to a new treaty negotiation because it requires advice and consent. Normally, a treaty amendment would be submitted to the Senate for its advice and consent as a subsequent treaty and would require approval by two-thirds of the senators present and voting. An amendment to a treaty could be approved by joint resolution if the Senate did not oppose such a course.

If the ABM Treaty is to remain viable over the next decade, it may require various amendments. It will almost certainly require numerous agreed interpretations between the two parties. Traditionally, agreed interpretations have not been submitted to the Senate for approval, although the Senate changed its practice when considering the SALT II Treaty. There has been no serious contention that the protocols and agreed statements reached under the ABM Treaty since 1974 should have been treated as amendments under U.S. law.

This relatively informal practice of the past may change. The ABM Treaty reinterpretation controversy and its impact on the INF Treaty ratification process have undermined trust between the two branches of government. The Senate will be much more likely to assert its full panoply of prerogatives in the future. As a consequence, modifications that could once have been treated as agreed statements not requiring Senate or congressional approval may now be elevated to the status of amendments, which invoke the full range of Senate procedure. The debate on the Sofaer Doctrine ensures that the Senate will pay particularly close attention to interpretations. Senators who oppose such agreements, or simply wish to assert the Senate's constitutional role in treaty making, may claim a particular interpretation should be dealt with as an amendment. Further, Congress will certainly insist that the executive comply with the Case Act requirements for reporting to Congress any modifications in the form of agreed interpretations, a practice that has been inconsistently followed in the past.

Although the dividing line between amendments and agreed statements remains far from clear, the Senate sought to establish a precedent in the INF Treaty ratification process. A distinction was made between "technical changes" and those that affect "fundamental obligations" of the Treaty.[35] Prior approval is not required for the former category, which includes minor, nonsubstantive changes that would improve implementation of the INF Treaty's protocols on on-site inspection and elimination. Any other modification, however, must be submitted to the Senate as an amendment. Although this approach will have to be interpreted on a case-by-case basis, it will probably lower the threshold for the type of modification the Senate believes requires congressional approval.

Conclusion

Managing the ABM Treaty regime in the 1990s will require adaptation of the Treaty's legal framework if the Treaty is to continue to mediate between the conflicting and mutual security interests of the United States and the Soviet Union. The viability of the treaty regime will in all likelihood depend on the willingness of its signatories to work together more closely in the future.

Without cooperative efforts, the pressures, both technological and political, within the United States to abandon the Treaty altogether may continue to rise. Central to such an effort will be greater specificity, in the form of mutually binding interpretations of key Treaty terms, such as "other physical principles" and of other gray areas. Such an undertaking will probably require a more productive dialogue, both within the U.S. government and with the Soviets, about the particular areas where greater specificity would be mutually beneficial. Finally, the executive and Congress, particularly the Senate leadership, will have to work together closely if the constitutional process is to deal constructively with efforts to manage the ABM Treaty regime.

Notes

1. The ABM Treaty, the agreed statements, the common understandings, and the unilateral statements are printed in the Appendix to this volume. The letters attached to each (e.g., Agreed Statement D) were added when the documents were submitted to the Senate.

2. The 1974 Protocol also appears in the Appendix.

3. Quoted in Gerard C. Smith, *Double Talk: The Story of SALT I* (Boston: University Press of America, 1985), pp. 485–86.

4. Readers familiar with the Treaty structure may wish to skip this part and go directly to "Threats to the ABM Treaty Regime" in this chapter.

5. This analysis is based on the traditional interpretation of the ABM Treaty, to which all administrations adhered until October 1985, when the Reagan administration sought to reinterpret the Treaty to permit unconstrained development and testing of space-based "future" systems. The reinterpretation is discussed below.

6. Article III was the most controversial of articles during the SALT I negotiations. Many of the arguments dealt with particular configurations to be allowed within each ABM deployment area, particularly the ABM radar rules for the two types of ABM systems. The most protracted issue, though, was the number of deployment areas allowed each side. The Soviet Union consistently urged one site for defense of each side's national capital area. The United States argued that defense of

ICBM sites should also be permitted because it enhanced deterrence and at different times formally proposed one, two, three, or four sites in each country. The final 1972 compromise was two sites for each party, one centered on its national capital and the other on ICBM silos. This allowance was reduced to one site in each country by the 1974 Protocol.

7. A formal submission for the record of the Senate Armed Services Committee on *The Military Implication of the ABM Treaty* (Hearings, 92d Cong., 2d sess., 1972, p. 377) provides in part that

> the SALT negotiating history clearly supports the following interpretation. The obligation not to develop such systems, devices, or warheads would be applicable only to that stage of development which follows laboratory development and testing. The prohibitions on development contained in the ABM Treaty would start at that part of the development process where field testing is initiated on either a prototype or breadboard model. It was understood by both sides that the prohibition on "development" applies to activities involved after a component moves from the laboratory development and testing stage to the field testing stage, wherever performed. The fact that early stages of the development process, such as laboratory testing, would pose problems for verification by national technical means is an important consideration in reaching this definition. Exchanges with the Soviet Delegation made clear that this definition is also the Soviet interpretation of the term "development."
>
> Consequently, there is adequate basis for the interpretation that development as used in Article V of the ABM Treaty and as applied to the budget categories in the DOD RDT&E [Department of Defense Research, Development, Test, and Evaluation] program places no constraints on research and on those aspects of exploratory and advanced development which precede field testing. Engineering development would clearly be prohibited.

8. During SALT I, the United States had a highly classified fixed land-based laser program under development, which was protected by the Treaty as negotiated.

9. The 1985 agreed statement has not been described in the open literature. As summarized in a 1985 unclassified report to Congress, the 1978 agreed statement provides that

> an interceptor missile is considered to be "tested in an ABM mode" if it has attempted to intercept (successfully or not) a strategic ballistic missile or its elements in flight trajectory. Likewise, a radar is considered to be "tested in an ABM mode" if it performs certain functions such as tracking and guiding an ABM interceptor missile or tracking strategic ballistic missiles or their elements in flight trajectory in conjunction with an ABM radar which is tracking and guiding an ABM interceptor missile. "Strategic ballistic missiles or their elements in flight trajectory" include ballistic target-missiles with the flight trajectory characteristics of strategic ballistic missiles or their elements over the portions of the flight trajectory involved in testing.

10. In response to a written question from Senator Percy on any "potential difficulties in identifying just what the specific purpose of the radar could be," Ambassador Gerard Smith provided a written reply for the record of the Committee on Foreign Relations (Hearings on *Strategic Arms Limitations Agreement*, 92d Cong., 2d sess., 1972, p. 54):

> *Answer*. We believe that national technical means of verification will be adequate to distinguish between ABM radars and air defense and space tracking radars. There are a number of parameters, such as location, orientation, size, power, and signal characteristics, which taken together, should provide sufficient information to make this distinction. If an ambiguous situation regarding radars should nevertheless arise, the situation could be clarified through discussions in the Standing Consultative Commission.

11. U.S. Unilateral Statement following ABM Treaty Review, Terry Shroeder, spokesman, U.S. delegation, August 31, 1988. See Matthew Bunn, "U.S., USSR Charge Violations at ABM Treaty Review Conference," *Arms Control Today*, November 1988, p. 25.

12. The *Report of the Strategic Defense Milestone Panel of the Defense Science Board* (the "Everett report"), April 13, 1988, suggests six steps in deployment of a ballistic missile defense, of which the first two would be Treaty-compliant. The Joint Chiefs of Staff (JCS) continue to support the military utility of the ABM Treaty. "Our view is that we should continue to abide by the ABM Treaty until it's clear that we should withdraw and for what purpose we should withdraw," said

General Robert T. Herres, vice chairman of the JCS, in testimony before the Senate and House Armed Services committees. "The only reason on the horizon for withdrawing from the ABM Treaty that we see would be . . . a deployment decision for 'phase one' of the 'Star Wars' program." John H. Cushman, Jr., "Beyond the Campaign, More Tests Await 'Star Wars,' " *New York Times,* October 16, 1988, p. E-4.

13. The Senate voted 81-0 that the Krasnoyarsk radar is a violation that must be corrected before the conclusion of any future agreement on strategic arms. *Congressional Record,* September 16, 1988, p. S12714. The House voted 418-0 that the Krasnoyarsk radar is a violation of the ABM Treaty. *Congressional Record,* May 7, 1987, p. H3278.

14. The Treaty limits radar for early warning of ballistic missiles to locations on the periphery of the country and to outward orientation. The Krasnoyarsk radar meets neither criterion.

15. The U.S. delegation in Geneva suggested a limit of fifteen "Star Wars" satellites in space at any one time, coupled with various notification provisions. The proposal would not apply to satellites used solely as sensors. See Michael Gordon, "U.S. Proposes Limit on 'Star Wars' Tests," *New York Times,* October 27, 1988, p. A-10.

16. After the president's "Star Wars" speech in March 1983, the Soviets grossly overstated the scope of the Treaty's prohibitions. At first, they said that "purposeful research" was prohibited by Article V(1), by which they apparently meant research on programs that, if continued, would be prohibited at a later stage. This position was flatly contradicted by the Treaty text, which never uses the term *research.* The Soviet posture was superficially supported by the Russian text of Article V, where the word for develop could be translated as "create," but the negotiating record makes clear that this approach was rejected at SALT I. By 1987 the Soviets had modified their position on the intended general scope of Article V(1) and asserted that they had adopted the traditional U.S. position.

17. Testimony before a joint hearing of the Senate Foreign Relations and Judiciary committees on *The ABM Treaty and the Constitution,* March 26, 1987, 100th Cong., 1st sess., p. 375.

18. Both international law and U.S. domestic law recognize that the subsequent practices of the parties, including their statements, provide evidence of their intent with regard to the meaning of a treaty. Senator Nunn found no evidence of Soviet practices or statements expressly embracing the reinterpretation. In fact, Nunn's review of documents revealed that the case for the reinterpretation was substantially weaker than the administration's previous analysis had indicated. He also found that the negotiating record contains substantial and credible information that the Soviet Union agreed that the development and testing of mobile and space-based exotics were banned. The preponderance of evidence, he concluded, supports the Senate's original understanding of the Treaty. Senator Sam Nunn, "Interpretation of the ABM Treaty—Part IV: An Examination of Judge Sofaer's Analysis of the Negotiating Record," *Congressional Record,* daily edition, May 19, 1987, pp. S6809–31.

19. Section 225 of the National Defense Authorization Act for Fiscal Years 1988 and 1989, Report 100–446, 100th Cong., 1st sess., 1987. Section 223 of the National Defense Authorization Act of Fiscal Year 1989, Report 100–989, 100th Cong., 2d sess., 1988.

20. In speaking to the American Society of Newspaper Editors on April 15, 1988, he said: "As far as what was presented to the Senate was concerned, it was what we call the 'narrow' interpretation. There is no question about that. And so Senator Nunn is absolutely correct on that point." Quoted in Matthew Bunn, "Nixon Supports Nunn on ABM Treaty," *Arms Control Today,* May 1988, p. 21.

21. *Report of the Strategic Defense Milestone Panel of the Defense Science Board* (the "Everett report"), April 13, 1988. This panel recommended that the Defense Department "define a technically optimum testing and deployment program" and "then adhere to that program except when Treaty constraints *unambiguously* require it do otherwise. The DOD should place the burden of proof on those who restrain the program."

22. See "The President's Report to the Congress on Soviet Noncompliance with Arms Control Agreements," January 23, 1984; October 18, 1984; February 1, 1985; December 23, 1985; March 10, 1987; December 2, 1987.

23. "The President's Report to the Congress on Soviet Noncompliance with Arms Control

Agreements,'' February 1, 1985; December 23, 1985. The Soviets agreed to dismantle some of this radar equipment as part of an agreement reached at The Special Consultative Commission in December 1988.

24. Statement of Robert Costello, under secretary of defense for acquisition, testimony before the Senate and House Armed Services committees, October 6, 1988.

25. See *Congressional Record*, daily edition, May 26, 1988. p. S6705.

26. See Eliot Marshall, ''The New Spy-in-the-Sky Race,'' *Washington Post*, December 27, 1987, p. C3; William J. Broad, ''New Clues on the Soviet Laser Complex,'' *New York Times*, October 23, 1987, p. A-14.

27. A recent study has proposed limiting the altitude of the target to 40 kilometers and its speed to 3 kilometers per second. See Ivo H. Daalder and Jeffrey Boutwell, ''TBMs and ATBMs: Arms Control Considerations,'' in Donald L. Hafner and John Roper, eds., *ATBMs and Western Security: Missile Defenses for Western Europe* (Boston: Ballinger Publishing Co., 1988), p. 192.

28. See 22 U.S.C. § 2573 (1982). See generally George Bunn, ''Missile Limitation: By Treaty or Otherwise?,'' *Columbia Law Review* 70 (1970):1.

29. During the full Senate's consideration of the INF Treaty, some key senators insisted that several matters be clarified in writing with the Soviets before the Senate moved to its final vote of approval. See *Congressional Record*, daily edition, May 17–27, 1988.

30. The Byrd-Biden amendment did not settle the debate over the ABM Treaty, for the administration could still argue that testimony before the Senate in 1972 was not clearly consistent with the traditional interpretation.

31. The under secretary of defense for acquisition, through a body called the Compliance Review Group, has been responsible for ensuring that SDI activities are consistent with the Treaty. Specific responsibilities are assigned by DOD Directive 5100.70, *Implementation of Strategic Arms Limitation Agreements*, January 9, 1973. DOD Instruction S-5100-72 establishes general instruction, guidelines, and procedures for ensuring compliance with existing arms control agreements.

32. From time to time, however, the federal courts may render decisions under trade, commerce, tax, or other international agreements and state principles of general relevance to arms control treaties. May and November 1988 decisions by Judge Greene of the District of Columbia federal district court is an example. The judge noted and rejected the Sofaer Doctrine under the facts of *Rainbow Navigation*, 686 F. Supp. 354 (D.D.C. 1988) and 699 F. Supp. 339 (D.D.C. 1988), in which the Justice Department sought to disavow representations made by the executive in testimony before a Senate committee and reflected in that committee's report, which was part of the ratification record. The Supreme Court has affirmed the authority of reliance on Senate ratification debates in interpreting treaties. *United States v. Stuart*, 57 L.W. 4263 (Feb. 28, 1989). However, concurring opinions by Justices Kennedy and Scalia, and a subsequent notice of appeal of *Rainbow Navigation* by the Justice Department, suggest that the role of Senate ratification debates in treaty interpretation may not yet be settled.

33. See American Law Institute, *Restatement of the Law, Second, Foreign Relations Law of the United States*, 1965, pp. 412–13.

34. 444 U.S. 996 (1979).

35. Senate Armed Services Committee, *NATO Defense and the INF Treaty*, 100th Cong., 2d sess., 1988, S. Rept. 100–312, pp. 25–26.

5

THE NATURE AND PURPOSE OF ABM RESEARCH

John C. Toomay and Robert T. Marsh

Background

FROM shortly before World War II until the early 1960s the United States's military research and development (R&D) program proceeded largely unconstrained by treaties and agreements. The defense R&D community probed the scientific and engineering disciplines broadly, seeking new means to conduct warfare more effectively and efficiently. The most promising applications were carried further, either into a preprototype demonstration or directly into engineering development of the ultimately desired military capability. Although Congress occasionally restricted R&D and deployment (as with chemical and biological weapons and, in the 1970s, the neutron bomb), in general, there were few restrictions on the type of research or nature of the capability pursued, as long as the end result was a cost-effective war-fighting capability.

The first significant constraints were those imposed by the nuclear test limitation treaties, which banned atmospheric testing of nuclear weapons and later limited the yield of those that could be tested underground. Since these constraints prohibited the full-scale operational testing of weapons of new design, nuclear weapon developers began to make more extensive use of simulation, component testing, and scaling from approved lower yield testing. In general, the restrictions did not significantly hinder advanced weapon design, development, and production. They did, however, limit testing and hence knowledge of the interaction of nuclear explosives with the upper atmosphere and space.

Another constraint was imposed by the 1967 treaty banning deployment of weapons of mass destruction in space. Since this treaty was promulgated in the early days of the military exploitation of space, and limited only deployment, its impact on R&D was hardly noticed. Preliminary studies had explored the feasibility and utility of nuclear space mines and orbital-based nuclear bombardment capabilities, but no actual research or development efforts had yet been planned. (The Soviets had progressed further into this area having tested a fractional orbit bombardment system.) Hence, the new constraints had minimal impact on the Defense Department research and development program.

A more difficult and complex constraint was imposed by the ABM Treaty in 1972, which not only restricts deployment of ABM systems to a relatively small number of fixed ground-based interceptors and supporting systems but limits research and development on follow-on ABM capabilities as well. R&D related to enhancements of the fixed ground-based systems is not significantly restricted, but testing must be conducted at ABM test ranges. For other basing concepts (e.g., land mobile, sea-based, or space-based), only early R&D may be conducted; advanced development and testing are restricted.

Between 1972 and 1984, Congress approved and the Defense Department conducted a modest ABM research and development program, expending several hundred million dollars annually. Under a clear policy of current and future Treaty compliance, the R&D effort was principally focused on enhancing fixed ground-based ABM capabilities. A working process was established to formulate and review the R&D program to ensure Treaty compliance. Several proposed programs, such as the nuclear version of the Navy SM-2 tactical missile defense program and the Trojan multiple warhead interceptor, were shelved in the interest of compliance. Since the advent of SDI in 1983, involving the expenditure of several billion dollars per year, there has been an understandable renewed interest in the goals, structure, and Treaty compliance aspects of the ABM R&D program. This chapter outlines alternative future ABM research and development programs based upon different overall ABM program goals and explores how the restrictions of the ABM Treaty would affect the achievement of these goals.

The Rationale for ABM Research

Potential ABM research and development programs cannot be assessed in isolation; they must be viewed in the context of overall national strategic defense policy. The overarching strategic objective—that of nuclear deterrence—has not changed substantively in the last thirty years. It has been maintained with a combination of deployed offensive nuclear forces and negotiated agreements.

The United States's deterrent posture has been and must be seamless and foolproof. Both our survivable redundant retaliatory forces and the ABM Treaty are pieces of the fabric.

The rationale for ABM R&D should be intimately tied to maintaining strategic deterrence over the long term. The efforts should seek to improve our capability, help us perceive and understand the ABM activities of our adversaries, and permit us to counter or thwart those actions that threaten the strategic balance. The traditional view has been that ABM R&D should support four goals:

- Seeking breakthrough ABM capabilities for the United States.
- Responding to a possible Soviet breakout.
- Ensuring against technological surprise.
- Assuring the penetration effectiveness of our offensive missile forces.

What are these goals, more specifically?

U.S. BREAKTHROUGHS

Most notions of ABM breakthrough envision giant space-based battle stations or similar exotic capabilities, with accompanying global hegemony. As used here, the term means *any advance enabling the final engineering development and deployment of an operationally effective and cost-effective missile defense system.* (Operational effectiveness and cost effectiveness are always hotly debated issues.) Technically feasible ABM system concepts have been proposed in the past, but there have always been more effective and less expensive means of accomplishing the same objectives. Examples include Safeguard,[1] which was partially deployed, and several more recently proposed ICBM silo defense systems.

Breakthrough advances could apply to ground-based, sea-based, or airborne systems as well as space-based ones. They could also apply to various kinds of systems with limited objectives, such as those for protection against accidental launches or any of the myriad system concepts for protecting valuable targets such as hardened missile silos, command centers, and other command, control, and communication facilities.

SOVIET BREAKOUT

The Soviets have pursued a vigorous and visible ABM research program, which includes a variety of new Treaty-compliant components in advanced stages of development: a new high-performance missile (Gazelle), an improved long-range missile (Galosh), and a new phased-array radar (Pushkino) around Moscow, high-performance interceptors and phased-array engagement radars at R&D sites, and increased numbers of large phased-array radars on the perimeter of the USSR.[2] The breakout concern is that the Soviets could rapidly deploy a nuclear-armed ground-based ABM system nationwide, achieving a substantial operational capability before the United States could respond, thereby severely affecting the strategic balance, if only temporarily. Although the alternative of improved offense forces is available, an ABM research and development program may be needed to allow the United States to deploy a matching nationwide capability.

The argument is that asymmetrical defense deployments are destabilizing and may very well be intolerable. If the Soviets alone had an ABM defense (especially a preferential defense[3]), the effectiveness of U.S. offensive forces would be degraded while the Soviets' devastating first-strike capability remained unopposed. It would be most destabilizing if the Soviets believed they had such an ABM capability, whether or not they were correct.

During the early 1970s, the United States tried to cope with potential Soviet breakout by maintaining the hard site defense program in a condition of immediate production readiness. That effort was soon abandoned, however, because of its very high costs (several hundred million dollars annually) compared with the readiness provided.

TECHNOLOGICAL SURPRISE

Technological surprise—a dramatic element in warfare from time immemorial—includes not only quantum changes in capability arising from completely new technology (as with the atomic bomb) but innovations involving existing technology (as with the English bowmen at Crecy and German panzers in the Lowlands). Examples relevant to the ABM problem would be a sudden substantial improvement in antisubmarine warfare or a practical measurement technique that could discriminate a missile warhead from its penetration aids. Keeping abreast of technological advances requires sufficient research in a broad spectrum of ABM technologies and concepts to understand their potential in future systems (including utility, impact, schedule, and costs). Analysis alone may be sufficient in some cases; in others, building and testing representative components or subsystems may be necessary. As a practical matter the United States cannot exhaustively explore all ABM-applicable technologies that the USSR might be developing. We must rely on the intelligence community to filter and provide cues. Unfortunately, some of the most damaging technological surprises might escape detection, and so an appropriate research program becomes vital.

OFFENSIVE SYSTEM DESIGN

If the United States is to ensure that its offensive forces can penetrate Soviet ABM defenses, it must understand both ABMs in general and Soviet ABMs in particular. The second task is an intelligence mission; the first requires that we design, build, and exercise critical features of ABM systems against which to test our penetration systems. Institutions and facilities to accomplish this already exist in our national test ranges. Advanced and highly capable sea-, ground-, and air-based sensors, backed by extensive signal and data processing, are operated there by highly qualified personnel. The sensors are not limited to the traditional ABM sensors, but their operations are treaty-compliant. They include radar, infrared, optical, ultraviolet, and ionizing radiation-sensing instruments. Historically, the test ranges have evolved with the technologies of strategic offense and defense. Many of them can be used to emulate either offense or defense. For the offense they act as a sophisticated defensive system; for the defense they are test beds for advanced acquisition, discrimination, and engagement technologies.

DOD Research—A Frame of Reference

What types and levels of R&D are required to meet the four objectives outlined above? How would such efforts jibe with the ABM Treaty regime? To answer these questions requires an understanding of the framework within which such programs will be conducted: the Department of Defense program for research, development, test, and evaluation (RDT&E).

The DOD R&D program, referred to as Program VI, comprises five categories: research (referred to as program 6.1), exploratory development (6.2), advanced development (6.3), engineering development (6.4), and management and support (6.5). The advanced development category is further subdivided into advanced technology demonstration (6.3A) and prototype demonstration (6.3B). Program 6.5 provides the support base to manage and conduct the R&D program and will not be discussed further.[4] Categories 6.1 through 6.4 are explained below.

Research (6.1) explores the laws of nature. It is composed of hundreds of programs of less than a million dollars each and involves substantial university participation. Projects should demonstrate potential application to future DOD needs. For fiscal year 1988, the 6.1 program amounts to about 2 percent of the overall DOD R&D budget, which is itself about 11 percent of the defense budget—a fairly steady percentage from year to year.

Exploratory development (6.2) nurtures critical technologies required to make feasible a variety of future systems concepts. Techniques and components may be designed, checked for function, and redesigned. These components are not major self-contained portions of a weapon system, but are critical items like microwave tubes, an aircraft control system, or a missile's first stage. Components may be put together as a "breadboard" of a subsystem or even a small system. A breadboard has the important functional parts in working order although not in final form and not in compliance with military specifications. It might be tested, if costs are not too high, in the regime in which it would eventually be deployed. Although there are exceptions, 6.2 efforts rarely exceed a few million dollars each; they may last from two to five years. The 6.2 program accounts for a little over 4 percent of the R&D budget.

Within advanced development (6.3), 6.3A efforts focus on demonstrating to the requirements and acquisition community that a certain technology has matured enough to be ready for potential systems application. In contrast to 6.3A projects, which can be viewed as proof-of-principle demonstrations, 6.3B programs are early functional prototype demonstrations of candidate weapon systems. They assemble all the technologies required in a particular system concept in a representation of their important functions and final form. Even though they do not represent the final design, such prototypes can be used to test and demonstrate the essential performance characteristics desired in the final system. Then reasonable extrapolations can be made to the final system characteristics, and engineering development can begin with reasonably low risk. If there are sufficient funds, more than one contractor may build prototypes, the winner being decided by a flyoff among the competing designs. It ordinarily takes approximately three years and several hundred million dollars to conduct a 6.3B program.

Engineering development programs (6.4) design, develop, and test the production prototype(s) of the desired operational system. The prototypes are designed and built to full military specifications, including the complex, extensive, and costly provisioning for producibility, operability, reliability, and maintainability over the lifetime of the system. Development and initial operational testing occur during this phase, rigorously confirming that the system meets its detailed performance specifications. Full-scale engineering development of a major system takes four to five years and costs several billion dollars. Most experienced developers would assert that a weapon system that will be required in substantial numbers must go through the equivalent of the engineering development phase if the acquisition effort is to be successful. The high level of activity, existence of prototypes, extensive testing in realistic environments, and the fact that it is a genuine system milestone make the commitment to full-scale engineering development an obvious candidate as a verification threshold for Treaty compliance.

Although the production and deployment phase of a weapon system is not considered to be R&D, it culminates the acquisition phase of weapon system development. As equipment comes off the production line it goes to an operational base where it becomes operationally useful. Further intensive testing, called operational test and evaluation (OT&E) is conducted, this time with operational personnel at the controls to ascertain that the system meets all of its operational requirements. The initial operational capability (IOC), the time when a significant number of systems is combat-ready, may occur in the same year as production commences. This is a rather vague, and sometimes political, milestone. Full operational capability (FOC), when the system is fully capable and ready, usually is reached three or four years after production begins.

The boundaries of these R&D categories are somewhat flexible in practice. For example, the Strategic Defense Initiative program, in its entirety, has been designated as advanced development, although it includes elements of basic research, exploratory development, and early advanced development. Because more funds are available for higher-numbered categories, there is a tendency toward upward migration (that is, advanced development funds are obtained for programs that would more properly be considered exploratory development, and so on). Furthermore, risky parts of programs in engineering development will often be backed up with subsidiary efforts in the 6.2 or 6.3 categories. Programs in production almost invariably involve continuing efforts—funded outside Program VI as operational systems development—that will lead to system changes. These programs may also include efforts that are improperly designated.

Although the Soviets undoubtedly have their own way of structuring research programs, the fundamental process must be the same as in the United States. The Soviet organizational equivalents of research, advanced development, engineering development, and production could be easily identified and a one-to-one correspondence established as points of reference for negotiations in a milieu that may be far more complex than that of SALT I and II. But because of their imprecision, R&D categories would probably not be useful as actual Treaty thresholds.

ABM Research and Treaty Compliance

Earlier we formulated four fundamental objectives for ABM R&D: seeking an ABM breakthrough, responding to a Soviet breakout, guarding against technological surprise, and supporting offensive system design. How might each goal lead to conflicts with Treaty compliance, and what ameliorating measures may be available?

The formulation of a breakthrough program is the most difficult of the four objectives. It is best exemplified by SDI as the program was originally described. All technologies that might contribute to the desired ABM capability were included. These technologies (including surveillance, command and control, tracking, seekers, propulsion, computing, kill mechanisms, kinetic weapons, and directed-energy) were aggregated under a mission-oriented management structure. The technologies were to be appropriately nurtured to fit into a preliminary system design. In parallel, preliminary system design studies (architecture studies) were undertaken to illuminate critical technologies that required maturation and demonstration. An iterative process of technology maturation and system concept exploration was foreseen, with the goal of converging to an operationally effective and cost-effective system. This approach is sound and logical if it is clear that the technology needed to achieve the ultimate goal is not near at hand. In the case of SDI, however, emphasis soon shifted to early deployment of a limited capability; thus the current program does not fit the breakthrough model discussed here.

Programs seeking a breakthrough can be pursued at a relatively slow, deliberate pace or conducted on a crash basis. Since funding alone can never guarantee success in a technology-intensive effort, it should be applied prudently and paced to the technology's maturation progress. As in any high-risk endeavor, failures may occur, requiring goal modification and/or program restructuring.

In its initial stages, a breakthrough research and development program would not violate ABM Treaty constraints. Only as promising technologies are demonstrated in an ABM system role, to confirm overall feasibility, do Treaty constraints become relevant. How soon this point is reached depends on the nature of the particular program.

An R&D program intended to hedge against breakout is of an entirely different nature. In simple terms, it is a deployment readiness program, as exemplified by the discontinued hard site defense program, in which the Department of Defense attempted to maintain a "warm base" to initiate production on short notice and proceed immediately to deployment. By the very nature of such a readiness program, the system design must be complete and proven. Moreover, it must employ a fixed ground-based configuration since no other configuration could be adequately tested and brought to production readiness under the Treaty constraints. The degree of readiness that can be achieved is theoretically limited only by the time required to deploy and activate the operational sites. In the extreme case, the components of the system would have all been produced and stored, as is permitted by the Treaty. Such a program would obviously be extremely costly. A posture of production readiness would be far less costly, though still very expensive, as the hard site program showed. Moving one step further backward, one could attempt to maintain a proven design that could be placed into production—recognizing that a rather lengthy period would be required for preparing the production facility and tooling.

A challenge of any breakout reaction program is keeping pace with the state of the art to assure the effectiveness of the readiness configuration. As sensors, interceptors, and communications and other components are improved, they must be fully tested, qualified, and incorporated into the production plan. It is not especially difficult to formulate an R&D program to improve this fixed ground-based ABM capability steadily. The principal challenge is determining how much readiness is desired, given its cost.

If a fixed ground-based system is deemed inadequate, however, the situation is transformed. Some of the proposed improvements to hard site defense (which had names like Low-Altitude Defense System [LoADS] and Sentry) involved mobile radars and interceptors and airborne, even spaceborne, adjuncts that could not be production-ready under the Treaty. To deploy a system with mobile components would require a crash program of development, test, and evaluation, as well as production. The time to deployment might be increased by from one to three years, depending on how close the system was brought to the edge of Treaty compliance before Soviet breakout began. Although this situation puts theoretical pressure on the Treaty, today's situation is prima facie evidence of its triviality. The United States backed off from a high level of readiness in the mid-1970s, and today, although we worry about the Soviets' vigorous ABM R&D program, the one we are pursuing has little prospect of even rudimentary deployment until the mid- to late 1990s.

Ensuring against technological surprise requires current knowledge of possible and probable Soviet capabilities. It requires a broad-fronted technological program of research, exploratory development, and some limited advanced development. The intelligence community must maintain special vigilance for indications of Soviet technical advances and must communicate effectively with ABM developers—seeking guidance for surveillance activities and providing cues to U.S. development activities. An adequate R&D program to avoid surprise resembles the broad-based exploratory activities of the SDI program but with no need to carry investigations much beyond proof of principle. Extensive system design work or preprototype demonstrations should not be necessary, and certainly not testing of an engineering development nature. It would be challenging, but possible, to formulate an appropriate treaty-compliant program.

The final goal an ABM R&D program must pursue is to assure the penetration effectiveness of our offensive missile force. Such efforts would aim at developing means for assured penetration, not ABM advances. Like attempts to avoid technological surprise, this program would also be highly dependent upon intelligence. Near-term R&D (i.e., engineering developments) would aim to improve U.S. capability against the confirmed capabilities of the existing Soviet ABM system and its near-term upgrades. Longer-term R&D (i.e., exploratory and advanced development) would be oriented to possible, more speculative advances in Soviet ABM capability. Such a program would have to explore all likely advances of Soviet ABM capability enough to allow U.S. developers to develop, design, and test appropriate countering penetration aids and techniques.

An effective penetration R&D program requires an adequate test capability. As long as the Soviets' ABM R&D program remains Treaty-compliant, U.S. national test ranges can be upgraded to serve as surrogates of their advanced capabilities. Testing advanced penetration capabilities against postulated non-compliant ABM capabilities is another matter, however, and would require substantial reliance on compliant component testing, analysis, and extrapolation. But considering U.S. intelligence capabilities to monitor advances in Soviet ABM, and the time required to develop and deploy likely noncompliant ABM advances, this testing limitation does not seem unduly severe.

Of the four objectives of ABM research discussed above, only the search for breakthroughs would require so much development and testing of new technologies that it would eventually exceed Treaty constraints. A response-to-breakout program could remain Treaty-compliant in a state of high readiness, assuming a conventional fixed ground-based system is involved but would obviously break the Treaty as deployment commences. A more advanced response would be less ready because of Treaty constraints, but the concern is not serious because alternate paths (e.g., penetration aids) are available. With respect to the remaining goals, the billions of dollars already spent in researching advanced technologies relevant to ABM sets the precedent that technology by itself does not violate Treaty constraints.

Summary

The United States has managed extensive Treaty-constrained ABM research programs ever since 1972. Of the four objectives of ABM research, two—avoiding technological surprise and knowing enough about ABMs to understand Soviet activities and to design our offensive systems—can be adequately supported within Treaty constraints. To seek a breakthrough might require modifying or withdrawing from the Treaty if we conclude that it is in the national interest to develop and deploy such a system. A breakout response can be pursued to the point of deployment—assuming that the system being readied for deployment is in itself Treaty-compliant. An advanced breakout response would be somewhat delayed by Treaty constraints. In any case, the United States has previously eschewed the high-readiness approach.

Although it has proved practical to manage ABM research in compliance with the Treaty, the constraints should eventually be revised or clarified to reflect evolving engineering and operational realities. Such revisions might either permit activities now forbidden or limit activities now unconstrained. Furthermore, we should continue to remind ourselves that the Treaty constraints are not sacrosanct. They were devised for security purposes. When security will be better served by adaptation, that should be undertaken.

Notes

1. The regional defense, deployed in the early 1970s in North Dakota, to defend the Minuteman ICBM fields in that vicinity.

2. *Soviet Military Power* (Washington, D.C.: U.S. Government Printing Office, 1988), pp. 55–57.

3. A preferential defense concentrates on saving a fraction of targets that the attacker must completely destroy. Since the attacker does not know which fraction will be defended, it must attack as if all were, thereby multiplying the number of weapons expended.

4. Research and development funds are also allocated to ongoing operational programs that have completed production or have production under way and are entering—or soon to enter—the inventory. These so-called operational system development funds, allocated to specific operational systems, are not considered to be in Program VI.

6

NON-ABM TECHNOLOGIES WITH ABM POTENTIAL

Richard L. Garwin and Theodore Jarvis, Jr.

THIS CHAPTER assesses potential ABM applications of technologies developed for other purposes. The primary emphasis will be on technologies whose future development or deployment seems to rub against the ABM Treaty and may be constrained by it. The six major areas examined will be (1) air defense, (2) antitactical ballistic missiles (ATBM), (3) offensive penetration aids, (4) antisatellite (ASAT) weapons and defense against antisatellite weapons (DSAT), (5) non-ABM sensors, and (6) civil uses of space. In each area we will ask:

- Would deployment of the particular system result in a significant ABM capability?
- Would deployment of the system create a significant base for breakout from the ABM Treaty?
- Would research and development (R&D) on the system erode the buffer time between observation of intent and the deployment of a significant ABM capability?

Systems purportedly developed for other purposes could be used to hide or mask ABM developments, a problem referred to in this book as relabeling. For example, ground-based missiles intended to shoot down satellites (ASAT systems) could be designed to have ABM capabilities as well.

Some technologies necessary to ABM systems are not verifiable and/or cannot be regulated by treaty, such as radiation-resistant space-based computers and communications. Moreover, it would be undesirable to restrict certain ABM-relevant but generally useful technologies such as rocket boosters capable of placing large mass in orbit at low cost, even though this technology is eminently observable.

If the existing ballistic missile force is not upgraded, it is inevitable that the general advance of civil and military technology will gradually improve potential ABM capability. A major concern of this volume is to assess the acceptability of such a development and to ask whether it can be offset within a regime based on the ABM Treaty or certain modifications thereof.

Air Defense

Sensors and weapons developed and deployed for defense against aircraft and cruise missiles have had minimal impact on the ABM Treaty thus far. In the future, however, air defense sensors and weapons could be developed that would affect the Treaty. Table 6-1 lists these current and possible future air defense technologies.

Most of the currently deployed air defense radars and interceptor aircraft and missiles have no ABM capabilities, but the most advanced surface-to-air interceptor missiles, such as the Soviet SA-12 and the U.S. Patriot, begin to approach the speed and maneuverability needed to attack lower-speed ballistic missiles. Moreover, space-based radars with the primary mission to detect low-observable aircraft and cruise missiles might also be able to detect ICBM launches (since microwave radars penetrate cloud cover) and track missile boosters and buses[1] with precision. Consider an engagement between a bal-

TABLE 6-1

Current and Possible Air Defense Technologies

	SENSORS	WEAPONS
Current	Microwave radar • Ground-based • Airborne	Interceptor • Aircraft • Missiles
	• Over-the-horizon (OTH) radar	
Possible	• Space-based radar • Space-based infrared	• Directed-energy weapons (DEW)

listic reentry vehicle (RV) and an advanced air defense modified for ABM intercept.[2]

The sequence of detection, tracking, and interception of a reentry vehicle by a modified air defense system (SA-12 or Patriot) is illustrated in figure 6-1. Assuming an RV trajectory at 30 degrees above the horizon, the first radar detection will take place as shown just beyond the point labeled "RV DETECTED. BEGINNING OF TRACKING" in figure 6-1. At 7 kilometers per second the RV will reach the target (assumed to be at the same place as the radar) about 29 seconds after detection. In this time, the air defense radar must acquire (detect and decide to attend to) the object, track, discriminate, and predict the trajectory of the RV, commit (launch) a ground-based interceptor, and correct the track of the interceptor to match the predicted intercept point and time. The radar tracks the reentry vehicle and associated lightweight decoys (balloons and chaff) down to an altitude of about 90 kilometers, where atmospheric drag effects should allow a crude discrimination of RVs from certain lightweight decoys. The radar then tracks the RV down to 70 kilometers' altitude (which takes about six seconds), at which point the interceptor is committed. For a nuclear-armed interceptor with a relatively large kill range against an RV within the atmosphere, this "command guidance" is all that is required. For a nonnuclear "hit-to-kill" interceptor, however, as is envisaged in some defense systems, the radar must bring the interceptor close enough in space and time so that it can guide itself into the target. The interceptor flies at 1 kilometer per second up along the reentry trajectory and intercepts at an altitude of around 9 kilometers or 27,000 feet.[3] The closing

FIGURE 6-1. Terminal Defense Time Line

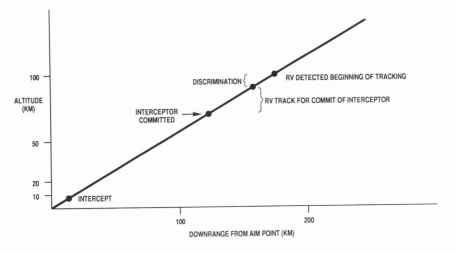

velocity is approximately 8 kilometers per second—much higher than normal air defense intercept speed.

Would a deployed air defense system have a significant ABM capability?

For several reasons, using an air defense system in this manner would not constitute an effective defense against ICBMs:

- Interception takes place at less than 10 kilometers' altitude, too low to protect many types of targets. If an RV were salvage-fused,[4] the resulting explosion would damage soft targets (i.e., ordinary buildings, people, vehicles) on the ground.
- Only a limited area can be defended.[5]
- If the offense employs better penetration aids or decoys that are not stripped out by the upper atmosphere, the defense will waste interceptors.
- A surface-to-air missile may be able to destroy a single nuclear-armed RV in this way. But the explosion of the RV would create a radar-opaque fireball that would mask the approach of a second RV coming in just higher than the altitude at which it could be intercepted.

A nuclear warhead on the interceptor would have a large kill radius against the RV and would increase the effectiveness of any given sortie. Nuclear warheads are employed in the operational Soviet ABM system around Moscow, as they were on the 100 interceptors deployed in the now-abandoned U.S. ABM system near Grand Forks, North Dakota. Whether the increased lethality of nuclear warheads offsets their cost and the logistic and operational difficulties is a question for detailed analysis.

Given some external means of cueing the radars (see note 2), the air defense system could offer some ABM defense capability if the interceptor guidance system were modified appropriately, if the interceptor speed were increased to 2 to 3 kilometers per second, and if the system had been tested in an ABM mode. SA-12 and Patriot interceptor upgrades may achieve this speed; the footprint of defense coverage (the actual region protected) would be limited to a diameter of 10 kilometers or less, however, and the system would be vulnerable to decoys, other penetration aids, and operational tactics such as maneuverable RVs, jammers, saturation attacks, and radar blackout. Just how significant an ABM defense this system could provide depends upon the nature of the deployment. A dense deployment of SA-12s around selected sites in the USSR (with external cueing) could be effective enough to require a substantial revision of attack plans for the case of moderate-scale attacks. Certainly such a system would not be the first, or even second, design choice for a robust ABM defense, but it might come at little extra cost to the air defense system, and it would add uncertainty to an attacker's problem.

Would deployment of an air defense system create a significant base for ABM Treaty breakout?

Even if air defense systems provide negligible ABM capability on their own, actual breakout from the Treaty by ABM deployment could be assisted by the use of another ABM defensive layer based on a high-performance air defense system (modified SA-12 or Patriot) as backup or reserve to attack leaders and to mop up stragglers. The strategic situation is asymmetric, as there are no Patriots operational in the United States and an increasing number of SA-12s are operational in the USSR.

Would research and development of air defense components and systems erode the buffer time for ABM breakout?

As mentioned above, air defense components are not in the mainstream of ABM development. While deployment of an advanced air defense system would provide some ABM capability, it is hard to argue that research and development of current air defense technology would materially reduce the buffer time between observation of intent and deployment of an effective ABM.

The Soviets have an incentive to explore and perhaps to deploy space-based radar in an effort to counter the U.S. stealth technology, which promises to make future U.S. bombers and cruise missiles difficult to detect with ground-based radar. Observation of large bombers from space, however, has little relevance to the problem of observing reentry vehicles and buses *in* space. Targets in space can be given appropriate shrouds for reducing radar signature, and in any case decoys can prevent intercept even if radar detection cannot be avoided. Unlike the aircraft situation, decoys and shrouds can accompany a warhead in space for many minutes, since there is no significant atmospheric drag. Furthermore, a space-based ABM radar would have to search a spherical shell many hundreds of kilometers thick, whereas an air defense radar would need to search only the thin shell of the earth's atmosphere to which aircraft are confined. As a result, space-based radar has far more potential for air defense than for ABM purposes. For ABM defense, space-based radar has its greatest potential in tracking and discrimination—not search.

On the other hand, space-based infrared sensors are likely to be less suitable for the air defense role than for ABM. Space-based infrared sensors can be deployed and oriented so that they can see buses and RVs (and decoys) in space, without seeing the energy from the earth's warm surface and atmosphere, but such satellites must view even high-altitude aircraft against clouds or the earth's surface. Unless some means can be found to observe the hot gas from the aircraft propulsion system, space-based infrared detection of high-altitude aircraft would require interrogation of very many small regions of the atmosphere for the presence of an aircraft, and this means vastly more sensors in the focal plane than space-based infrared would need for ABM purposes. In sum, space-based *infrared* sensors for air defense have a much more difficult task that do those for ABM and are therefore not likely to be used for air defense purposes. If they were, tests in an air defense mode are not particularly relevant to ABM capability.

Neither the current U.S. bomber threat to the Soviet Union nor rational Soviet air defense improvements against planned U.S. forces are likely to provoke significant SAM advances toward ABM capability. The problem is complex, however, with a small real and a larger imaginary component. For example, consider the short-range attack missile (SRAM), which has long been deployed as a penetration aid for the U.S. bomber force. This rocket-propelled, nuclear-armed weapon is launched from the aircraft either on a level trajectory sustained by body lift or on a longer-range "semiballistic" trajectory. SRAM's penetration of air defenses is aided by its sleek shape, sharp nose, and supersonic speed. A future penetration aid program for aircraft, if unconstrained by cost or reason, might test a super-SRAM with ICBM-like speed. Such a development would legitimize testing of SAM systems in a mode to oppose super-SRAM, which would be difficult to distinguish from a test "in ABM mode."

Antitactical Ballistic Missile Systems

Research, development, and deployment of an ATBM system would significantly affect the ABM Treaty even though the technical parameters for intercepting tactical and strategic ballistic missiles are different. The most significant difference is the velocity of the target reentry vehicle. In figure 6-2 the variation of reentry velocity for missiles with minimum-energy trajectory is shown as a function of range. Other trajectories (lofted or depressed) would require more energy and hence would have a higher reentry velocity for a given range.

The distinction between tactical and strategic missiles was less clear before the INF Treaty. The longer-range tactical missiles (SS-20, for example) overlapped in range and velocity the shorter-range strategic missiles (SS-N-6, for example). With the INF limitation of tactical ballistic missiles to less than 500 kilometers, there is no longer an overlap. As figure 6-2 shows, velocities up to about 2 kilometers per second are to be expected for tactical ballistic missiles and 5 kilometers per second or more for SLBMs and ICBMs. The INF Treaty probably reduces the magnitude of the ABM Treaty problems arising from ATBM by reducing the need for and the incentive to build ATBM systems.

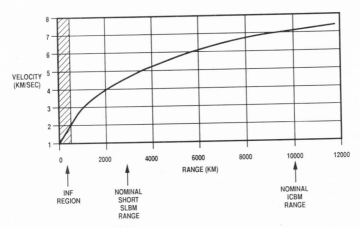

FIGURE 6-2. Velocity of Reentry Vehicle As a Function of Range for Vacuum, Minimum-energy Trajectory

Would a deployed defense against tactical ballistic missiles have a significant ABM capability?

Some components (radars and interceptors) designed as part of a system to intercept tactical ballistic missiles would certainly have some capability in an ABM system against strategic ballistic missiles, particularly against older SLBMs or even modern SLBMs launched at short range. However, the velocity range of an ATBM system, though higher than that of an air defense system, would remain directly lower than for an ABM system, and this difference could be detected. Any attempt to deploy an ATBM system in the nation's interior could be detected by national technical means (NTM) and would clearly be a subterfuge, since no tactical ballistic missile (TBM) threat is possible in the deep interior. ATBM deployment aimed at reinforcing SAM systems by providing a capability to handle longer-range air-launched missiles than now exist could be a relabeling problem. On balance, however, vigilant surveillance should ensure that ATBM deployments remain wedded to their mission and would not compromise ICBM attacks at normal, long range.

Would deployment of an ATBM be a significant base for breakout?

Both the United States and the USSR have tested some (presumably) modified air defense components in an ATBM mode. Although the lessons learned from such testing would be of some use for ABMs, it is quite unlikely that designs would be directly transferable. However, testing during ATBM development might provide a basis for generalized testing of higher-powered radars and faster interceptors than would be justified for the pure air defense mission. The USSR could, in principle, build a very high performance interceptor, test it only against 2 kilometers per second targets, and call it protection for Soviet troops in East Germany. The process could be observed by national technical means, and the payoff would be limited.

More futuristic ATBM capability may be restrained by the ABM Treaty. For instance, boost-phase intercept of a tactical missile is similar to boost-phase intercept of an ICBM and could be tested under the ABM Treaty, but only from either of the two ABM test sites permitted to each side. Very "hot" interceptors (of high acceleration and speed) could be developed for terminal and late midcourse intercept of tactical missiles, but analogous efforts are allowed with little restriction for ABMs.[6] Therefore, as the Treaty stands, some modest progress could be made toward disallowed ABM systems through legitimate development of ATBM systems, but it would fall far short of the performance needed to be directly applicable to ABMs.

Offensive Penetration Aids

An ABM Treaty regime is less vulnerable to breakout or to clandestine ABM systems if each side has penetration aids that can nullify an ABM system. To what extent can one side perfect offensive penetration aids to counter potential ABM systems without providing a base for deployment of its own ABM system? Under Article VI of the ABM Treaty, each party undertakes

> not to give missiles, launchers, or radars, other than ABM interceptor missiles, ABM launchers, or ABM radars, capabilities to counter strategic ballistic missiles or their elements in flight trajectory, and not to test them in an ABM mode. . . .

Thus it is perfectly all right for the United States or the Soviet Union to test offensive penetration aids against real ABM radars, lasers, and interceptors based at (or launched on suborbital trajectory from) one of the two agreed-upon ABM test sites allowed each nation. Similarly, it would be perfectly within the bounds of the ABM Treaty to use an instrumentation radar at the ABM test site to generate waveforms similar to those of an *adversary* radar in order to determine the adequacy of penetration aids and countermeasures.

This clause seems to have been intended to reduce the potential for Treaty breakout by barring the modification of any *deployed* non-ABM systems. Because the SA-12 may eventually see wide deployment as an air defense system, it is *not* all right for the Soviet Union to test an SA-12 SAM system, even at an ABM test site, against ICBMs, even if the purpose of the test is to develop means of penetrating similar U.S. defenses. There is a potential compliance problem here. Suppose the Soviets tested penetration aids that they asserted were intended for use against the U.S. Patriot system radar, while the United States charged that the Soviets had tried to simulate U.S. penetration aids and test them against the SA-12 radar, not the Patriot radar. Would the disagreement be important? How could one resolve it? If one side had chosen to break out of the ABM Treaty using a widely deployed set of air defenses as a base, such testing would be crucial, making the disagreement important indeed. Unfortunately, there seems to be no way of resolving the intent of ambiguous tests by limited external measurements of waveforms or other observable phenomena. For example, radars often have a battle mode using a frequency or pulse waveform not exhibited in exercises (in the hope that jammers and other electronic countermeasures will not be deployed by the other side against the actual wartime operating mode). The actual battle mode of the defensive radar is probably a secret closely held in the defense establishment. Therefore, even if the offense (for purposes of conducting a test at its ABM test site) managed by espionage to learn the battle mode or frequency of the other side's defensive radar, it would not demonstrate this in a test, increasing the difficulty of demonstrating or verifying that the activity is really one of perfecting penetration aids against the advanced air defense of the other side, rather than augmenting the capability of one's own air defense radars against the strategic RVs of the other side.

As one last example of offensive penetration aids that could be developed without threatening the ABM Treaty, imagine an attempt to test countermeasures to an orbiting laser radar. Such an orbiting system capable of replacing the normal ABM radar is obviously banned by the ABM Treaty, but it might be prudent to explore its potential and to develop countermeasures to the laser radar in case of breakout by the other side. In support of such a program, the offense might wish to study the performance of candidate countermeasures (optical corner reflectors, balloons, and the like) against a system of similar capability. To simulate the performance of the potential radar against a particular target, the test device need not have the power or agility to cover a vast number of potential targets at the same time. A more limited system, incapable of replacing the ABM radar, could be used as an adjunct to the permitted ABM system and certainly could be tested at an ABM test range. It could be mounted on an aircraft as an Airborne Optical Adjunct (AOA), or it could be lifted as a rocket probe in support of the permitted ABM site. The laser radar could be used to send pulses of light (similar to those that might be used in a powerful deployed system) against the reentry vehicle and decoys, as part of the testing of penetration aids. One could perfect and deploy the penetration aids without coming close to the development (much less the manufacture and deployment) of orbiting laser radar.

Chapter 5 argues that a reasonable offensive ability to penetrate ABM systems (by development and deployment of penetration aids) can be maintained without conflict with the Treaty; in agreement with that judgment, we show here how an advanced penetration aids program can be accommodated within the Treaty framework.

Would deployment of offensive penetration aids create a significant base for breakout?

The kinds of penetration aids that are directly associated with offensive missiles (decoys, chaff, etc.) are clearly not a threat to the ABM Treaty. In themselves, they do not constitute a defense component. One could consider an antisatellite weapon as a kind of penetration aid; these are discussed in the next section. Protection for U.S. satellites threatened by antisatellite capabilities is discussed in the DSAT section.

Would research, development, and test of penetration aids reduce the buffer time for defense breakout?

Research, development, testing, and deployment of penetration aids would not be Treaty problems. Testing, however, creates an opportunity to mask development and testing of sensing systems "based on other physical principles," which could be of concern to the Treaty. We believe, however, that the intent of such tests could be inferred from observable characteristics of the sensors involved. As discussed above, the power and beam agility needed for a real defense would far exceed the capabilities required for testing penetration aids or for technical intelligence.

ASAT and DSAT

Clearly an antisatellite system can be deployed without injuring the ABM Treaty. (See chapter 8.) The Soviet co-orbital interceptor and the U.S. homing vehicle launched from an F-15, for example, have little ABM capability because of their design. Similarly, space mines would have little impact on the ABM Treaty because neither their research and development nor their deployment would solve significant ABM problems. Certain other kinds of ASAT weapons could have an ABM capability.

INTERCEPTORS

Galosh and the Exoatmospheric Reentry Vehicle Interceptor System (ERIS)[7] interceptors would have both ASAT and ABM capability. Thus restrictions on numbers and locations should apply to types of interceptors and not to the labels attached to them. Although the United States was developing a direct-ascent nonnuclear ASAT weapon for launch from an F-15 aircraft, and the Soviets have long had a ground-launched co-orbital pellet-warhead ASAT weapon, neither of these could be imagined to have any ABM capability. A more suitable ASAT system would be a direct-ascent, nonnuclear, large interceptor more like that tested by the U.S. Army in 1985, but its performance and the likely number of such weapons would provide little capability in comparison with the set of high-performance interceptors needed for ABM.

In principle, space-based interceptors could be used for ASAT purposes, but they are peculiarly unsuitable and costly in comparison with ground-launched systems, except in the very special (and especially low performance) case of space mines.

DIRECTED-ENERGY WEAPONS (DEWS)

Development of directed-energy weapon technology (for example, either space-based or ground-based lasers) for purposes other than ABM would clearly be a major step toward ABM capability. The power and brightness[8] of directed-energy weapons determines their military use. Figure 6-3 shows the relationships among laser brightness, range from laser to target, and typical target damage thresholds. With steady laser light, existing satellites could be damaged by overheating of thin temperature-control surface films and of the solar cells used to provide electrical power. No more than about 0.3 watts per square centimeter is tolerable for some tens of seconds on a normal satellite. (The

FIGURE 6-3. Laser Brightness for Damage As Function of Target Hardness and Range

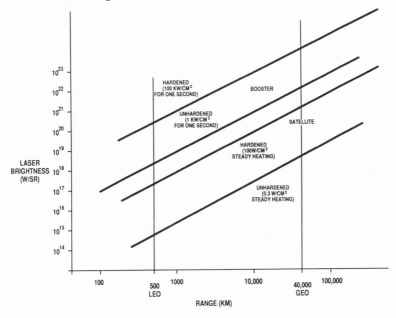

sun provides heat at a rate of about 0.1 watt per square centimeter [W/cm²].) For antisatellite use of a laser, the brightness corresponding to a power density of 0.3 W/cm² ranges from 8×10^{14} to 5×10^{18} watts per steradian as the range varies from low earth orbit (LEO) (~ 500-kilometers' range) to geosynchronous equatorial orbit (GEO) (40,000-kilometers' range).[9]

Power densities on the order of 1,000 W/cm² could be sufficient to destroy unhardened boosters in one second. Thus, as figure 6-3 shows, a directed-energy weapon bright enough to destroy satellites in geostationary orbit (i.e., delivering 0.3 W/cm² to them) could destroy about one unhardened booster every two seconds of beam dwell time at a range of 1,000 kilometers. To destroy hardened boosters at this same 1,000-kilometers range at a rate of one per second might require power densities of 100,000 W/cm², corresponding to laser brightness of 10^{21} watts per steradian. There is little overlap in capability between the ground-based laser that might destroy a passing LEO satellite with 0.3 W/cm² at a range of 500 kilometers and an ABM-capable laser. Direct laser-heat destruction of reentry vehicles either during reentry or in late midcourse would not be feasible since RVs are normally superhardened to resist the fiery heat of reentry and because clear atmosphere in the area under nuclear attack cannot be anticipated. In any case, a ground-based laser ABM capability of this type could be approached totally with the ABM Treaty and tested at an ABM test site, without subterfuge; it would then be an ineffective ABM (deployable only at the permitted site), and it could not be deployed elsewhere as an ASAT.

The situation is more worrisome if the ground-based laser is required to counter a satellite in geosynchronous orbit (40,000-kilometer range) hardened to withstand, say, 100 W/cm². The required brightness of 1.6×10^{21} W/steradian would clearly threaten unhardened boosters (being able to kill one every 10 seconds at 40,000-kilometer range, or 10 per second at a 4,000-kilometer range.[10] Thus the deployment of ASAT lasers might provoke the hardening of satellites with heat shields, reflectors, and the like, legitimizing deployment of more powerful ASAT lasers that would be ABM capable, and thus bringing about a direct confrontation with the ABM Treaty (unless the laser were located at an ABM test range and had no space-based components).

How big a step toward ABM capability would be represented by a ground-based laser that could destroy a satellite in low orbit? A deployed ASAT would constitute a significant ABM capability only if teamed with an entire infrastructure of tracking and command and control needed to intercept many uncooperative targets. Relay mirrors in GEO would be required to switch rapidly from target to target for boosters beyond the horizon, and ''fighting mirrors'' in LEO, at an average distance of perhaps 2,000 kilometers from the target boosters, would focus the laser light to 400 times[11] the intensity available from the relay mirrors in GEO.

How much of this necessary infrastructure could be observed by intelligence systems in conjunction with some potential observed and tested ground-based laser ASAT? The answer would depend very much on the importance the observing side placed on the strategic capability under investigation. With national technical means in use for the last decade or more, one could probably infer from the construction effort that a large device was being developed and perhaps guess at the technology being used. One could infer the power *into* the test site, but perhaps not the laser power *emitted* by the test site. It might be possible (though by no means easy) to build large test installations that were undetectable by NTM. The detection of ground-based lasers is discussed further in chapter 5.

Using NTM alone, the United States could have a few satellites capable of observing a considerable number of designated sites in the Soviet Union, using fiber-optic or other focal-plane feeds to enable a single collecting mirror to watch many designated sites simultaneously.[12] Alternatively (or additionally), one could watch from ground sites or from satellites the relatively few Soviet satellites that might serve as cooperative relay mirrors or targets for ground-based lasers in the clandestine evolution of ABM capability (or of a quick-acting ASAT capability that would not require waiting until the target satellite passed near the laser site). By observing the heating rate of a target satellite, one might estimate the beam power density at the target to within a factor of three. To disguise such a test as something else might be possible, and one could not tell the difference between a beam that had been misleadingly defocused to reduce laser power density and a beam running at "best" focus; the size of the beam at the target would not be evident if it extended beyond the target satellite itself.

The compatibility of various non-ABM sensors with the ABM Treaty regime is addressed in a following section; this paragraph considers the utility and acceptability of actual SDI sensors that might be deployed to observe the activity of ground-based lasers and to verify that they remain within ABM Treaty limits. The new-generation U.S. early-warning satellite program incorporates some of the elements of the BSTS (Boost Surveillance and Tracking System) being developed under the SDI program and will presumably take its own place in GEO. Another element of space-defense systems as planned for SDI is the SSTS (Space Surveillance and Tracking System), which would observe the mid-course flight of reentry vehicles and decoys by using long-wavelength infrared (LWIR) radar emitted from objects even at room temperature. Could BSTS and SSTS possibly provide useful information about Soviet tests to space of ground-based lasers? It is important to recognize that the requirements for BSTS and SSTS differ from those needed for a peacetime intelligence role of observing unannounced tests of ground-based lasers against cooperative satellites. The latter role does not require survivability against attack, robustness against jamming, or the sensor and communication capability to observe thousands of simultaneous launches or millions of objects in space. The deployment of BSTS or SSTS in this verification role would be transparent relabeling.[13]

Defense against Antisatellite Weapons

Passive defenses for satellites (such as hardening, hiding, or proliferation) and decoys for satellites do not provide in themselves any ABM capability. Active defenses include electronic warfare, maneuvering, and shooting back with short-range interceptors. Of these defenses, only the last might affect the ABM Treaty. Suppose a country deployed and tested interceptors on board a satellite, supposedly to protect that satellite. The relevance of the design to ABM would depend to a considerable extent on the velocity of the on-board interceptors. High-velocity interceptors (say 7 kilometers per second) would, with proper seeker heads, have a real ABM capability. If the velocity were low, say 1 kilometer per second, the interceptors would not be able to reach many offensive boosters and hence would have little or no direct use as an ABM system.

A militarily significant set of space-based interceptors cannot credibly be deployed aboard satellites under the label of "self defense of benign satellites." The latter role would need only perhaps 1 percent of the number of satellites and 1 percent of the mass on orbit of that required for an ABM system. National technical means could readily detect this kind of relabeling.

In contrast to deployment, *development* of a militarily significant space-based interceptor (SBI) might be carried out under the label of satellite self-defense. Although timing, target characteristics, command and control, sensors, and interceptor characteristics for defense against ASAT weapons are quite different from those for ABM, it would be difficult to distinguish counter-ASAT SBI allowed under the ABM Treaty from the prohibited ABM SBI without close observation, such as might be obtained on the space-based test range discussed in chapter 8.

Would deployment of ASAT and DSAT weapons have a significant ABM capability?

A nation could choose to deploy ostensible ASAT or DSAT weapons that, in sufficient numbers and qualities, could approach an ABM capability. Examples are high-speed direct-ascent antisatellite interceptor rockets and space-based lasers. Relabeling, as discussed in chapter 2, is a serious concern here.

Would deployment of ASAT and DSAT weapons create a significant base for breakout?

Certain deployments might not constitute a significant ABM capability but could, depending on national interest and the design approach selected, create a modest base for breakout. The space-deployed components might well be very vulnerable to countermeasures, however.

Would research, development, and testing of ASAT and DSAT systems erode the buffer time for a significant ABM capability?

ASAT and DSAT weapons could erode the buffer time between observation of intent and deployment of an ABM capability. Directed-energy weapons that we already know how to build would be needed in such numbers that deployment time would be an adequate buffer. For the most powerful ABM-capable DEWs about which we know the least, the research, development, and testing time may exceed the probable deployment time. In this judgment we are guided by the American Physical Society study group on DEWs, which states that "even in the best of circumstances, a decade or more of intensive research would be required to provide the technical knowledge needed for an informed decision about the potential effectiveness and survivability of directed-energy weapon systems." To prohibit all such research and development, however, is probably undesirable and certainly infeasible without an implausible degree of on-site inspection.

Non-ABM Sensors

A number of sensors that have been or could be developed for other non-ABM purposes also have ABM potential. The discussion here is organized by sensor type rather than mission. Table 6-2 shows the applicability of sensor type to various ABM mission areas.[14] The significance of each entry in the table is indicated in the discussion below.

TABLE 6-2

Applicability of Sensor Types to Mission

	SENSOR TYPE				
MISSION	*Ground-Based Radar*	*Space-Based Radar*	*Short-Wavelength Infrared*	*Long-Wavelength Infrared*	*Laser Radar*
Warning and Assessment	Yes	Yes	Yes	Yes?	No
Space Track	Yes	Yes	Yes	Yes	?
Technical Intelligence	Yes	Yes	Yes	Yes	Yes

GROUND-BASED RADARS

Typical frequencies and locations for ground-based radars used to perform various missions are shown in table 6-3.

UHF frequencies are well suited for surveillance as well as for warning and acquisition. Higher frequencies such as L and X band will have sharper beams for a given radar size and hence can achieve better angular measurements of target position for technical intelligence and precision tracking and guidance for ABM fire control.

Large and powerful ground-based phased-array radars, such as the four PAVE PAWS and three BMEWS (ballistic missile early warning system) radars, are used to provide warning and assessment of a ballistic missile attack on the United States and, in peacetime, to track orbiting objects in space. In theory, a missile launch would already have been detected by an infrared sensor on board a satellite; the radars would provide confirmation. The radars play an important role in national security by providing continuing information that no attack by strategic ballistic missiles is under way.

Such radars, however, depending on their siting and software, can also perform other functions including ABM battle management. To ensure against

TABLE 6-3

Comparison of Frequencies and Locations
for Ground-Based Radars

	TYPICAL FREQUENCY	TYPICAL LOCATION
Surveillance and Warning	UHF	National perimeter looking outward
Space Track	UHF	National perimeter looking outward
National Technical Means	L Band	Near foreign test ranges
ABM Radars	Acquisition and track UHF	Operational: not defended targets
	Fire control X band	Test: at national ranges

their use in this role, the ABM Treaty provides that they are to be deployed only at the periphery of the national territory, looking outward. Large phased-array radars deployed in the interior might be used for battle management, since they could view reentry vehicles as they reentered the atmosphere. The Treaty's strict limitations on deployment location are designed to ensure that such radars perform only the early-warning function.

It might seem that, even if sited in accordance with Treaty limitations, the BMEWS and PAVE PAWS radars (and their Soviet equivalents) could provide sufficient track accuracy to cue an air defense radar to perform ABM acquisition, as discussed earlier in this chapter. However, they probably could not guide an interceptor to an incoming reentry vehicle and certainly would be overwhelmed by the ABM requirements of countering a large raid. The radars were not designed for control and management of many interceptors at a time, and the many engagement radars needed to conduct the actual intercept with command-guided interceptors cannot be deployed under the ABM Treaty. Interceptors with infrared self-guiding sensors might be able to conduct intercepts above the atmosphere (particularly if nuclear armed), if launched on valid threat assessment from early-warning radars. The penetration capability of the offense would then depend on the use of decoys or other penetration aids. But in any event, because the radars are on the periphery, they could not be counted on to survive and function beyond the early-warning stage.

Unilateral Statement D of the ABM Treaty states that "since Hen House radars [Soviet ballistic missile early-warning radars] can detect and track ballistic missile warheads at great distances, they have a significant ABM potential. Accordingly, the United States would regard any increase in the defenses of such radars by surface-to-air missiles as inconsistent with an agreement."

ABM radars—defined by the Treaty as those "constructed and deployed for an ABM role, or of a type tested in an ABM mode"—are limited in number and location. The limitations ensure that such radars can be deployed only in support of a permitted ground-based ABM site or at a permitted test range. The Treaty exempts from all siting or other limitations large phased-array radars used for space track or NTM. Since it is impossible to be sure, using NTM, that a particular radar is being used solely for these purposes, large early warning radars are limited by the Treaty to the perimeter of the nation, facing out, except as indicated above. The Krasnoyarsk radar is identical in construction to a large phased-array early-warning ABM radar at Pechora, but it is in the interior and consequently violates the ABM Treaty.[15]

SWIR SENSORS

Since the 1960s, U.S. satellites in geosynchronous orbit have provided early warning of missile launch almost anywhere in the world by observing the radiant energy produced by the burning plume of rocket exhaust. Energetic boosters can easily be tracked even against the warm background of the earth by shortwave-length infrared (SWIR) sensors on board satellites. Such sensor satellites can provide an important early indication of attack by ballistic missiles. Track accuracy on the order of tens of kilometers would be sufficient to establish which parts of a large country, such as the United States, were under attack and which were not. It would not be possible, however, to pinpoint the intended impact points of multiple RVs from a single rocket, because the postboost vehicle aims the individual RVs after booster burnout, typically over a region of 100 kilometers or more. The postboost vehicle has much lower thrust and radiated power than the rocket booster and is normally invisible to the SWIR sensors that detect rocket launch.

SWIR sensors have long been used for warning of missile launch, but they cannot perform all ABM functions. From geosynchronous orbit, they can detect the region from which a booster has been launched, and they can track the booster. As discussed above and in chapter 9, they could predict RV impact points only for those attacking missiles that do not have a bus. Although SWIR sensors may track a booster with sufficient accuracy to cue a homing sensor aboard a space-based interceptor (or to cue a fine-track sensor aboard some future directed-energy weapon), they would not ordinarily be able to track the much weaker rocket plume of a bus dispensing RVs and thus could not support bus intercept with either DEW or SBI. A passive infrared satellite that is larger or more capable than needed for early warning would be a potential ABM component. The effectiveness of a satellite sensor can be assessed in terms of the mirror diameter and quality, focal-plane material and configuration, and on-board data processing. Figure 6-4 shows the lower limit for mirror diameter (aperture) required to achieve a given resolution at given ranges for a given wavelength of radiation. Although only one factor, diffraction limit, is shown here, one can conclude with the chapter 9 data that aperture diameters under 1 meter can provide kilometer-class accuracy for shortwavelength infrared sensors at geosynchronous equatorial orbit and for long-wavelength sensors in low earth orbit.

Because the actual performance depends on focal-plane material and design, it is not likely that external observations of sensor satellites could provide a basis for estimating level of performance. In contrast, for ground-based radars such as Krasnoyarsk, location, size, and intent are externally observable. Cooperative revelation and verification of satellite technical characteristics could, in principle, provide assurance that a space-based sensor's capability was limited to early warning.[16]

The accuracy indicated above is sufficient to get an interceptor near enough to a booster to intercept it either with a nuclear warhead above the atmosphere or

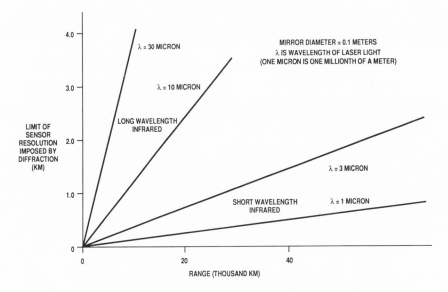

FIGURE 6-4. Diffraction Limit As Function of Range, Wavelength and Aperture

by a homing mechanism on the interceptor. The accuracy is not sufficient to put a laser or other directed-energy weapon on the target. The DEW would need its own tracking and small-area acquisition (search) sensors, if only because even speed-of-light weapons must be pointed ahead of the target to compensate for target or DEW motion; this tracking sensor could be cued by the SWIR satellite.

LWIR SENSORS

LWIR sensors on board satellites could be used to track "warm" (typically at least room temperature) objects against a cold space background, providing useful technical intelligence on a variety of foreign technical developments in space. They could also perform a space-track function, although a satellite can usually be tracked by ground-based sensors observing sunlight reflected from the satellite. Unlike SWIR sensors, LWIR sensors could monitor the release of reentry vehicles from postboost vehicles, because they can detect objects emitting no radiation other than heat from their surfaces at room temperature. Thus they could improve warning and assessment of missile attack.

Just how much resolution would be needed for an effective midcourse defense depends on the particular sensor design, but the purpose of passive infrared sensors used in an ABM system would be to get homing interceptors near the RVs after release from the postboost vehicle or to provide approximate target location for fine-tracking sensors on a directed-energy weapon. For this purpose, large mirrors are not required, as figure 6-4 shows.

A LWIR or SWIR satellite sufficiently sensitive and accurate to gather technical intelligence and to provide early warning could have some potential use for ABM, especially to cue ground-based systems. Actual ABM utility would depend on the survivability of the satellite and its sensor, a question that does not arise in its peacetime role and that is, for the most part, not considered explicitly in the ABM Treaty. Verification of lack of ABM capability would require direct access to highly sensitive design and test information.

SPACE-BASED RADAR

Space-based laser radar (LADAR) has no search capability because of its very narrow beam. The LADARs would be used for precision tracking and for discriminating warheads from decoys, but their capability seems readily countered by simple optical "corner reflectors"[17] that in very small sizes can provide signals much larger than those of reentry vehicles or other objects in space.[18]

LADAR could be used as part of a boost-phase defense to find the "hard body" of the booster in the enormously dispersed rocket plume. It might be argued that a LADAR in this role is an adjunct and not an ABM component, since the LADAR cannot replace an ABM radar; but this argument is as misleading as the suggestion that an ABM radar can be permitted at an arbitrary site if it is made up of two non-ABM radars—each of which might be considered only as an adjunct.[19]

Would deployment of sensor systems create a significant base for breakout?

Sensors by themselves do not constitute a defense, although they could contribute to one. A shortwavelength infrared sensor might provide useful information for a boost-phase defense; however, the sensor weight is trivial compared with that of the space-based weapons needed to constitute a significant defense; the lead time or buffer time (and launch cost) to deploy space-based interceptors is correspondingly much greater than that for sensors.

Long-wavelength infrared sensors could, in principle, cue air defense radars. They could not, however, guide SA-12 or Patriot-class interceptors to a target; these interceptors must operate below about 30 kilometers, and the sensor can track objects only above 100 kilometers against a dark sky background. (Otherwise, the detectors would be swamped with thermal radiation from the earth's atmosphere.) In principle, satellites in GEO equipped with shortwavelength infrared sensors, or even optical sensors operating in the visible region of the spectrum, could observe RVs as they reentered the atmosphere and could follow them down to any layer of dense cloud.

It is hardly likely, however, that an effective terminal defense could be based on this ability to track RVs. Typical sensor look intervals are too long to permit accurate measurement and prediction of drag effects on RVs and decoys.

LADARs might provide more frequent position measurements, but formidable agility would be required to handle, say, a thousand objects simultaneously. Finally, uncertain cloud top height would lead to an uncertain lower altitude limit on object tracking.

Passive infrared satellites existed in 1972, although they are not mentioned in the ABM Treaty. Presumably the value they contribute to strategic stability by providing early warning of offensive launch was considered more significant than their effect in reducing buffer time to an ABM deployment. But since SWIR satellites could replace ABM radars for boost-phase intercept and for intercept on reentry, and LWIR satellites could support intercept by space-based rockets or DEW, what protection is offered by the ABM Treaty, given that it permits testing of the technical principles involved by similar sensors mounted on probes launched from ABM test sites?

Whether deployment of the BSTS and SSTS would constitute a violation of the ABM Treaty is an open question. An ABM application would require greater survivability and higher output data rates for larger numbers of objects being tracked, but these criteria do not easily lend themselves to a clear and visible distinction between "allowed" and "not allowed." BSTS could, together with radar, provide highly credible warning of enemy attack, and SSTS could provide significant verification of technical characteristics of strategic offense missiles limited by potential arms control treaties.

Whether BSTS or SSTS could "substitute" for a ground-based ABM radar is also arguable. Like the ABM radar, either could contribute to ABM-related functions (e.g., surveillance, assessment, track). However, design details for hypothetical interceptors in hypothetical engagements would be required to compare performance of defenses with ABM radars against those with space-based sensors.[20]

Would research, development, and testing of sensors erode the buffer time for breakout with a significant ABM capability?

The development and testing of sensors are unlikely to erode buffer time to ABM breakout significantly. As discussed above, large radars can be developed and tested at national test ranges. As a general rule, phased-array radars evolve by steady improvements in power efficiency, bandwidth, and processing. There have been no revolutionary improvements in radar performance that produced immediate large improvements in defense system performance. A nation planning defense breakout would probably choose the highest-performance radar that could confidently be built consistent with interceptor research development and deployment schedules.

Once developed, spaceborne infrared sensing capabilities probably could be deployed more quickly than the interceptor systems or other weapons they would guide. Because passive infrared detection satellites existed at the time the Treaty was signed, research, development, and testing of improved versions will continue, presumably subject only to the limitation of Article V "not to develop ABM systems or components which are . . . space-based." We have suggested that satellites observing the boost phase are analogous to early-warning radars located in the periphery and facing out, so long as there is no capability for *destroying* missiles in boost phase; satellites capable of tracking in midcourse, however, might impinge on the Treaty, as discussed earlier.

Civil Space Activities

The uses of space that have become classical in the last few decades—navigation, communications, weather, observation, and such applications as direct broadcasting of television—have no relevance to the ABM Treaty. Several other space-related technologies that will emerge in the future will also have little bearing on the Treaty. For example, nuclear reactors on deep-space probes have no more than an auxiliary support function for space-based ABM systems. In themselves, they cannot be regarded as bumping up against the ABM Treaty, although nuclear reactors in space might be controlled for other (e.g., environmental) purposes. Nuclear reactors do not seem necessary for any civil use thus far identified; photovoltaic or solar-dynamic power (heat engines on board satellites) seem a preferable approach. Thus, nuclear reactors in earth orbit could be prohibited without loss of important benefits, in the interest of strengthening the ABM Treaty buffer against deployment of apparently serious ABM capability.

Very-long-baseline interferometry (VLBI) presents no conflict with the ABM Treaty. This extraordinary advance in radio astronomy is already, from earth, yielding pictures of the universe with resolution better than that available from any optical telescope. In the future, the displaced antennas for VLBI would be specialized to receive signals from a great distance and would be linked by a communication means (radio or laser) of considerable bandwidth capability. VLBI will not generate ABM-relevant technology, however.

Nor will space stations pose problems for Treaty compliance. Space stations at most add people to a possibly ABM-related technology or activity. What people contribute (aside from a possible role in construction) is intelligence informed by vision, and they can do that equally well from the ground, requiring very limited communication to receive the same visual display they would see in a space station and to relay commands. As for space colonies, they are not a realistic probability within the time covered by the treaty regime now being considered.

Three types of civil space activities—space telescopes, solar-power satellites, and laser-powered launch—were examined further for possible implications for the ABM Treaty regime.

SPACE TELESCOPES

Space telescopes for scientific uses may be built with large mirrors, perhaps up to 10 meters in diameter. (The NASA space telescope ready for launch has a 2.4-meter-diameter mirror.) The Strategic Defense Initiative Organization (SDIO) has contributed substantially to the support of adaptive optics, and future scientific space optics may very well be lightweight, with wavefront error sensors and actuators that preserve the overall mirror figure to the requisite accuracy of a few hundredths of a wavelength. An astronomical telescope will not have power sources beyond a few kilowatts, perhaps for cooling high-sensitivity infrared sensors, and its mirror could not be used to transmit significant laser power.

Astrometrical telescopes formerly had a single or relatively few sensors, but telescopes (whether based in space or on the ground) can be made more productive in many cases by great increases in the number of sensors in the focal plane where the image of distant objects is formed; astronomical telescopes using film have the equivalent of very many sensors in the focal plane. How, then, is a large space telescope (LST) to be distinguished from an optical sensor satellite that might "be capable of substituting for an ABM radar"? Although the diameter of the mirrors might be similar in the two cases, astronomical telescopes are not designed for rapid re-aiming and would have a lighter structure, much less on-board electrical power, and probably limited bandwidth communications to the ground. An astronomical telescope might have some protection against micrometeors but, for example, no laser or nuclear hardening and no ability to maneuver rapidly in orbit to aid its survivability against ASAT.

Would deployment of large space telescopes result in a significant ABM capability?

The astronomical community cannot afford the number of LSTs required to provide any ABM capability; hence limiting LSTs in LEO to a declared and small number would ensure that they contribute no significant ABM capability. Furthermore, the LST would be unclassified, and its datalink would not be robust against jamming or destruction. Since such telescopes are not allowed to be "tested in an ABM mode," they would have no capability unless they were essentially identical to an ABM-capable sensor that *had* been tested in an ABM mode. The same considerations hold for Soviet large space telescopes—if designed for scientific investigation, they would have no ABM capability. Of course, a real ABM laser or sensor could be relabeled a "scientific telescope" and might even have an LST mounted on it for camouflage, but ABM capability would derive from the ABM component and not the LST.

Would deployment of large space telescopes create a significant base for breakout?

Deployment of LSTs in space would provide no base for breakout from the Treaty unless they already provided an ABM capability. If one believed that an LST deployment lacked actual capability only because there were no interceptors, then such a deployment, by definition, would provide a significant base for breakout to be achieved by deploying interceptors. But we assert that large space telescopes will not contribute significant ABM capability, with or without interceptors (and this conclusion is strengthened by the fragility and vulnerability of the LST).

Would R&D on large space telescopes erode the buffer time sought by the ABM Treaty?

Like the general advance of technology, R&D on large space telescopes somewhat erode the buffer time sought by the ABM Treaty, but the erosion would be relatively minor in comparison with the effect on R&D on large ABM sensors that could be conducted even under the most restrictive interpretation of the ABM Treaty.

SOLAR-POWER SATELLITES

The possibility of deploying large solar-power-collecting satellites has been discussed in the United States for almost twenty years. Such satellites would intercept solar energy in space at the rate of about 1 kilowatt per square meter and transform it, at an efficiency ranging from 10 to 50 percent, to electrical energy, which would then be converted to microwave or laser power and focused on a rectifying antenna or other receiving structure on the ground. Specific proposals have been made for systems to produce some 6,000 megawatts of electrical power, which with an overall 20 percent efficiency would require a collector in space occupying some 30 square kilometers. The satellite would presumably be in geosynchronous orbit, and if the microwave power density at the surface of the earth was limited to 10 kW/m^2, a receiving antenna of 1 square kilometer would be required.[21] At a wavelength of 10 centimeters, a transmitting antenna on the satellite of some 4-kilometer diameter would be required. There is some Soviet interest in this approach, although such proposals in the United States have not been able to pass the test of economic competitiveness with other sources of electrical power.

Would deployment of solar-power-transfer satellites result in a significant ABM capability?

Solar-power systems (SPS) that rely on a microwave downlink have little relevance to the ABM Treaty. The microwave power density provided by a 4-kilometer-diameter transmitting antenna is insufficient to do any damage to a military system shielded by even the thin aluminum foil, and it would be prohibitively expensive to provide a higher concentration of microwave energy. A *laser* power downlink, however, would provide ABM capability, although a very vulnerable one. Thus research on a laser downlink would erode the buffer period sought by the Treaty.

LASER-POWERED LAUNCH TECHNOLOGY

Ground-based lasers might provide a means of launching satellites or deep-space probes. Powerful lasers on the ground would heat inert propellant material in the rocket as it rose through the atmosphere and into space. The propellant could be contained in a heating chamber and expelled through a standard rocket nozzle, or repeated intense laser pulses could ablate (evaporate) it from a flat plate at the base of the rocket.

To minimize the absorption of laser light as it traversed the atmosphere, such a system might involve a relay satellite in geosynchronous orbit and a number of focusing mirrors in low earth orbit to provide flexibility for delivering energy to the rocket powered by the ground-based laser. It is not the pressure of the light itself, but the driving of material off the rocket at high speed that would provide recoil momentum to the body, just as in normal rocket propulsion.

Two approaches are possible. One involves an ordinary combustion chamber into which laser light is fed, to heat an effluent material. Hydrogen gas, provided with a contaminant for absorbing light, would be an efficient propulsion medium, but such a system has no advantage over ordinary rocket propulsion. For launch of satellites to low earth orbit, there can be no energy saving over the normal rocket, which in this role can convert more than 30 percent of the propellant energy to kinetic energy of payload in LEO. Providing the energy from the ground does little to reduce the mass or cost of the rocket, compared with providing both expulsion mass and chemical energy in the fuel, so there is no possibility of recovering the cost of the laser system.

The second approach has more promise. A flat plate of specially designed ablative material would be illuminated with carefully timed pulses of intense laser light. Successive pulses might differ in wavelength to continue to deposit energy in the blown-off material so that it can achieve very high blowoff speeds perpendicular to the ablating plate—kinetic energy per gram blown off large compared with the thermal energy at any containable temperature. This approach, however, would be useful only for speeds far in excess of satellite and ICBM needs.

In the ABM-useful velocity regime, there is no potential benefit associated with laser propulsion. Nevertheless, supporters of such an approach have called for funding related work within the SDIO budget.

Would deployment of laser-powered launch systems result in a significant ABM capability?

The deployment of laser-powered launch systems would result in a significant ABM weapon capability simply by directing the laser beam via relay and mission mirrors onto the adversary ICBM in boost phase. Or if the laser-launch facility did not provide a significant capability (because some sensors were missing from the system, for example), then it would certainly provide a significant base for breakout. To launch 10 tons into low earth orbit (8 kilometers per second velocity gain) in 320 seconds (during which time the vehicle would have moved under constant acceleration some 1,500 kilometers) would require the transfer to the payload of some 320 gigajoules of kinetic energy; that is, the payload would have to gain kinetic energy at the rate of 1 gigawatt. (This is the power output of a large civil nuclear power station.) The lasers proposed for space defense would have power outputs on the order of 0.1 gigawatt, and not 1.0 gigawatt. Furthermore, one can hardly conceive of a laser-rocket efficiency much better than 50 percent, and even that would require a 2-gigawatt laser source, if all the laser light traversed the atmosphere without scattering or loss. If one assumes a tenfold loss of laser light in traversing the atmosphere and spilling over at the relay mirror, a laser of 20 gigawatts would be required as a source. In fact, it would be remarkable to obtain a laser efficiency of 30 percent, which would require a prime power input of some 70 gigawatts during launch, and hence a laser enormously overpowered even for the space-defense role.

Such an enormous program would offer no possibility of benefit for satellite launch, since ordinary rocket fuel energy is converted to satellite kinetic energy at 30 to 50 percent efficiency. But, even a laser-launch facility capable of launching 100-kilogram satellites to LEO (via GEO relay and LEO focusing satellites) would constitute much of the boost-phase intercept component of a full ABM system.

Would R&D on laser-launch erode the buffer time sought by the ABM Treaty?

Research on laser-launch capability would erode the ABM Treaty's buffer time. A full demonstration adequate to decide whether to go ahead on a commercial laser-launch facility would involve a GEO relay and at least one LEO focusing mirror. Such a system would require only replication to constitute a significant ABM component capable of substituting for ground-based interceptors. Such a system would be a clear example of relabeling, as discussed earlier in this chapter.

Summary

We have considered how development and deployment of systems and technologies conducted for non-ABM purposes might affect the ABM Treaty regime. In general, systems for air defense and defense against tactical ballistic missiles would not directly lead to a significant ABM capability. With additional sensors for cueing of air defense radars, with the possibility of fitting nuclear warheads to interceptors, and with modifications to interceptor seekers and control software, these systems could provide a limited capability to intercept a small or cooperative attack. Such makeshift ABM deployments could readily be overcome by offensive tactics and penetration aids such as decoys, jammers, and the like. Widespread deployment of such non-ABM defenses as a backup or reserve, as discussed earlier, would reduce the buffer time for deployment of a minimal breakout system. Although the USSR has a large, sophisticated air defense system in place while the United States has none and is not likely to get one, the ABM relevance of this system must be assessed in detail, as indicated above.

Development, testing, and deployment of penetration aids for offensive missiles do not erode, but rather reinforce, the buffer against an ABM defense. The development of sensors or discrimination means could be hidden under or masked by the testing of offensive penetration aids, but such activities could more readily be conducted overtly and are permitted by the ABM Treaty, except as they pertain to covert improvement in ABM capabilities of air defense or ATBM systems.

Although certain ASAT and DSAT approaches pose no problems for an ABM Treaty regime, others might do so—for example, lasers and defensive interceptors on board satellites. Development and possible deployment of such interceptors could well lead to difficulty for the ABM Treaty and could reduce buffer time for ABM breakout. Although outright prohibition of ASAT and limitation of DSAT may or may not be desirable on their own merits, if individual agreed orbiting test ranges are created in a loosening of the ABM Treaty, as discussed in chapter 8, ASAT activity might be limited to these ranges.

Large ground-based phased-array radars and infrared sensors on satellites can furnish useful information for a defense against ballistic missiles. However, they have legitimate and important missions quite independent of any defense. For instance, they can provide warning and assessment of enemy attack by ballistic missiles, track objects in space, and provide technical intelligence that reduces uncertainty of foreign offensive capabilities.

Large phased-array radars for ballistic missile early warning are limited by the ABM Treaty to the periphery of the national territory, where they are further restricted to face outward, and to a single small deployment region in the nation's interior. As such, they provide neither an ABM capability nor a base for one.

Of the civil space activities discussed here, only laser-powered launch of satellites and space probes appears to have any conflict with the ABM Treaty. The deployment of even a single such facility must be judged capable of substituting for an ABM component.

Notes

1. A bus is the low-thrust spacecraft initially containing all the warheads and the precision guidance system, which maneuvers in midcourse flight to drop off each warhead with precisely the right velocity to strike its designated target.

2. The radar could be cued and pointed in the right direction by an external source such as a larger, fixed radar or an infrared track from an aircraft or a satellite. If the air defense radar was not cued and instead had to search the entire sky, the average detection range would be much reduced, perhaps to only a few tens of kilometers, and intercept would be impossible. In searching the entire sky, a radar must distribute its pulses throughout a solid angle perhaps 1,000 times larger than if it is properly cued; thus if the whole region is to be scanned in the same time, the actual target receives only 1/1,000 the pulse energy, and the range is reduced by a factor of 5.6 (detected signal goes down in proportion to range to the fourth power). Alternatively, if pulses of the same energy and repetition rate are used, it takes 1,000 times longer to search the larger solid angle, and average time to detection is delayed. Chapter 7 examines the need for cueing in more detail.

3. The calculations underlying these numbers have been simplified for clarity. The RV is taken to move at constant velocity of 7 kilometers per second with a reentry angle of 30 degrees, and the interceptor at constant velocity of 1 kilometer per second.

4. That is, arranged to provide a full nuclear explosion at the instant it is struck by the nonnuclear-kill interceptor. In general, salvage fusing is not feasible against nuclear-kill interceptors, whose warhead killing action penetrates at the speed of light. But a "ladder down" tactic against nuclear-armed interceptors provides much of the same benefit to the attacker as does salvage fusing; planned detonation of successive warheads at decreasing altitudes along the trajectory denies the defense enough precision tracking time to intercept before the warhead detonates or (finally) reaches its target.

5. Nose-on intercepts, as shown in the figure, are relatively easy, since, for example, higher than nominal drag on the incoming RV slides the intercept point back up along the intercept line so that only the time of intercept is affected. Cross-range intercepts are harder, because the time necessary for relatively slow interceptors to reach the path of fast RV targets further delays the time of intercept and allows the RV to explode at a lower altitude, closer to its intended target. Considerable divert capability and maneuver are needed to intercept an RV slowing rapidly and not perfectly predictably because of atmospheric drag.

The defender could commit an interceptor on the basis of tracking by a sensor external to the air defense system, before the radar detects the RV. This approach requires interceptor commit before the effect of atmospheric drag can be useful for discrimination of decoys; the offense need use only enough decoys to exhaust the local stock of interceptors.

6. If developed to have ABM capability, however, such interceptors could not be deployed except at the permitted site.

7. For description, please refer to the Glossary.

8. Brightness *B* is typically expressed in watts per steradian, with 4π steradian of solid angle filling a sphere. If the brightness is limited only by the unavoidable angular spread by "diffraction" of light from the finite exit mirror of the laser system, $B = PA/\lambda^2$, where *P* is the steady output power of the laser in watts, *A* is the area of the exit aperture in square meters, and λ is the wavelength of the laser light (in meters). See also chapter 8.

9. Note that satellites would need to resist steady illumination for 100 seconds or more in a pass over a ground laser, so the survivability thresholds are given in illuminating power per square centimeter of satellite surface. Significant ABM capability can be obtained only if destructive energy is delivered in a short time, since the booster flight time is limited, and many boosters must be destroyed in that time. For that reason, the lethality threshold of missiles is often given in watt-seconds (or kilowatt-seconds—kilojoules) per square centimeter; at the risk of some confusion, we show this in figure 6-3 on the assumption of 1 second illumination time.

10. This result can be obtained simply by recognizing that the power density or local heating at the "best focus" of a light beam falls off precisely as the square of the distance from the mirror. At a range of 4,000 kilometers, the assumed laser would produce 10 kilowatts per square centimeter and so could deliver the assumed 1 kilowatt-seconds per square centimeter to a unhardened booster in 0.1 second. Of course, it could kill boosters at a steady rate of 10 per second only if the laser retarget time was considerably less than 0.1 second, which is a difficult goal to achieve with the required mirror diameter.

11. A mirror of the same size as that at GEO would have the same diffraction spread in angle, but at $\frac{1}{20}$ the range, the spot would be $(\frac{1}{20})^2$ or $\frac{1}{400}$ the area.

12. *Nature*, September 9, 1988, p. 124. In essence, a number of detectors can be situated in a camera film-plane exactly where the images of the suspected sites appear.

13. In actuality, the BSTS is probably harmless to the ABM Treaty regime, since it is little more than a modern version of the early-warning launch-detection satellite in operation at the time the ABM Treaty entered into force in 1972. The SSTS both in principle and in capability (if it is fully developed and deployed) could play the role of an ABM radar and presumably would not be permitted under the ABM Treaty. If there were some compelling non-ABM peacetime role for SSTS (and ABM Treaty verification is not it), SSTS might be deployed only if it were assuredly vulnerable—for instance, by cooperative mining.

14. For example, LWIR satellites are judged to be of questionable utility for warning and assessment, because the booster is far easier to detect from its SWIR emissions against cloud and earth background than it is from the much smaller amount of long-wave infrared emitted. Furthermore, the relatively low altitude of burnout increases the number of non-earth-viewing LWIR satellites that would be required to see boosters without competition from the LWIR radiated from the earth.

15. A visit to the Krasnoyarsk radar by a U.S. group in 1987 confirms that the radar is years from completion. President Gorbachev has stated formally that the radar has been given to the Soviet Academy of Sciences to be turned into an international space research establishment.

16. For instance, focal-plane resolution of 10 kilometers or a frame rate of one picture per 10 seconds or more.

17. Small reflective cube corners send light directly back to the illuminating source. Because of this directional reflection, a corner reflector will reflect as much light as a sphere or disk of diameter S if the corner reflector itself has diameter $(\lambda S)^{0.5}$. For $S = 1$ meter and $\lambda = 1$ micrometer, the corner reflector need only be 1 millimeter in diameter to return as much light as a sphere or plate a million times its area.

18. In principle, coherent laser radar might distinguish RVs from decoys by the detailed velocity structure of the spinning RV, as evidenced in the Doppler pattern of LADAR returns from a very small interval in range. Such a costly, sensitive detection system, however, can be negated by providing randomly moving surface features on balloon-enclosed RVs ("fronds") and on decoy balloons as well. See, for instance, the chapter by R. L. Garwin, "The Soviet Response: New Missiles and Countermeasures" in *Empty Promise—The Growing Case Against Star Wars* by the

Union of Concerned Scientists, edited by J. Tirman (Boston: Beacon Press, 1986). Interactive discrimination can also be countered, as Garwin describes; in any case, the space-based pulsed-laser capability required to discriminate millions of decoys seems at least as demanding as the laser weapons that would actually kill thousands of boosters in boost phase. Since such a LADAR might "substitute for ABM radars" against the current threat, its deployment could not be judged compliant to the ABM Treaty.

19. Space-based microwave radars can provide detailed measurements on space objects. Chirped or other high-bandwidth pulses, combined with range-gated Doppler processing, can detect some fine structure of targets and decoys, but both laser and microwave radars are subject to similar contermeasures such as corner reflectors and variable surface features. In general, because the signal usable by an active sensor such as radar or LADAR diminishes with the fourth power of the distance to the target, and the signal for a passive LWIR or SWIR sensor diminishes only as the square, radars have more application for relatively short-range tasks than for surveillance of a large fraction of the earth's surface.

20. If the United States or USSR wished to deploy large satellites for nominally peaceful purposes (without negotiating in detail their technical characteristics), their peaceful nature could be assured by allowing the other side to place an explosive charge and communication package on board. The on-board charge could be detonated by its owner at any time (but legitimately only at the outbreak of war); there would be communications of modest capability for this purpose and for housekeeping, and detonation could be made automatic if the communication channel were rendered unusable (e.g., by covering the small special antenna on the satellite). Some mutual inspection and verification of the package containing the on-board charge would be needed, but such an approach could obviate excessively detailed information transfer about satellite function. This is an example of an ASAT capability with no ABM function at all; it is also the next step in the old proverb "Trust, but verify." Unfamiliar and thus "unrealistic," this option may appear more reasonable on further thought.

21. People would have to be excluded from a region several times this diameter to limit the nonionizing radiation exposure to tolerable levels.

7

GROUND-BASED ABM SYSTEMS

Thomas H. Johnson

T O SOME EXTENT the distinction denoting some ABM systems as ground-based is arbitrarily drawn, since virtually all ground-based systems now contemplated use space-based elements in some way, if only for warning. Ground-based laser systems require space-based mirrors to attack ICBMs in all but the terminal phases of their trajectories and would be more effective using them even there. Also, many advanced ground-based concepts employ airborne elements, an addition that may not be substantive but that can be confusing in the context of the ABM Treaty. For practical purposes then, let us specify ground-based systems as ones in which the rockets or the lasers that actually intercept missiles or reentry vehicles are on the ground when the attack begins; the presence of system elements elsewhere is irrelevant. This definition is somewhat different from the Treaty's, which states that ground-based systems comprise interceptors, launchers, and radars on the ground, and nothing more anywhere.

Discussion of ground-based systems is complicated by the fact that their various components span the possible states of development. Thus, some components, such as radars and rockets carrying nuclear weapons, are fully developed, and their performance has been well evaluated. Some components, such as homing hit-to-kill (kinetic-energy) interceptors, although not yet ready for deployment, are in advance states of development. Although one cannot yet predict how well they would perform as ABM components, one can be reasonably confident in predicting their essential characteristics of testing and operation, particularly as they affect questions of verification. Finally, some components are based on technologies that are still in the transition from science to engineering; high-power lasers and many of their supporting systems are in this category. Considerable uncertainty exists concerning their eventual capabilities and modes of testing and hence the effectiveness of precise means of verification.

Partly in response to such uncertainties, the approach taken here to verification questions is a conservative one: use as few precise, quantitative limits as possible and apply them only where they can be measured confidently and at reasonable cost. Do not try to constrain things that are not really threatening, and do not try to restrain technology that can be developed in laboratories. And avoid intentionally ambiguous generalities in definitions; they are not effective as a means of dealing with the uncertainty of technological projections.

As discussed in chapter 2, three criteria are important in identifying matters of military concern. The first is the prevention of militarily threatening ABM deployments. This criterion is generally taken in this chapter to denote the "free ride" case of chapter 2—that is, the ability to intercept confidently more than 10 percent of the opponent's full ballistic missile force; this might be translated into an ability to defend preferentially a small but important set of military targets against even very large attacks. The second criterion is to prevent the other side from creating a base from which to deploy a militarily threatening ABM defense. The third criterion, relabeling of non-ABM systems, is especially relevant to certain classes of ground-based systems. The third criterion simply amounts to applying the first two criteria to non-ABM systems: is the ostensibly non-ABM-capable air defense, ASAT, or other system actually ABM-capable to the point of being able to intercept 10 percent of ballistic reentry vehicles (or to break up large, structured attacks against hardened targets), or is it de facto a base for a breakout deployment of a more extensive and more capable system?

Realistic military discussions of ballistic missile defense operations become extremely complex, even when only mature, and thus reasonably well understood, technologies are involved. A great many uncertainties attend even the most tested components, not merely individual reliabilities, but questions of how well components will interact while under attack; command, control, and communications limitations; assumptions about the nature of the attack itself and about the penetration capabilities of the offensive missiles; personalities of the common chain under very strict time limitations; and great uncertainties in the effects of nuclear weapons detonating in the atmosphere, particularly large-yield weapons intentionally detonated by the attacker. All of these uncertainties lead to two distinct frames of mind (called the "offense conservative" and "defense conservative" views) as to the effectiveness of the defense. The offense planner must assume it will work as well as its components will allow; the defense planner must assume that his side's least favorable estimates of penetration apply.

This chapter adopts the offense conservative view; that is, it assumes that everything fielded works up to its estimated capability. This amounts to a sure-safe criterion in terms of the effectiveness of the Treaty and generally favors a set of strict limitations on ABM-related technologies. If the Treaty successfully constrains offense-conservative systems, then certainly it has prevented the development of the defense one wishes to prevent. It is also assumed here that relatively high offensive force levels are maintained.

Background

An ABM engagement is commonly discussed as occurring in five stages: search and acquisition; track; discrimination; interceptor fly-out; and target destruction ("kill"). The search and acquisition function generally requires sensors that can scan fairly large volumes of space over very long ranges and reliably detect the presence of all potential targets. These targets must then be tracked by the original sensor or their positions handed off to a different sensor for tracking. Tracking for several seconds makes it possible to predict the targets' trajectories and assists in identifying the signals picked up by the sensors from various nontargets (such as remnant booster pieces). Using tracking and other information, the ABM system must then determine which of the objects in the sky are threats that must be engaged. The interceptor must take a finite amount of time to fly to its intercept point in the target's trajectory. It must then be able to get sufficiently close to ensure that its warhead—a nuclear weapon, an explosive and shrapnel charge, or the body of the interceptor itself—destroys the target.

Each of these five stages is the object of rigorous research in the application of new technologies, methods that might fundamentally change the capabilities of ABM systems. Search and acquisition is currently performed by high-power, broad-beamed, low-frequency, phased-array radars. The angular extent and range of the search mandate the high powers; at the wavelengths most efficient for search, the result is large, vulnerable facilities, of which each nation has only a few. Research is under way to replace these radars with various kinds of new subsystems, most of them operating on "other physical principals"—primarily infrared or optical wavelength detection. Such sensors can be much smaller and can be mounted on airplanes or on satellites. Verification of their presence and operation can be made difficult because of their size and because, unlike radar, they are passive sensors: they do not radiate energy, but operate on natural or reflected radiation from the target itself. And being airborne or space-based, if they are used for target acquisition rather than for early warning, they explicitly violate the terms of the Treaty.

The track function might also be performed or augmented with passive sensors or with new kinds of optical radars. More conventional, microwave-frequency radars remain the best option for this function. Technical progress is being made in this area also. The radars currently being designed for the U.S. SDI system, Terminal Imaging Radar (TIR), for example, operate around 10 gigahertz, with about 10,000 transmit/receive modules. They will reach power-aperture products 1 million to 2 million watt-meters squared, insufficient for search and acquisition but excellent for tracking.[1] Efforts to build radars of yet higher frequencies (about 30 gigahertz) are hampered both by technological difficulties in generating the beams and by the fact that such frequencies propagate poorly through the atmosphere, particularly if it happens to rain.

Reentry vehicles (RVs) can be discriminated from some kinds of decoys as the attacking warheads pass from an altitude of about 100 kilometers to about 70 kilometers, since atmospheric drag will slow the lighter decoys more than it will the reentry vehicles themselves. Low-altitude terminal-defense systems are designed to take advantage of this natural aid to discrimination, but low-altitude engagement makes their timelines short and restricts the area on the ground (the "footprint") that can be protected by a particular battery of missiles. Most of the sensor technologies discussed so far are being studied for use in decoy discrimination.

Decoy discrimination is the key technical problem of ABM and is in essence little closer to a militarily workable solution than it was thirty years ago. Passive infrared and optical techniques remain under intense study but at present seem unlikely to provide unambiguous discrimination against an opponent with carefully designed decoys. The excellent phase stability[2] of the higher-frequency radars such as TIR is being studied for use in discrimination also, but such subtle discrimination techniques are especially susceptible to offensive countermeasures and so introduce a potentially endless measure-countermeasure game that makes it impossible to evaluate the effectiveness of one's defense system. Other possibilities, both active (e.g., reflected laser light) and interactive (e.g., pushing slightly on reentry vehicles and decoys with directed-energy beams), are also being explored.

Interceptor fly-out can be made almost instantaneous if directed-energy weapons can perform the function of interceptors; specific fly-out considerations would then be replaced by beam-handling considerations. Any such working components are far in the future, however. For long-range, high-altitude intercepts, moderate acceleration, high-burnout-velocity missiles are appropriate; in the more stressful environment below 50 kilometers, intercepts must be performed by high-acceleration missiles with lower burnout velocities.

Although small nuclear weapons are politically unfashionable for intercep-tors, they remain the only warheads with convincing lethality for low-altitude interceptions. Outside the atmosphere, homing vehicles may permit nonnuclear target distinction, although one good way of achieving a cost-exchange advantage with such homers (lofting several small missiles on one large missile) is forbidden by the ABM Treaty.

The vast number of possible combinations of these technologies and their descendants virtually prohibits an unequivocal judgment concerning the effectiveness and relative significance of any particular configuration. However, by assessing how certain ways of solving various problems would influence the general effectiveness of ABM operations, we can get some comparative measures of the importance of various advances. Such measures can then be combined with our judgments about the cost and confidence of verifying restrictions on those advances. In the spirit of the Treaty, we would like to prevent the development or evolution of defenses that require the offense to deploy penetration aids (such as reentry vehicle decoys) to maintain confidence in its deterrent forces.

Existing ABM Systems

The ABM system currently deployed around Moscow (and being expanded up to the allowed 100 interceptors allowed by the Treaty) is not militarily meaningful. It does not interfere substantively with the United States's ability to destroy targets in the Moscow area, certainly not enough to protect the city against a large attack. For example, the United States could simply spend 100 extra warheads to exhaust the interceptors in the system by attacking them (since they cannot be mobile or deceptively based), then proceed with the attack against undefended targets. In practice, a combination of offensive penetration aids on ICBMs and simultaneous attack with submarine-launched ballistic missile (SLBM) warheads (also assisted by penetration aids) could probably make the attack effective with fewer than 100 warheads lost to the defense, even assuming a preferential defense,[3] because the current system is susceptible even to relatively crude penetration aids.

The Moscow ABM is also easily verifiable in its current deployment. The United States knows how many launchers there are and has observed test firings of the missiles. The radars are spatially deployed in accordance with the Treaty's provisions for defense of a capital.

In short, this system does not pose a threat either militarily or politically (that is, a threat to the Treaty). Further, there is no reason even to try to restrict Treaty-consistent upgrades (higher-frequency radar akin to missile-site radars, for example) of the Moscow system. Such upgrades could include new missiles (or new combinations of missiles) and new high-performance, high-frequency radars. As long as the number of missiles is not increased beyond the prescribed limit, they can be exhausted; and as long as the radars are not made mobile or proliferated or hidden, they can be targeted.

A more complicated question is posed by the frequently discussed notion of ABM breakout, which suggests a widespread deployment (either nationwide or at many key military targets) of the technology and components of the current Moscow system. Missile and radar production lines are open; we do not know how many system components of any type have already been produced and stored. If the Soviets began only now to produce and field a widespread system, they would be several years ahead of any comparable action by the United States. The United States has no ABM system of any kind fully engineered, let alone in actual production.

Therefore, we must accept that the physical possibility of a breakout exists as an option to Soviet planners. That breakout could already be fully prepared for by secret stockpiling, or it could occur if the Soviets decide to take advantage of their ability to deploy a proliferated system in less time than the United States could deploy one, for whatever reason. Such a proliferation of a very large number (say, several thousand) of interceptors, along with several hundred radars (perhaps mobile ones), could be very worrisome to U.S. attack planners and expensive for the United States to counteract. Nevertheless, because of the performance limits of the Moscow ABM technology, particularly in stressful nuclear attack environments, it is highly unlikely that any such ABM proliferation would actually undermine the credibility of the U.S. nuclear deterrent. Effective penetration aids, even without large increases in force size, could be deployed and could provide high confidence of successful attacks in most cases.

Still, U.S. offensive planners would be highly unlikely to settle for penetration aids alone in the face of extensive defenses. The pressure for force increases in various categories would be extreme; it could be argued that such increases were necessary to guarantee success across the broad range of the most critical military targets.

Hence, from the Soviet point of view, proliferation of the Moscow ABM system cannot present a terribly attractive option, purely on its own military terms. Such an effort would be extremely expensive. Site preparation and deployment would be conspicuous and time-consuming enough to allow the United States to respond effectively. It would not confer a decisive military advantage, even in its limited objective. Extensive calculations by U.S. defensive planners all reinforce the conclusion that penetration aids and large numbers of attacking warheads could succeed against even well-defended targets using this technology, especially with preferential targeting. The Soviets' defense conservative calculations could hardly be much more optimistic. An actual deployment would require expensive testing and upgrade (mobile radars, for example) after the commitment was made, so that even the Soviets' own measure of military effectiveness could not be firmly established until after the political and military costs of proceeding had been accepted. And, finally, such a move would undoubtedly spur a new round of offensive escalation by the United States.

In sum, a breakout threat does exist and will continue to be a possibility, and no verification measures or agreements under the existing ABM Treaty can remove that threat. If the components to support a breakout have already been produced and stored, a more restrictive treaty regime will not help either. But breakout is not a potent military threat in the near term and can be made even less threatening later on.[4] What can be done is to provide both political and military incentives to the Soviets to reinforce adherence to the existing treaty regime. The political incentives could include less rhetoric about future breakouts by the United States using new ABM technologies, more rhetoric about the virtues of a stable treaty regime and a coupling of offensive reductions to maintenance of Treaty restrictives under improved controls. The military incentives could include a robust penetration aids development program to weaken any Soviet conception of a favorable marginal effectiveness of broad defenses of military targets. To test the practical effectiveness of penetration aids developed in such a program, the United States would need to operate a functional prototype terminal-defense system capable of emulating key characteristics of the Moscow system and its future upgrades. Execution of the detailed engineering to construct and upgrade such a functional prototype could provide an additional military incentive to maintain the Treaty, since it would reduce considerably the lead-time-to-deployment advantage of a Soviet breakout.

One application of existing ABM technologies that has been widely discussed is a small system to protect against accidental launches of offensive missiles (the jargon is Accidental Launch Protection System, or ALPS). The threat in such a case would presumably be no more than about three missiles' worth of RVs, since a larger-scale launch purely by accident is generally regarded as unlikely. This definition of accidental launch must be distinguished for unauthorized launch, in which the threat would comprise much larger numbers of missiles (as from a submarine commander launching his entire battery). Dealing with unauthorized launch would require a robust system well beyond Treaty-limited capabilities.

As for a true ALPS, to get nationwide coverage from a Treaty-limited 100-interceptor system it would be necessary to commit interceptors to reentry vehicles while the RVs were still at high altitude (otherwise the footprint of the defense would be too small). Such intercepts could be performed either by kinetic kill or by nuclear warheads and remain entirely Treaty-consistent. But the nationwide effectiveness of that system would rely either on the absence of offensive decoys or on a currently nonexistent scheme to discriminate reentry vehicles from decoys. Attempting to solve the discrimination problem with space-based sensors would immediately conflict with the terms of the Treaty, as would enlarging the footprint for terminal intercepts by raising the number of interceptor launch sites (and the number of interceptors). In addition, radars in North Dakota have too high a horizon (they cannot see the attacking reentry vehicles far enough away) to perform acquisition and track handoff for the ALPS interceptors. BMEWs and PAVE PAWS radars, which might technically perform this function, are forbidden to do so by the ABM Treaty.

In sum, the public attention to ALPS has been generated by the suggestion of an application of existing (or nearly existing) ABM technology within the constraints of the ABM Treaty, so that actual defense system integration and operation experience can be obtained without overwhelming financial or political costs. But, as described above, an effective ALPS cannot be built within the constraints of the Treaty.

Upgrades to Existing ABM Systems

Although certain upgrades are allowed under the Treaty, other improvements now being developed or studied raise questions of compliance. These upgrades do not directly change the characteristics of either interceptors or radars; the Treaty limits the former only numerically. For the latter, limitations on number and mobility of deployed systems are easily verifiable (although the question of stockpiling remains, as discussed above, problematic). The power-aperture product limit as defined in the Treaty (3×10^6 watt-meters squared) is verifiable only in an approximate sense by national technical means. That is, we can have confidence of estimates of this product for a given radar only within about a factor of three to four. Nevertheless, for deployed systems this degree of confidence is sufficient. The key elements of the deployed systems, the acquisition radars of significantly greater power, are appropriately limited in number or location by the Treaty, and those deployments are easy to verify. If the Soviets developed mobile engagement radars of such high power that they could themselves also perform the target acquisition function, the testing of such radars (deployed anywhere except in the National Command Authority defense) should be detectable as a Treaty violation, because their powers would be so far above the Treaty limit.[5]

Thus, the real issues in upgrades to existing ABM systems have to do with the integration of more advanced kinds of sensor systems, both active and passive. Passive optics means primarily infrared optical systems that are airborne, space-based, or launched on rockets and are used either to assist or to replace radars for target acquisition, tracking, or discrimination. To the extent that they could perform acquisition, such systems could alleviate the defense's reliance on large perimeter acquisition radars, a key vulnerability. To the extent that they could track, such systems could obviate the numerical limits on deployed battle management radars and could improve the performance of the entire defense in nuclear engagement environments. And to the extent that they could discriminate incoming reentry vehicles from decoys, such systems might permit the terminal defense to engage the attackers at higher altitudes, increasing the effectiveness of the defense by enlarging both the battle space and the interception opportunities.

All this makes passive optics sound threatening. Nevertheless, our judgment is that such components do not present sensible objects of further control under the present ABM Treaty regime. There are three reasons for this judgment.

The first reason has to do with verification. The use of passive optics in partial or even full-scale testing could be masked by extensive, simultaneous radar testing over a wide area, especially if the telemetry were encrypted; the airplane containing the optics (and its encrypted messages) could be explained as part of an alternative command system. One might never know that optical signals were being used for acquisition or battle management, and one certainly could not tell how much the system logic depended upon optics or radar. The monitoring of test target sets for optical acquisition and tracking would necessarily involve very deep guesswork, and the presence of optical sensors on board test aircraft could not be verified without placing observers on those aircraft.

The second reason is essentially juridical. If infrared systems are used only as adjuncts to improve the performance of radars (by, for instance, eliminating problems of blackout from ionization produced by detonations), then it is not clear that their use is forbidden by the Treaty. As suggested above, use in this mode during tests may be impossible to distinguish from use in a forbidden mode (substituting for radars).

The third reason has to do with military effectiveness. Assisting or even replacing either acquisition or battle management radars does not make an otherwise Treaty-limited ABM defense significantly more difficult to overcome (there would still be only 100 interceptors). Nor does performance improvement in either acquisition or battle management change the basic calculus of ABM breakout; a response with both penetration aids and offensive increases would be likely to follow, but those actions should fully maintain confidence in the U.S. deterrent. An infrared optical system that could actually discriminate decoys from reentry vehicles well outside the atmosphere would indeed be worrisome and might change the United States's estimate of its ability to penetrate a widely proliferated defense. But experimentation on passive infrared discrimination has been under way for some time now, and as discussed earlier, such methods seem unlikely to be sufficient to do the job, particularly against an offensive threat tailored to deal with such optics.

This last point suggests the major problem in analysis of what is conceptually the other main category of improvements to existing terminal ABM systems: *active* optical components. Such components consist primarily of lasers of various wavelengths, from infrared through visible to ultraviolet. Such lasers could be airborne, space-based, rocketborne, or even, for some battle management scenarios, ground-based.

Because of their inherently narrow fields of view, lasers are of no use in target acquisition. Nor do they offer any strong advantages as battle management sensors (compared with radars and passive optics), since advantages of wavelength and precision are somewhat offset by the additional command and control problems of pointing and tracking and by the limitations imposed by weather and atmospheric contaminations.

But, for the third application of new optical components—decoy discrimination—lasers cannot yet be dismissed. Because of problems with weather it is unlikely that such lasers would be ground-based, but it remains conceivable, though far from demonstrated, that airborne, space-based, or rocketborne lasers could be used to eliminate some large fraction of decoys from an incoming threat cloud. If the reentry vehicles can be unambiguously discriminated at long ranges, it might be possible to destroy them outside the atmosphere (either by hit-to-kill interceptors or by nuclear weapons) at favorable exchange ratios. Thus, if active optics could develop a discrimination capability, an ABM system otherwise based essentially on existing components and technologies could become much more threatening. Coupled with the possibility of Soviet breakout, this presents a disturbing prospect.

The first two difficulties discussed above for passive optics—verification and distinction between adjunct and component—also arise, to a lesser extent, with active optics. But since radar and passive optics cannot accomplish decoy discrimination on a really meaningful scale, performing this task with active optics would amount to conferring a whole new capability with a new component, clarifying the Treaty issue by eliminating the option of claiming that the new elements are merely adjuncts to allowed components. The verification problem would be less difficult for active than for passive optics.

Development and verification of a military capability to discriminate decoys with such lasers would require extensive series of tests against moderately large clouds of decoys. Since we already monitor ICBM testing, and since ICBM tests with multiple decoy releases are rare, the United States should be able to concentrate its monitoring resources effectively to diagnose such tests. And proper monitoring, particularly using space-based assets, should be able to detect the scattered radiation from the discrimination lasers (even though they are of low power compared with laser weapons), since the cloud of target reentry vehicles and decoys tells one precisely where to look. Because a successful test series would itself quickly provide a base for deployment (since the other major components of a system exist), it is important to clarify this issue in advance with the Soviets that any such tests constitute a violation of the ABM Treaty (Article V).

Advanced Technology ABM

The one candidate being seriously discussed as a replacement for interceptor rockets in an advanced-technology, ground-based ABM role is directed-energy weapons. Within this broad category, only high-power lasers require serious consideration. Ground-based charged-particle beams can be dispensed with because they cannot propagate far enough; at realistic power levels the damage mechanism of radio-frequency weapons is too uncertain.

As the 1987 study of the American Physical Society[6] explained, laser-weapon development will require many years to demonstrate an ABM capability, many more to create a base for deployment. In short, the problem is not particularly pressing. Agreeing to restrict large-scale development tests to announced test ranges will ease verification of the general level of technology development, which at the current stage is appropriate. The most stressing environment is one in which, as at present, ground-based laser antisatellite weapons (ASATs) are not the subject of any treaty. Such ASATs are discussed below as one of the principal relabeling problems through which systems for other military missions might grow to ABM capability. Meanwhile, ABM-related limitations on the characteristics of ground-based lasers seem premature; in any case, such limitations would not be verifiable without site visits, though certain characteristics of tests conducted with the laser might be verified.

Antisatellite Weapons (ASATs)

DIRECT-ASCENT ROCKETS

Flexible, effective, direct-ascent ASATs will have some residual ABM capability, because the engagement parameters require similar capabilities: high burnout velocities and cross-range maneuver. Furthermore, testing of such ASATs will remain, even with relatively full knowledge of the test conditions, somewhat ambiguous. Whether such a test meets the tester's own criterion of utility in an ABM mode can only be guessed. Some parameters of the antisatellite test engagement will always prove to be somewhat different from a true ICBM intercept, but the observer and tester may (and probably will) disagree as to whether the test performance scales reliable to ABM capability. Hence, such tests could be a potential breeding ground of difficulties with the

Treaty and its specific application. Deployment, not testing, of direct-ascent ASATs is the issue of greatest importance, since ABM interceptors may be tested openly under the Treaty anyway.

Permitting full development of direct-ascent ASATs poses some minor Treaty issues. A separate bilateral agreement on two points could ease matters considerably. First, the United States and the USSR should agree that all such tests be conducted with single-warhead ASAT missiles against single orbital targets. Second, such testing should occur only on identified ASAT test ranges to simplify verification of the first point. With carefully monitored tests limited to single targets, even highly capable direct-ascent ASAT rockets do not offer more of a base for deployment than do existing ABM interceptors. In fact, given the additional requirements for radar, optical, and integration development and testing, the ASAT system itself would be well behind the Soviet Galosh and Gazelle interceptors as candidates for ABM proliferation. Of course, if the interceptor missiles were sufficiently close in performance to Galosh, one might argue that ASAT deployments in large numbers were simply a ploy to exceed the Treaty's numerical limit on interceptors and sites. One might then propose, as some have, to limit the ASAT rockets' burnout velocity or divert capability[7] to prevent such relabeling.

In my view, such additional limitations pose an unnecessary quagmire for negotiations and cooperation. In the first place, the possibility that many Galosh missiles have already been stockpiled, or are being stockpiled today, exists now and cannot be ruled out in the foreseeable future. Using ASAT as a mask to accomplish this same end seems unnecessarily complex and expensive; limiting the number of deployed ASAT missiles leaves open the same questions that limiting the number of deployed ABM missiles has left open. In the second place, imposing limitations on the performance of deployed ASATs might easily degrade the ASAT system's capability in a way unacceptable to the ASAT developer. If the goal is to stop ASAT, it will be more effective to negotiate an ASAT treaty directly, rather than use the ABM Treaty as an indirect, expedient means to a different, controversial goal. In the third place, the problem of the proliferation of dual-capable interceptors is much more sensibly and straightfor-wardly handled by limiting the sites themselves, not the missiles. Thus, one might agree with the Soviets to deploy ASAT missiles at only a few (say, three) particular sites and on those sites to permit only a few (say, ten) individual launchers. Such limitations could be negotiated to satisfy both nations' ASAT mission requirements, yet restrict the base for ABM relabeling.

LASERS

Ground-based laser ASATs for attacking satellites in low earth orbit (LEO) provide an intermediate development objective en route to both ABM lasers and high-altitude (geosynchronous and beyond) ASATs. These latter two categories have approximately the same requirements, that is somewhat beyond 100 megawatts and, consequently, at this stage in their development, present essentially equivalent technical goals.[8] LEO ASATs require about ten times less power. Thus, ground-based LEO ASAT lasers suggest a base for development, rather than for deployment, of a laser ABM defense. Yet they remain a concern simply because the characteristics and even existence of such lasers are very difficult, if not impossible, to verify confidently. Thus it may be possible to pass surreptitiously into the development stage for the high-power device. The concern is not great, since the roughly tenfold increase in power from a LEO ASAT to an entry-level ABM laser will take at least a few years to accomplish, and several more years would be needed for system integration. Construction and testing on the requisite scale would be virtually impossible to conceal. Nevertheless, the issue continues to receive considerable attention and so is worth examining. A technical background to the issues is provided in chapter 6.

A continuous-wave laser, operating in the infrared anywhere from roughly 1 to 10 microns wavelength (depending upon the choice of lasing medium) would require a minimum power between 2 and 10 megawatts off the final telescope mirror (beam detector) to provide a useful military capability as a LEO ASAT. We define that capability as lethal fluence delivered to satellites at 1,000-kilometers' altitude and 1,000-kilometers' cross-range from the laser's location.[9] A repetitively pulsed ultraviolet excimer laser would require essentially the same power, and a single-pulse excimer (which causes damage by impulse loading, rather than by deposition of thermal energy) would require an output energy in the range 5 to 10 megajoules.

For most of the candidate lasers for this mission, devices of this size could be constructed in buildings the size of airplane hangars[10] and powered (in most locations) from existing electric grids. Thus their construction and laboratory testing could be carried out entirely surreptitiously. Operation as an ASAT requires (for all but the very longest, least attractive wavelengths) some form of point-ahead compensation.[11] This compensation is an extremely difficult problem, whose solution will require accurate testing against well-instrumented, satellite-borne targets. Whether such tests can be performed completely surreptitiously is problematic, but in practical terms the answer is probably yes.

To find such a test, one would look for one of two things (assuming the telemetry has been encrypted and disguised): laser light scattered by the atmosphere in the beam's upward passage or laser light scattered off the target during the test. With no knowledge of the laser's ground location, the first approach would be incredibly difficult and expensive. The United States would need a fleet of satellites constantly examining the sky over the entire USSR looking for a signal whose wavelength would be uncertain over almost two orders of magnitude and whose strength would be uncertain over perhaps four orders of magnitude. The second indicator, laser light scattered off the target, might seem more promising, since the number of Soviet satellites is smaller than the number of hangar-sized buildings in the USSR. Unfortunately, though, we do not know all the functions of even existing Soviet satellites. Thus, this verification method would require that the United States develop monitoring methods (such as direct observation from other satellites) for all Soviet satellites all the time, for a signal of highly uncertain (as before) wavelength and strength (signal strength here would be even more uncertain, since presumably the Soviets would design their target to capture as much of the incident beam as possible). More important, the Soviets launch satellites at a rate several times that of the United States. The United States would be unlikely to be willing to launch new laser-spy satellites immediately following every new Soviet launch, to prevent them from doing second- or third-orbit laser ASAT tests on a new target satellite, then quietly switching the target satellite to some benign function. Nor does the threat merit anything close to such an effort.

Ground-based lasers may indeed represent a real threat to LEO satellites, which may or may not be a good reason to discuss an ASAT limitation treaty (complicated by the verification problems described above). But for ABM missions, lasers of ASAT size merely advance the technology toward some still-distant possibility of performing missile defense. In the absence of a negotiated ASAT ban, it would be useful to encourage cooperative rules on laser development to keep some track of the state of technology, but it would be misleading to call this an urgent problem.

In the first place, one might agree to conduct ASAT tests only on designated ASAT ranges, which might or might not coincide with existing ABM ranges. Because of the verification problem, such an agreement would not provide an absolute guarantee against cheating, but it would promote a cooperative arms control position, especially since the main concern is not achievement of ASAT-level powers, but further development to ABM levels. By restricting the lasers at such sites to 20 megawatts or 20 megajoules class, one could control the advance of relevant ABM technology without limiting development of ASAT capability.

Ground-based laser ASATs would be far more effective if used in combination with space-based mirrors to increase their cross-range capabilities (and the variety of angles from which they could attack shielded satellites). Tests of such systems should be restricted to test ranges and to single-bounce scenarios (only one orbiting mirror involved) against orbiting targets. Such tests, because of their complex geometries, should be easy to monitor when carried out at announced test sites and, because the particular nature of space mirrors should permit their identification and observation, might also prove detectable from secret laser sites, although confidence in such detection would always remain problematic. The possibility of such detection, in the presence of a cooperative ASAT regime, should act as a deterrent to extensive surreptitious programs.

High-altitude ASAT lasers, and ABM-capable lasers, will be so large and will have exorbitant power requirements that they will be virtually impossible to conceal. For instance, a 100-megawatt laser facility would require delivered electrical power of more than 1 gigawatt, the equivalent of the electric power requirement of a moderately large city. Some designs even conceive such lasers as powered by their own hydroelectric dams. Development and testing of a high-altitude ASAT laser would simultaneously create a base for deployment of a laser ABM system. To limit this base as much as possible, no space mirror tests at the high power levels should be allowed. No more than one such site should be permitted (about seven would be necessary for an entry-level ABM capability), and on-site inspection and presence should be required during operational testing. A strict numerical limit on such tests (two to four per year) against single scoring satellites might also be imposed.

SAM Upgrade

Because many Soviet surface-to-air missile (SAM) interceptors and mobile radars already exist, SAM upgrade to ABM capability has long been a subject of public discussion and dispute in the United States. To some extent, this concern shows a lack of perspective, since proliferation of the far more effective Soviet Galosh-based ABM system is a more disturbing possibility. Nevertheless, additional Galosh missiles are hypothetical, whereas many SA-10s already exist in the field. The advent of the SA-12 system, which has demonstrated the technical characteristics to intercept tactical ballistic missiles, has made the issue a major consideration in evaluating the future of the ABM Treaty. The SA-12, particularly the version with the larger (Giant) interceptor, probably does have some residual capabilities against older and slower types of SLBMs and ICBMs, by virtue of its high (for a SAM) burnout velocity, mobile phased-array radar, and relatively large payload (inferred). The U.S. counterpart, Patriot, probably has similar overall residual capability, with a somewhat slower missile but a somewhat more powerful radar. The questions are, How great is this residual capability? and how much can it be improved? If the answer to the first question, or to the two combined, is ''a lot,'' then such systems (and Patriot and the SA-12 in particular) should be redefined by agreement as ABM systems; otherwise they could completely undercut the Treaty.

The present U.S. understanding of these systems suggests they have two important limitations. The power-aperture products of their mobile radars are vastly insufficient to perform acquisition and long-range track of ballistic missiles; and the interceptors are not sufficiently fast or agile to intercept low-drag (high ballistic coefficient) reentry vehicles. Since the SA-12 and Patriot are clearly at the top of their class in terms of performance, limitations that apply to them should prove effective for other existing, deployed SAMs.

Air defense missiles used in terminal ABM modes would be constrained by both the radar's and the missile's capabilities to low-altitude intercepts. Once an offensive reentry vehicle has been acquired and identified as a real target (discriminated), the tracking radar must have sufficient power to track it accurately for a few seconds at the longest practical range, allowing the ABM computers to predict its trajectory and determine a defense intercept. The interceptor missile then must have sufficient time to reach that point, given its finite fly-out velocity.

The footprint of the defense (the actual area protected) is determined by the range and altitude of the intercept point, and the footprint is of course the capability that we wish to specify for the defense. Thus, for a given intercept point, a faster missile will allow more time for the radar to perform its mission and thereby accommodate a lower power-aperture product. Conversely, a radar that can complete its track and prediction tasks at longer range (which implies a large power-aperture product) allows the defense to operate with a somewhat slower missile. Estimation of these trade-offs is complex, since required increases in power-aperture product are proportional to the cube (third power) of increases in range, and since incoming reentry vehicles are generally moving three to four times as fast as SAM interceptors. Details of these trade-offs are discussed in chapter 6, and a sample time line showing track and intercept is presented in figure 6.1.

As discussed above and in chapter 6, search and acquisition are the most demanding of the radar's tasks in terms of power-aperture product. The phased-array radar of Patriot has a product in the neighborhood of 50,000 watt-meters squared, that of the SA-12 is somewhat less. This level is vastly insufficient to search even for ICBMs, let alone SLBMs (whose search requirements are greater since they may come from many different directions, the attack corridors from opposing ICBM fields are generally known). Three possibilities remain for performing acquisition: existing large-perimeter radar facilities of both the United States and USSR; new acquisition sensors, such as airborne or satellite-borne infrared sensors, which would hand off acquisition data to the air defense track radars; or internetting of the numerous track radars themselves (or others like them).

If neither side finds the magic spell to discriminate reentry vehicles from decoys above the atmosphere, the situation is relatively straightforward. Discrimination and track functions can begin roughly as the incoming RVs reach 100 kilometers' altitude, and radar discrimination in the atmosphere should permit commitment of attacking interceptors to particular targets at altitudes of roughly 70 kilometers. Since modern, low-drag ("high-beta") reentry vehicles descend at about 7 kilometers per second until they reach altitudes of 25 kilometers, and since both Patriot and SA-12 have burnout velocities in the 2-kilometers-per-second regime, the intercepts will all occur below about 20 kilometers. The power-aperture products of both radars are sufficient to perform track for such intercepts against current reentry vehicles (assuming no penetration aids such as low radar cross sections, jamming, or electronic spoofing).

In this scenario, the dominant problem is to provide acquisition and discrimination functions to the battle management system that directs the interceptors. Neither nation's large-perimeter acquisition radars (LPARs)—large, vulnerable, and located close to oceans—can be relied upon to provide this information if a real attack (as opposed to an accidental launch) is under way. This leaves two possibilities: internetting existing air defense radars or providing acquisition by other means. In either case, handoff or internetting would require substantial computational capability, extensive communications, and extensive testing. This testing, which would involve many radars radiating at once and communicating with one another (and, in the case of optical acquisition, with airplanes or satellites), should be so extensive as to be detectable and thus verifiable. It would be the electronic equivalent of a broad field exercise.

Although development of higher power-aperture radars for air defense would decrease the required number and internetting of radars, even a fivefold or greater increase would leave the radars far short of the capacity to do their own search and acquisition; increasing the radars' frequency does not change this situation. Moreover, communications between radars and optical platforms in tests against ballistic missiles would reveal a Treaty violation, since those systems themselves violate the ABM Treaty when tested as components. Thus, coupling existing SAMs to new, space-based optics does not present a viable means of circumventing the ABM Treaty; rather, it conflicts directly with the terms of the Treaty, assuming that one has solved the problem of definition in distinguishing between ABM testing and ATBM testing. Current practice is to apply the so-called "Foster box" to the performance characteristics (velocity, reentry angle, etc.) of the reentry vehicle being intercepted.[12] This approach is workable and has the virtue of being widely accepted as a criterion. Finally, one can continue expanding a SAM upgrade threat by postulating yet larger and larger air defense radars until they actually attain ABM capability; but one must then ask, would such radars actually be built and deployed for air defense? If either side were to deploy and test new, large ABM radars, calling them air defense radars would confuse no one. The problem is rather the residual capability of real air defense systems.

Assuming that search and acquisition have been provided to the SAM system, what capability would the defender emphasize to improve its ABM capability further? With the commit altitude fixed by discrimination, the importance of handoff from Treaty-forbidden, space-based optical systems is reduced; further assume that the interceptors' lethality has been increased by using nuclear warheads, which the Treaty permits. The next important improvement would be in the interceptor's characteristics, to provide sufficient dynamic margin to intercept high-performance reentry vehicles, partly by enlarging the battle space by intercepting higher. Other attractive improvements would include increasing the numbers of radars (to increase search capability and to provide survivability through redundancy); raising the operating frequency of the radars (to allow them to perform track and battle management in the presence of countermeasures); and increasing the power-aperture products of the radars (for additional performance margin). This last possible improvement is the most frequently discussed avenue for limiting SAM upgrade, but the discussion above suggests that other means would be more important.

This still leaves the possibility that the SAMs represent a base for deployment of a more extensive system. The best way to prevent the establishment of such a base is to limit deployed SAM interceptors to burnout velocities of 3 kilometers per second or less.[13] That limit will permit all existing SAMs, including Patriot and SA-12s; it is high enough to permit fully effective air defense systems[14]; and it is even high enough to allow one to consider seriously systems that intercept most tactical ballistic missiles. But such a limit will prevent the deployment of an interceptor system capable of dealing with high-performance RVs unless the discrimination problem is solved in a way that allows handoff to the system's battle management at much greater ranges (requiring an increase in SAM radar power also). The possibility of a residual capability against some slower ICBM reentry vehicles (Minuteman II, for example) will remain. But the small fraction of such reentry vehicles, together with scenario ambiguities and performance uncertainties, will prevent this residual capability from approaching a militarily meaningful ABM defense by our criteria.

Even if an effective solution is found to the decoy discrimination problem, search and acquisition remain a dominant consideration in SAM upgrade. As discussed in chapter 6 and above, solving search and acquisition with airborne or spaced-based optics—the most likely method— is forbidden by the Treaty and is verifiable during testing. Once the search problem was solved, then improvements in SAM radars (both power and frequency) could allow SAM missiles to commit to launch earlier and thus perform more distant and more effective intercepts. Even so, the ranges for such intercepts using existing SAM missiles would provide only a marginal overall system improvement. Significantly better performance would require improving both the mobile radars and the interceptors—in short, transmogrifying the air defense into a de facto ABM system.

More Restrictive Regime

If the greatest substantial (as opposed to speculative) threat to the ABM Treaty's stability were judged to be the possibility of proliferation of existing systems, then the first sensible move toward a more restrictive regime might be to ban the allowed 100-interceptor systems and the agreed test ranges. This would not absolutely remove the threat of a breakout, but the threat would diminish as time passed: operational experience with and confidence in the fielded Moscow system would decay, and no such experience could be acquired with a U.S. system. Equally important, the technical capabilities of the fielded system would become increasingly obsolete. These same comments obviously apply to the most restrictive regime, a zero-ABM in which research as well as deployment is banned.

If deployed systems are still permitted, one should focus next on the relabeling prospects, both ASAT and SAM upgrade. The most straightforward step would be to ban ASATs; but militarily, ASATs are, as we have said, a separate and different problem (rhetoric about "arms races in space" to the contrary notwithstanding). One might, however, restrict ASATs to ground-based rockets, which are generally similar to the permitted, deployed ABM systems. This restriction would not prevent development of a LEO laser ASAT (for the verification reasons discussed above), but it would force all high-power laser testing and deployment into covert channels, slowing progress toward an ABM laser.

But such progress, as noted above, is already pretty slow. For that reason and, more important, to prevent extended Treaty controversies that undermine mutual trust and cooperation, detailed limits on ground-based ABM laser development parameters (brightness, for example) seem pointless, if not actually counterproductive.

Finally, a more restrictive regime relative to SAM upgrade would have to impose fairly draconian limits on either the number of deployed radars and interceptors or the power-aperture product of individual SAM radars. Any such measures would run into the same conceptual problem as an ASAT ban: they would interfere with a separate military mission (in this case a more legitimate one, because of its clear necessity to conventional warfare). Compared with the USSR, a significantly larger fraction of U.S. nuclear deterrent forces remains in bombers and cruise missiles; compared with the United States, the Soviets expend vastly larger sums in air defense. As long as these conditions hold true, the USSR can hardly be expected to accept ABM restrictions that also hamstring air defense capabilities.

Thus there are few (if any) strongly attractive options for a more restrictive regime governing ground-based systems, given the negotiating capital that would have to be expended and the potential loss of cooperative will[15]. This conclusion is a testament to, rather than a criticism of, the 1972 ABM Treaty. There are certainly issues within the existing regime to be clarified by mutual agreement, particularly with respect to lasers under Agreed Statement D, as discussed above and in other chapters. But these adjustments can be made relatively straightforwardly.

Several other, more ambitious measures for maintaining the Treaty's strength as technology introduces new capabilities in particular areas of ABM or ABM-related performance have been discussed. The more important of these, such as restricting ASATs to direct-ascent interceptors, limiting the burnout velocity of SAMs, and eventually forbidding ABM deployments entirely, offer potentially attractive options in the future. Because of present realities of the military situation, none of these steps is urgently needed now.

Notes

1. Search and acquisition require radar power broadcast over a large volume of space, so this capability scales with the product of radar power and antenna area. Tracking requires only a particular power level to reach a given range and to overcome noise sources that may mask the target; the antenna area is no longer a major consideration in scaling the performance.

2. This property opens the possibility of using the radar signal to create the equivalent of photographic images of the reentry vehicles and decoys.

3. That is, one in which the interceptors are assigned to defend only some subset of the targets, so the attacker does not know which are well-defended and which are undefended.

4. This conclusion may not be true in the event of extremely deep cuts—90 percent or more—in offensive forces. Obviously, in such a situation defense becomes much more important, and the offensive and defensive forces must be considered together in fashioning an agreement.

5. The possibility remains that the Soviets could net together many allowed radars to perform target acquisition. This case is technically identical to netting together their air defense radars, which are already mobile and so is discussed under the rubric below.

6. N. Bloembergen et al., "Science and Technology of Directed Energy Weapons," *Reviews of Modern Physics* 59, no. 3, pt. 2 (July 1987).

7. Divert capability: a rocket's ability to move suddenly some distance off its established trajectory to intercept a target. An interceptor's trajectory will generally carry it close to its target but will leave some finite miss distance for which this lateral "divert" motion must correct.

8. See, for example, chapter 6. In figure 6-1, the required laser brightness to destroy a satellite at synchronous altitude is approximately the same as that required to kill an unhardened booster at 1,000 kilometers.

9. The power levels quoted above assume 100 seconds of illumination for this mission requirement.

10. Free-electron lasers (FELs) are an exception here, since their accelerators, wigglers, and optics sections would be hundreds of meters long. Although the United States is attempting to build such a laser, there is no evidence that the Soviet Union is doing so, too.

11. The beam will become distorted in passing through the atmosphere because of air turbulence and other effects, and this distortion must be corrected for if the beam's full energy is to be deposited on target. In addition, during the time it takes the laser beam to get from the ground to a satellite at, say, 500 kilometers, the satellite will have moved more than 10 meters. The laser must "lead" the satellite just as a hunter leads a duck, and the air whose distortion effects are compensated must be

the air between the laser and the satellite's future position. Measurement of the state of this column of air is extremely difficult.

12. The "Foster box" is a particular set of missile characteristics used by then Defense Director of Research and Engineering John S. Foster, Jr., to define ICBMs in ABM testing. The values were mentioned by Dr. Foster in congressional testimony in 1969 and have been generally applied since.

13. This number should not be confused with a frequently discussed 3-kilometer-per-second upper velocity of target missiles, proposed to define what testing "in an ABM mode" means.

14. That is, if the interceptors can have burnout velocities in the range 2 to 3 kilometers per second, an air defense system will certainly be limited by other performance parameters.

15. Even a zero-ABM regime, which is certainly in principle negotiable, poses a problematic balance of costs and benefits. The breakout threat, as discussed above, would continue to exist; research in technologies for advanced ABM systems (optical sensors, directed-energy weapons, high-performance missiles) would continue under other guises, and the political contention over SAM upgrade would become more significant. The principal gain would be to slow progress toward more advanced, and presumably more tempting, defensive systems—progress that (in military terms) is not particularly worrisome at present.

8

LIMITATIONS AND ALLOWANCES FOR SPACE-BASED WEAPONS

Ashton B. Carter

THE STRATEGIC DEFENSE INITIATIVE'S emphasis on space-based weapons abruptly posed the question of whether and how the ABM Treaty's limitations applied to such advanced ABM concepts. The Soviet Union has maintained that answering this question should be the agenda for the Geneva Defense and Space negotiations. Though the United States has tended to emphasize the "transition" to widespread ABM deployments as the proper topic of negotiation, it has agreed with the Soviets that the Treaty does not define clear limitations on space ABMs. The results has been an upswelling of policy attention to the compliance of the SDI's space-based tests with the ABM Treaty.

The Department of Defense has generally declined on policy grounds to contribute its technical expertise to any wide-ranging analysis of how the treaty regime's limits should apply to advanced ABMs. The resulting void has been partially filled by lawyers debating the strictness or permissiveness of the regime in very general terms. Other analyses have begun by trying to discern what the 1972 ABM Treaty negotiators wrote, said, meant to say, or intended. In fact the 1972 negotiators seem to have had no alternative but to view detailed treatment of future ABMs as premature and to leave it to future negotiations. Such technical specifics as have been proposed by Soviet and Western analysts typically define thresholds of capability for exotic test articles like lasers. These thresholds have too often focused on individual components divorced from the military setting in which they would be deployed and on technical parameters characterizing test devices without regard to how the tests would be conducted. Above all, discussion by U.S. proponents and detractors of SDI alike has focused on the limits to be placed on U.S. testing, without attention to future *Soviet* ABM testing.

This chapter focuses on how the technical limitations on testing of space weapons for ABM can be made consistent with the full range of U.S. military interests.[1] It assumes the United States wishes to remain within the treaty regime for the time being, but it does not assume that the 1972 ABM Treaty's language or legal categories are necessarily sufficient for what is, after all, a slightly different problem from the one faced by the 1972 negotiators.

A comprehensive analysis of all hypothetical future space weapon technologies and military applications would be far too complex to undertake here. Fortunately, reality will be less complicated than today's viewgraphs, with their myriad possibilities, suggest. Only a subset of the technological candidates for ABM space weapons will arrive at serious testing, development, or deployment. The wisest course is probably to follow the 1972 drafters' lead and defer some especially speculative problems to a future time, by which they will have either come into focus or proved irrelevant. This chapter aims to develop a more general framework, to be used in formulating rules regarding particular types of weapons and tests as they arise. We begin by describing the rules as they apply today.

The ABM Treaty's drafters expected that the United States and the Soviet Union would adapt the ban on ABM deployment to new generations of technology, so long as both sides believed a ban was in their national security interest. This chapter closes by sketching three different paths for such adaptation. The first hews closely to the text of the 1972 ABM Treaty and to the way the United States interprets it today. The second path is more restrictive than the ABM Treaty, the third path more permissive. All three paths, however, are intended to be compatible with the underlying military purposes of the treaty regime as sketched in chapter 2.

The Current Situation

Today the United States is obeying the traditional interpretation of the ABM Treaty. Where the Treaty is not explicit about which space tests are allowed and which are not, Defense Department compliance officials and lawyers necessarily make their own interpretations, balancing the Strategic Defense Initiative Organization's (SDIO's) desires to perform experiments unfettered by Treaty restrictions against U.S. legal obligations and the fear of setting a precedent that allows too much latitude for analogous Soviet testing. The ambiguities involved in making these compliance judgments indicate the areas where additional clarification is desirable.

FOUR TYPES OF SPACE TESTING

Much attention attaches to the characteristics of weapons involved in space testing (thresholds), but from the viewpoint of the traditional interpretation, the mode in which the test occurs is key to determining legal compliance. Technically useful space testing can be conducted in four modes (see figure 8-1):

1. *Full-up ABM Test.* In a full-up test of a space-based ABM concept, a weapon in stable orbit intercepts a strategic ballistic missile in boost or postboost phase. This is a test of a ''space-based'' ABM in what is clearly an ''ABM mode,'' and it is forbidden by the traditional interpretation no matter how weak the strength of the laser or other weapon: there is no threshold.

FIGURE 8-1. Four Types of Tests of Space Weapons   *In a full-up ABM test (a), a weapon in stable orbit attacks a strategic ballistic missile in boost or postboost phase. A lofted test (b) differs from a full-up test in that the weapon is lofted into space for a few minutes on a suborbital trajectory; it is not based in space. In the ASAT test (c), both weapon and target (which may fire a rocket motor during the test to resemble a missile booster) are placed in stable orbit before the test. In the air defense test (d), a space laser illuminates an airplane or drone in flight or an instrumented target on the ground.*

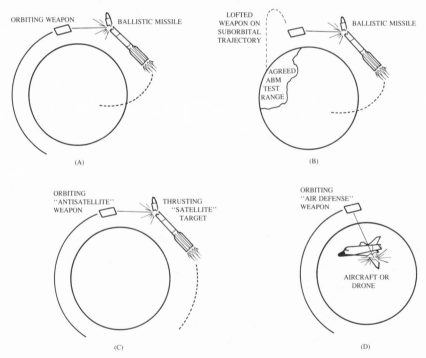

Less clear is whether the Treaty's restrictions apply if the target is not actually destroyed. Suppose, for example, that a space-based laser illuminates an ascending strategic booster but does not destroy it, either because the laser is operated at low power or with the optics defocused, or because the test target is specially hardened. Since nuclear ABM interceptors have been tested for many years without the actual detonation of a defensive nuclear warhead, it would seem that the defensive weapon might qualify as "tested in an ABM mode" even if it did not operate at full power. Moreover, tests are subject to Treaty restrictions regardless of whether they succeed.[2] A test in which a space-based laser points at an ascending booster at low power might therefore be judged illegal. In any event, the SDIO has no acknowledged plans to test laser weapons (as opposed to laser radars and designators) in this way.

Can Treaty violation be avoided by substituting a nonstrategic ballistic missile—say, a theater ballistic missile—for a strategic missile? Seemingly not, according to Paul H. Nitze, special adviser to the president and secretary of state for arms control matters. As long as the test target has the "flight trajectory characteristics of a strategic ballistic missile or its elements over that portion of the flight trajectory involved in the test," as an intermediate-range missile would have during boost phase, the test is "in an ABM mode."[3] Further along the trajectory, both the United States and the Soviet Union have seemingly made a distinction between the faster flight of strategic missile reentry vehicles (RVs) and the slower flight of shorter-range RVs, since both sides have tested air defense systems against short-range RVs, and the ABM Treaty would forbid such tests against a "strategic ballistic missile." But the boost phase of an intermediate-range missile closely resembles that of a strategic missile.

2. *Lofted Test.* In a lofted test the weapon that performs the boost-phase intercept is not placed in orbit but flies into space for a few minutes while the test is conducted and then reenters the atmosphere. If the weapon is lofted from an agreed ABM test range, it is considered to be a ground-based ABM, not a space-based ABM. A lofted test is legal (in the current U.S. view) no matter how powerful the weapon; again, there is no threshold. The SDIO plans to test early versions of its space-based interceptor (SBI) in this way.

The United States set the precedent in the 1970s for the interpretation that an ABM component is not space-based unless it is placed in stable orbit, when it assessed the Treaty compliance of lofted testing of the infrared Probe. The Probe, which was continued by the SDIO as the Ground Surveillance and Tracking System (GSTS), is an infrared sensor for acquiring and tracking RVs, mounted on a small rocket. Cued by warning satellites that Soviet ICBMs had been launched, the Probe was supposed to fly from the United States on a suborbital trajectory that would give it a better view of the unfolding attack than a ground-based radar would have. Information from the Probe could then be used to direct traditional ground-based interceptors against the attacking RVs.

A lofted SBI test differs from the Probe precedent in two respects. First, the SBI would most likely be space-based and not ground-based in its deployed form, even though it could be tested from the ground. The Probe and GSTS would truly be ground-based components. Second, SBI is a component of a boost-phase defense with inherent nationwide coverage, whereas the Probe was a component of midcourse and terminal defenses with limited reach. (It would not be possible to justify testing either the Probe or the SBI to support the 100-interceptor deployment allowed by the Treaty, since neither device is an allowed component of that defense.)

3. *ASAT Test.* In an antisatellite (ASAT) test, a weapon in orbit intercepts a target that is also orbiting rather than ascending from the earth as a missile booster does. A satellite target can easily be made to resemble the postboost vehicle of a strategic ballistic missile, which thrusts only intermittently and at low thrust levels. If the satellite target is equipped with a large booster motor, it can also be made to resemble the second or third stages of a strategic missile booster. SDI reportedly plans to test a space-based laser called Zenith Star against a thrusting satellite target.

By developing and deploying its own ASAT interceptor, the Soviet Union has implicitly accepted the United States's view that testing in an ASAT mode can be different from testing in an ABM mode. Under the traditional interpretation of the ABM Treaty, ASAT testing is subject to a threshold, however. Article VI of the Treaty forbids upgrading non-ABM systems to give them "capabilities to counter strategic ballistic missiles." A weapon tested in the ASAT mode must therefore not cross a threshold that would qualify it as "ABM-capable." The parties to the Treaty have not agreed how this threshold is to be defined.

4. *Air Defense Test.* In what might loosely be called an air defense test, a space-based laser (or other weapon capable of penetrating the atmosphere) illuminates an airplane or pilotless drone aircraft in flight or an instrumented target on the ground. Like ASATs, such air defense weapons must not be "ABM-capable"; a threshold is implied.

VERIFICATION

The United States requires that tests of space-based weapons be compatible with the (traditional) interpretation of the ABM Treaty (in its view) but does not require that the technical basis of its legal judgments be verifiable by the Soviet Union. For example, since SDIO plans to test the space-based Zenith Star laser in the ASAT mode, its designers must hobble the laser in some way so it does not have ABM capability. But the limitations imposed on the test weapon to make it incapable of ABM might not be detectable by Soviet national technical means (NTM) of verification. Designing test weapons so that they visibly comply with the Treaty and clearly could not be easily upgraded to ABM capability with, so to speak, the flip of a switch would be burdensome for ABM developers. Yet if the Soviet Union followed our practices, the United States would find it impossible to verify Soviet Treaty compliance.

It is unclear how verifiable the rules of the Treaty regime need to be to satisfy the United States. A requirement of strict verifiability would present novel problems in the case of space weapons, because actual and potential means of monitoring space testing are not nearly as well analyzed as means of monitoring traditional ABM testing.

THE BROAD INTERPRETATION

The broad interpretation of the ABM Treaty, like the traditional interpretation, lacks technical specificity. But the general differences between the two interpretations are clear. Under the broad interpretation, full-up testing of directed-energy weapons from space would be legal. Full-up testing of space-based interceptors would also *not* be allowed unless SBIs were judged not to be "interceptors" in the sense intended by the 1972 ABM Treaty but, rather, novel weapons based, like lasers and particle beams, on "other physical principles" (OPP). The argument that SBIs are OPP would have to rest on either or both of the facts that SBIs have (1) nonnuclear warheads instead of nuclear warheads and (2) infrared homing guidance instead of radar command guidance like the Safeguard system of 1972. By the same argument, the SDI's ground-based interceptors—the Exoatmospheric Reentry Vehicle Interceptor System (ERIS) and the High Endoatmospheric Defense Interceptor (HEDI)—would also be OPP. In effect, the broad interpretation, with such a broad definition of OPP, would exclude *all* weapons in the SDI from the testing limitations of the Treaty. But if ERIS is declared to be OPP, then a 100-ERIS Accidental Launch Protection System (ALPS) at Grand Forks would not be legal, since the Treaty only allows deployment of true "interceptors." Thus although the broad interpretation opens the way to expanded space testing, when combined with a claim that new-technology interceptors are OPP it also creates new restrictions on ground deployments.

The broad interpretation would permit complete *development* of space-based components and systems (i.e., progression from test articles to production-model prototypes). Only *deployment* of space weapons based on other physical principles would remain forbidden. Proponents of the broad interpretation have not specified what buffer would remain between allowed development and testing of space weapons and creation of a base for rapid breakout deployment. This buffer is also unclear under the traditional interpretation, as we shall see, but it is thinner under the broad interpretation.

Key Technical Issues for Space-Based ABMs

Before turning to ways in which a more specific set of rules applying to space-based ABMs might be devised, a necessary preliminary is to define appropriate measures of ABM capability, breakout potential, and verifiability for ABM space weapons.

MEASURES OF ABM CAPABILITY FOR SPACE-BASED WEAPONS

Rules against Soviet breakout cannot be based solely on the technical parameters characterizing the capability of space weapons to serve as ABMs. Nevertheless, these technical parameters are meaningful in the context of deployment or testing practices.

Space-based interceptors. A useful space-based interceptor for boost- or postboost-phase ABM must have two key subsystems: a homing warhead with on-board homing sensor, guidance system, and divert rocket motors for terminal maneuvers; and axial propulsion to carry the warhead far from the carrier satellite from which it is launched within the short boost and postboost phases of its target. The key characteristics of an SBI test from the point of view of developing the homing subsystem are the relative velocity of the warhead and the target; the extent to which the target resembles a ballistic missile booster, with its exhaust plume; and the geometry of the intercept with respect to the direction of flight of the target booster and the position of the earth. The key parameter for the axial propulsion rocket motor is the velocity it imparts to the warhead relative to the carrier satellite, called δv ("delta vee") for "change in velocity (relative to the launch platform)."

The Soviets could move toward breakout deployment of SBIs in either of two ways: development and testing of SBI ABMs, followed by breakout deployment; or deployment of SBI ASATs, followed by rapid upgrade to ABM capability. A number of U.S. and Soviet analysts have suggested that treaty regime limits on SBIs be expressed in terms of δv. An SBI must have a δv of at least 6 to 8 kilometers per second to be useful for boost-phase ABM. With a smaller δv, each carrier satellite could make intercepts only in its immediate vicinity, so that a larger number of satellites would be required to provide worldwide boost-phase coverage. The ABM potential of a constellation of SBIs increases both with the number, N, of deployed interceptors and with δv, and for many configurations of attacking boosters is roughly proportional to $N(\delta v)^2$.[4] An adequate SBI ASAT deployment, on the other hand, need not have a large value of $N(\delta v)^2$: the number of satellite targets for an ASAT would be smaller than the number of booster targets for an ABM, and the times available to attack satellites is much longer than the duration of the boost and postboost phases of a ballistic missile. Thus a rule limiting SBI ASAT deployments to small values[5] of $N(\delta v)^2$ (or some other appropriate function of N and δv representing the constellation's ABM potential) would ensure that they had negligible ABM potential without unduly limiting their usefulness as ASATs. A stronger constraint on ASAT upgrade would involve placing a separate limit of, say, 1 kilometer per second on δv itself.

However, a limit on testing or deploying SBIs at δv's greater than 1 kilometer per second would not necessarily prevent the Soviets from developing an ABM-capable SBI. Experiments to develop homing warheads and axial propulsion could be conducted separately, although the two subsystems would need to be integrated in a production-model prototype. Homing warhead tests against thrusting satellites in the ASAT mode would allow developers to explore the warhead's performance against a realistic target over the full range of ABM closing velocity (i.e., the relative velocity between the warhead and the *target*) *even if the SBI warhead were dispatched from its carrier satellite at low* δv.[6] A limit on δv alone, therefore, would not guarantee that ABM-capable homing warheads could not be developed. The axial propulsion subsystem could then be developed in ground test stand firings and in space tests conducted without the homing warhead. In the end, both pieces of an ABM-capable SBI would have been developed. Thus if it were considered essential to prevent development of ABM-capable SBIs to preserve the buffer against breakout, it would be necessary to forbid SBI testing in the ASAT mode and the lofted mode, at least against thrusting targets.

The case of the δv limit for SBIs illustrates the inadequacy of thinking in terms of capability thresholds for test devices without reference to how the test is conducted. Testing practices and target characteristics, not velocity thresholds, are the most important focus for a treaty regime seeking to place limits on SBI ABM. If SBI testing is first restricted to certain modes (such as the ASAT mode against nonthrusting targets) so that development of SBI ASATs is still permitted, an additional limit on the δv of SBI ASATs (1 kilometer per second or so) might become useful to inhibit ASAT upgrading. This restriction should be conditional on high rates of acceleration, since nonweapon spacecraft regularly blast off from low earth orbit with δv greater than 1 kilometer per second[7] but do not require high acceleration. Thus the regime might limit space objects from maneuvering with δv more than 1 kilometer per second only if their acceleration exceeds ten times the acceleration of gravity (10 g's).[8]

Space lasers and mirror relays. The rate at which a space laser weapon can destroy targets at a given range, and thus its ABM capability, is determined in large part by its brightness. Numerically, brightness equals the power of the laser beam divided by the size of the diverging cone into which the weapon's mirror can focus the beam. The power of the laser is its energy output per second, measured in watts. Cone size is measured in steradians, a unit of measurement similar to the square degrees of angle obtained by multiplying the angular width of the cone by its angular height. A threshold on laser brightness is thus expressed in watts per steradian. Brightness is similarly a measure of the lethality of a mirror relay satellite that does not generate its own energy but that collects and refocuses energy generated by a laser on the ground or on another satellite.

If the laser (or relay) emits energy in pulses rather than a continuous beam, its effective brightness is just the energy of each pulse (in joules; one watt equals one joule per second) times the number of pulses per second, divided by the cone size (in steradians). If a pulsed laser could emit extremely energetic but short pulses, a target booster might be destroyed by the so-called impulse-kill mechanism rather than by scorching, as with a continuous beam.[9] Treaty regime rules for such a pulsed laser might therefore define both an effective brightness threshold *and* a separate threshold on the number of joules per steradian that could be emitted in a single pulse.

Brightness has attracted attention as a threshold parameter because of its intuitive appeal and theoretical elegance, but in fact the ABM capability of a space-based laser (SBL) is determined by more numerous and more complex parameters. The number of boosters of a given type that an SBL can engage in a given period of time depends not only on how long it takes to kill each booster (determined largely by brightness[10]) but on how long it takes to slew from one target to another (a function of the pointing mechanism's slew angular acceleration, maximum slew angular velocity, and resettle time) and the supply of energy aboard the satellite (chemical reactants or stored electrical source). The acquisition, pointing, and tracking system that directs the beam to the target's location is a complex subsystem whose ABM capability is characterized by its own array of thresholds. Moreover, Treaty limits on brightness can be replaced or augmented by limits on laser power and mirror size. These parameters differ in their verifiability and in their importance for constraining development of ABMs and upgrading of other systems. The following discussion uses brightness as an illustrative proxy for a complex set of potential technical limitations on space lasers and relays.

As with SBIs, testing practices for laser weapons are at least as important as the parameters characterizing the test devices. Once again, there are two routes the Soviet Union could take to break out: development of SBL ABM followed by rapid deployment, and deployment of SBL ASATs or SBL air defense weapons followed by upgrade.

ABM defense against a responsive opponent would probably require space lasers brighter than 10^{22} watts per steradian.[11] But the United States must be concerned about Soviet lasers much less bright than this. As explained in chapter 2, the United States needs to ensure that today's deployed offensive missiles could penetrate a Soviet breakout SBL deployment with minimal modifications. Performance against Minuteman, MX/Peacekeeper, and Trident missiles thus determines whether an SBL is "ABM capable" for the purposes of U.S. security under the Treaty regime. The amount of heating these currently deployed missiles could tolerate without damage or disruption is unknown (and differs from the amount that the Soviet Union could be confident would destroy them). We shall assume the United States would need to worry only about Soviet lasers that could deposit more than a "sure-safe" flux of 140 watts per square centimeter (1,000 times the flux of the noonday sun at the earth's surface) on a target at a range of more than 500 kilometers. By this standard, Soviet SBLs would be ABM-capable if their brightness exceeded 4×10^{17} watts per steradian. Thus the U.S. threshold of concern about Soviet lasers under the ABM Treaty is fully 25,000 times less than the ABM developers' goal of 10^{22} watts per steradian. U.S. concerns under the ABM Treaty are dominated by the potential of Soviet SBLs to threaten even a small portion of today's deterrent force; SDIO aims to intercept a large fraction of a future hardened Soviet ICBM force.

To impede Soviet development of ABM-capable lasers (if this were deemed necessary), the United States would need to negotiate rules for the Treaty regime that forbid testing of SBLs with brightness approaching 4×10^{17} watts per steradian in the full-up mode, the ASAT mode (at least when such tests involve thrusting targets), and the lofted mode.[12] To prevent upgrade of SBL ASATs and SBL air defense weapons, the number of deployed SBLs should be limited so that the constellation has negligible ABM capability.[13]

SBLs have also been proposed as a means of discriminating RVs from light decoys in midcourse flight by popping, warming, or nudging the decoys. Such an "active discriminator" would have to be quite bright, since it could devote only a short time to each of the many objects it has to illuminate. Though an SBL discriminator might be legally characterized as an adjunct rather than an ABM component, it would probably be brighter than the threshold for ABM capability. Development of laser discriminators would therefore be affected by constraints on laser weapons.

Particle-beam weapons. A particle-beam weapon's (PBW's) lethality is determined by the energy of the particles (in electron volts), the number of particles emitted per second (in amperes), and the size of the cone into which the beam can be focused (determined by the particle accelerator, focusing magnets, and neutralizer). One can define the brightness of a PBW just as for a laser: the power in watts is the particle energy times the number of particles per second (multiplying volts times amperes gives watts), and the cone size is measured in steradians.

The numerical thresholds for ABM capability would be about the same as the laser thresholds if the PBW has to heat its target to destroy it. But if the United States is worried about the potential of Soviet PBWs to disrupt electronic components in Minuteman, MX/Peacekeeper, or Trident missiles,[14] a threshold 1,000 to 10,000 times lower would be appropriate. PBW discriminators would probably need to be almost as bright as PBW thermal-kill ABMs.

THE BUFFER AGAINST BREAKOUT

As explained in chapter 2, the United States needs to ensure that a comfortable buffer of conspicuous and time-consuming Soviet deployment activity stands between allowed Soviet testing of ABMs, or deployment of space weapons for other military purposes (ASAT or air defense), and achievement of a meaningful defense against today's U.S. offensive missiles. If the Soviet Union broke out of the treaty regime, the United States would use the buffer period to prepare its missile force to penetrate the Soviet defense.

The process of developing and deploying a breakout system involves many technical steps, from proof-of-principle experiments with preprototype components to checkout and integration of the final deployed system. In general, the longer it would take the Soviet Union to deploy a defense based on a certain weapon technology, the less need there is to constrain the development and testing of that technology. Thus, using the rough rules of thumb for the buffer proposed in chapter 2, if the United States believed the Soviets would need at least two years to deploy a defensive system capable of intercepting 10 percent of the current U.S. missile force, it could afford to allow the Soviets to develop and test the components of the defense fully. But if the process of deployment itself is not an adequate buffer against breakout, then the treaty regime must attempt to prevent the Soviet Union from completing the development, testing, and manufacturing of components. Constraints on development and testing do not necessarily create a well-defined buffer, however: it would not be easy to assess whether the Soviet Union could complete the development of a prototype SBI if it were permitted to conduct only lofted, ASAT, and air defense mode tests; or to assess whether a laser tested at 10^{17} watts per steradian could easily be scaled up to higher brightness.

The negotiators of the 1972 ABM Treaty seem to have regarded the conspicuous and time-consuming process of deploying ground-based defenses as an adequate buffer, since they permitted development and full-scale testing (as well as limited deployment) of such defenses. Since the manufacturing of individual components would be difficult to monitor, the 1972 negotiators presumably thought the buffer was provided by the lengthy processes of site preparation and construction—particularly construction of large radars.

Deployment of space-based ABMs entails the conspicuous activity of launching satellites. ABM weapon satellites would be placed in near-polar (70- to 80-degree inclination angle) low earth orbits.[15] The Soviet Union's ability to place payload into these orbits thus establishes a lower limit on the time required to complete a breakout deployment. Unfortunately, this minimum time is quite short, at least for a first-generation defense of limited capability.

The weight of a Soviet breakout deployment would depend on its state of technology and its military capability. The SDIO has proposed a Phase I deployment for the United States that includes a space-based tier consisting of several thousand interceptors. SDIO system architects estimate that deployment of the Phase I partial defense would involve launching a total of 1 million to 2 million kilograms into low earth orbit. Follow-on phases involving directed-energy weapons have estimated weights of 7.2 million to 18.6 million kilograms, and far-term deployments as much as 80 million kilograms.[16] Phase I is designed to intercept about 10 percent of the Soviet ICBM arsenal. According to chapter 2, the United States will want to be sure that it would take the Soviet Union at least two years to deploy a system like Phase I. If this buffer is to be accounted for entirely by limitations on Soviet launch rate, the Soviet Union cannot be allowed to possess a launch capacity in excess of about 1.0 million kilograms over two years, or 0.5 million kilograms per year.[17]

Today the Soviet Union has already achieved this annual launch capacity, placing about 0.5 million kilograms into low earth orbit in about 100 separate launches.[18] (By contrast, U.S. plans before the *Challenger* accident called for placing about 0.2 million kilograms into orbit annually in about 20 launches.) Soviet launch capacity is shared among its military space program, civil missions (scientific, manned, and planetary), and commercial missions (communications, weather, remote sensing). To avoid having to shut down its other space programs, lift capacity in excess of their requirements would have to be found for launching a breakout ABM. Assuming 0.5 million kilograms for non-ABM launches and another 0.5 million kilograms for a Phase I-type ABM, the Soviet Union would need about 1 million kilograms per year of launch capacity to threaten the United States with rapid breakout.

The U.S. Department of Defense expects Soviet lift capacity to increase steadily over the next two decades, from 0.5 million kilograms per year today to 1 million kilograms per year in the early 1990s, and to almost 2 million kilograms per year by 2005.[19] Almost all of this growth is accounted for by the new Soviet heavy-lift launch vehicle, the SL-X-17 or Energiya, which might be able to place as much as 0.1 million kilograms into orbit on each launch. The

Defense Department's estimates of Soviet future lift capacity amount to guessing how many Energiyas could be launched every year.[20]

Limitations of spacelift capacity place significant constraints on Soviet breakout potential. Given the Energiya heavy lifter, however, it is not possible to prove that launch-rate limitations by themselves guarantee the United States an adequate buffer against rapid deployment of a crude SBI system like Phase I. Weights of directed-energy ABMs are even more speculative: they could be much heavier than Phase I (if composed, for example, of chemical lasers) or about the same weight as Phase I (if composed of relay mirrors and ground-based lasers). The Soviet Union, on the other hand, can be quite certain over the next decade that the United States could not deploy a space-based ABM quickly: the U.S. heavy lifter, the Advanced Launch System, could not be operational until the late 1990s.

If Soviet lift capacity does not by itself provide a fully convincing buffer, the United States has two alternatives. The first, more familiar, possibility is to craft a regime that forbids the Soviet Union to complete developmental testing of production-model prototypes of space ABM weapons. The second alternative is to negotiate limits on launch capacity, possibly focusing the limitations on the number of Energiya launch pads, the size of assembly buildings connected to the pads by rail or heavy road, manufacturing sites and transport facilities for the lifter's enormous stages, and facilities for producing, transporting, and storing liquid hydrogen fuel.

VERIFICATION

As Soviet weapons for ABM-related testing and for other military purposes appear in space in coming decades, the United States will be striving to replicate for these space activities the intelligence capabilities it possesses for monitoring Soviet military activities on the ground. These new capabilities will be necessary whether the ABM Treaty regime is in force or not. But if the treaty regime is in force, its rules should be crafted so that adherence to them is verifiable.[21]

For more than thirty years the United States has built up its capability to monitor activity at Soviet ABM and strategic offensive missile ranges. Realistically, capabilities to monitor space activities will have to evolve over a comparable period. One reason the United States has been able to afford the NTM and analytic resources to monitor ABM, SALT, INF, and START agreements is that the Soviet Union conducts its missile tests year after year in much the same places and in much the same way. Consequently data collection can focus on the current test ranges. The United States would not collect as much information about the test of a Soviet offensive missile launched over the South Pole, for example, as about one launched from Plesetsk to the Kamchatka Peninsula.

Devising a practical scheme for monitoring Soviet compliance in space is therefore not just a matter of identifying advanced remote sensing technologies that could in principle detect laser light and other exotic signatures. The treaty regime must also constrain Soviet testing practices (in part by setting an example with U.S. testing practices) so that monitoring is operationally feasible and affordable.

Thus, for example, the rules could require that any permitted tests (full-up, lofted, ASAT, or air defense) be conducted along each nation's traditional ICBM and submarine-launched ballistic missile test ranges or from an agreed ABM test range. A more restrictive rule would require that all space weapons approaching ABM capability be tested in agreed orbiting test ranges (discussed further below). Other operational aids to verification include prior notification of certain types of tests, prior description of tests, inspection of test devices on the ground before launch, and restrictions on concealment tactics such as telemetry encryption.

The United States can use a variety of monitoring technologies if Soviet space tests can be constrained so as to make these techniques operationally practical. The richest two generic sources of information on Soviet spacecraft would probably be telemetry and imagery. Electronic signals emitted by space test vehicles might include beacons for tracking them and radio broadcasts of the output of on-board sensors and diagnostic equipment. Images could be collected from the ground in sunlight or by illuminating the satellites with laser light or radar; or one satellite could be photographed from another.

The velocity and acceleration of SBIs might be determined from the arrival times and Doppler shifts of their radio emissions, much as navigators use the Transit or Navstar Global Positioning System satellite signals to measure their position and velocity on the ground. Ground-based radars could also track test objects if the tests were confined to regions of space visible to U.S. radars. Last, space-track sensors akin to the SDI's Space Surveillance and Tracking System (SSTS) could aid in tracking SBIs. The mass of an SBI, on the other hand, would normally be difficult to measure unless details of its rocket motors were known or its rocket exhaust were carefully measured.[22]

Because the beams from directed-energy weapons of potential ABM capability would be quite narrow, it is unlikely that monitoring satellites would be in the beam at the time of a test. Instead, energy reflected or scattered outside of the narrow beam cone (by the edges of the laser-focusing mirror or particle-beam neutralizer, by space junk, by the target, or by the earth's atmosphere) would have to be used to characterize the weapon (laser wavelength or particle energy) and perhaps make a rough guess at its power. Further information about power might come from observing the combustion products from chemical power sources as they were vented into space or from detecting the electrical emanations from electrically pumped lasers, from particle-beam accelerators, and from rail guns. A laser's wavelength can be determined by collecting scattered light; inspection on the ground or imagery in space could reveal the size of its mirror. This information would make it possible to estimate the size of the cone into which the laser can focus its light; if its power can also be estimated, its brightness can be calculated.

It is not possible to render in advance a general judgment on the quality or adequacy of the technical information the United States will have about Soviet space weapons. ABM Treaty regime rules crafted to ease monitoring would constrain the time, place, and manner of tests; ban methods of concealment and deception; and perhaps permit prelaunch inspection of certain payloads. After that, the United States will need to make an investment in an evolving technical collection system commensurate with its concern about Soviet breakthrough and tuned to the weapon technologies the Soviets choose to emphasize. Negotiated properly, the treaty regime's rules will enhance American understanding of Soviet military space activities in general.

Adaptations within the ABM Treaty Framework

One approach to adapting the ABM Treaty regime to space weapons is to proceed from the practices of the past seventeen years, confirming areas of implicit agreement and clarifying ambiguities that have arisen. Such adaptations can be made in the areas of testing practices, thresholds, and aids to monitoring. Adopting some or all of the following steps would be compatible with this approach:

TESTING PRACTICES

1. Confirm the traditional, narrow interpretation of the 1972 Treaty, which forbids full-up tests of all types of space-based ABM weapons, whether interceptors or directed-energy weapons.
2. Include simulated or attempted intercepts in the ban on full-up tests to prevent close flyby SBI tests, laser tests at low power or against artificially hardened target boosters, and other means of circumvention.
3. Confirm that full-up tests against nonstrategic boosters are also banned, arguing that shorter-range missiles closely resemble strategic missiles during their boost phase.
4. Confirm the legality of lofted tests against thrusting targets, arguing that they conform to the 1972 ABM Treaty's language if performed from the ground at agreed test ranges. Alternatively, agree to forbid lofted tests, arguing that the weapons tested in this way would be space-based in their deployed

configuration, would constitute a defense of inherent nationwide reach, and could not be deployed as part of the allowed 100-interceptor local defense.

5. Confirm the legality of ASAT mode and air defense mode tests.
6. Forbid ASAT tests against thrusting satellites as too similar to full-up testing.

THRESHOLDS

7. Define the thresholds implied by Article VI, which says that ASATs and air defenses should not be ABM-capable. These thresholds can be designed to apply to the ABM capabilities of individual test articles (for example, thresholds on the brightness of space-based lasers) or to the ABM capability and upgrade potential of deployed ASAT and air defense systems (for example, limits on N or $N(\delta v)^2$ for SBI ASATs).

AIDS TO MONITORING

8. Forbid telemetry encryption or other specified means of interference with NTM during tests of space weapons in all allowed ABM-related modes.
9. Require that tests of space weapons in all allowed modes be conducted from or along customary ICBM and SLBM test ranges and agreed ABM test ranges or from space weapons passing over those ranges.

Adaptations outside the ABM Treaty Framework: More Restrictive

A second approach to clarification would resolve all ambiguities and uncertainties associated with future technologies in favor of greater restrictiveness. Though not quite a ban on space weapons, this approach is a virtual ban on space-*based* weapons. To create a thick and unambiguous buffer against ABM breakout, these rules suppress ABM experimentation, together with development and deployment of space-based ASATs and air defense weapons. In addition to the rules listed above, this approach might include the following:

1. Forbid lofted tests (and possibly close agreed ABM ground test ranges altogether, eliminating allowed 100-interceptor deployments as a consequence).
2. Forbid ASAT mode tests against thrusting and nonthrusting targets. (A ban on tests against nonthrusting satellites would not forbid all antisatellite weapons. Ground-based ASATs and space mines would still be permitted.)
3. Ban nuclear reactors in space.[23]
4. Place limits on spacelift capability, including production and stockpiling of

heavy-lift vehicles and their assembly and launch facilities, to preclude rapid breakout.

5. Require prior announcement of tests of space weapons.
6. Require prior description of tests of space weapons.
7. Require prelaunch inspection of payloads involved in space weapon tests.[24]

Adaptations outside the ABM Treaty Framework: More Permissive

The 1972 ABM Treaty restricts testing of space-based ABMs much more harshly than testing of ground-based ABMs. The Treaty allows realistic testing and development of fixed ground-based defenses but no full-up testing of space-based ABMs. The third approach to adaptation for the 1990s is to reconcile these two standards by creating an agreed orbiting test range (AOTR) analogous to the 1972 ABM Treaty's agreed ground test ranges. After all, this argument would go, it is no easier (and might well be *more* difficult) to break out and deploy space-based defenses rapidly than it is to deploy ground-based defenses; both sides have apparently been comfortable that ground testing did not erode the buffer, so why not allow space testing? This approach is, in effect, an implementation of the Reagan administration's "broad" interpretation of the ABM Treaty, though with due attention to preserving some buffer against rapid breakout. The extra permissiveness accorded Soviet ABM testers in this approach is only compatible with U.S. security, of course, if there is such a buffer.

Rules are needed, first, to define the location and scope of the AOTR. The 1972 ABM Treaty places certain analogous restrictions on test activities at the agreed ground test ranges.[25] Other rules are needed to define what testing can be done on the AOTR. A third set of rules would define what kinds of tests can be done only on the range and not elsewhere in space.

LOCATION AND SCOPE OF THE AOTR

The simplest of the many possible ways to define an AOTR is for each side to specify an orbital slot by altitude (assuming circular orbit), inclination, and longitude and time of ascending node. The AOTR could consist of a single space structure in the specified orbit to which all test weapons were docked, but a more practical scheme would merely require that all articles on the range remain within a tight cluster of, say, a 50-kilometer radius. The AOTR should be at about the same altitude—500 to 700 kilometers—where space-based ABM weapons would be deployed. The AOTR orbit should be inclined so that the range passes over each side's ICBM and SLBM test ranges and ABM test ranges. New equipment could be added to the range and old equipment removed from it.

ACTIVITIES ON THE AOTR

Full-up ABM tests and development of space-based ABM weapons would be permitted, subject only to rules of the following sorts:

1. Space-based interceptors, rail guns, lasers, particle-beam weapons, relay mirrors, and other devices to counter strategic ballistic missiles in any phase of their flight must be located on the AOTR and may not be based in space or placed in space in any other manner.

2. Sensors that are capable of ABM search, acquisition, tracking, discrimination, or weapon-pointing functions, or that participate in AOTR testing, need not be placed on the AOTR. All such sensors must be declared, however, and the number of sensor-carrying spacecraft should not exceed, say, five.

3. The ballistic missiles that serve as test targets must be launched along their customary test ranges, and all intercepts must occur along these ranges. This restriction will allow the United States to make effective use of existing NTM in monitoring and evaluating Soviet tests.

4. Devices of a type previously tested from the AOTR may not be placed in space in any manner other than on the AOTR.

5. Only one device of each type (SBI, mirror, chemical laser, particle accelerator, etc.) may be on the AOTR at a time. A decommissioned test device must be deorbited before another device of the same type can take its place.

6. In particular, multiple SBIs or carrier vehicles for multiple SBIs may not be placed on the AOTR.

7. Further measures to ensure a buffer against breakout might include additional limits on the capabilities of devices on the range, so that the AOTR itself does not have any militarily threatening ABM capability as it passes over the other side's territory. Likewise, additional limits might be needed for activities on the AOTR that erode the buffer between exploration and deployment of ABM technology. Last, deployments of space weapons for ASAT or air defense not in association with the AOTR would have to be restricted to prevent upgrade to ABM capability.

8. To ensure an adequate understanding of Soviet ABM developments, the AOTR agreement could include aids to monitoring. Since the orbit of the AOTR would remain the same, the United States could fully instrument the Soviet AOTR as the years went by, much as it has instrumented Soviet ICBM and SLBM test ranges over a period of thirty years. The costs of monitoring might thereby be made acceptable. U.S. sensor satellites could position themselves close enough to the Soviet AOTR to take pictures; collect radio signals, weapon emissions, and effluents; and so forth. All this could be

permitted by agreement. Encryption of telemetry and other specified types of interference with U.S. monitoring could be forbidden. Finally, rules could require prior announcement of tests, prior description of tests, and/or inspection of test articles (to the extent consistent with U.S. security requirements) before placement on the range.

ACTIVITIES OUTSIDE THE AOTR

No technical activity with ABM potential should be allowed except in association with the AOTR, implying rules of the following types:

1. No ABM-capable weapons could be placed in space except on the AOTR. This restriction implies a set of thresholds for defining ABM capability, such as: δv of greater than 1 kilometer per second at an acceleration of more than 10 g's for SBIs; brightness greater than 4×10^{17} watts per steradian for directed-energy weapons; or other appropriate thresholds.
2. Development of space-based ASATs or air defense weapons, and all tests of such weapons, could be confined to the AOTR; moreover, such weapons should not be tested in the full-up ABM mode.
3. Deployments of space-based ASATs or air defenses would be restricted so that they had no meaningful ABM capability and could not be upgraded to ABM capability quickly. Thus SBI ASAT deployments might be limited to 50 interceptors ($N = 50$), or to a total $N(\delta v)^2$ of a few hundred square kilometers per square second.
4. Weapons deployed for ASAT or air defense could not be tested in the full-up ABM mode.

Conclusion

This chapter defines three general approaches to specifying prohibited and permitted ABM-related weapon testing in space. The first approach is to apply the language of the 1972 ABM Treaty, and its interpretation over the last seventeen years, to space weapons, translating the Treaty's legal language into technical specifics where necessary. The second, more restrictive, approach bans more kinds of space weapons tests than the Treaty alone would ban. The third approach is more permissive, allowing a great deal of space testing subject only to certain measures designed to allay fears of rapid breakout deployment. Although only the first approach is fully consistent with the language of the 1972 ABM Treaty, *all three approaches are intended to preserve a buffer against rapid breakout or leakout attainment of a significant ABM capability.* Such a buffer is the key national security guarantee for any party to a treaty regime banning ABM deployment, as explained in chapter 2.

If the United States and the Soviet Union continue to agree not to deploy ABMs and choose to clarify the limits on space weapons that such a ban implies, their negotiators will find that the technical and military facts afford them considerable latitude.

First, there is latitude about where to draw the line between permitted and prohibited testing and deployment of space weapons. On the one hand, development of space-based ABMs is an inherently conspicuous and time-consuming process, and neither side truly needs to worry that the other could break out quickly with more than a nuisance-level defense. Thus the regime can safely be fairly permissive. On the other hand, a great deal of technical work bearing on the feasibility of space-based ABM can be accomplished without extensive space testing. Thus the regime can safely be fairly restrictive. The technical facts do not by themselves prescribe where to draw the line between permitted and prohibited activities. That the line be clarified is probably more important than where it is drawn. A clear line allows the U.S. SDIO to plan its experiments well in advance and with clear congressional and public consensus as to their legality. A clear line also expresses the fact that the United States cannot afford to forgo improvements in its missile forces, much less to reduce them dramatically through arms control, unless Soviet ABM-related activities are limited so as to pose no imminent threat to the ability of these U.S. forces to reach their targets.

Second, there is latitude in time. Few exotic weapon technologies are pressing at the limits of significant ABM capability today. And though many technologies will be explored, few of them will survive to the stage of serious preprototype development. Comprehensive and technically precise agreements will not be necessary soon.

In short the technical and military facts would permit a variety of policy approaches. That latitude can make for acrimonious disagreement over matters of little actual importance to national security, but it also gives scope for creative defense and arms control policy.

Notes

1. This discussion draws upon and in places updates Ashton B. Carter, "The Structure of Possible U.S.-Soviet Agreements Regarding Missile Defense," paper presented to the Aspen Strategy Group, William Perry and Brent Scowcroft, co-chairs, in Aspen, Colorado, August 1986 and published in Joseph S. Nye, Jr., and James A. Schear, eds., *On the Defensive?: The Future of SDI* (Lanham, MD: University Press of America, 1988).

2. Paul H. Nitze cites a classified agreed statement of 1978 as providing that "an interceptor missile" is considered to be "tested in an ABM mode if it has *attempted* to intercept a strategic ballistic missile or its elements in flight trajectory" (emphasis added). See "Permitted and Prohibited Activities under the ABM Treaty," speech before the International Law Weekend Group, October 31, 1986 (Department of State, Bureau of Public Affairs, *Current Policy Bulletin* No. 886).

3. Ibid.

4. The radius of action of each SBI is δv multiplied by the time interval between location of the ascending booster and the end of its postboost phase. The square of the radius of action multiplied by pi gives the area of the earth's surface "covered" by the defensive SBI. The number of SBIs multiplied by the coverage area of each measures the thickness of coverage over each ICBM silo field or SLBM patrol area. Against some configurations of offensive boosters, the constellation's ABM potential is more a complicated function of N and δv.

5. A limit of a few hundred square kilometers per square second would ensure that Soviet SBIs could not intercept more than a few tens of U.S. SLBMs and ICBMs, guaranteeing an essentially "free ride" to U.S. missiles.

6. By orbiting in opposite directions, the target satellite and SBI launcher satellite would approach each other at high relative velocity (see figure 1).

7. Communications satellites require a total δv of 6 kilometers per second to move from an initial inclined low earth "parking" orbit to their geosynchronous equatorial deployment orbits. Planetary probes depart from low earth orbit with at least 3.5-kilometers-per-second velocity change.

8. Another threshold parameter for SBIs has occasionally been discussed: a *lower* limit on the *mass*, M, of the homing warhead. Since the launch cost of an SBI constellation is proportional to the constellation's total mass, NM, the threshold would permit the Soviets to test only large-mass "clunkers" that would be too expensive to deploy. One problem with a mass threshold is verifiability (see below); another is ease of upgrade.

9. In impulse kill, such a large amount of energy is delivered to the skin of the booster in a short time that the skin explodes, sending an impulsive shock through the booster.

10. The interaction of a laser beam with a booster body can be complex, and harmful effects may depend on other features of the laser beam than just the rate of energy deposition per unit area.

11. The American Physical Society's Study Group on the Science and Technology of Directed-Energy Weapons suggested that reasonably rapid thermal structural kill of a *hardened* booster might require an energy flux in excess of 300 kilowatts per square centimeter. At 2,000-kilometer range, this requires a laser of brightness greater than 10^{22} watts per steradian.

12. Bright lasers and even relay mirrors, unlike SBIs, might be too heavy and unwieldy to test in the lofted mode.

13. The limit might be phrased, for example, as a limit on the number of laser ASATs multiplied by their brightness, analogous to the $N(\delta v)^2$ limit for SBI ASATs.

14. Ashton B. Carter, "Directed Energy Missile Defense in Space," Background Paper of the Congressional Office of Technology Assessment, OTA-BP-ISC-26 (Washington, D.C.: U.S. Government Printing Office, April 1984), pp. 29–30.

15. A small number of sensor and battle-management satellites would be in higher orbits.

16. U.S. Congress, Office of Technology Assessment, *SDI: Technology, Survivability, and Software*, OTA-ISC-353 (Washington, D.C.: U.S. Government Printing Office, May 1988), p. 149.

17. The lift capability of space-launch vehicles is usually denoted by the mass they can place into low (185 kilometers) earth orbit if launched due eastward into inclined orbits, when the earth's eastward rotation assists the attainment of orbital velocity. Launch into near-polar inclinations with less assist from the earth's rotation entails a sacrifice of payload weight, typically of about 25 percent. This variation will be ignored in the following calculations since few of the other numbers are known to within 25 percent.

18. U.S. Department of Defense, *The Soviet Space Challenge*, November 1987.

19. Ibid.

20. Other factors besides weight to orbit would influence Energiya's ability to deploy a breakout ABM, including the availability of personnel to support launch operations, the ability of upper stages to distribute many satellites carried aloft in one launch to different orbits, and so on.

21. Today Defense Department lawyers and compliance officials must certify that U.S. ABM tests comply with the Treaty (as the United States interprets it), but not that the Soviet Union can collect all the facts that go into making that certification with their national technical means.

22. The principle of the equivalence of inertial and gravitational mass means that objects of

different mass can follow the same trajectories in space. The same inconvenient principle lies behind the well-publicized difficulties with measuring the throw-weight of Soviet offensive missiles.

23. The ban would not apply to nonreactor nuclear power sources or to reactors used for agreed civil space missions, such as interplanetary probes.

24. Only spacecraft associated with ABM testing would presumably be made subject to inspection, in order to protect the secrecy of other U.S. national security missions.

25. These restrictions govern the number of ABM launchers allowed at the range (fifteen), mobility, multiple warheads on defensive interceptors, rapid reload of launchers, and transfer of technology developed on the range to third countries.

9

LIMITS ON ANTIMISSILE
SENSOR SYSTEMS

*John E. Pike and Barry E. Fridling**

AN ABM SENSOR is a device that detects, tracks, or identifies ballistic missile boosters, postboost vehicles, reentry vehicles (RVs), and decoys. From the beginning of the ABM Treaty regime, sensors have presented ambiguities and have been a major focus for issues of compliance. Thus, although they are also discussed in chapters 6 and 7, sensors merit separate consideration here.

The Treaty, which lists the ABM radar as an example of a component, prohibits sea, air, space, and mobile-land basing for all listed ABM components or devices capable of substituting for them. One of the principal concerns in the Treaty negotiations of 1972 was large phased-array radars, which could serve some ABM functions but had other uses as well, in particular, early warning. These radars were conspicuous and thoroughly verifiable. Because of the long time required for construction (several years in most cases), such radars provided a long-lead-time indicator for breakout from the treaty regime. The Treaty defines strict location and orientation limits to keep ABM radars from being "relabeled" as early-warning radars, thereby creating a base for a nationwide ABM system. These limitations apply to all phased-array radars above a specified power-aperture product, except for those used for space tracking and national technical means of verification (NTM).

* Dr. Fridling's contribution to this article was independent from his position as a staff member of the Institute for Defense Analyses, and its publication does not indicate endorsement by IDA of the views expressed herein.

Newer sensor systems present some of the same and several new problems, and limits may be more difficult to craft. As with large phased-array radars, the newer sensor systems are a long-lead-time item in the development of an antimissile system. Many of these new sensors might require years of testing that could provide advance indication of impending ABM system deployment.

Unfortunately, the newer technologies pose a fundamentally greater verification challenge than did the radars of 1972. Large phased-array radars emit powerful signals that are readily verifiable by national technical means, and in many cases their relatively short operating ranges permit ready association of the radar with other antimissile test activities. But many of the newer technologies are passive, emitting no detectable signature; of those technologies that do emit signals, many would be difficult to detect. In addition, most of these new technologies operate over ranges that would make it difficult to associate the sensor with other antimissile activities.

Sensors present the classic dual-use problem. As chapter 6 indicates, sensors have many non-ABM and even nonmilitary uses. And sensors designed for other missions may have substantial ABM capability. In many cases, ABM sensors are hard to distinguish from other sensors. The development or deployment of certain non-ABM sensors that have, or could be rapidly upgraded to, ABM capability might threaten the treaty regime by eroding the buffer that the Treaty provides. Therefore sensors remain a subject requiring Treaty clarification and possible adaptation.

If research and development are to go forward without undermining the treaty regime, the parties must find ways to deal with the ABM potential of a number of sensors, planned or in operation for legitimate non-ABM use or for ABM research purposes. A sensor's ABM capability should be measured against today's offensive forces, strengthened perhaps by readily implemented countermeasures, since, as Carter argues in chapter 2, neither party should have to prepare aggressively against breakout by the other in order to gain the benefits of the Treaty.

A sensor's ABM capability depends in part on its relationship to other sensors needed to create an effective ABM surveillance, tracking, discrimination, and fire control system. As chapter 4 points out, no one sensor is likely to perform all these functions. But the same was true in 1972, when the Treaty was adopted. ABM systems then current in both the Soviet Union and the United States used at least two different types of radars to perform the necessary surveillance, tracking, discrimination, and fire control functions. Therefore, the fact that a single type of sensor cannot perform all these functions does not necessarily mean that it is not "capable of substituting for" an ABM radar.

A further consideration is the state of development of associated interceptor systems. Concerns about the ABM capabilities of sensor systems are directly related to the availability of interceptors that could use data from these sensors. The presence of an extensive space-based sensor network that could provide long-range target tracking information could increase concerns about the possibility of upgrading antiaircraft or antitactical ballistic missile systems (permitted under the Treaty) to have capabilities against strategic ballistic missiles. Conversely, very stringent limits on the development, testing, and deployment of interceptors might alleviate concerns over the newer sensor technologies.

There are critical policy choices to be made about sensors. This chapter attempts to provide both the information and options to guide wise decisions. The initial sections of the chapter provide an introduction to the operating principles of these systems, and the readers who are familiar with this area may wish to turn to the subsequent policy discussion.

ABM Sensor Functions

Sensors serve one or more of four general functions:

- Surveillance and acquisition (together called "search")
- Track
- Discrimination, and
- Fire control (sometimes called "engagement")

One device may perform more than one of these functions. For instance, phased-array radars generally can simultaneously track individual targets while maintaining surveillance over broad areas of space.

Surveillance and acquisition sensors maintain a constant watch over large regions of space to detect and localize objects of interest. This function is also required for other non-ABM missions, such as early warning. For ABM sensors, the task is continuous coverage of likely missile launch locations or regions in space through which missiles and their warheads would pass to reach their target. Search sensors may also provide precise tracking and identification information, or those functions may be performed by other sensors more appropriate to the mission, usually after being cued by the search sensor.

Tracking sensors determine a target's trajectory—its position as a function of time—through a sequence of measurements. This function is also required for other missions such as Treaty compliance verification and satellite tracking. ABM tracking sensors must determine the trajectories of as many as several thousand missiles, several tens of thousands of reentry vehicles, and several hundreds of thousands of decoys, against a background cluttered by natural phenomena and nuclear explosions. The precise trajectory of these targets must be determined and updated frequently so that interceptor weapons can be properly assigned. The quality of the track information required from the sensor depends on the purpose for which the information is used.

Discrimination sensors seek to distinguish threatening from nonthreatening objects. For an ABM system, the discrimination sensors would separate Soviet reentry vehicles carrying nuclear warheads from decoys, chaff, and aerosol clouds and find RVs hidden by antisimulation deception techniques. For instance,

- Traffic decoys, such as light balloons inflated in space, attempt to congest the defense battle management system by forcing the ABM sensors to keep track of large numbers of objects. Chaff and aerosol clouds can be numerous and extend over a large region of space, masking the location of actual RVs to radar and optical sensors, respectively. Traffic decoys, designed only to keep the system busy, are not intended to fool sophisticated discrimination processing.
- Replica decoys have nearly the same size and shape (but not mass) of actual RVs and may have the same optical and thermal properties.[1] Some decoys of this type are designed to duplicate the deployment kinematics as well as the aerodynamic properties of real RVs.
- Antisimulation techniques involve enclosing RVs within balloons and proliferating similar but empty balloons as replica decoys.

Fire control sensors are required to guide ABM interceptors to their targets. The interceptor may be guided directly (command guidance), by the sensor's illumination reflected from the target (semiactive homing guidance), or by the interceptor's own passive or active sensors (autonomous or active guidance). Directed-energy weapons (DEWs) require a different type of fire control: precision pointing and tracking. Because directed-energy weapons must make use of very small-diameter beams, target locations would have to be known at least as precisely as the diameter of the beams.

ABM Sensor Types

Each phase of the ballistic trajectory presents sensors with different conditions and phenomena. ABM sensor technologies fall within three broad types: passive, active, and interactive. Active and passive sensors are of potential interest for performing the full range of surveillance, tracking, discrimination, and fire control functions, while interactive sensors are primarily limited to the discrimination function.

The surveillance capability of active and passive sensors depends on (1) their ability to detect targets, (2) the area they can view in a single instant, and (3) the rate at which they can scan large areas. The ability of these sensors to perform the other three functions (tracking, discrimination, and fire control) also depends on the sensor's resolution: the minimum separation distance at which two objects can be discerned as distinct. Resolution is determined by the sensor's aperture (the size of the radar antenna or telescope mirror) and operating frequency or wavelength. (Frequency, which is proportional to the inverse of wavelength, is the measure used in discussing microwave radars; wavelength is used in discussing optical systems such as passive infrared sensors and laser radars.) Larger apertures and higher operating frequencies (or shorter operating wavelengths) improve resolution and thus performance of these functions. In the case of optical sensors, which include those operating both at visible and other wavelengths, resolution is also determined by the characteristics of the sensor's detector, in the same way that fine-grained camera film produces clearer pictures than coarse-grained film.

Factors beside the physics of these devices influence the performance of a sensor system. Management of the huge amounts of information typical of an ABM engagement—both the coordination of the various sensor and weapon elements of the system (battle management) and sensor data processing—often dominates the physical characteristics of the devices. Battle management and data processing issues are less familiar to most policymakers and often more difficult to grasp.[2]

In the arms control context, however, physical characteristics are more significant, because they may be verifiable, while battle management capability is not. For this reason, the discussion below is primarily about physics, rather than information processing. The abilities attributed to sensors and sensing techniques are theoretical and not necessarily achievable in practice. In practice, engineering limits and design compromises frequently result in system performance that is significantly less than the theoretical ideal.

PASSIVE OPTICAL SENSORS

A passive sensor system relies solely on radiation emitted by the object to be observed. Because the objects under observation (ballistic missile boosters and booster plumes, postboost vehicles, reentry vehicles, and decoys) emit thermal (largely infrared) radiation, passive optical sensors can be used for search and track and to discriminate targets from decoys.

Following the boost phase, passive discrimination of warheads from decoys would rely on the existence of detectable differences between real and decoy targets. For instance, during midcourse, light balloon decoys would cool off much more rapidly than heavy warheads. The temperature difference, or a difference in the rate of change of temperature, could be detected unless the offense took countermeasures such as placing small heaters in the empty balloons or insulating balloons that enclosed warheads.

Passive sensors are usually classified according to their operating wavelength, which is a function of the temperature of the targets they are tracking. High-temperature targets such as missile exhaust plumes emit copiously in the shortwave infrared (SWIR) band, which has wavelengths somewhat longer than visible light, while cooler reentry vehicles primarily emit in the long-wave infrared (LWIR) band. Given the dependence of system performance on operating wavelength, these two bands are discussed separately. The midwavelength infrared (MWIR) band, with characteristics between these two bands, can also be used for antimissile sensors.

Advances in infrared (IR) sensors may involve improvements in detector qualities such as sensitivity, reduced vulnerability to radiation from nuclear detonations; detector focal-plane arrays that scan faster or even stare; and improved on-board computer resources. Increased sensitivity would result from more sensitive, cooled detectors. The refrigerators for these systems, known as cryo-coolers, may require kilowatts or tens of kilowatts of power. Improved radiation hardness, in addition to enhancing the survivability of the sensor itself, could lead to less noise on the detectors and thus reduce the masking of targets by radiation from the debris from a nuclear detonation.

Because sensor resolution is one component in tracking error, improvements in resolution may result in improved tracks. Tracking accuracy can also be improved by using very high density focal-plane arrays, typically with hundreds of thousands of detectors, as compared to the commonly reported several thousand detectors in the current early-warning satellites of the Defense Support Program (DSP).[3] Such improvements in focal-plane arrays are the major source of enhanced performance of these sensors, primarily because they permit much more frequent track updates. Although focal-plane array sizes are planned to increase as much as a thousandfold, apertures will grow by less than a factor of ten.

Shortwavelength Infrared (SWIR) Sensors. During the boost portion of a ballistic missile's trajectory, the rocket's intensely burning fuel provides a very strong SWIR signal. A sensor looking down on the earth for this signal would need an optical aperture large enough to collect a sufficiently strong signal to register with the sensor's detectors and with sufficient spatial resolution so that solar-reflected energy from water and clouds would be less than the signal from the rocket plume. The very large signal from the first booster stage of an ICBM is readily observed from satellites in geostationary earth orbits (GEO) with relatively small apertures and hence coarse spatial resolutions.[4]

Surveillance and tracking of the weaker signals from the second and third booster stages of ICBMs and the first booster stage of submarine-launched ballistic missiles (SLBMs) require significantly greater sensitivity. One meter aperture optics in GEO should be adequate for reliable detection of even these weaker signals, according to estimates in the American Physical Society report.[5]

In principle, data from such a passive sensor observing the boost phase could, in combination with other sources, be used to derive the launch points, number, type, and general trajectories of attacking missiles, but not their final destinations. Determination of the number of missiles launched would depend on the geographical separation of the launch points. The several kilometers that typically separate silo-based missiles could permit such a determination, while launches of mobile missiles in less widely dispersed cluster (or launches of missiles from a single submarine) could confound such a determination. Knowledge of the type of missile deployed in a particular silo field, derived in peacetime by national technical means, could be used to deduce the type of missile detected by such sensors, but again, mobile and submarine-launched missile launches might elude classification. The quality of trajectory determination would depend on the rate at which good data points were acquired on the missile's position during boost phase. Staring sensors with focal-plane arrays consisting of hundreds of thousands of pixels, which would continuously view the missile's flight corridor and rapidly (perhaps several times each second) generate updates on its trajectory, could provide accurate boost-phase tracks. Scanning sensors (using much smaller focal-plane arrays) would provide tracking data at intervals on the order of many seconds.

The SDI program's Boost Surveillance and Tracking System (BSTS) satellite sensor will, Pike believes,[6] have much larger aperture than current DSP early-warning satellites. In addition, it may have a very large focal-plane array, permitting it to stare continuously at the earth, rather than scanning sections intermittently, several times each minute, as does the DSP, according to published reports.[7] Thus, Pike believes, in contrast to the three active satellites of the DSP system, the dozen or so satellites that will constitute the BSTS constellation could quickly acquire the tracking points needed for an accurate computation of each missile's trajectory.[8]

Information on the location of a booster plume derived from SWIR sensors in GEO is unlikely to be sufficient to aim directed-energy weapons, which must be aimed at the booster itself, rather than the plume. The localization information, however, might be used to cue interceptors equipped with on-board terminal homing sensors.

Long-Wavelength Infrared Sensors (LWIR). After propulsion ceases, passive sensors must rely on radiation from the postboost vehicle, reentry vehicles, and decoys, which emit long-wavelength infrared radiation with a characteristic temperature of about 300 degrees Kelvin, the same as earth.[9] Thus LWIR sensors would require sensitive detector arrays and large optics, and they must look above earth's horizon to see their targets. The effective range of these sensors, and thus the total number of sensors required, is constrained by this "above-the-horizon" requirement and is limited by the apogee of the objects that must be tracked, as well as the operating altitude of the sensor itself. Satellites in high-altitude orbits could be tracked by a handful of sensor satellites. ICBM RVs, with apogees over 1,000 kilometers, could be tracked by a constellation of tens of satellites (potentially on the order of 100 might be needed), while shorter-range (and depressed trajectory) missiles might require many more sensor satellites.

Sensors looking for RVs above the LWIR bright background could be in near-earth orbit, lofted into space by rockets, or based on aircraft operating at altitudes above 10 kilometers, where the water vapor in the atmosphere becomes sparse. The United States currently has a program for each of these modes.

The Space Surveillance and Tracking System (SSTS) is an SDI LWIR sensor for postboost and midcourse. In its initial configuration, which Pike believes will consist of ten to twenty satellites,[10] each with an aperture of more than 1 meter,[11] the SSTS would perform the tracking necessary to commit weapon systems, such as the space-based interceptors (SBI) and Exoatmospheric Reentry Vehicle Interceptor System (ERIS). Pike believes[12] that earlier plans had called for a constellation of as many as eighty more capable satellites, each with a 2.5-meter aperture, that would also perform discrimination functions. The Ground Surveillance and Tracking System (GSTS) is a rocket-launched LWIR sensor system. The Airborne Optical Adjunct (AOA) will carry an LWIR sensor for high-altitude operations. As of the end of the Reagan administration, the AOA was seen as a major test program to resolve many of the passive sensor issues related to all midcourse sensor systems. Pike believes that both GSTS[13] and AOA[14] will carry meter-class optics.

Unlike radars, passive systems such as these cannot directly measure target range. However, three-dimensional tracking is made possible by combining a series of azimuth and elevation measurements with the knowledge that the object is in an elliptical trajectory with the earth at one focus of this ellipse. The number of observations required is determined by the effects of imperfect resolution, other measurement and sensor errors, and target density. The American Physical Society report stated that typically ten to twenty looks spread over a 50- to 100-second interval would be necessary but might not be sufficient.

The information from a single sensor could be adequate to guide interceptors close enough to their targets for on-board guidance to be effective. But, just as with SWIR sensors, single-platform LWIR sensors do not have the precision-tracking capability necessary for fire control of directed-energy weapons, even if the latter are based on the same platform. To accomplish the necessary resolution and enable the sensor to operate from a reasonable distance of thousands of kilometers, the optical apertures would have to exceed 10 meters in diameter, which would result in a very cumbersome, costly, and vulnerable system. In the absence of countermeasures such as tethered pairs of balloons, the correlation of target track data from several separate sensors could, in principle, provide the precise trajectory information needed for interception.[15] In practice, however, the wide spatial dispersal of these sensors, as well as the resulting large communication loads and other operational difficulties (including countermeasures) might make it difficult to correlate target tracks from separate sensor platforms.

LWIR sensors cannot discriminate targets by high-resolution imaging at useful ranges. However, LWIR target signatures might provide discrimination information, based on the differing thermal signatures of warheads and decoys. Massive warheads possess considerable thermal inertia and thus would remain at nearly room temperature during their flight. Simple decoys such as empty balloons would quickly cool off.

As indicated earlier, however, battery-powered heaters could be placed inside empty balloons to compensate for this effect. Moreover, there would be no observable temperature difference between a properly insulated balloon enclosing an RV and an empty balloon. The American Physical Society study group was persuaded that, in the face of such a responsive threat, LWIR techniques alone cannot do the entire job of discrimination, and "passive thermal sensing is likely to be limited to the establishment of coarse tracks of all objects in mid-course, followed by . . . hand over to sophisticated discrimination methods."[16]

ACTIVE SENSORS: MICROWAVE AND LASER RADARS

Active sensors, such as microwave and optical laser radars, illuminate objects in order to detect or track targets or to measure certain important properties by analyzing the reflected signal. Active sensors can be used for surveillance, track, discrimination, and fire control. Their greatest utility lies in precision tracking and discrimination. Active sensors may be capable of discrimination if the signature of an RV is sufficiently different from that of the accompanying decoys. Cross-section histories, fine-grained Doppler measurements, polarization measurements, inverse synthetic aperture imaging, and length measurements may all be used. However, in each case, troublesome countermeasures might impede the capabilities of such sensors.

Microwave radars typically have operational ranges between 1,000 and 5,000 kilometers from their target, which restricts them to basing on the ground or in near-earth orbit. Basing radars in space could pose operational problems, because large apertures are required to obtain good angular resolution at long microwave wavelengths—on the order of the many tens of meters required by ground-based large phased-array radars. However, somewhat smaller apertures might be permitted by the use of higher-frequency millimeter wavelengths (not possible for ground-based radars since the atmosphere is comparatively opaque at these frequencies). Although the instantaneous angle resolution of radars is poor compared with the potential of some optical systems, the position of the observed object can be accurately determined by combining the information of several radars. A single radar can achieve the same result by synthetic aperture processing, in which the orbital motion of the radar satellite is used to synthesize a higher-resolution image, with a resolution that could get nearly as good as that of the operating frequency of the radar (centimeters or millimeters). Another technique is inverse synthetic aperture processing, in which the target's motion is used. However, the utility of these techniques could be compromised by countermeasures, such as fronds or other intentional fluctuations in the target's surface.

The capacity of a radar to illuminate a relatively large volume of space simultaneously is useful because it could rapidly detect the many RVs and decoys deployed by a postboost vehicle during the separation. The range and radial velocity of the many objects in the field of view could then be determined by range-Doppler processing. If these measurements are sufficiently fine-grained, some discrimination could result. Such discrimination could be countered by equipping postboost vehicles equipped with a radar-jamming capacity, using shrouds to prevent the radar from observing the deployments during the separation phase or altering postboost vehicle deployment maneuvers.

Synthetic and inverse synthetic aperture processing can also achieve some discrimination. If not challenged with effective countermeasures, it could be capable of seeing small details and measuring with great precision various motions of the objects.

Laser radars would operate in the band between near ultraviolet (UV), 0.25 micron, and near infrared (IR), 1 micron. Because of their narrow beams, laser radars would have to scan very rapidly to perform the search function, which may prove difficult in practice. They are a leading candidate to provide precision tracking and discrimination measurements of objects acquired by other sensors. Multikilowatt lasers and meter-class aperture receivers could track over ranges of a few thousand kilometers.[17]

Lasers with a mosaic of receiver elements, transmitter average powers in the tens of kilowatts, operating in very short pulses (nanoseconds), over distances of several thousand kilometers, could achieve much reduced scan times and many looks per second. Like radars, such lasers might also discriminate using range-Doppler techniques, distinguishing RVs from decoys on the basis of differences in their rotation or surface motion, although antisimulation through intentional perturbations could deny this technique.

INTERACTIVE SENSORS

To discriminate threatening targets from decoys may require determining an object's intrinsic characteristics, such as mass, uranium or plutonium content, or the presence of chemical explosives or electronics. Four general interactive, perturbing methods might be used to sense these properties remotely:

- Physical disruption of the structures of decoys;
- Heating the decoy with a laser and observing the rate at which the object cools;
- Measuring mass by delivering an impulse to the target and then observing the resulting change in motion; and
- Penetrating the target with energetic primary particles and then determining the target composition (and/or mass) by measuring the total flux and/or spectrum of the scattered secondary radiation.

When some device (other than the atmosphere) is used to apply an impulse to the target or deliver discriminating radiation against it, the perturbation is called interactive. If discrimination is achieved, it is called interactive discrimination.

The traditional method of interactive discrimination involves the physical disruption or destruction of decoys. Balloon simulation or antisimulation decoys above the atmosphere would be severely damaged or distorted by the recoil from the blowoff of a micron-thick surface layer exploded by the x-ray flux of a high-yield nuclear burst over a range of many tens of kilometers, while reentry vehicles would remain intact except at much shorter ranges. Unfortunately, such nuclear bursts could also severely impair the functioning of the sensors that would be needed subsequently to track the remaining RVs.

If the passive emissions of objects alone are not sufficient for discrimination, then heating the object with a laser may improve matters. This technique, known as laser tagging, could be used to cope with decoys that employ small heaters in balloons to simulate the presence of warheads. Laser tagging operates from the premise that empty balloons would reradiate the laser's heat much more rapidly than warheads or simple antisimulation decoys containing warheads; the tactic might prove of little help in the face of more sophisticated insulated balloons.

Lasers could be used to destroy lightweight traffic decoys and simple antisimulation balloons. Laser vaporization typically requires some 1 to 10 kilojoules per gram. To vaporize a 1-kilogram traffic decoy totally, then, would require about 1 to 10 megajoules of laser energy absorbed. A single 10-megawatt laser would thus require between 10,000 and 100,000 seconds to destroy a notional threat cloud of 100,000 decoys (ignoring the time to slew the laser from one target to another, which could significantly increase the total time required).

Since the entire midcourse phase lasts for no more than twenty-five minutes (or 1,500 seconds), between 60 and 600 such lasers could be required to complete this task within the available time. A somewhat larger number of lasers would have to be in orbit to accomplish this mission, since some laser platforms would be on the wrong side of the earth to participate in the battle, although the absentee ratio would be less than one in ten, the factor usually posited for boost-phase engagements. These very rough calculations suggest that the number of lasers required for this form of interactive discrimination could range from approximately the number required for boost-phase engagement to a fraction of that number (in practice, the same lasers could be used for both boost-phase engagement of boosters and midcourse interactive discrimination).

Lasers could also be used to induce motion by impulse transfer. To change the target's velocity about 10 centimeters per second would require a laser pulse energy of some tens of kilojoules spread over some 1,000 square centimeters. Such laser impulse vaporization may require substantially less energy than laser vaporization (and correspondingly less powerful lasers or small numbers of lasers than in the previous calculation). However, the effectiveness of this technique may be reduced by various countermeasures, such as the use of very large balloons, reflective balloon coatings, and balloon coatings of differing compositions.

Particle beams could be used in the midcourse phase as an interactive discrimination device. All materials emit gamma rays, x-rays, and neutrons when irradiated with high-energy particles. Since the secondary particle production will scale approximately with the target mass, a particle beam could be used to estimate the target mass by monitoring the quantity (and perhaps spectra) of the induced secondary emissions. For example, a neutral particle beam will penetrate through several centimeters of aluminum. It will thus produce observable secondary radiation when it strikes a warhead (which is much thicker than this depth), but it will pass through the very thin skin of a balloon decoy without much interaction and production of observable secondary radiation. The operational attractiveness of such systems is compromised by the probable requirement for a large number of expensive particle-beam generator satellites, which could constitute an attractive target for attack by offensive forces.

How These Sensors Fit Together to Perform an ABM Function

The detection and tracking of ICBM boosters by passive SWIR satellites in GEO would find three principal uses in an ABM system. First, the tracking information could be sufficient for a battle management system to assign and launch terminal homing space-based interceptors. The capability of the homing sensor located on the interceptor would establish one requirement on the tracking accuracy of the sensor. Second, the satellites could cue precision tracking and pointing sensors for a boost-phase directed-energy weapon. Third, the satellite could cue and even hand over tracks to midcourse sensors.

From booster burnout to about halfway along the ballistic trajectory, detection and tracking would be performed by space-based sensors in near-earth orbit, or perhaps LWIR sensors launched from ground bases or submarines after early detection of an attack, as well as possibly forward deployed air-based sensor platforms. LWIR sensors or phased-array radars in near-earth orbit could search wide areas of space for targets and provide tracking information to assign and launch space- or ground-based interceptors with autonomous homing capability. Laser radars could provide enough precision tracking to aim directed-energy weapons for midcourse intercept, if mounted on the same platform as the DEWs.

After about the midway point of ballistic flight, ground-based and air-based sensors could search and track with sufficient accuracy for space-based and ground-based terminal homing interceptors. Radars and lasers could provide fire control illumination for interceptors with semiactive terminal guidance.

The ability to discriminate RVs from decoys during the exoatmospheric portion of flight is utterly crucial to the performance of an ABM system. Therefore, experiments are expected to play a critical role in providing the hard data necessary to judge the capability of passive discrimination techniques, with or without laser tagging. If discrimination is to be accomplished by observing bussing operations, microwave and optical radars must be space-based in order to illuminate postboost vehicles at the critical times. High-resolution microwave space-based imaging radars may or may not rule out the use of replica decoys but would probably be defeated by antisimulation decoys. Interactive-laser and particle-beam discrimination techniques may or may not hold the promise of defeating antisimulation decoys, but these approaches involve large, expensive satellites that may be unacceptably vulnerable to defense suppression attacks.

Treaty Limits on and Adaptations for Sensors

At the time the ABM Treaty was signed, large phased-array radars were the principal sensor of concern. They were also the "long pole in the tent," since their construction required a number of years. Sensors remain a long-lead-time element of an antimissile system. Although constraints on interception systems may provide an adequate cushion against breakout, two independent buffers provide more security than a single one. And the long development cycles for sensors make them an appropriate focus for arms control limits.

Defining limits and Treaty adaptations for ABM-capable sensors in the 1990s involves a complex interaction of technical, practical, military, and negotiating judgments. Policymakers will have to be concerned about sensors that could perform long-range surveillance, tracking, and discrimination. The effort to impose limits should focus on potentially realizable components that could erode the Treaty's buffer. All the sensors discussed above could perform one or more ABM functions if they were sufficiently powerful. In evaluating proposals to limit sensor testing and development, the policymaker should consider

- Possible Treaty clarifications to reduce ambiguities.
- The type of limits that might be imposed, including limits on sensor testing in an ABM mode, sensor capability, and the number of deployed sensor platforms.
- The verifiability of any limit, both by NTM alone and with potential improvements in verification through cooperative measures.
- The existence and capabilities of other sensors and weapons needed to perform the complete ABM function.

POSSIBLE TREATY CLARIFICATIONS

Article V of the ABM Treaty prohibits development and testing of space-based ABM "components" (as well as systems), so one relevant question is "When is a sensor a 'component'?" As noted in chapter 4, the parties discussed the difference between a "component" and an "adjunct" during the Treaty negotiations. The only example of an adjunct mentioned in those discussions was a small optical telescope that might be used to help point an ABM radar. Since such a device would not by itself have any meaningful ABM capability, the inference was that it would not be subject to Treaty limits.

On the other hand, a sensor need not be capable of performing the entire gamut of surveillance, tracking, discrimination, and fire control functions in order to be a "component" capable of substituting for a 1972 ABM radar. As noted above, the radars then in use did not perform all these functions individually either. Thus, the Treaty is not clear whether space-based sensors that are ABM capable but have not been tested in an ABM mode are prohibited by Article V of the Treaty. It seems tolerably clear that microwave imaging satellites in excess of 3 million watts-square meter power-aperture product cannot be deployed in space, except for space track or NTM purposes. Moreover, if the sensor is capable of substituting for a ground-based ABM radar then it cannot be space-based, whatever its power-aperture. But the concept "capable of substituting for" is as vague as the concept of "component." As chapter 4 points out, this is an area for clarification and definition.

"TESTING IN AN ABM MODE"

In 1972, verification of testing in an ABM mode was a fairly straightforward process. The operation of a radar could be monitored by NTM. The concurrent launch of an interceptor and the flight of the target reentry vehicle could also be monitored. Although it was not absolutely clear that the air defense radars were operating in association with them, these activities provided a relatively unambiguous basis for defining "tested in an ABM mode."

The new passive optical ABM technologies pose a greater challenge for determining whether a device has been "tested in an ABM mode." Since passive sensors do not emit signals, it is difficult to determine whether they are being operated in association with an antimissile test. A further complication arises from the very long ranges of passive sensors. Satellites at geosynchronous orbit can observe nearly half of the earth's surface. Associating such a satellite with an ABM test would be impossible. Thus, although the focus on "testing in an ABM mode" may be appropriate for shorter-range active sensor systems such as radars, it is less useful as a way of imposing limits on longer-range passive systems.

LIMITS ON SENSOR CAPABILITY

A useful limit on sensor capability must reliably distinguish between permissible non-ABM activity and actions that threaten the Treaty buffer. The limit must also be one that can be satisfactorily verified. In assessing the acceptability of development and deployment of certain sensor programs, the United States cannot simply make a unilateral judgment about the ABM capability of its own systems. The question is whether a look-alike Soviet program would present performance ambiguities that could not be resolved by NTM. Several planned U.S. programs, such as AOA, BSTS, and SSTS may present ambiguities of this kind. In such a case, the United States would not be satisfied to rely on assurances from the Soviets about the capability of their sensors based on their unilateral evaluation, as Graybeal and McFate point out in chapter 10. Such a situation is a candidate for the imposition of some sort of objective limits. But if an agreed threshold cannot be policed by NTM, supplementary verification measures will be necessary; that is, the parties must share basic design information, operational data, or cooperative testing practices.

Early-warning satellites. One of the most immediate challenges is the question of potential upgrades to early-warning satellite systems. The BSTS satellite system is currently under consideration as an eventual replacement for the current DSP system.

One might conclude that any difference between existing early-warning satellites and early-warning satellites capable of an ABM surveillance and tracking function, such as BSTS, is not militarily significant because the buffer to ABM capability is not seriously eroded. Any additional capability provided by BSTS might not be important because no weapons that could make use of the information have been or could be deployed except by violating the ABM Treaty in a very obvious manner, with long lead time.

However, as noted above, the additional capability of BSTS may be potentially militarily significant. One could ask whether an optical aperture threshold is useful to distinguish between satellites having permissible early-warning capability and those that could perform more demanding ABM functions. Garwin and Jarvis, in chapter 6, note that aperture diameters under 1 meter will provide kilometer-class accuracy for shortwavelength infrared sensors at geosynchronous orbit, depending on the focal-plane material and design. This resolution would in turn be sufficient to perform some types of ABM acquisition and tracking. Thus, even the 1-meter aperture limit might be of limited utility unless accompanied by inspection to ensure that the ABM performance limits are not approached.

The size of the optical aperture is one characteristic that clearly differentiates DSP from BSTS, according to Pike,[18] and might be used in general to distinguish between an ABM-capable satellite and one that is useful only for early warning. This threshold may also be one of the more readily verifiable by national technical means. DSP is commonly reported as having optical apertures in the 1-meter range,[19] and BSTS several times this size. Although the orders of magnitude improvement in focal-plane array capabilities is a major source of difference in the performance of these two systems, a threshold of 1 meter could predictably limit the capabilities of future satellites.

Current NTM will not be able to verify a 1-meter threshold. To measure the size of an optical aperture some 40,000 kilometers from the earth with an accuracy of tens of centimeters from ground-based observation could require a single telescope with an unrealistic optical diameter of many tens of meters. A ground-based optical interferometer, combining the images from several telescopes for improved resolution, might provide a means to verify this threshold. Although this would require the construction of new facilities, the technique is currently in use in the astronomical community, which suggests that the cost of such a facility could be a few hundred million dollars.[20] The performance of the system depends on the perfection of various advanced image-processing techniques, such as the illumination of the object of interest with a very short duration low-power laser pulse, to provide means of atmospheric compensation.

Otherwise, the aperture itself, as well as the internal characteristics, might require additional methods of verification. These could include inspector satellites and cooperative methods such as prelaunch inspection (see chapter 10).

Surveillance and tracking satellites. Another planned U.S. program, the SSTS, is being developed for midcourse RV tracking. SSTS will also have a space surveillance and tracking capability, as well as some ability to track the elements of strategic missiles in the boost phase of their flight. The policymaker will ask whether an SSTS LWIR satellite could have enough ABM capability to cause a worrisome erosion of the buffer.

Some would argue that the potential ABM capability of a space-based tracking system, such as SSTS, outweighs all other concerns. First, the widely deployed Soviet surface-to-air missile (SAM) batteries could use tracking information from the SSTS to achieve improved ABM performance. With a capable Soviet space-track system in place, the United States might perceive the threat of rapid SAM upgrades as substantially reducing the buffer against the creation of militarily significant ABM capabilities. On the other hand, assessments by Garwin and Jarvis in chapter 6 and Johnson in chapter 7 maintain that current SAM systems have only limited capability to intercept modern, high-performance RVs, even with additional discrimination and tracking capability.

Second, if the Soviets were covertly stockpiling Moscow-type ABM interceptors, as well as rapidly deployable radars, the availability of a space-based sensor system such as SSTS might also reduce the buffer. Johnson argues in chapter 7 that site preparation and deployment might be sufficiently conspicuous and time-consuming to allow the United States to respond effectively.

Third, breakout deployment with advanced ground-based, ERIS- and High Endoatmospheric Defense Interceptor-type (HEDI) missiles or space-based weapons is also of great concern. These weapons could arguably be supported by a space-based space-track system such as SSTS. But deployment of these weapons might also be conspicuous and time-consuming, perhaps sufficiently so to maintain the buffer.

It is possible that in practice there may be no obvious difference between a non-ABM space-track satellite and an ABM satellite for midcourse tracking. If that were so, a regime with no constraints on testing and development of such sensors might arise more from necessity than from choice; the alternative, on this assumption, would be to prevent any potential ABM capability by forgoing space-based space track.

On the other hand, if there were observable differences between ABM midcourse tracking and non-ABM space-based space track, many of the same difficulties would arise as in the case of early-warning sensors. The use of satellites for non-ABM purposes such as satellite tracking would affect the bounds at which ABM parameters could be set. The technical capabilities of permitted systems, such as aperture size or power-aperture product, place a practical lower limit on any threshold that might be drawn now and in the future.

Yet there would be a small possibility of verifying the actual capability of the satellite by NTM alone.

Likewise, if air-based IR sensors are to be limited, then it will be necessary to find some method to distinguish ABM sensors from range instrumentation devices, experimental proof-of-principle devices, infrared astronomy devices, and radar adjuncts.

Discrimination sensors. Active and interactive sensors appear to be the only conceivable candidates for the discrimination function, although their actual potential for performing this mission is as yet unclear. The ABM capabilities of microwave imaging satellites could be limited by constraining their power and aperture in order to restrict their effective range, as with the 3 million watts-square meter power-aperture product limit currently in the ABM Treaty. Higher-power laser tagging devices might be covered by brightness threshold limits, particularly if combined with restrictions on testing modes. Limits on high-power laser and particle-beam discrimination devices would have to be considered in conjunction with brightness and situational limits on laser and particle-beam weapons. (Since these sensors have little apparent non-ABM application, and may be more readily monitored than passive sensors, there seems to be little to lose in the way of non-ABM missions in imposing limits that would result in banning these types completely.)

Passive optical sensors may or may not turn out to be capable of discrimination. But it would not be easy to define limits on development and testing intended to resolve these uncertainties. Experiments with ground-based optical probes lofted into space, which would be important to this end, are currently regarded as permitted, if they are launched from an agreed test range. Passive optical sensors designed for "instrumentation," NTM, or space surveillance and tracking could all gather important and useful data on the issue. If these experiments should indicate that passive optical discrimination can be performed, deployed passive sensors might be converted to the discrimination mission in very short order. If some class of platforms and experiments are to be allowed, then criteria would have to be developed to measure the ABM capability of the platform and determine the modes in which its use in ABM experiments would be permitted.

Although passive IR sensors in a discrimination role may be susceptible to countermeasures, both superpowers might have to make nontrivial efforts to reassure themselves of the fidelity of their simulation and antisimulation decoys. In the absence of a compelling rationale for giving free rein to space-based sensors, it might be prudent to clarify the existing Treaty limitations and avoid the threat inflation that might accompany efforts by both parties to maintain confidence in their countermeasures programs.

Fire control sensors. Low-power laser radars appear to hold considerable promise for the fire control of space-based directed-energy weapons. Limits on such systems would have to distinguish them from low-power laser communication devices and other scientific devices of similar design and capabilities. Although it may be possible to devise conditions on the testing of such devices, their small size, small signature in testing, and physical similarity to other systems are cause for pessimism.

THE QUESTION OF APERTURES

A major issue in devising limits on space-based sensors is the usefulness of limits on the mirror apertures of passive and active sensors. There are three classes of mirror apertures that may be distinguished on the basis of their military potential and their potential for verification.

Submeter apertures (mirrors with diameters less than 1 meter) encompass a very broad range of nonmilitary and non-ABM functions, as well as certain ABM functions such as some types of fire control systems. The small size of such devices, as well as the near-impossibility of distinguishing ABM-related devices from other devices, renders verification effectively impossible. Thus, there is little that arms control can do to constrain such devices.

Meter-class apertures encompass mirrors with diameters from somewhat less than 1 meter to a few meters (without being too precise, this upper limit might be imagined to be in the neighborhood of perhaps 2 meters). Sensors in this class include both non-ABM systems, such as early-warning satellites, and some systems developed for ABM applications. It is questionable whether meaningful and verifiable distinctions can be drawn between individual non-ABM and ABM sensors with apertures in this range. If such distinctions are not possible, decisions on other limitations on ABM systems (particularly kill mechanisms and possible ground-based radars) will have to acknowledge the ABM capabilities inherent in these systems (although concerns about such capabilities might be tempered by a pessimistic assessment of their performance in the face of countermeasures).

Multimeter-class sensors would have apertures larger than those of the preceding class. Such devices could have significant ABM capabilities (tempered by degradation by various countermeasures). With the exception of a few scientific applications, apertures of this class do not appear at present to have military applications outside ABM systems. However, despite the initial enthusiasm on the part of the SDI program for sensors of this class, it is not apparent that they will be tested or deployed for ABM purposes either. Although verifiable limits might be devised to limit multimeter-class ABM sensors while permitting smaller non-ABM sensors, the comfort that could be drawn from such limits may prove rather small, at least in the near term. In the longer run, however, this might provide a hedge against the resurrection of plans for more ambitious sensor systems.

SYSTEM LIMITS

Sensor developments and deployments can reduce the breakout time from the ABM Treaty. Other than limiting the sensors themselves along the lines discussed above, there are two possible, somewhat contradictory avenues to compensate for sensors. First, the vulnerability of space-based sensors to antisatellite attack may counterbalance any threat they may pose to the buffer. Although the importance of space-based sensors may be large in peacetime, vulnerability to relatively modest ASAT will limit their wartime role, and hence their significance in breakout. In fact, large-scale deployments of tactically important space-based sensors act as incentive to further ASAT development. Many but not all types of antisatellite weapons at least share technology with antimissile weapons. Therein lies the basis for the contradiction.

A second approach to compensating for sensors is to tighten limits on ABM weapons beyond those that have been in force for the last sixteen years in order to have the same amount of protection against breakout. However, tight limits on ABM weapons are bound to limit many types of ASATs, which in turn *decreases* satellite vulnerability.

If loosening up on sensor restrictions threatens to undermine the breakout protection offered by the ABM Treaty, then some tighter than previous limits on ABM weapons will have to compensate. And some have suggested that there may also be a role for ASATs not covered by these tighter limits, such as agreement to space mine ABM-relevant space-based sensors.

Limits on and Adaptations for Sensors: The Three Approaches

This section derives concrete proposals from the foregoing analysis and organizes them in terms of the three approaches to maintaining the treaty regime outlined in earlier chapters.

ADAPTATIONS TO MAINTAIN PRESENT TREATY LEVELS OF
RESTRAINT

The premise underlying this category of adaptations is to fortify the ABM Treaty's rules on sensors to prevent any erosion in the buffer against rapid breakout that might be caused by sensor developments. The broad implications of this approach would involve

- Preventing where possible additional deployment of long-range search and track capability without greatly increasing the restrictions imposed on sensors for other missions, and
- Preventing, to the extent possible, the development of discrimination sensors.

Specific adaptations might include the following:

1. Restrict the ABM capability of passive optical satellites in geosynchronous orbit by limiting to five the number of such passive optical satellites that could be operational at any one time. Agreed deactivation procedures would be required to permit differentiation between Treaty-accountable operational satellites and inoperable satellites that would not count against this limit. Satellites at geosynchronous altitudes have orbital lives of millions of years, and the propellant required to cause them to reenter the Earth's atmosphere at the end of their operational lives could result in an unacceptable (potentially a fourfold) increase in the propellant needed to place such satellites in their operational orbit. Even the Soviet early-warning satellites that operate in semisynchronous orbits with perigees of only a few hundred kilometers have orbital lifetimes that greatly exceed the operational lifetime of the spacecraft themselves. Deactivation might be achieved by detaching the large solar arrays from these satellites at the end of their operational lives. In conjunction with the proposed ban on nuclear power sources in space (see point 7 below), such an agreement could effectively preclude the covert accumulation of an excess number of such satellites.

2. Limit the ABM capability of passive optical satellites in near-earth orbit by restricting the total number of passive optical satellites in space to the number (perhaps four) that would be required for satellite tracking, precluding the deployment of the tens of satellites that would be needed for an ABM system. This limit would likewise require agreed deactivation procedures of the type previously outlined. Cooperative inspection measures, for example, would be required to distinguish between satellites in near-earth orbit serving national technical means of verification from those that were part of a space-track network or were supporting programs to develop ABM capability by collecting data and performing proof-of-principle experiments.

3. Limit the presence of aircraft-based passive optical systems at ABM test ranges and/or prohibit their operation in conjunction with ABM interceptor tests.

4. Limit the optical aperture in all the systems mentioned in the previous sections to perhaps 2 meters. Pike believes[21] this would permit the deployment of satellites such as the currently planned version of BSTS, which might be used for improved early warning and verification, while precluding

the deployment of much larger satellites contemplated at the outset of the SDI program that could have more significant ABM capabilities. Exceptions may be required to permit scientific and other satellites with larger apertures. (This suggestion does not prejudge the question of whether BSTS should be regarded as consistent with the ABM Treaty but rather indicates that a clarification of the Treaty could result in such a conclusion.)

5. Prohibit the use of lasers during ABM tests for any purpose other than weapons tests, if those are allowed.
6. Prohibit the use of particle beams during ABM tests for any purpose other than weapons tests, if those are allowed.
7. Ban nuclear power sources in space. These power sources could be required for some types of very capable ABM sensor systems (including space-based microwave radars and particle-beam generators).

ADAPTATIONS TO ACHIEVE A MORE RESTRICTIVE TREATY REGIME

This category of adaptations would aim to strengthen the preventive provisions of the ABM Treaty's rules on sensors, to inhibit significant progress toward exploring the feasibility of strategic defenses by preventing the development and testing of key technologies. The rules set forth in the previous category would be supplemented to cover current technologies and programs more completely. This approach would involve

- Acting to prevent deployment of long-range search and track capability without regard to the restrictions imposed on sensors for other missions, and
- Preventing the development of discrimination sensors.

Specific adaptations would be as follows:

1. Prohibit the use of ground-launched probes lofted into space to collect experimental data even though they are currently permitted by the ABM Treaty when they are launched from agreed test ranges. All ABM testing would be banned, which in turn would require cooperative inspection measures.
2. Establish more restrictive rules on the number and optical aperture size of sensors in both geostationary and near-earth orbits and on aircraft.

ADAPTATIONS TO PERMIT A MORE PERMISSIVE TREATY REGIME

Three assumptions underlie this category of adaptations. First, it is of national importance to be able to accomplish a number of non-ABM missions and explore the feasibility of strategic defenses. Second, there are no meaningful, militarily significant limits that can be effectively imposed on passive optical sensors. Last, limits on weapon systems are more appropriate and meaningful and provide an adequate buffer against rapid breakout from the Treaty. The broad implications of this approach would involve

- Permitting a great deal of space-based long-range search and track capability and
- Restricting discrimination sensors to proof-of-principle experiments.

Specific adaptations would be as follows:

1. Place no restrictions on the testing or deployment of space-based passive optical sensors in geostationary orbit.
2. Permit a small number of space-based space-track sensors without regard to optical aperture size.
3. Permit a small number of aircraft-based optical platforms without restriction.
4. Define, where appropriate, laser and particle-beam thresholds of ABM weapons capability to include devices used to discriminate targets; permit operation of these devices only in agreed modes.
5. Establish cooperative measures that would limit the use of lasers, including those not covered by the weapons threshold (such as laser communication, radars, and tagging devices), to specific circumstances, so that each side can better measure ABM capability.
6. If an agreed orbital test is created, as per chapter 8, then all sensors participating in agreed orbiting test range (AOTR) testing should be declared.

Conclusion

Just as with the radars in 1972, the passive optical, active, and interactive sensors of future systems pose serious problems for an effective treaty regime. These sensor systems, based on aircraft and in space, may prove much more capable than their ground-based predecessors, and they will be much more difficult to verify with existing national technical means.

This does not mean that testing and development of sensors should be permitted to run free, although in some cases, loosening up on sensors may not undermine the buffer against the deployment of militarily significant ABM capabilities. In either case, more stringent constraints on weapons testing may be needed to compensate for the difficulties of limiting sensors.

Notes

1. The report by the American Physical Society describes typical replica decoys as "objects erected or inflated in space which have surface areas and shapes matching the radar cross sections and the long wave infrared emissions of reentry vehicles." *Report to the American Physical Society of the Study Group on Science and Technology of Directed Energy Weapons,* April 1987, p. 322.

2. See, for instance, Charles A. Zraket, "Uncertainties in Building a Strategic Defense," *Science* 235 (March 27, 1987): pp. 1600–1606.

3. *Jane's Spaceflight Directory 1987* (London and New York: Jane's Publishing, Inc., 1987), p. 353.

4. On the order of 10 × 10 square kilometers according to the American Physical Society report, p. 312.

5. In this case the sensor field of view would be reduced to about 2 × 2 square kilometers. The calculations for these estimates can be found in the American Physical Society report, pp. 311–312. It estimates that the signal from second and third stages of ICBMs and the first stages of SLBMs would be about 4 percent of the signal from first stages of ICBMs; a 10:1 signal-to-noise ratio is assumed.

6. "SDIO Sees ASAT Self-Protection in Midcourse Sensors, SBI," *Aerospace Daily*, September 22, 1987, p. 457, describes BSTS as having a diameter of 16 feet. An artist's concept of BSTS published in "Lockheed Designs Satellite System for Boost Surveillance and Tracking," *Aviation Week & Space Technology,* February 1, 1988, p. 45, shows that the BSTS sensor aperture is of comparable dimensions.

7. *Jane's Spaceflight Directory 1987*, supra n. 3.

8. "BSTS Plans Outlined," *Defense Daily*, October 25, 1988, p. 204.

9. For comparison, the temperature in degrees Celsius equals the Kelvin temperature minus 273.16.

10. "SDIO Scales Back Space Sensor Design," *SDI Monitor*, December 26, 1988, pp. 294–5.

11. "SDIO Scales Back Space Sensor Design," *Military Space,* December 19, 1988, p. 3, reports that SSTS will have an aperture "50% smaller than the 2.5 meter" design originally studied.

12. Ibid.

13. *Report to the Congress on the Strategic Defense System Architecture* (Washington, DC: SDI Organization, January 1988), p. A-6.

14. "Missile Tracker" (photo released by the Defense Department, November 17, 1988) indicates scale of AOA sensor.

15. Tethered balloons are balloons connected together so as to remain in proximity.

16. American Physical Society report, p. 326.

17. American Physical Society report, p. 314 and p. 321.

18. See endnotes discussing BSTS aperture.

19. *Jane's Spaceflight Directory 1987*, supra n.3.

20. Based on the costs of new astronomical facilities, see "Europe's Astronomy Machine," *Sky & Telescope,* May 1988, pp. 471–75.

21. See endnotes discussing BSTS aperture.

IO

ASSESSING VERIFICATION AND COMPLIANCE

Sidney N. Graybeal and Patricia Bliss McFate

RMS CONTROL has played an important role in U.S. strategic planning and foreign policy over the past thirty years. The ABM Treaty is one of the most significant arms control achievements and should remain a key foundation for future agreements. The Treaty poses unique verification problems, however. Unlike most other arms control agreements, which focus primarily on limiting or eliminating categories of weapons, the Treaty focuses on development and testing activities associated with achieving an ABM capability or mission.

Although verification and compliance were not major considerations in ratifying the ABM Treaty, they will be dominant factors in maintaining and enhancing its viability in the 1990s. Because of technological advances in weapons and weapon systems since 1972, the verification process associated with the Treaty will not only need to include the determination of compliance with existing provisions of the agreement, but also policy decisions about what constitutes effective verification of the agreement in the light of new technologies, the design and negotiation of new verification regimes to meet security requirements, the implementation of updated clarifications and additional verification provisions, and the determination of appropriate responses to ambiguous situations or clear noncompliance with specific provisions of the Treaty. This view of verification as an all-encompassing process going beyond monitoring and evaluation into the areas of design of new regimes and responses for noncompliance applies to other arms control agreements in effect or under negotiation at this time.

This chapter provides some background on verification issues, highlights recent advances or precedents in the modes of verification, delineates verification and compliance issues associated with maintaining a viable ABM Treaty, and suggests some specific courses of action.

Background

As the United States prepared for and negotiated the ABM Treaty, it had several serious verification concerns, related to upgrading surface-to-air missiles (SAMs) to give them an ABM capability, controlling the ABM system potential of large phased-array radars, banning mobile ABM systems and components, and limiting future (exotic) ABM systems and components. U.S. monitoring capabilities and potential compliance problems were important considerations in deriving and negotiating specific treaty language associated with these concerns. For example, in the case of SAM upgrade, there was considerable debate over whether to define ''tested in an ABM mode'' in specific quantitative terms or in broad, general terms. Specificity would have been useful for U.S. program managers, but engineers could design around any series of particular criteria. General language (the chosen option) permitted flexibility both in system engineering and in challenging testing activities associated with the extensive Soviet SAM programs, which if upgraded to ABM capable systems could undermine the agreement.

Some ABM Treaty compliance questions began to emerge in 1975 and have been the subject of exchanges in the Standing Consultative Commission (SCC) and other forums. The early issues were resolved either by Soviet responses or actions or by agreed statements clarifying the ABM Treaty language and negotiating record (e.g., the still-classified 1978 Agreed Statement clarifying certain aspects of ''tested in an ABM mode''). Beginning in 1981, the Reagan administration highlighted Soviet ABM Treaty compliance issues. The Krasnoyarsk radar is a clear-cut violation of the ABM Treaty and as such has provided a basis for raising and exaggerating other, less clear Soviet activities; Reagan administration compliance reports have alleged that the Soviet government is ''preparing to break out of the ABM Treaty.''

President Reagan's SDI, launched in 1983, has generated a whole new set of U.S. compliance questions, specifically how much research, development, testing, production, and deployment can be carried out without violating the ABM Treaty. When Pentagon personnel questioned the extent to which the ABM Treaty limited research, development, and testing of ''future'' ABM components and systems based on ''other physical principles,'' the matter was referred to the Department of State's legal adviser, Judge Abraham Sofaer; he came up with an innovative reinterpretation of the ABM Treaty that would permit unlimited research, development, and testing of ABM components and systems based on "other physical principles." His reinterpretation has not been accepted by most ABM Treaty negotiators, by the Senate, which ratified the Treaty, or by the Soviets, with whom the Treaty was negotiated. Consequently, the SDI Organization (SDIO) has been directed by the administration and Congress to conduct its programs in compliance with the traditional ("narrow" or "restrictive") interpretation of the Treaty. However, as noted in previous chapters, technologies applicable to ballistic missile defense (BMD) are advancing rapidly and raising legitimate compliance questions even under the restrictive interpretation. Needed clarification of ABM Treaty terms and their applications will generate additional verification considerations; the nature and scope of these verification issues will depend, in large part, on the agreed-upon wording and intent of these clarifications. Thus, verification and compliance will play an increasingly important role in the formulation and implementation of an ABM Treaty regime in the 1990s.

VERIFICATION CRITERIA

What constitutes "adequate" or "effective" verification? The latter term, used in the Reagan administration, seems to emphasize the production of a desired effect and at least implies the use of more demanding standards than a criterion of adequacy, which was the term used during the three previous administrations. In fact, there is very little difference in the application of these terms: judgments on adequate or effective verification depend on the nature and scope of the provisions of the agreement, the nation's monitoring capabilities and limitations, and one's view of the strategic forces required to maintain deterrence.

Both the Carter and Reagan administrations used the criterion of *military significance* in assessing the adequacy or effectiveness of a verification regime. In January 1988, testifying before the Senate, Ambassador Paul Nitze described the INF Treaty verification regime as "effective," meaning that, "if the other side moves beyond the limits of the Treaty in any militarily significant way, we would be able to detect such a violation in time to respond effectively and thereby to deny the other side the benefit of violation."[1] Harold Brown, secretary of defense in the Carter administration, employed essentially the same definition during the SALT II hearings when he explained that "any Soviet cheating which would pose a significant military risk or affect the Strategic Balance would be detected by our intelligence in time to respond effectively."[2] The criterion of military significance is compatible with a verification regime relying primarily on national technical means (NTM)[3] of verification complemented by cooperative measures.

Because arms control agreements are essentially political instruments, however, any violations—real or perceived—can take on major political significance. There is no such thing as foolproof or "100 percent" verification;

attempting to detect and identify all possible violations is neither possible nor worth the effort. Nevertheless, some provisions require verification not because they are militarily significant, but because they demonstrate overall compliance. Designing a verification regime to meet the criterion of political significance, however, would demand extremely stringent and intrusive provisions that are not essential to our national security.

Some believe there should also be a standard for judging compliance based on self-determination (sometimes called the criterion of "legal significance"). By this standard, one side could declare that certain of its activities complied with the ABM Treaty on the basis of knowledge not available to the other side through NTM. Such a criterion suggests that we police ourselves; specifically, it claims that the United States is obeying U.S. law or Treaty interpretation, and thus is it not necessary to explain to the Soviets (or the world) why we reached that conclusion. In our view, such "legal" approaches lead to a double standard that is not in the overall U.S. interest and indeed would be a fatal blow to the Treaty. It is essential that each party applies the same performance standards to its activities and is held accountable by the other side.

VERIFICATION PRECEDENTS FOR THE 1990s

NTM provided a basis for verifying strategic arms control agreements in the 1960s and 1970s. Intelligence collection and analysis capabilities have continued to be the foundation for monitoring arms control agreements and the key element in achieving effective verification. The SALT I ABM Treaty and the Interim Agreement limiting launchers for intercontinental and submarine-launched ballistic missiles (ICBMs and SLBMs) relied exclusively on NTM. The SALT II agreement, signed in 1979 but never ratified, provided more extensive limitations on strategic offensive forces; verification was based on NTM supplemented by "counting rules" to assist in monitoring reentry vehicle (RV) limitations. SALT I and SALT II focused on limiting *deployed* strategic weapon systems by counting their launchers rather than the total inventory of deployed and nondeployed strategic nuclear delivery vehicles (SNDVs) and their launchers, many of which are now mobile.

The evolution of arms control verification from the Surprise Attack Conference of 1958 to the current START negotiations suggests some lessons for the design of an ABM Treaty verification regime for the 1990s. The U.S proposal in the Surprise Attack Conference would have allowed about six U.S.-operated radars in the USSR to provide a thirty-minute warning of a surprise attack using fixed land-based ICBMs. The Soviets were not interested, in part because they did not want U.S.-manned radars on Soviet territory. In the 1964 Eighteen Nation Disarmament Conference, the United States proposed a freeze on SNDVs that would be verified by extensive on-site inspections (OSIs). The Soviets denounced the proposal as intelligence collection and regularly thereafter conveyed to U.S. negotiators their concerns over intrusive inspections.

Two developments enabled U.S. officials to overcome these concerns: the advent of reliable satellite photo-reconnaissance and the change in negotiating focus from SNDVs to their launchers. Thus at SALT I, the United States proposed limiting silos and submarines from which ICBMs and SLBMs would be fired. SALT II continued to focus on launchers for ICBMs and SLBMs and added limits on heavy bombers. SALT I and II relied on NTM for verification; the United States and the Soviet Union both possessed extensive NTM capabilities, and neither side pressed for OSIs. As the INF and START negotiations focused on total inventories of deployed and nondeployed delivery vehicles and their launchers, NTM were not considered adequate for ''effective'' verification; beginning with INF, NTM has been supplemented by extensive cooperative measures including OSIs.

The term *on-site inspection* covers a spectrum of activities including individual or team visits and the placement of sensors around the perimeter of or inside installations of particular interest. Inspections may be routinely permitted or conducted on an individual or a challenge basis:

- A routine inspection of declared facilities is one expressly permitted under the terms of an agreement; it does not imply suspicion of a violation.
- A challenge inspection of either a declared facility or a suspect site need not require supporting evidence of a violation under the terms of an agreement, although the party issuing the challenge might feel obliged to furnish such evidence to generate public and diplomatic support for its request. Unlike routinely permitted visits, challenge inspections suggest serious concerns over compliance and are thus more politically charged. Indeed, it is not clear that challenge inspections can be termed cooperative measures, since they seem more adversarial than cooperative in nature.
- A country may also invite inspection teams to visit an area or facility in order to improve its political standing, dispel concerns over noncompliance, or facilitate resolution of problems that have arisen. An important precedent for invitational inspections was the September 1987 visit of a U.S. congressional delegation to a Soviet radar site near Krasnoyarsk and a subsequent visit by U.S. government officials to Gomel to check on the status of ABM radars.

With this broad menu of choices, the wide popular support for on-site inspections may seem warranted. A closer review of the benefits and risks of inspections, however, suggests important distinctions. Routine inspections have clear benefits and limited risks, but challenge inspections offer very limited or uncertain benefits, along with substantial risks to U.S. security. Invitational inspections occupy an intermediate position.

A brief review of INF and START verification will disclose significant advances in verification procedures that could be relevant to an ABM regime for the 1990s. The INF Treaty requires the United States and the Soviet Union to eliminate all intermediate-range ground-based missiles (range between 1,000 and 5,500 kilometers), all shorter-range ground-based missiles (range between 500 and 1,000 kilometers), associated launchers, equipment, support facilities, and operating bases worldwide within a three-year period. Some 1,752 Soviet missiles and 867 U.S. missiles are to be eliminated, either by prescribed destruction procedures or by firing; their warheads and guidance systems are removed prior to their eliminations. The Treaty also bans flight testing and productions of these missiles, as well as production of their launchers.

Even with the elimination of whole classes of missiles and their supporting equipment and facilities along with flight-testing and production bans, the INF Treaty and associated documents comprise an extremely stringent verification regime. The verification provisions include:

1. A detailed exchange of data, updated periodically, on the location of missile support facilities, the number of missiles and launchers at those facilities, and technical parameters of those systems;

2. Continuing notification of movement of missiles and launchers between declared facilities;

3. An initial baseline inspection to verify the number of missiles and launchers at all facilities declared in the data exchange;

4. An elimination inspection to verify the destruction of missiles and launchers;

5. Close-out inspections to verify that the Treaty-prohibited activities have ceased at each of the declared facilities;

6. Short-notice on-site inspections for thirteen years at declared and formerly declared facilities;

7. The right of the United States to monitor the Soviet SS-25 ICBM final-assembly facility at Votkinsk around the clock for thirteen years to ensure it is not being used for SS-20 assembly;

8. Noninterference with national technical means;

9. Enhancement of national technical means—specifically, six times a year, the Soviets must, on six hours' notice, open the roofs of those SS-25 garages that are not subject to on-site inspection in order to show that no SS-20s are concealed within and must display the SS-25 launchers in the open; and

10. The establishment of a Special Verification Commission, which can be convened at the request of either side to resolve problems relating to compliance with the Treaty.

The INF Treaty contains the most extensive and rigorous verification provisions ever negotiated for any arms control agreement, and its implementation will be costly in both dollars and personnel. In our view, the provisions are probably more stringent than needed to protect U.S. security but were necessary to obtain ratification in the current political environment. The Treaty is far from totally verifiable, however; for example, the ban on production of ground-launched cruise missiles (GLCMs) can be circumvented by converting sea-launched and air-launched cruise missiles (SLCMs and ALCMs), which are not limited, into GLCMs. Nevertheless, the INF Treaty provides a useful precedent for a more complex and militarily significant START agreement, which will include a markedly more demanding verification regime with commensurate increases in the resources required for its implementation. We also believe that there are many valuable lessons to be learned during the implementation of the numerous cooperative measures established by the INF Treaty. These lessons should be learned *before* formulating and negotiating a verification regime for a START agreement; they will also be useful for designing an ABM Treaty verification regime for the 1990s.

The nature and the scope of a START agreement have been agreed upon in the December 1987 and May-June 1988 joint U.S.-Soviet Summit Statements. Each side will be limited to 1,600 strategic nuclear delivery vehicles with a total of 6,000 warheads. A maximum of 4,900 warheads may be on ICBMs and SLBMs, with no more than 1,540 warheads on 154 heavy ICBMs within this limit. These limits will reduce Soviet aggregate ICBM and SLBM throw-weight by 50 percent. The summit statements also include the framework for START verification; this framework builds upon the provisions of the INF Treaty and, at a minimum, will include

- Weapon systems database and data exchange;
- Baseline inspections;
- Elimination inspections;
- Continuous portal monitoring of critical production and support facilities;
- Short-notice on-site inspection of declared locations;
- Short-notice on-site inspection, in accordance with agreed-upon procedures, of locations where either side considers covert activities involving strategic offensive arms could be occurring (often referred to as Suspect Site Inspections);
- Procedures to confirm the number of warheads on deployed ballistic missiles, including OSIs;
- Provisions prohibiting concealment or other activities that impede verification by national technical means and
- Cooperative measures to enhance NTM.

A START agreement will pose serious verification problems. Both rail- and road-mobile ICBMs are difficult to detect and count; rail-mobile missiles in particular can be disguised as ordinary rail cars in the USSR. Sea-launched cruise missiles present an extremely difficult—if not impossible—monitoring task if the agreement limits only nuclear-armed SLCMs, because they are externally indistinguishable from their conventionally armed counterparts. In addition SLCMs can be deployed on almost any surface ship or submarine. Some have suggested that a combination of tagging and OSIs might provide a solution to the SLCM verification problem; this is yet to be proven. *Deployed* nuclear-armed air-launched cruise missiles will be limited, and verification will be accompanied by "counting rules" (that is, an agreed number of deployed ALCMs per heavy bomber). ALCMs also pose the problem of differentiation between those that are and are not nuclear-armed. Verifying the range of both SCLMs and ALCMs will be difficult, particularly if telemetry is not available. Ballistic missile warhead limits will also involve counting rules, the accuracy of which must be verified. START may include limits on ballistic missile throw-weight, which will pose additional verification requirements.

In our view, it should be possible to formulate verification procedures for road- and rail-mobile ICBMs and throw-weight limits compatible with the criterion of military significance. The most difficult START verification problems will arise in monitoring nuclear-armed SLCMs and ALCMs with no limits on their conventional counterparts, even with cooperative measures and on-site inspection procedures. The manner in which these complex verification issues are resolved could affect both the nature of the ABM Treaty and its verification regime in the 1990s.

The short-notice OSIs of *declared* facilities over the thirteen-year period will build confidence in the INF agreement, making cheating more difficult and costly, and provide a useful deterrent to militarily significant cheating. These inspections will pose some risk of acquiring information irrelevant to the INF agreement that might impair the security of the inspected side, but not nearly as much as do the proposed START inspections. The joint U.S.-Soviet summit statements speak of "the right to implement, in accordance with agreed-upon procedures, short-notice inspections at locations where either side considers covert deployment, production, storage or repair of strategic offensive arms could be occurring." This language essentially permits short-notice challenge inspections—anywhere and anytime—of suspect sites in a START verification regime, which is not a possibility under the INF Treaty. Clearly a START verification regime will be far more extensive than that for the INF Treaty, and its implementation will require far greater resources and experience.

ABM Treaty Verification: Historical Issues and Present Concerns

Although verification was not a dominant issue in the negotiating and ratification process, some rather serious ambiguities and compliance issues have arisen over sixteen years of experience with the ABM Treaty. Chapter 3 discusses the major problems related to Treaty provisions. In our view, compliance issues with potential military significance require U.S. attention and prompt resolution. To date, the only potential compliance issues that meet this criterion are those associated with the Soviets' ability to upgrade rapidly a portion of their extensive SAM system, giving it effective ABM capability. Ambiguous Soviet activities such as testing SAM components in an ABM mode, mobile ABM-capable radars, and rapid reloading of likely ABM launchers have potential military significance; the Krasnoyarsk radar and the two radars outside an electronics plant at Gomel do not meet this criterion.

The 1978 and 1985 Agreed Statements made major strides toward clarifying what was meant by "tested in an ABM mode" and the use of radars. Unfortunately, both statements are classified and unavailable to many persons concerned about the Treaty and its future. In our view, all past arms control agreements should be declassified, and all future agreements unclassified, and both should be made readily available to the concerned public. The Treaty is incomplete without the agreed statements, and it is difficult to design an ABM Treaty regime for the 1990s without knowing the Treaty's full meaning.

Some observers appear to be concerned that the Soviets are preparing an ABM defense of their territory and may abrogate or break out of the ABM Treaty. We find little evidence to support this concern and very few persuasive reasons why the Soviets should abandon the ABM Treaty anytime in this or the next decade. In fact, the Soviets have many pragmatic reasons to maintain the Treaty even if they do not subscribe to U.S. views about its contribution to strategic stability:

- They can accomplish many of their ballistic missile defense objectives through legal circumventions of the ABM Treaty (e.g., antitactical ballistic missiles [ATBMs] that may have some BMD capabilities and their extensive air defense and civil defense programs).
- They know that the current U.S. SDI program will run directly into the ABM Treaty in about three to four years, or sooner. Then the United States will have to press for amendments or accept the adverse political consequences of withdrawing from the Treaty.
- They find the ABM Treaty a useful tool in their anti-SDI campaign, which is widespread both in the United States and in Europe.

- They are worried about U.S. technical capabilities. Why should they remove any real or perceived limitations on or inhibitions to the development or expansion of these capabilities?
- The ABM Treaty is considered the cornerstone of arms control. With the current Soviet public relations campaign and their interest in and initiatives for arms control, why would they undermine their own efforts by abandoning the ABM Treaty?

If the United States were truly concerned about a near-term Soviet breakout from the ABM Treaty, one would expect to see an extensive U.S. penetration aids program associated with strategic ballistic missiles. In fact, the current U.S. penetration aids program does not convey a serious concern. Nevertheless, the ABM Treaty verification regime for the 1990s should focus attention and major resources on detecting, identifying, and assessing any Soviet actions suggesting preparation for a breakout, and United States should develop means to safeguard against or counter a possible breakout.

Although no current ABM Treaty compliance issues are militarily significant, in our view, all outstanding compliance questions must be resolved in a mutually satisfactory manner if we are to design an acceptable and durable ABM Treaty verification regime for the 1990s. The Krasnoyarsk radar is the most visible, clear violation of the ABM Treaty even though its military significance is minimal; a mutually satisfactory solution must be found in order to keep this conspicuous irritant from becoming an untreatable wound. The Soviets should dismantle the Krasnoyarsk radar in accordance with the procedures worked out in the Standing Consultative Commission for the dismantlement or destruction of large phased-array ABM radars. This action should be taken independent of other compliance issues.

In general, it is undesirable to link compliance issues. Each issue should be considered on its own merits; a side is either in compliance with or in violation of an agreement. Linkage can be detrimental in that all compliance issues are not of equal importance. It can lead to both sides agreeing with each other to violate a treaty, thus undermining both the treaty and the arms control process.

Application of Verification Precedents to the ABM Treaty Regime for the 1990s

Although NTM has been adequate to detect Soviet compliance and noncompliance with the ABM Treaty to date, NTM alone will probably not provide the effective verification required for maintaining the Treaty into the 1990s, because of the many advances in technologies and the related testing requirements.

Verification of the ABM Treaty was based on NTM with no required cooperative measures. There was no effort to limit research that could not be verified by NTM, and the dividing line between "research" and "development" was the point at which specific activities became visible in principle to NTM. Although battle management is a critical aspect of ABM system effectiveness, its components and capabilities cannot be verified by NTM; they were not limited by the ABM Treaty, and thus they are not a verification challenge. At the same time, the U.S. recognized that antisatellite (ASAT) and antitactical ballistic missile (ATBM) systems have some ABM capabilities; however, it was decided not to attempt to limit such systems in the Treaty. With advances in technologies applicable to ASAT and ATBM systems, their potential ABM capabilities have increased significantly, along with the verification problems associated with determining these capabilities. Clearly future ASAT and ATBM systems could provide a means of circumventing the ABM Treaty limitations.

As the technologies associated with ABM components and systems have advanced, pressures have increased to perform some research, testing, and development activities that could be considered inconsistent with the ABM Treaty. With regard to proposed SDI tests, some people argue that if the Soviet NTM cannot observe an activity, then it is permitted even if the test per se is inconsistent with the Treaty. If the Soviets were discovered pursuing such a course of action, the United States would be raising compliance issues potentially more significant than any existing ones, including the Krasnoyarsk radar.

If the ABM Treaty is to remain viable in the 1990s, the two sides must observe both its provisions and its intent. Basic research is not limited, but the application of that research to ABM systems or components is covered by the Treaty whether or not it is observable by NTM. Neither the Congress nor the public would accept U.S. or Soviet activities inconsistent with the provisions of the Treaty. It is essential that the United States avoid a double standard; it should not limit itself more than it does the Soviets (as in the case of ATBM testing), nor should it take actions to which it would object if they were taken by the Soviets. The danger of creating a double standard could be minimized in the United States by sharing information or combining functions of the Department of Defense, which is responsible for U.S. compliance, and the Intelligence Community, which is responsible for monitoring Soviet activities and providing the data used to make verification judgments.

In designing an ABM Treaty verification regime for the 1990s, it is desirable to assess the potential applications of the verification provisions of the ratified INF Treaty and the emerging START agreement. Although the ABM Treaty verification problems are quite different, the verification regimes associated with the INF and START agreements represent significant advances in applying cooperative measures, including OSIs, to complement NTM; these advances should help enhance the future viability of the ABM Treaty.

Many of the specific verification problems associated with the advancing ballistic missile defense technologies have been covered in previous chapters. Here we will focus on how the verification precedents encompassed in the INF and START agreements may be applicable to ABM Treaty verification and future compliance issues.

NATIONAL TECHNICAL MEANS

With or without any arms control agreements, the U.S. requires extensive knowledge about Soviet military capabilities and intentions. Arms control verification costs involve the *incremental* collection system capabilities and analytical resources required to monitor agreements.

Although NTM will continue to be the foundation for arms control verification, significant modifications and advances will be required to meet the ABM Treaty regime verification challenges of the 1990s. Major advances are being made in verification technology, specifically as applied to NTM. Although much of this technology is classified, it is apparent from open sources that enhanced NTM will be capable of meeting many but not all future ABM Treaty verification needs. Several of SDI's sensor technologies draw on NTM background and will also have NTM applications.

Thus, in designing an "effective" ABM Treaty verification regime for the 1990s, primary reliance should be placed on NTM, and its effectiveness should be judged by the criterion of military significance. If NTM supplemented by cooperative measures cannot provide effective verification, the United States should formulate and fund appropriate military research and development programs as hedges or safeguards against potential Soviet noncompliance.

To date, NTM have focused primarily on activities on the ground. With the advent of space-based ABM sensors, components, and systems, NTM must be capable of providing data on the nature and characteristics of activities in space. For example, is a space-based laser capable of destroying ballistic missiles, or is it only capable of discriminating between reentry vehicles and decoys? (The latter would be permitted, while the former would be a violation of the ABM Treaty.) What is the difference between a space-based laser for antisatellite purposes, a space-based laser for air defense, and a space-based laser for ballistic missile defense? The problem is further complicated if the laser has variable power (i.e., its brightness can be adjusted as needed to identify or to destroy different targets). A critical question is whether NTM will be capable of detecting and measuring the brightness of space-based lasers precisely enough to make these determinations, or whether NTM will depend upon observation of what happens to a target during an actual test.

From a verification viewpoint, it is usually better to focus on ABM testing modes than on specific numerical thresholds, which can be designed around.

Ground-based lasers (GBLs) can be used in an ABM role, either engaging the reentry vehicle directly or using "relay mirrors" overhead, and "fighting mirrors" near the ICBM and SLBM launch points. The effectiveness of a GBL will depend on both the power output of the beam and the size of the relay and fighting mirrors. GBLs can also have an ASAT capability. If a GBL is going to be used in both ABM and ASAT modes, it would be necessary to test the GBL in an ABM mode before testing it as an ASAT. Article VI of the ABM Treaty prohibits giving other than ABM systems "capabilities to counter strategic ballistic missiles or their elements in flight trajectory, and not to test them in an ABM mode"[4]; thus, first testing the GBL as an ASAT would preclude its subsequent use as an ABM. Such testing in either an ABM or ASAT role would probably be verifiable by NTM.

There will also be questions regarding the capabilities of the Boost Surveillance and Tracking System (BSTS) and Space Surveillance and Tracking System (SSTS) sensors: could they substitute for ABM radars, or are they performing only as sensors and thus adjuncts to the ABM system? To answer these questions and to accomplish similar tasks will require additional NTM and modifications to existing collection and analysis capabilities.

DATA EXCHANGES

The INF Treaty and the tentative START agreement call for comprehensive exchanges of data on the numbers, locations, and characteristics of the limited missile systems and their supporting equipment and facilities. A similar approach should be applied to the complex verification problems associated with the ABM Treaty regime in the 1990s. Such data exchanges could be extremely useful for "conventional" and "futuristic" (e.g., free-electron laser) ground-based and "futuristic" space-based ABM components and systems. For example, the nature and characteristics of ground-based ABM radars would assist in determining their mobility, and their permissibility under the Treaty. Similarly, characteristics of ABM missiles and their launchers could help resolve the "rapid reload" issue, since the Treaty prohibits rapid reload of ABM launchers. However, this issue becomes complicated with the use of GBLs in an ABM mode, inasmuch as ground-based lasers possess a reload capability by their very nature.

Given the difficulties of acquiring definitive information on space-based ABM sensors, ABM test devices, ASAT systems, and other non-ABM components and systems through NTM, any exchange of data on the size, performance characteristics, and locations of these items would facilitate and enhance NTM capabilities. Some critics, of course, will argue that "you cannot trust the Russians or the data they provide," that NTM will not be able to confirm or deny the accuracy of the provided data, and that these exchanges will be of little value.

We strongly disagree with this view; if the two sides value the utility of the ABM Treaty, there will be little incentive to provide erroneous information, particularly since such misinformation may be revealed by NTM or other sources. Nevertheless, reciprocal audits of the provided data will be required to maintain the ABM Treaty, whether in periods of détente or of cold war.

ON-SITE INSPECTIONS

Perhaps the most significant recent verification breakthrough has been the Soviet government's acceptance of on-site inspection in the INF and START agreements. Such inspections of declared facilities and invitational inspections to remove ambiguities provide unique opportunities for supplementing the verification capabilities of NTM and thus would make it easier to achieve an effective ABM regime in the 1990s. For example, agreed OSIs of what might be regarded as ABM sensors and components, before they were launched into space, would provide invaluable information on their performance capabilities and thus remove much of the burden placed on NTM. Similarly, a side could use invitational OSIs to dispel ambiguities surrounding either ground-based or planned space-based ABM components, systems, or facilities. OSIs would also be useful in confirming any questionable information contained in the data exchanges.

OSIs of the interiors of many facilities and prelaunch OSIs of certain satellite payloads would pose serious security problems and would therefore be unacceptable to the United States and probably the USSR. However, OSIs involving inspectors and sensors could be useful for determining certain activities; for example, if there were limitations on space-based power sources (such as nuclear reactors for particle-beam devices and/or space-based infrared sensors), prelaunch inspections involving radiation-monitoring devices exterior to the payload would confirm the presence or absence of a nuclear reactor without compromising sensitive characteristics of the payload. Other technological tools have potential applications to OSI; for example, major advances in tagging techniques could enhance OSIs and monitoring by NTM.

Challenge inspections of suspect sites (SSIs) are unlikely to contribute to effective verification of the ABM Treaty, given that the Soviets will never allow U.S. inspectors to acquire definitive data on a serious violation. In addition, SSIs would be detrimental to U.S. security because the Soviets would be able to target sensitive facilities and activities for inspection; U.S. refusal of an inspection could confirm the sensitivity of the facilities, generate reciprocal refusals on the part of the Soviets, and undermine the utility of cooperative measures in general.

NOTIFICATIONS

The acceptance of prior notification of missile movements and activities in the Accident Measures Agreement, INF, and START provides another useful precedent for the ABM Treaty regime. For example, given advance notifications of planned ground- and space-based ABM tests, NTM collection efforts could be focused on acquiring the information needed for assuring compliance with the Treaty. Such notifications could also remove uncertainties about Soviet ground- and space-based ABM activities and the ability to differentiate between ABM, ASAT, and ATBM testing. Should the ABM Treaty be amended to permit either the testing or limited deployment of space-based ABM components or systems, prior notification of the nature, scope, and magnitude of such testing or deployments would be useful to avoid misinterpretation or overreaction to such activities.

NONINTERFERENCE WITH NTM

With technological advances and the movement of more and more activities and satellites into space for enhanced NTM, improved sensors for early warning, and possible ABM components (SDI, Phase I), it becomes increasingly important to reinforce the "noninterference with NTM" provisions of the ABM Treaty. It may even be desirable to extend the noninterference concept beyond that of "providing assurance of compliance with the provisions of this Treaty" to encompass other space-based assets such as early-warning satellites of the BSTS type. For enhanced verification in the 1990s, it would also be beneficial to assure access to telemetric data associated with all space-based ABM sensors, components, and systems; this would require an agreement on a telemetry access provision involving no denial of telemetry by encryption or other means.

ENHANCING NTM

In addition to the already mentioned means of improving NTM, there are useful precedents for making more information readily available to overhead reconnaissance by removing covers or leaving objects in the open for extended periods. Such cooperation could be useful for making measurements of ground-based lasers and their potential power output; certain of these cooperative acts could preclude the need for some OSIs.

SYNERGISTIC EFFECT

Because of synergy between cooperative measures and NTM, the whole of verification will always be greater than the sum of its component parts. NTM will provide specific information for focusing OSIs on suspect activities or facilities; conversely, OSIs can provide information for clarifying and/or directing NTM. In certain cases, improved NTM may preclude the OSI; on the other hand, some OSIs may substitute for NTM. With advance notifications of specific testing, NTM could focus on critical activities. Data exchanges could provide useful information on ABM systems and related facilities that could complement and reinforce data from NTM. These synergistic effects could become very important in assessing the ABM Treaty verification regime for the 1990s.

Verification Regimes for Alternative Adaptations of the ABM Treaty

In chapter 8, Carter describes three alternative adaptations of the ban on ABM deployment based on new technologies in the 1990s. The first assumes that the traditional interpretation of the ABM Treaty is observed; the second and third take more restrictive and more permissive views, respectively, of the Treaty's limitations.

Our chapter has addressed the ABM Treaty verification regime in the 1990s, applying the original interpretation and taking into account technological advances that will complicate monitoring problems. The more restrictive approach, a virtual ban on space-based weapons, would simplify verification problems, inasmuch as it is easier to monitor a ban than to keep track of permitted activities or measure thresholds. This approach also requires prior announcement and descriptions and prelaunch inspections, which facilitate effective verification.

The more permissive approach would permit the creation of an agreed orbiting test range (AOTR) analogous to the Treaty's agreed ground test ranges and could raise the issue of the "broad" interpretation of the Treaty. Such an approach would require defining the location and scope of the AOTR, setting rules for permitted and prohibited testing in the AOTR, and agreeing on which tests can be performed only on the AOTR. This approach would pose major verification problems. It would be extremely difficult and costly to acquire the collection systems necessary to monitor the various permitted activities in the AOTR. It would also be necessary to assure that such activities were not conducted elsewhere in space—a not insignificant task—as is necessary under the traditional interpretation of the Treaty.

The Role of the Standing Consultative Commission (SCC)

The ABM Treaty established the SCC to promote its objectives and implement its provisions. To date, the SCC's activities have centered on compliance issues and implementation agreements such as the dismantling or destruction procedures and the 1978 and 1985 Agreed Statements. The SCC is also charged to "consider, as appropriate, possible proposals for further increasing the viability of this Treaty, including proposals for amendments in accordance with the provisions of this Treaty."[5] Thus the SCC is a proper forum for clarifying the application of advancing technologies to the ABM Treaty and for proposing amendments to the Treaty where appropriate to accommodate these technologies.

As a forum for clarification, the SCC (or the ongoing Nuclear and Space Talks) could specify appropriate parameters that would measure the performance of a particular technology. It could establish "figures of merit" (capability levels to accomplish certain technological tasks) such that system performance above these levels would constitute violations of the agreement; this would also define what constitutes "tested in an ABM mode." The United States and the USSR could unilaterally specify threshold values beyond which concern would be triggered. The SCC could also review programs periodically to determine if the threshold values set earlier should be altered or if new figures of merit should be defined.

The SCC was also charged with implementing SALT II and resolving its compliance issues. The INF Treaty established a Special Verification Commission (SVC) to resolve compliance questions and agree upon measures to improve the viability and effectiveness of that treaty. The functions and operations of the SCC and the SVC are essentially the same; in fact, since the SCC has proven to be an effective forum for implementing bilateral strategic arms control agreements and for resolving most compliance issues, we do not see the need to establish a separate body for the INF Treaty. It would be more cost effective and efficient to combine the SVC and the SCC into a single body responsible for handling implementation and compliance issues for the ABM Treaty, the INF Treaty, a START agreement, and any other future bilateral agreements with the Soviet Union. The role and functions of the SCC in implementing the ABM Treaty regime in the 1990s should encompass the activities associated with proposed OSIs—a role being handled for the INF Treaty by the On-Site Inspection Agency (OSIA)—and with the suggested prior notifications—a function of the Nuclear Risk Reduction Centers (NRRCs) for the INF Treaty. The original concept of the SCC included these types of functions; they should not be separated in any future ABM Treaty verification regime.

Costs of Verification

Significant costs will be associated with an ABM Treaty verification regime for the 1990s. The nature and scope of these costs—involving monetary, technological, and human resources, organizational changes, and management information systems—will depend largely on the requirements to enhance NTM and the extent to which the INF and START verification precedents are incorporated in the ABM Treaty regime (specifically, the inclusion of data exchanges, notifications, on-site inspections, and implementation mechanisms).[6]

There is considerable controversy over what constitutes effective verification and the price to be paid for it. To judge the effectiveness of a verification regime for the ABM Treaty in terms of military significance is consistent with U.S. security and will avoid unrealistic verification requirements and exorbitant costs.

Summary

The increasingly important role of arms control in national security, the recent verification precedents, and the urgent need to strengthen the ABM Treaty afford unique opportunities to advance U.S. and world security by pursuing further arms control agreements including an ABM Treaty regime for the 1990s.

Because the ABM Treaty places certain limits on development and testing, it will become increasingly difficult to verify as new technologies are developed and as testing moves into space. Adaptation of the ABM Treaty to accommodate these new technologies will make verification more exacting—not because criteria are more exacting but because the technological developments and their testing are harder to monitor.

National technical means remain the foundation of arms control verification. Although the United States continues to make major improvements in the monitoring capabilities of NTM and in the data reduction and analytical capabilities of the Intelligence Community, these improvements may not be adequate for the ABM Treaty verification regime in the 1990s. The Soviets are evincing an increased willingness to accept—and in some cases are taking the lead in proposing—extensive cooperative measures, including on-site inspections, which open new and promising avenues for enhancing verification and thus strengthening the Treaty.

Cooperative measures will help, but OSIs are a mixed blessing. They may help increase transparency of weapons and associated activities that are difficult to monitor with NTMs, but certain types of OSIs pose serious security problems. Also, the OSIs themselves may create opportunities for disagreements and disputes that could undermine both the Treaty and U.S.-Soviet relations.

With verifiable limits on strategic offensive forces, there is an urgent need to maintain and strengthen the ABM Treaty by clarifying ambiguities, removing compliance issues, and applying mutually agreed verifiable constraints on the application of new technolgies.

Notes

1. U.S. Congress, Senate, Committee on Foreign Relations, *The INF Treaty,* 100th Cong., 2d sess., April 14, 1988, p. 41.

2. U.S. Congress Senate, Committee on Foreign Relations, *The SALT II Treaty, Hearings,* pt. 2, 96th Cong., 1st sess., July, 16–19, 1979, pp. 239–40.

3. National technical means consist of the primary systems used to monitor compliance with treaty provisions and include the basic intelligence collection systems such as photo-reconnaisance satellites and air-, sea-, and ground-based systems.

4. ABM Treaty, Article VI (a), p. 8.

5. ABM Treaty, Article XIII (1) (f) p. 11. Chapter 11 of this book describes the powers and experience of the SCC in managing compliance issues and Treaty implementation.

6. For an analysis of costs and benefits associated with the INF Treaty and the proposed START agreement, see Patricia Bliss McFate and Sidney N. Graybeal, ''The Price for Effective Verification in an Era of Expanding Arms Control,'' *The Annals of the American Academy of Political and Social Science* 500 (November 1988): 73–90.

II

LIVING UNDER A TREATY REGIME: COMPLIANCE, INTERPRETATION, AND ADAPTATION

Abram Chayes and Antonia Handler Chayes

A S THIS STUDY testifies, the conclusion of an arms control agreement is not the end of the story. In an important sense it is only the beginning. When the ABM Treaty entered into force on October 3, 1972, it initiated an ongoing process of implementation that requires continuous attention from civilian and military officials at all levels of government.

The only element of the implementation process that has received continuing focused attention has been the verification of the agreement.[1] Verification, however, is not an end in itself. It produces an enormous volume of information and intelligence to be analyzed, assessed, and acted upon. These monitoring and surveillance activities have three functions: (1) inducing compliance with Treaty obligations, (2) interpreting the Treaty, and (3) adapting the Treaty to a changing technological and political environment. Although these functions can be distinguished analytically, they are inevitably intertwined in practice. All involve an intensive process of continuous negotiation and political interaction.

A dominating reality is that neither party has any way to compel the other to comply with its conception of Treaty requirements—except for the familiar means of diplomatic pressure. Like questions of interpretation and adaptation, compliance issues can be resolved only by agreement between the parties—express or tacit—on the significance of the situation and what must be done.

If one party should persist in conduct that the other regards as unacceptable, it would undermine the fabric of the Treaty, and the regime would collapse. Given the political investment on both sides and the consequences of abrogation, such an outcome is highly unlikely—unless overall relations between the parties had gravely deteriorated, in which case termination of the Treaty would be only an incidental consequence.[2]

This state of affairs may seem unsatisfactory, especially to Americans, who are accustomed to judicial enforcement of government obligations. But at present, there seems to be no escape from it. The essential premise of living under the ABM Treaty—or any other arms control agreement and most international agreements—is the absence of any coercive means of enforcing the obligations the parties have undertaken.[3] The task is to develop and strengthen other processes that will perform the three functions of inducing compliance, interpreting the Treaty, and adapting it. Such processes are "legal," in the sense that the issues and argumentation will be framed in terms of the legal obligations imposed by the Treaty. But equally they are "political," in the sense that the only means of enforcement is the mobilization of political pressures against the other party.

The trouble-free treaty has yet to be written. No drafters, no matter how prescient, can anticipate and deal with all the issues that will arise once the agreement is in operation. Many problems of meaning surface only when the agreement is applied to specific circumstances. Sometimes issues cannot be settled in the negotiations and are deliberately left ambiguous. The technological and political context changes. Since there are no means for imposing an interpretation on an unwilling party, each side remains free, over a broad range, to maintain its own view of disputed conduct. What one may characterize as a violation, the other may plausibly regard as or colorably claim to be permitted behavior. Experience under the ABM Treaty amply illustrates these propositions.

As a result, the maintenance of an effective treaty relationship entails a continuing negotiation between the parties. Like an ongoing commercial relationship, the ABM Treaty regime must rely on negotiation and other informal means to settle disputes and adapt the agreement to a changing situation.[4] Commercial joint endeavors—joint ventures, long-term supply contracts, collective bargaining agreements—develop ways less adversarial and confrontational than adjudication to interpret the underlying agreements and adapt them to changing circumstances. Even in the private sphere, disputes are not referred to an outsider but are worked out between the parties. A lawsuit is not so much a way of resolving disputes as of liquidating a relationship that has collapsed.

It has not been easy to achieve this kind of adjustment process under the ABM Treaty. The relationship between the United States and the Soviet Union has been adversarial and volatile. Much more than that between co-venturers, it is marked by suspicion and hostility. It lacks a history and framework of common interests. Each of the partners tends to regard compliance disputes as evidence of the other's bad faith rather than as an inevitable part of living under a treaty regime. Thus, they have not been able to establish reliable modes of adjustment and settlement.

Treaty Draftsmanship and Dispute Settlement

In its conduct of arms control negotiations, the United States has sought to avoid potential disputes by careful draftsmanship to eliminate ambiguities in the treaty text. U.S. negotiators have insisted on increasingly precise and detailed formulation of treaty obligations. The Limited Test Ban Treaty (LTBT) (1963) contains five articles and covers two pages. The ABM Treaty has sixteen articles covering four pages, with another three pages of agreed statements and common understandings. SALT II (1979) has nineteen articles and is twenty-two pages long, with five pages of attachments. The INF Treaty contains seventeen articles, a memorandum of understanding on the initial database and a protocol on verification, totaling more than 100 pages, not counting assorted maps, photographs, and diagrams.

A second device to avoid ambiguity is the formulation of prophylactic or "bright line" rules—clear rules that can be applied more or less automatically, without exercising judgment or weighing relevant considerations.[5] An example is the ABM Treaty provision prohibiting deployment of early-warning radars except on the periphery of the country and oriented outward. Any particular radar sited elsewhere would not necessarily be militarily threatening. But a set of such radars deployed at interior sites and linked together might have ABM battle management capability. The siting limitations in the Treaty permit the use of radars for early warning, while forestalling potentially threatening deployments, without requiring subjective assessments of the purpose of each radar.

Similarly, in SALT II the parties dealt with certain weapons system capability issues by arbitrary "counting rules." If an intercontinental or submarine-launched ballistic missile (ICBM or SLBM) is tested with multiple independently targeted reentry vehicles (MIRVs), all missiles of that class will be counted as MIRVed.[6]

All the rules establishing mathematical and technical parameters discussed in chapters 6, 7, and 8 are examples of bright line rules. Regulations governing cooperative verification measures likewise have their share of such rules.

Yet the techniques of textual specificity and bright line rules create problems of their own. Prophylactic rules are inherently underinclusive or overinclusive.

If they are underinclusive, they fail to control some undesirable activity. If they are overinclusive, they forbid some conduct that may be harmless and inconsistent with the underlying purpose of the rule. In such cases, arguments for strict enforcement may be resisted on the ground that only "legal technicalities" are at stake. The Krasnoyarsk radar episode illustrates the political dilemmas of dealing with violations that cross the bright line but are not intrinsically harmful.

Likewise, specificity cannot cure the inherent ambiguity of general categories in which any norm, no matter how detailed, must be phrased. Disputes about meaning simply take place at the more specific level, and the arguments become increasingly technical. Thus, the SALT II Treaty contained a detailed definition of throw-weight as the sum of three specific components.[7] This detail did not prevent extended and acidulous controversy between the parties about whether the "telemetry package," which was not mentioned in the definition, should or should not be included in the calculation. As specificity increases, so does the tension between the strict letter of the text and the underlying purpose or "spirit" of the Treaty. The Internal Revenue Code, said to be the most specific and detailed body of American law, spawns a vast array of loopholes that require continuous legislative and administrative correction.

The treaty creates a high-density legal environment for both American and Soviet military establishments, much like a corporation in a highly regulated industry. Like such corporations, a military organization is charged with an operational task—conducting a research and development program or preparing to carry out a specified mission in the event of war. It may monitor compliance with great or lesser care; its purpose is not to obey the law in some abstract sense, but to achieve the assigned objective. The question of compliance with law arises secondarily, usually when a lawyer, or the treaty partner, raises a question about the applicability of treaty constraints to particular activities undertaken in pursuit of the military objective.[8] The immediate response is rarely to abandon the program. As in business, lawyers will try to find a way to help the organization accomplish its task, either by suggesting marginal modifications in the planned action or by developing a defensible construction of the applicable legal provisions that permits it. Going forward with the program is not necessarily a deliberate or devious attempt to circumvent the rules, but it is often seen as such by outsiders. At that point a compliance dispute arises.

These observations are illustrated by the compliance disputes that have emerged over the past decade under SALT I and SALT II. The Krasnoyarsk radar exemplifies the violation of a bright line prophylactic rule. It is sited some 400 miles from the Soviet–Mongolian border rather than "on the periphery of the national territory"; and its orientation is northeast, across Siberia, rather than outward, as required by the Treaty. Nevertheless, it is hard to fashion an appropriate response to this violation. It is of little military significance and would not justify withdrawal from the Treaty. United States protests have had some, but thus far only partial effect: the Soviets ceased equipping the radar and opened it to inspection by a U.S. congressional delegation. More recently they have turned the radar over to the Soviet Academy of Sciences to devise a peaceful international use.[9] This has not been acceptable to the United States, which has insisted on complete dismantlement.[10] At the close of the Reagan administration, officials were still considering whether to declare the violation a "material breach," which they contend would provide some basis for reprisal.[11]

Disputes about compliance with bright line rules often revolve around the quality and interpretation of the evidence. For example, the United States charged that the SS-25 ICBM being deployed as part of a Soviet "modernization" program was really a prohibited "new" missile. The SALT II Treaty states that a missile will be regarded as new if it exceeds the length, diameter, launch-weight or throw-weight of the original by more than 5 percent.[12] Although the administration has decided that the parameter has been exceeded, its evidence is not conclusive. Indeed, there are differences of opinion within the U.S. government.[13] Such differences are often present, given the range of error inherent in remote observation or calculation under conditions of uncertainty. Thus, even though the rule defining a "new" missile can be expressed mathematically in the Treaty text, the "true" dimensions of a test weapon, from the point of view of the observer, can only be a matter of judgment in evaluating ambiguous evidence.

Equally difficult problems arise when the drafters forgo specificity in favor of general standards, as is illustrated by the dispute over telemetry encryption under SALT II. Article XV(3) prohibits only encryption that "impedes verification of compliance with the provisions of the Treaty."[14] The difficulty is that the announced standard cannot be as easily applied to particular fact situations with the certainty of a bright line rule. The continuing dispute about Soviet encryption illustrates how much room remains for argument about whether the particular level of encryption does or does not impede verification.[15] Thus neither precise, bright line rules nor standards embodying broader purposes can by themselves avoid compliance disputes.

The Evolution of the U.S. Approach to Compliance

THE LAW ENFORCEMENT MODEL

The U.S. approach to institutional arrangements for dispute settlement has changed drastically over the four decades of arms control negotiations. At first, the United States adopted what might be called a law enforcement model of verification and compliance, as exemplified by the 1945 Baruch Plan for the control of atomic energy after World War II.[16] This plan would have created an international agency to control all fissionable material, existing weapons, and peaceful uses of atomic energy. The agency would have been vested with sweeping powers to investigate violations of the agreement. Violations were to be "stigmatized as international crimes" and visited with "condign punishment," to be imposed by a Security Council in which no member would have a veto. "Penalization is essential," Baruch said, "if peace is to be more than a feverish interlude between wars."

Although the Baruch Plan was launched on the crest of the post–World War II wave of enthusiasm for international institutions, it could not overcome the inherent resistance of the nation-state system to centralized coercive enforcement. In today's more fragmented world, it is hard to conceive that any great power would consider relinquishing sovereignty to the extent of permitting an outside entity to fully investigate highly sensitive activities central to its national security, much less allow an outside arbiter to resolve interpretative issues or impose sanctions. Yet the echoes of the law enforcement model continue to sound in U.S. attitudes toward treaty compliance. The concept of challenge inspections (anytime, anywhere) is an example of that model.

THE UNILATERAL MONITORING MODEL

The LTBT, the first arms control agreement between the United States and the Soviet Union, prohibited nuclear testing in the atmosphere, in outer space, and under water. A crucial feature of the agreement was reliance on unilateral monitoring by each party to verify compliance. By excluding underground tests, which the United States believed could not be accurately monitored, the treaty bypassed the contentious issues of inspection. Tests in the atmosphere, under water, or in outer space would be conspicuous. U.S. concerns about compliance and enforcement were satisfied for the moment. The process was reciprocal in that each party relied on its own resources to audit treaty-relevant activities of the other. It was neither joint nor explicitly cooperative, although it was implicit from the beginning that each party would tolerate, and not interfere with, certain monitoring efforts of the other.

Reliance on national technical means (NTM) of verification, implicit in the LTBT, was made explicit in the ABM Treaty. Article XII specifically recognized national technical means of verification as the method of "providing assurance of compliance with the provisions of the Treaty." In addition, by undertaking "not to interfere with the national technical means of verification of the other party" and "not to use deliberate concealment measures which impede verification by national technical means," the implicit cooperation was also made explicit. These obligations are carried forward in later treaties.[17]

The LTBT also marked the end of the U.S. effort to secure international sanctions in case of violations. Instead, the parties incorporated a right to withdraw to protect themselves against breach or significant change of circumstances. Soviet insistence on the "inherent right" of a sovereign to withdraw from a treaty at any time led to a broad, unilateral withdrawal clause: "Each Party shall in exercising its national sovereignty have the right to withdraw from the Treaty if it decides that extraordinary events, related to the subject matter of this Treaty, have jeopardized the supreme interests of its country."[18]

This withdrawal clause has also been repeated with only slight modifications in all subsequent arms control agreements.

The unilateral monitoring model of the LTBT contained no provisions for settlement of compliance disputes. Disputes arose, however, under the treaty prohibition against explosions that "cause radioactive debris to be present outside the territorial limits of the [testing] State."[19] The LTBT does not define *present* or *radioactive debris* (the word in the Russian text is more akin to *fallout*). Both sides conducted underground tests that released radioactive material, and each claimed that radioactivity from the other's test had been detected beyond its borders. Diplomatic exchanges failed to resolve all these issues. The 1987 Noncompliance Report issued by the Reagan administration still maintains that some of the Soviet venting incidents violate the LTBT.

TOWARD A DISPUTE SETTLEMENT MODEL

The ABM Treaty is the first arms control agreement to address the problem of dispute settlement. As described in chapter 10, the Treaty established a specialized institution, the Standing Consultative Commission (SCC), to "consider questions concerning compliance with the obligations assumed and related situations which may be considered ambiguous."[20]

There was hope that the SCC—a permanent institution with jurisdiction over a broad range of issues—might provide a framework for resolving disputes and working out adjustments needed for successful management of the treaty regime. In addition to its authority to deal with day-to-day issues arising under the Treaty, Article XIII(f) and (g) give the SCC a particularly broad role in the area of treaty amendments and new proposals for strategic arms limitation. Yet, despite the wide range of Treaty management issues within its purview, the SCC was granted no separate institutional authority and, not surprisingly, no enforcement powers.

The charter of the SCC emphasizes the voluntary character of the exercise. Article XIII(1)(b) contains an obligation to "provide on a voluntary basis such information as either Party considers necessary to assure confidence in compliance with the obligations assumed." The provision reflects a tension between the SCC's need for evidence and information to perform its tasks and the unwillingness of suspicious adversaries to bind themselves to produce possibly sensitive information.

The SCC was conceived as a confidential institution, sheltered from public political scrutiny—an instrument of the parties. Its scope has been circumscribed to insulate it from broader political issues to enable it to work out issues of treaty interpretation and compliance. It never had the attributes of a neutral body. Under its regulations, proceedings are private and cannot be made public without mutual consent. The USSR has been particularly sensitive on this point. The confidentiality requirement creates another dilemma. Privacy is necessary for effective operation of the SCC, but public information is necessary to ensure public confidence in its work, at least in the United States.

The SCC commissioners are government representatives acting under detailed instructions, heavily negotiated within the bureaucracies of each nation. They have scant freedom of action. With some continuity of personnnel over the years, the delegations have developed a body of practice and experience. But the parties have not encouraged evolution toward a more substantial or independent institution.

Successes and Failures: What the SCC Has Done

Because of the confidentiality rule, there is no published record or unclassified history of SCC activities. Some concrete cases have been discussed in official and unofficial reports, but even here, classification precludes a full account. Appraisal is more difficult still because the performance of the SCC has become an element in the broader political debate of the past decade on arms control policy and objectives.

Official reports and the sparse literature suggest that the history of the SCC can be divided into two periods, mirroring the overall relationship of the superpowers. From 1973 to 1980, coinciding roughly with the period of détente, the Nixon, Ford, and Carter administrations expressed satisfaction with the performance of the SCC. The one report on compliance published by the Carter administration (in 1979 during the SALT II debate) conveys the impression that the SCC had been successful in resolving the issues submitted to it.[21]

The Reagan administration took a much dimmer view of the SCC's record in resolving compliance disputes. The noncompliance reports to Congress, issued annually since 1984, reveal that the atmosphere in the SCC has been confrontational, not cooperative. Until 1987, Soviet explanations were often conclusory and uninformative, and the United States regarded many of them as simply implausible.

For the first time, the United States went public on issues that had been discussed in the SCC, making increasingly strident accusation of Soviet violations of the ABM Treaty and SALT II. The Soviets responded with countercharges and reopened issues the United States thought had long been settled.[22]

The Reagan administration was outspoken in its disparagement of the SCC. Assistant Secretary of Defense Richard Perle, in a 1985 memorandum urging a policy of proportionate response to Soviet noncompliance, excoriated the SCC for failure to correct violations, arguing that the result was to legitimate violative behavior. "Far from resolving disputes over compliance, the SCC has become a diplomatic carpet under which Soviet violations have been continuously swept, an Orwellian memory-hole into which our concerns have been dumped like yesterday's trash."[23] Critics charged, in turn, that the administration had not employed the SCC in good faith and had not sought constructive solutions with due regard to its special institutional capacities and limitations.

In the INF Treaty, the United States decided to start from scratch with a new organizational structure, although it is patterned on the SCC. Article XIII creates a Special Verification Commission, within the framework of which the parties will meet "to resolve questions relating to compliance." The Nuclear Risk Reduction Centers—created by a different agreement and for a different purpose—are to administer notifications, database updates, requests for inspections and other information exchange activities. Still a third agency inside the U.S. government will conduct on-site inspections. Diffusion of responsibility threatens to complicate both verification and dispute resolution by creating unnecessary communications problems and turf fights.[24]

Nevertheless, the public record suggests that over sixteen years, the SCC has handled a number of cases with varying degrees of success. Even though it has never made an institutional decision, it has been the vehicle for resolving some controversial compliance issues and has dealt with some matters of treaty interpretation not unlike those that will be needed to adapt the ABM Treaty to technological developments. The methods and approaches used fall roughly into four categories, with considerable overlap.

1. Warning. The SCC is a channel through which one party can put the other on notice that it is concerned about certain conduct. In the early days of the ABM Treaty, the USSR dismantled a number of launchers before agreed dismantling proceduires had been formulated. Although the launchers were completely dismantled, the process did not conform to the procedures ultimately adopted. The United States raised the point in the SCC, stating that it would insist upon the agreed procedures in the future. The U.S. action appears to have been designed to alert the Soviets to U.S. surveillance capability and to the importance it attached to strict compliance.[25]

2. Cessation of questioned activities. A simple and relatively unembarrassing way for a party to respond to the other's challenge without admitting violation is to stop the questioned activity. The process has been likened to a consent decree, by which a party agrees to stop the activity complained of without admitting wrongdoing. When the United States raised questions under Article VI of the ABM Treaty about the activation of Soviet SA-5 radars at test ranges, the Soviets admitted nothing, but in a few weeks, the practice stopped.[26]

Although the situation has not yet been finally resolved, recent Soviet conduct on Krasnoyarsk is of this character. Work stopped on the installation without any acknowledgment that it violates the Treaty.

3. Explanation and exchange of information. The SCC was originally expected to operate primarily by factual clarification of ambiguous activity. When one party raised an issue, the other would come forward with information and explanation showing the nature and purpose of the challenged activity. Since each side would have extensive, though not complete information about the other, each would be able to evaluate the accuracy of the explanation. But in practice, since information is provided only "on a voluntary basis," performance has been less than satisfactory on this score.

Nevertheless, some sensitive compliance questions have been clarified by factual exchange. In 1973, the United States observed activity associated with existing ICBM sites that it thought might indicate the construction of new launchers in violation of the Interim Agreement. The Soviets explained that the installations observed were hardened launch-control facilities and provided supporting information and data. U.S. surveillance later confirmed the Soviet explanation.[27]

On other occasions, notably the construction of the Krasnoyarsk radar, the Soviets have offered conclusory explanations and steadfastly refused to elaborate. This kind of stonewalling, needless to say, does not promote resolution. With repetitive sparring, relations within the SCC deteriorate while the dispute festers.

4. Elaborating and interpreting treaty provisions. Both SALT I and SALT II charged the SCC with developing agreed procedures for dismantling or destroying weapons scheduled to be eliminated. These tasks were carried out successfully for SALT I, and the SCC has been able to adjust disputes concerning compliance with agreed schedules and procedures. It has produced more than ten procedural protocols and agreed statements, including a set of procedures on accident prevention measures. Both parties have provided and accepted notifications of dismantlements in businesslike exchanges at the beginning of each SCC session.

The long-drawn-out negotiation on testing of air defense systems "in an ABM mode"[28] is the most relevant of the SCC activities for the present study, because it deals with the impact of dual-purpose technologies on the treaty regime. Even in the absence of an explicit delegation of authority, the SCC succeeded in developing an agreed interpretation of the applicable Treaty provision.

When the ABM Treaty was negotiated, the United States feared the Soviets might achieve a rapid breakout to a nationwide system by upgrading the capabilities of antiaircraft missile defenses. The Treaty contains general prohibitions against "building a base" for a nationwide defense (Article I) and "testing in an ABM mode" (Article VI). But the Soviets would not agree to specific treaty language prohibiting the testing of air defense radar against incoming missiles, a necessary preliminary if the radars were to be upgraded. The United States incorporated its more specific strictures on testing in a formal unilateral statement delivered at the final negotiating session in Helsinki, but not accepted by the Soviets.[29]

After the Treaty went into effect, U.S. surveillance indicated that air defense radar was being activated simultaneously with antiballistic missile tests. Soon after the first complaints in the SCC, the joint testing ceased—an example of the consent decree behavior discussed above. However, the United States pressed for an explicit clarification of the meaning of the phrase "testing in an ABM mode." In 1978, the SCC produced an agreed statement on the subject, and in 1985, at the height of the Reagan administration attack on the SCC, the statement was further refined in a common understanding to take account of certain operations not covered by the earlier language.

Agreed statements and common understandings can be used not only for resolving disputes over the interpretation of the Treaty but also for adapting it to changing circumstances. In fact, it is not altogether clear which way the "SAM upgrade" episode should be characterized. In any case, the agreed statement and common understanding that were produced have one important defect. Although they embody international obligations of the United States, they remain classified. There is no apparent reason why they should still be unavailable to the interested public. To the extent that the Soviets were concerned about their confidentiality in the past, it should be possible now to introduce some *glasnost* in line with their new thinking.

In some areas covered by Article XIII, the SCC has been almost completely inactive. The five-year reviews in 1977 and 1982 were perfunctory. The SCC has not been a test bed for the development of new treaty ideas or amendments. No suggestions for "further increasing the viability of the . . . Treaty" have emerged.[30] In fact, there have been complaints that the U.S. delegation to the Geneva arms control negotiations does not take advantage of the U.S. commissioners' experience about the kinds of issues and language that might give rise to difficulties.

Here, as elsewhere, it is somewhat anomalous to criticize the SCC as an institution, since it is only an instrument of the governments that compose it and labors under the inherent limitations of any dispute settlement institution that is wholly controlled by the parties. Since its only power is to negotiate, it can resolve controversies only when the parties are willing to negotiate in good faith. Given the inherently suspicious and adversarial relationship between the super-powers, neither side has an enviable record on this score. When these characteristics dominate, the institution may become little more than another arena for strategic behavior.

The Ongoing Negotiation Process

Although the SCC is an important institutional innovation, it is not the only mechanism available for dispute settlement and adaptation under the ABM Treaty. It is a part—a relatively low-level element—of the continuing negotiating process that surrounds arms control agreements between the United States and the Soviet Union. Indeed the strategic relationship as a whole can be viewed as an extended and continuous negotiating process. A major preoccupation in this process is the management of compliance, interpretation, and adaptation questions that arise under the ABM Treaty and other arms control agreements.

These efforts take place in various arenas. If strategic arms negotiations are proceeding on a more or less continuous basis, as they have been for the past two decades, issues of compliance and interpretation can be handled in that forum. Ordinary diplomatic channels are also open. After a long interval, a series of fairly regular meetings between foreign ministers or heads of state was resumed in the latter part of the Reagan administration in which arms control issues have been an important item on the agenda.

One way of avoiding disputes is for one party to set a conspicuously pointed unilateral example of acceptable behavior. If the controversial issue does not represent an urgent threat, the best course may simply be, as in other types of disputes, to make the position clear and wait it out for a while.

It is important that this range of choice should be more explicitly and systematically recognized as part of the normal process for implementing a regulatory treaty. These forums and methods are not mutually exclusive; work often proceeds in several at once. If an impasse arises in one forum, it may be bypassed by referring the issue to another.

All of these methods have been used in the past. Two interpretative issues that arose under SALT I and had been considered without avail in the SCC—the definition of a heavy missile and the Soviet complaint about environmental shelters over U.S. ICBMs—were referred to the SALT II negotiations, which the United States regarded as a better forum. Ultimately they were resolved there, although a special agreement at the last minute between U.S. Secretary of State Cyrus Vance and Soviet Ambassador Anatoly Dobrynin was needed to put the environmental shelters finally to rest.[31] The U.S. statement in September 1988 that it would not sign a START agreement until the matter of Krasnoyarsk is resolved[32] suggests that this dispute will also most probably be settled in the arms control negotiations at Geneva, if not at the summit.

On the other hand, there are disadvantages to drawing a clear-cut compliance dispute into the overall negotiation process. It becomes hostage to the schedule and agenda of the larger negotiations. It is less likely to be settled on the merits as a question of interpretation and more likely to be compromised or traded off against other issues on the table.

Ordinary diplomatic channels are probably best used as a backup forum, to reinforce what is going on elsewhere. The whole range of U.S. compliance concerns was reviewed regularly, it is said, with Ambassador Dobrinyin during his tenure. Yet, although diplomatic channels are ad hoc and flexible, they are also subject to all the vagaries and delays of normal diplomatic intercourse. Interpretative issues under arms control agreements must take their place in line among all the other questions, large and small, at issue between the two countries.

The results that emerge from these processes are recorded in a variety of ways without very clear legal lines of demarcation between them. At one end, informal agreements between the parties may be embodied in exchanges of notes or meaningful silence. The Interim Agreement on Limitation of Offensive Weapons was extended beyond its original expiration date by coordinated (and carefully negotiated) unilateral statements of policy on both sides. In the same way, the parties committed themselves to abide by the SALT II limits despite the Senate's failure to ratify the Treaty.

A more formal modality is the bilateral agreed statement interpreting a treaty provision. As indicated, this was the method used to resolve the SAM upgrade issue. At the other extreme, formal amendments to a treaty must be submitted to the Senate. A protocol reducing the number of permitted ABM sites from two to one was treated as a new treaty subject to Senate advice and consent.

Most constitutional lawyers take the position that approval by majority vote of both houses of Congress is legally equivalent to approval by a two-thirds vote of the Senate. Yet when President Carter hinted he might submit SALT II for approval by both houses if the Senate proved recalcitrant, the outcry from Capitol Hill quickly persuaded him to abandon the idea.

The most important distinction, as a practical matter, is between adjustments that can be agreed to by the executive branch alone and those that would require the advice and consent of the Senate or approval of both houses of Congress. Here, too, there are no bright line rules, and nomenclature is not a reliable guide. The more important the subject matter, the more likely Congress is to demand and be given a role. But this is by no means a perfect indicator of the solemnity of the treatment that will be accorded. Political considerations, foreign and domestic, are important as always. The final provisions governing environmental shelters over ICBM silos, as noted, became part of the SALT II Treaty, although they could easily have been handled as an agreed interpretation or even less formally, by cessation, without any written acknowledgment.[33]

If an agreement can be said to ''reduce or limit the Armed Forces or armaments of the United States,'' Article 33 of the Arms Control and Disarmament Act requires that it be submitted to Congress.[34] Again, there is no authoritative procedure for determining whether an agreement meets this criterion. For example, it could be argued that limits on testing of the kinds outlined in chapters 7, 8, and 9 do not reduce or limit U.S. armaments. On the other hand, since test limitations might ultimately prevent development and deployment of certain types of weapons—and indeed are designed to do so—they might be considered subject to the requirements of Article 33. If such an issue should arise, it would be resolved by a test of political wills between the president and Congress, as was the case with President Carter's gambit on SALT II.

When treaty language provides a handle, there is a strong tendency to classify adjustments as ''interpretations.'' These do not require a congressional vote since, within broad limits, the president has the power to interpret treaties. Thus limitations on the altitude of space tests or on laser brightness might be considered refinements of the Treaty prohibition against ''testing in the ABM mode.'' It would be harder, but not wholly implausible, to apply the same treatment to an agreement to permit space testing only in an orbital test bed.

Treaty proponents are reluctant to use the formal amendment process because it risks opening up a broader range of issues than those in the immediate dispute. It may not be so easy to avoid this route in the future, however. The controversy over the reinterpretation of the ABM Treaty has awakened Senate sensibilities and may presage an insistence on its constitutional role in treaty adjustments that might otherwise have been handled by the executive alone.

Conclusion

Although disputes are endemic to arms control agreements, even if both parties are seeking to comply in good faith, the need for ongoing negotiations is seldom recognized. The process of dispute settlement has received very little systematic attention from the arms control community. Diplomats take refuge in their ability to devise solutions ad hoc. Scientists and technicians may be repelled by the vague and imprecise formulations of process thinkers. Moreover, it must be admitted that even good process is no guarantee of good results. If either of the parties is determined not to reach agreement, the best institutional arrangements in the world cannot compel it. Conversely, if the parties have the will to settle, little by way of formal institutional structure may be needed to reach a solution.

Yet process can make a difference in the broad range of situations where neither intransigence nor harmony prevails. Considerable theoretical and practical work has now been done on alternative approaches to this process in situations where the objective is to create, rather than to divide, joint gains.[35] A variety of techniques have been developed to make the negotiating process more flexible. These new approaches should be exploited in the U.S.-USSR negotiations and in interagency negotiations within the U.S. government as well.

The foregoing discussion does not lead to sharp and clear-cut recommendations, but certain general conclusions emerge that may guide future action and decision.

1. The SCC, a specialized, confidential channel for the Treaty parties, should be the forum of choice for raising questions of interpretation, adaptation, and adjustment under the ABM Treaty, at least in the first instance. The Treaty designed it to perform these functions. The parties have accepted an obligation to consult in this forum at regular intervals and under agreed procedures. Properly used, the SCC can ensure that genuine questions of interpretation are discussed in confidence and in a relatively nonconfrontational mode. The political stakes and commitment on both sides can be kept low while the problem is explored on a technical and expert basis.

2. The SCC should *not* be used to resolve formal charges of treaty violation made by either party, although it would normally vet such issues before they reached the point of a formal accusation. The SCC is not an adjudicatory institution. It cannot pronounce judgment on disputed issues of fact or treaty interpretation. It does not have the authority or the means to resolve adversarial confrontations. The attempt to use the SCC for these purposes is bound to fail and to create acrimony that will make it harder for the institution to perform its proper functions.

   Formal charges of violation raise the political stakes involved in any dispute enough to require a more overtly political forum—for example, a meeting of foreign ministers or the Geneva negotiating process.

3. If the SCC is reserved for its proper negotiating role, a number of concrete steps would strengthen it for its tasks.

   (a) *Consolidate dispute settlement functions under all arms control agreements.* In our view, SCC-type functions under all arms control treaties should, as far as possible, be consolidated in a single overarching agency, not scattered among many. This does not mean that each treaty should not develop specialized and expert staffs. But some degree of overall integration would permit the cumulation of experience under several treaties and create a corps of experts in the process of treaty interpretation and adaptation. Although the creation of the INF Special Verification Commission was an unfortunate move in the opposite direction, the damage could be minimized by appointing the same officials to serve on both commissions.

(b) *Give the SCC some institutional permanence.* The SCC could be given a degree of autonomous influence by establishing a permanent location and assigning relatively permanent personnel on both sides. Continuity of experience and personal relationships generated in such a setting could contribute to a more flexible and straightforward approach to settling disputes within the institution.

(c) *Begin to consider some form of third-party involvement.* Would the attendance of third parties help discipline the ongoing negotiating process or simply invite posturing by the parties? General Secretary Gorbachev has hinted at a willingness to permit outsiders to become involved in arms control verification, but there has been no serious discussion about the phase of the verification and compliance process where a third party might serve a useful and mediating function. This is worth considerable thinking and discussion between the United States and Soviet Union, but there are arguments against broadening the special, confidential channel that the SCC is supposed to provide. It first needs to recapture its initial purpose.[36]

(d) *Create a stronger obligation for the parties to provide information.* In an era of improving U.S.-USSR relations, it should be possible to give more bite to the obligation of the parties to provide information to the SCC. Under the existing provision, which dates from 1972, the parties agree to give information with respect to compliance issues only "on a voluntary basis." A good deal of data has been exchanged between the two countries since then. The Soviets have become more accustomed to the idea of talking about numbers in the presence of civilians, even American civilians. It may be too much to expect that the parties would accept a binding obligation to produce relevant information. Indeed, it is not clear that such an obligation would be desirable, since it would provide large-scale opportunities for adversarial and intelligence game-playing. It might be possible, however, to develop some sort of express understanding that the parties will ordinarily provide enough detailed information to permit a fair appraisal of questions before the SCC.

(e) *Provide public reports on the work of the SCC.* The SCC could not function under a sunshine law; diplomats must have a degree of privacy and freedom from intrusion to adjust delicate and sensitive questions. At the same time, it is hard to maintain public confidence when the SCC is known only through (possibly one-sided) versions leaked in the face of the obligation of confidentiality.

Nothing inherent in the process, however, requires the results to be kept secret. At a minimum, each commissioner should issue a public report after each session. The U.S. commissioner's report should be transmitted to Congress, where it could form the basis of appropriate oversight hearings. Formal agreements reached in the SCC, such as the agreed statements on SAM testing, should be made public as a matter of course. It is unacceptable that the extent of U.S. obligations under the Treaty is not available to the public.

4. U.S. bureaucratic procedures should be reviewed and revised to reflect the conception of compliance, interpretation, and adjustment as essentially a negotiating rather than an adjudicative process. The current tendency is to treat compliance and interpretative issues as zero-sum games in which one party wins and the other loses. The result is an overly confrontational posture.

Positional bargaining is reinforced by the internal procedures for developing U.S. negotiating positions. At present, these positions are hammered out in complex and formal intragency negotiations, often at a relatively low level, that are as adversarial and confrontative as the U.S.-USSR interchange. The results are embodied in written instructions from which the negotiator cannot deviate without permission. Once reached, these positions are very hard to modify. Indeed, the delegation commonly includes representatives from the agencies involved to ensure that their bureaucratic interests are protected. Intervention at the cabinet level or even higher may be necessary to make any changes.

It might help to achieve a thoroughgoing resolution of ambiguous positions inside the bureaucracy, at sufficiently high levels first. Possible Soviet responses should also be canvassed at a high level, not after the fact. As a first step in what should be a thorough revamping, the appointment of a senior member of the National Security Council arms control staff to chair these interagency processes might help to shape U.S. positions that are more creative, flexible, and responsive.

5. The United States should abandon its present double standard on compliance issues. Today, responsibility for ABM Treaty interpretation is not centralized within the U.S. government. Defense Department lawyers review SDI activities to ensure that they are treaty-compliant. Arms Control and Disarmament Agency (ACDA) personnel monitor Soviet activities. Not surprisingly, the standards applied by the two organizations diverge. SDI

tests are approved if the device is considered incapable of performing an ABM function (for instance, if the test is conducted at power levels lower than required to destroy an ICBM), even if the incapacity cannot be verified by Soviet national technical means. ACDA, however, would regard a similar Soviet test as a violation. Responsibility for treaty interpretation should be vested in a single agency to eliminate this double standard.

By the same token, positions of U.S. negotiators in the various forums should be coordinated and consistent. In particular, the negotiating team in the Geneva negotiations has not taken full advantage of the information and experience of the SCC commissioners on the same or similar issues. The need for coordination will be even greater if, as in the INF Treaty, consultative organizations are multiplied.

6. Neither increasing specificity of draftsmanship nor intrusive on-site inspection should be pursued as an end in itself. To a considerable degree, both reflect the law enforcement conception of arms control, which has proved unworkable. Specificity of language cannot eliminate ambiguity. The cost of detailed procedures for on-site inspection, both in money and in the multiplication of procedural disputes, may exceed the returns in increased assurance of compliance. Careful case-by-case decision is needed to ensure that additional specificity in a particular clause or a particular form of on-site inspection will actually improve the management of the treaty regime. On-site inspection may turn out to be more important as a way for one party to reassure the other than as a means for finding smoking guns—as a dispute settlement rather than a verification device. A rudimentary example is Gorbachev's invitation to U.S. scientists to visit Krasnoyarsk.

The problems of living under a treaty regime are fundamentally attitudinal and intellectual. The most important requirement is for both the government and the public to recognize that disputes about compliance, interpretation, and adaptation are inevitable. Just as there is no way to draft a treaty that avoids interpretative questions, there is no clear-cut method for disposing of compliance issues or conflicts of interpretation once they arise. Dispute settlement will continue to be difficult, complicated, and politically sensitive. A grasp of these basic realities could greatly improve management of the ABM Treaty regime.

Notes

1. Problems associated with ABM Treaty verification are discussed in chapter 10.

2. The Reagan administration has searched for an intermediate ground. Theoretically it should be possible to threaten or even carry out some form of proportionate response, as Richard Perle advocated. See *Responding to Soviet Violations Policy* (RSVP) *Study,* Secretary of Defense, December 1985, memorandum to the president from the secretary of defense. But this creates a

considerable problem inasmuch as if the responsive action were accepted by the other side, rather than serving to bring it into line, the parties would have in effect rewritten the Treaty without going through the necessary ratification process that the U.S. Constitution requires. The Treaty provides for withdrawal but does not provide for lesser steps. The stated intention of the Reagan administration to declare the Krasnoyarsk radar as a material breach raises the very problems of amending the Treaty. See Ralph Earle II and John Rhinelander, "The Krasnoyarsk Radar: A 'Material Breach'?" *Arms Control Today* 18 (September 1988): 11.

3. Even in cases where the parties submit the agreements to an independent arbiter, the tribunal has no means of enforcing its judgment.

4. In a speech delivered at Harvard University, senior arms control adviser Paul Nitze echoed this sentiment when he stated that if we are to "ensure that the stability provided by the ABM Treaty will be retained, . . . an effort should be made to avoid further disputes and future compliance problems by negotiating a clarification of technical activity under the ABM Treaty." Paul Nitze, "The Nuclear and Space Talks: The Reagan Legacy and the Path Ahead," speech to the Harvard University Strategy and Arms Control Seminar, unpublished, November 30, 1988.

5. To the extent a rule approaches these conditions it is said to be "formally realizable." See Duncan Kennedy, "Form and Substance in Private Law Adjudication," *Harvard Law Review* 89 (1976): 1685. Such rules are common in any legal system. Examples include speed limits, and voting age. Specificity in drafting strives to attain this quality of formal realizeability.

6. Article II(5) First Agreed Statement, First Common Understanding.

7. Article IV(7), Second Agreed Statement.

8. The structure to assure compliance with the ABM Treaty was established in the Office of the Secretary of Defense in 1972 and continues to function today under the auspices of the Office of Strategy, Arms Control, and Compliance. In its annual report to Congress, the Strategic Defense Initiative Organization has a section on the legal compliance justification for each SDI activity. That has turned out to be a very controversial section of the report, in part because the legal interpretation of the Treaty has been so politicized (see chapter 4). DOD environmental compliance efforts have also been highly politically charged upon occasion and represent similar tensions between performing the mission and complying with the law. For a judicial view of this tension, see *Concerned about Trident v. Rumfield*, 555 F.2d 817.

9. Michael Gordon, "Soviet Offers U.S. Inspections of Additional Radar," *New York Times*, October 29, 1987; David Remnick, "Moscow Offers Disputed Radar for Research," *Washington Post*, October 25, 1988, p. A-25.

10. Paul Lewis, "U.S. Ties Arms Deal to a Soviet Radar," *New York Times*, September 1, 1988, p. A-9.

11. A material breach according to the Vienna Convention on the Law of Treaties is one that undermines the fundamental purpose of the Treaty. If that were the case, it would appear that the only option available to the president consistent with the Senate's constitutional role in the Senate's treaty process would be to abrogate rather than take "proportionate" reprisals.

12. Article IV(9), First Agreed Statement and First Common Understanding. A separate charge of violation was that the missile violated the treaty requirement that in a single-warhead missile, the warhead should be at least 50 percent of the throw-weight. This issue involves questions of evidence and interpretation similar to those discussed in the text and is similarly incapable of authoritative resolution, despite the apparent precision of the treaty requirement. Article IV(10), Third Agreed Statement, par. (c).

13. Gloria Duffy, ed., *Compliance and the Future of Arms Control* (Stanford: The Center for International Security and Arms Control and Global Outlook, 1988), pp. 64–71.

14. Article XV(3), Second Common Understanding.

15. In this case, the uncertainties were exacerbated because the United States refused to discuss particular fact situations in which it contended the rule was applicable. On principle, it did not want to validate other encryption and was concerned that embarking on any such discussions with the Soviets would betray sources and methods of intelligence collection, see Strobe Talbott, *Endgame*, (N.Y.: Harper and Row, 1979), pp. 194–202 and 237–44.

16. See *The Baruch Plan: Statement by the U.S. Representative to the U.N. Atomic Energy Commission*, Documents on Disarmament 1945–59, 7 (Washington, D.C.: U.S. Department of State, 1960) and *Second Report on the U.N. Atomic Energy Commission to the Security Council*, September 11, 1947, Documents on Disarmament 1945–59, 93 (Washington, D.C.: U.S. Department of State, 1960).

17. ABM, Article XII. Identical provisions appear in the Interim Agreement, Article V, and SALT II, Article XV.

18. Article IV. The Treaty required three months' advance notice of withdrawal, extended in later agreements to six months. ABM Treaty, Article XV; SALT II, Article XIX.

19. LTBT, Article I(1)(b).

20. ABM Treaty, Article XIII.

21. *Compliance with SALT I Agreements, Bureau of Public Affairs*, Special Report No. 55, (Washington, D.C.: U.S. Department of State, July 1979).

22. "TASS Statement Denounces U.S. 'Smear Campaign,' " *Foreign Broadcast Information Service* (*FBIS*) December 30, 1985.

23. See RSVP, n. 2

24. See chapter 10.

25. *Compliance with SALT Agreements, Bureau of Public Affairs*, supra n. 21. Special Report No. 55.

26. Ibid.

27. Ibid.

28. ABM Treaty, Article VI(a).

29. ABM Treaty, Unilateral Statement B. The statement shows that the United States itself was not ready to accept a comprehensive formula, since it exempted "[r]adars used for purposes such as range safety or instrumentation."

30. ABM Treaty, Article XIII(1)(f).

31. See Talbott, *Endgame*, pp. 273–76.

32. Paul Lewis, "U.S. Ties Arms Deal to a Soviet Radar," *New York Times*, September 1, 1988, p. A-9.

33. Talbott, *Engame*, p. 117.

34. Arms Control and Disarmament Act, United States Code 22 (1982 edition): Section 2573.

35. See Howard Raiffa, Roger Fisher, David Lax, and James Sebienius, *The Art and Science of Negotiation* (Cambridge: Harvard University Press, 1982), and Roger Fisher and William Ury, *Getting to Yes* (New York: Penguin Books, 1981).

36. See Phillip Trimble, "Beyond Verification: The Next Steps in Arms Control," *Harvard Law Review* 102 (1989): 885.

12

MANAGING THE ABM TREATY REGIME: ISSUES AND OPTIONS

Albert Carnesale

THIS BOOK explores ways in which the ABM Treaty regime could adapt to changes in the technological and political environment.[1] The authors believe that a regime of the kind currently in effect should be preserved for the foreseeable future, but readers need not share that view to see value in maintaining a regime shaped in ways that will best serve U.S. national security interests.

Surely, Americans would prefer a world in which the United States enjoyed complete freedom to pursue defenses against ballistic missiles and the Soviet Union suffered severe constraints on its ABM activities. Just as surely, the Soviets would prefer that they had widespread and highly effective ballistic missile defenses and the United States was barred from achieving comparable capabilities. Although each side would favor being far less vulnerable than the other side to ballistic missile attack, each recognizes that the other side would never permit the emergence of so lopsided a strategic balance.

In the real word, either both nations will subject themselves to an agreed regime regulating their behavior with regard to ballistic missile defenses, or both will abjure such agreement and be free to pursue their independent ABM objectives.

The ABM Treaty of 1972 represents a joint selection by the United States and the Soviet Union of a world in which neither side can approach deployment of a defensive system that would threaten the ability of a significant portion of the other side's ballistic missiles to penetrate to their assigned targets.

Two decades is a long time, especially in the worlds of high technology and high politics. But twenty years have passed since formal negotiations on the ABM Treaty began, and technology has evolved substantially. The relevant technological advancements achieved or in sight include ground-based phased-array radars with advanced signal processing, permitting more rapid deployment of a widespread ABM defense; infrared sensors so small they can be carried aboard an ABM interceptor missile and guide it directly to impact with an incoming reentry vehicle (RV), perhaps eliminating the need for nuclear intercepts, ground-based radars, or both; advanced antitactical ballistic missile and antisatellite systems with some inherent capability for defense against strategic ballistic missiles; space-based sensors capable of surveillance, detection, and tracking; and space-based weapons, ranging from chemical rockets to exotic lasers, capable of destroying ballistic missiles in the boost phase of flight. Applying the general language of the Treaty to these new devices is a difficult and complex task.

Marked political changes also have taken place, both within the United States and the Soviet Union and in the relationship between them. President Reagan's Strategic Defense Initiative, General Secretary Gorbachev's *glasnost* and *perestroika,* the Soviet radar at Krasnoyarsk and the U.S. radars at Thule and Fylingdales Moor, the extensive and intrusive verification measures incorporated in the U.S.-Soviet treaty banning intermediate-range nuclear missiles, the growth on both sides in the number of warheads carried by strategic ballistic missiles, and the absence of an agreement requiring reductions in strategic offensive arms—these and other political factors, like their technological counterparts, pose important challenges and opportunities for the ABM Treaty regime.

Objectives for the Treaty Regime

Although the primary goals of the ABM Treaty regime are military in nature, the regime is intended to serve economic and diplomatic purposes as well.

MILITARY OBJECTIVES

A fundamental U.S. arms control objective is to maintain meaningful constraints on Soviet arms. Such constraints come at the price of comparable constraints on American forces. So it is with the ABM Treaty. The military benefits to the United States are the constraints imposed on Soviet ABM programs, while the military costs are derived from the constraints imposed on our own ABM programs. As in all matters, we seek to maximize the net benefits—that is, the difference between benefits and costs. Thus far, the United States has seen greater military value in restricting Soviet ABM deployments than in permitting extensive U.S. ABM deployments. (In other words, symmetric constraints on U.S. and Soviet deployments are viewed by us as providing a net military benefit to the United States.) It is likely that the Soviets similarly perceive greater value to themselves in restricting U.S. ABM efforts than in freeing their own; otherwise they would not continue to adhere to the Treaty. Arms control is not a zero-sum game.

Deterrence rests in large part on the ability of a substantial portion of U.S. strategic offensive forces to survive a Soviet first strike and penetrate to their targets. Deployment of an extensive ABM system in the United States probably would enhance the survivability of America's land-based retaliatory forces and strategic command, control, and communication systems. This would have a positive effect of deterrence. But a widespread Soviet ABM system would reduce the penetration of surviving U.S. forces—ICBMs and SLBMs directly, and bombers and cruise missiles indirectly (by interfering with precursor ballistic missile attacks on Soviet air defenses)—thereby weakening deterrence. Most analysts would agree that an ABM system based on currently available technologies probably would be less effective against a well-coordinated first strike than against a ragged retaliatory attack. If so, the protection afforded to a defender's retaliatory forces by widespread ABM would be more than offset by the effect of the other side's comparable ABM system in repelling the retaliatory response. That is, with current technologies, equally capable widespread ABM on both sides probably would undermine deterrence.

The primary U.S. military objective of the ABM Treaty regime, then, must be to prevent the Soviet Union from deploying an ABM system that could significantly degrade a U.S. retaliatory attack or otherwise interfere with important goals to be met by U.S. missile forces. Second, the regime should provide a time buffer (i.e., the time interval between our observing evidence that the Soviets had abandoned the ABM Treaty and their achievement of a militarily threatening ABM deployment) sufficient to permit the United States to take compensating counteractions. Third, the regime should guard against the Soviets reducing the buffer or actually achieving a militarily threatening ABM capability by "relabeling"—that is, by providing ABM capability to military systems primarily or ostensibly intended for other purposes (e.g., warning systems, antitactical ballistic missile systems, air defense systems, and antisatellite systems).

Views differ on what would constitute unacceptable degradation of U.S. retaliatory capability and on how long the time buffer need be. For example, a satisfactory buffer might be established if it would take the Soviet Union

- At least five years to create a defense that could intercept 50 percent of the warheads that would survive an attack on current U.S. strategic forces, and
- At least two years to create a defense that could intercept 10 percent of the warheads that would survive an attack on current U.S. strategic forces.

These illustrative standards could be relaxed if the United States were to accept lower levels of damage to Soviet targets, or deployed (or stood ready quickly to deploy) effective countermeasures (such as penetration aids and/or additional offensive missiles) to a plausible Soviet ABM system.

ECONOMIC OBJECTIVES

Ballistic missile defenses involve two kinds of economic costs: (1) the cost of one's own defensive system; and (2) the cost of any countermeasures taken to penetrate or circumvent the adversary's defensive system. The cost of a U.S. ABM system depends upon the objectives to be served (e.g., What is to be defended? how well? for how long?), the offensive threat to be countered, the defensive technologies available, the performance characteristics and costs of the major components, and the nature and extent of the overall system. The cost of countering Soviet ABM depends upon the objectives set for U.S. offensive forces (e.g., What is to be attacked? to achieve what degree of damage? how quickly? under what conditions?), the defenses to be countered, the offensive technologies available, the costs of alternative countermeasures, and the nature and extent of the offensive responses. None of these fundamental parameters is now known. Little is to be gained by arguing about how much the hypothetical defense or offensive countermeasures to it would cost, and even less by quibbling about which of the two unknown costs is the greater.

What is clear is that if both sides choose to deploy ABM, then each will be burdened with very high costs, covering both defenses and offensive counter-measures. A successful ABM Treaty regime would minimize not only these costs, but also the costs of hedging against possible circumvention, withdrawal, and abrogation of the regime by the other side.

POLITICAL AND DIPLOMATIC OBJECTIVES

The ABM Treaty is by far the most important accomplishment of twenty years of nearly continuous arms control negotiations between the superpowers. Unilateral termination of the accord surely would alter the course of U.S. and Soviet approaches to strategic forces, both defensive and offensive. To the extent that progress in arms control is in reality (as it is in public perception) a barometer of broader U.S.-Soviet cooperation, abandonment of the ABM Treaty could be a harbinger of stormy superpower relations.

America's allies value the ABM Treaty as a symbol of the strategic status quo—a condition in which for more than four decades the world has been free of global war. Prospective changes in that status quo are viewed with suspicion and met with resistance. The French, British, and Chinese have a special interest in maintaining the ABM Treaty. Their missile forces now can penetrate with high confidence to virtually any target in the Soviet Union. If the Soviets were to deploy ABM systems at a level much higher than that permitted by the ABM Treaty, the Chinese, British, and French independent deterrent forces might well be seriously undermined long before U.S. forces were affected.

Allies, neutrals, and adversaries alike see value in the ABM Treaty. It assures them that the United States and the Soviet Union are no less vulnerable to nuclear holocaust than are the other nations of the world. In a global nuclear war, the superpowers would be the first, and probably the worst, victims. If either or both nuclear giants were to abandon the ABM Treaty, others would almost certainly believe that the likelihood of nuclear war had increased. Maintaining a stable ABM Treaty regime is seen as a positive contribution by virtually every nation on earth.

Issues Arising under the Current Regime

The elements of an ABM Treaty regime can be divided roughly into two categories: (1) rules governing research, development, testing, and deployment of ABM-capable systems and components; and (2) processes by which these rules are to be interpreted, implemented, and modified. Elements in the former group are primarily technological in nature; those in the latter category focus largely on institutional and procedural aspects.

TECHNOLOGICAL ISSUES

Deployment is strictly limited by the ABM Treaty. Each side agrees "not to deploy ABM systems for defense of the territory of its country and not to provide a base for such a defense." (Unlike most aspects of domestic and international law, the approach of the ABM Treaty with respect to deployments is based on the principle that what is not expressly permitted is prohibited. Indeed, Article III of the Treaty begins "Each Party undertakes not to deploy ABM systems or their components except that . . ." and then specifies the permitted deployments.) Even the permitted deployments are severely constrained. Each side may deploy a limited number of ABM components at either its national capital or an ICBM deployment field. ABM components based on exotic technologies (such as lasers, particle beams, or infrared sensors) and capable of substituting for ABM launchers, interceptors, or radars may not be deployed at all.

To prevent the achievement of meaningful defenses against ballistic missiles through deployment of technically related systems or components primarily or ostensibly intended for other purposes (such as air defense systems, antitactical ballistic missile [ATBM] systems, antisatellite [ASAT] systems, and sensors for warning of missile attack), the Treaty prohibits providing such non-ABM systems with the capability "to counter strategic ballistic missiles or their elements in flight trajectory." Also banned is the testing of non-ABM components "in an ABM mode." Of particular concern at the time of the Treaty negotiations were large phased-array radars. This problem was dealt with by confining ABM radars to authorized ABM deployment areas and ABM test ranges and by prohibiting each side's deployment of "future radars for early warning of strategic ballistic missile attack except at locations along the periphery of its national territory and oriented outward." Exempted from all constraints are radars for tracking objects in space or for use as national technical means (NTM) of verification.[2]

The Treaty imposes no restraints on research per se; indeed, the word *research* does not appear in the Treaty text. As was anticipated at the time of agreement, both sides have pursued vigorous ABM research programs.

In an attempt to prevent creation of a base for rapid deployment of a widespread ABM system, development and testing of ABM systems and components are constrained. Specifically, the Treaty includes an undertaking "not to develop, test or deploy ABM systems or components which are sea-based, air-based, space-based, or mobile land-based." Only fixed land-based components can move beyond research to development and testing, and the permitted testing may take place only at agreed test ranges.[3]

The technological issues associated with the current regime raise a number of ambiguities and differences in interpretation of the Treaty. These will be examined first. Other major issues are divided into three categories: ground-based systems, space-based weapons, and exotic sensors. Challenges and opportunities of a more political nature are addressed subsequently.

Ambiguities and interpretations

Many of the key concepts and terms employed in the Treaty remain imprecisely defined. Listing these ambiguous notions is a convenient way of summarizing the difficulty of translating the general concepts in the Treaty into specific technical terms. This does not imply, however, that achievement of mutually agreed, explicit, precise definitions is the best way to resolve these issues. Several questions are of particular concern: What constitutes ABM capability? What characterizes a "defense of the territory" of the United States or the USSR, or a "base for such a defense"? How is research to be distinguished from development and testing? What is meant by "tested in an ABM mode"? What differentiates an ABM component from a subcomponent or an adjunct? Each of these issues is examined briefly below.

ABM capability. Air defense systems, ATBM systems, satellite defense systems, and early-warning sensor systems share some of the central technological characteristics of ABM systems and, in principle, have some inherent capability "to counter strategic ballistic missiles in flight trajectory." Just how much ABM capability must a system or component primarily or ostensibly intended for one of these other missions have before it would be considered to violate the Treaty? How should the parties approach this issue? Should "ABM capability" be defined in terms of specific technical characteristics of devices that might be part of an ABM system? If so, by what process would these definitions be updated to keep abreast of technological change? How would compliance be verified?

Territorial defense. Each party to the ABM Treaty agrees to forgo an ABM defense of the "territory of its country," as well as a "base for such a defense." At what point does deployment of systems with some ABM capability constitute a territorial defense or the base for one? For example, would 100 long-range ABM interceptor missiles equipped with on-board infrared sensors and based at either the national capital or an ICBM field, but capable of protecting the entire nation against a very limited attack, be seen as either a territorial defense or a base for one? Would the provision be violated by an extensive deployment of highly capable large phased-array radars on the perimeter of the country (ostensibly for early warning) and in the interior (ostensibly tracking objects in space)?

Research versus development and testing. The line between "research" and "development and testing" is an important one, for the Treaty imposes strict constraints on the latter and none on the former. The conceptual dividing line was based primarily on verification considerations. Relying solely on NTM, neither side could know with confidence what was going on inside the other's laboratories. National technical means come into play only when a component moves from the laboratory into the field. For purposes of the Treaty, *development* refers to those activities that take place after the laboratory stage, and *testing* refers to field testing of a prototype or breadboard model. This distinction appears to be working fairly well for land-based components, because research on such components ordinarily is confined to laboratory buildings. But some research on space-based components would be conducted in space. Where, in this case, would the line between permitted research and prohibited development and testing of space-based systems and components be drawn? By what process would the parties redraw the line to accommodate advances in technology?

Testing in an ABM mode. Any interceptor missile or radar that has been "tested in ABM mode" is considered to be an ABM component and is subject to Treaty constraints on such components. Although two still-classified statements (1978 and 1985) agreed to by both parties to the Treaty help clarify what is meant by "tested in an ABM mode," important ambiguities remain. In light of the potential similarities in testing modes for ABM systems and, for example, ATBM and ASAT systems, more precise definition of the phrase "tested in an ABM mode" may be necessary.

ABM components. Restrictions on ABM components apply to those launchers, interceptor missiles, and radars "constructed and deployed for an ABM role or of a type tested in an ABM mode" and to devices "based on other physical principles" and "capable of substituting for" ABM launchers, ABM interceptors, and ABM radars. The constraints do not apply to subcomponents or to adjuncts incapable of substituting for ABM components.

This arrangement gives rise to two kinds of problems. First, two or more distinct devices, none of which by itself would be capable of substituting for an ABM launcher, interceptor, or radar, could in combination have such a capability. For example, separate sensors might each be incapable of performing all of the necessary ABM sensor functions (i.e., surveillance, acquisition, tracking, discrimination, and fire control), but together might be fully capable of doing so. Should each of the individual sensors be subject to Treaty constraints? Could all be deployed without limit?

The second kind of problem arises from devices claimed to be subcomponents or adjuncts that might be indistinguishable by NTM from ABM components. For example, a long-wave infrared sensor aboard an airplane (such as the United States's Airborne Optical Adjunct) might be used to detect, track, and discriminate among ballistic targets and to provide these data for use by a ground-based ABM radar guiding an ABM interceptor missile to an incoming reentry vehicle. Would it be verifiable by NTM that the airborne sensor system could not also guide the interceptor missile to its target and therefore would not be "capable of substituting for" an ABM radar? Which side should bear the burden of proof of compliance or noncompliance?

Ground-based systems

The distinction between ground-based and space-based systems and components is not as clear as it might appear to be. All of the so-called ground-based systems currently deployed or under investigation employ space-based sensors for prompt early warning of ballistic missile attack, and some would make greater use of such sensors. A ground-based laser might be used in conjunction with space-based mirror relays to attack a ballistic missile in boost phase. Together, but not alone, the laser and mirrors would be capable of substituting for an ABM interceptor missile. Should this combined "ABM component" be classified as ground-based, space-based, neither, or both? The basing question arises also with regard to sensors and interceptors that were designed for deployment in space but would be tested from the ground in a lofted mode.

Should such testing from an ABM test range be considered a permitted test of a ground-based component or a prohibited test of a space-based component?

Although no satisfactory answer to the basing question has been identified, for purposes of this discussion we find it helpful to consider in the category of ground-based systems any ABM system in which the weapons (such as interceptor missiles or lasers) that damage or destroy the offensive ballistic missiles or reentry vehicles are expected to be on the ground when the attack begins.

Current ground-based ABM technologies. The current ABM deployment around Moscow does not pose a militarily significant barrier to penetration by U.S. retaliatory forces. Concerns about Soviet ABM systems employing currently available technology focus on the possibility of a Soviet decision to abrogate the ABM Treaty and rapidly deploy additional ABM launchers, interceptors, and radars. The military significance of an ABM breakout would depend strongly on the pace of deployment. Because mobile components that had been produced and stockpiled in advance could be deployed rapidly enough to present a significant threat, the ABM Treaty prohibits their development and testing, as well as their deployment. It is agreed that the ban on mobiles extends to all but "permanent fixed types," but there is no agreement on how readily and rapidly transportable a component must be before it is considered to be mobile.

Advanced ground-based ABM technologies. Advanced technologies might be employed to augment or replace ABM radars or ABM interceptor missiles. For example, either airborne optical sensors or miniature infrared sensors aboard self-guided interceptor missiles could, in combination with space-based sensors, perform the functions of ABM battle management radars. This raises concerns about the adequacy of Treaty constraints on sensors other than traditional ABM radars.

Ground-based directed-energy weapons, particularly high-power lasers, in principle might be able to substitute for ABM interceptor missiles. Development and testing of such devices is permitted at agreed test ranges, but deployment is prohibited. If such devices eventually could be designed to be effective, the two sides could choose to amend the Treaty to permit their limited deployment. But if the devices could be deployed rapidly, they could pose a significant breakout threat. Does this potential concern warrant further restrictions on the development and testing of land-based directed-energy weapons?

Dual-use technologies. Of the ground-based systems for performing military missions other than ballistic missile defense, ASAT, ATBM, and air defense systems have the most potential ABM capability.

Direct-ascent rockets and ground-based high-power lasers suitable to use in an ASAT role will unavoidably have some inherent ABM capability. Moreover, the testing of such devices in an ASAT mode could be difficult (especially for the other side) to distinguish from testing in an ABM mode. For these reasons, it has been suggested that such types of ASAT systems be banned or that their performance characteristics be restricted. Of course, constraints on ASAT systems have other benefits and costs quite unrelated to the ABM Treaty.

Systems for defense against aircraft are widely deployed in the Soviet Union, and some of these can also defend against tactical ballistic missiles. These systems include mobile launchers for surface-to-air missiles (SAMs) and mobile radars. Over time, modernization of these air defense and ATBM networks improves their performance characteristics and brings them closer to the threshold of ABM capability. Accordingly, those most concerned about the problem of SAM upgrade express interest in constraining the performance parameters of air defense and ATBM systems.

Expanded deployment. Some believe that the ABM Treaty should be amended to permit deployment of ground-based ABM systems beyond current Treaty limits. Two military missions are of particular interest: local defense of retaliatory forces, particularly ICBMs; and area defense of the United States against very small attacks that might be launched by accident. It remains to be seen whether future ABM systems designed to perform these missions would be militarily sound, cost effective, and Treaty-compliant. Analysts generally (although not universally) agree that the ABM technologies available now do not warrant deployment beyond current Treaty limits.

Effective ground-based defense of ICBMs almost surely would require the use of mobile components, and effective ground-based nationwide defense against accidental launches probably would require use of early-warning radars in an ABM mode, deployment of ABM components at several sites, and/or the use of components based on other physical principles (e.g., infrared search sensors and homing sensors on board interceptor missiles) and capable of substituting for ABM radars. Thus, full achievement of either of these defensive missions probably would require modification of the 1972 Treaty regime and would shorten the time buffer to a thick nationwide ABM deployment.

Space-based weapons

Space-based ABM systems and components are directly affected by the dispute over the "traditional" versus "broad" interpretations of the ABM Treaty. Both interpretations prohibit deployment of space-based ABM systems and components, regardless of the technologies employed. The traditional interpretation additionally prohibits the development and testing of all space-based ABM systems and components (although it remains unclear as to just what constitutes ABM capability). The broad interpretation differs in that it would permit development and testing of space-based ABM systems and components provided that they were based on other physical principles. Under either interpretation, challenges to the ABM Treaty regime arise from technological advances and increased interest in space-based weapons for ABM and other military missions.

Measures of ABM capability. As indicated above, the ABM Treaty provides little guidance for determining the point at which space-based weapons such as interceptors, lasers and mirror relays, and particle-beam weapons are ABM-capable. Yet, such definitions can be essential to determining whether a particular device is a space-based "ABM component" and thus subject to the constraints embodied in the Treaty.

Proposed rules designed to assess and constrain the ABM capability of space-based weapons are of two general types: restrictions on testing practices, and threshold limits on technical parameters. Testing might be restricted to certain modes—for example, to an ASAT mode against a nonthrusting target, to a lofted mode, or to an agreed orbiting test range. Threshold limits might be placed separately or in combination on the maximum velocity at which a space-based interceptor may depart from its carrier satellite, the brightness of space-based lasers, the size of space-based mirrors, or the number of weapons in orbit.

Buffer against breakout. Constraints on development and testing of space-based weapons are designed to ensure a buffer against ABM breakout. If such activity were completely unrestricted, the time available to respond to breakout would depend primarily on the pace of deployment. For space-based ABM systems, deployment entails the conspicuous activity of launching satellites. To extend the time required for breakout deployment, constraints might be placed on space launch capacity, possibly focusing the limitations on facilities for producing, transporting, and launching large booster rockets. Thus, constraining the speed with which space-based ABM components could be deployed would mitigate the need to limit their development and testing. Of course, constraints on space launch capacity could impinge upon non-ABM space activities, both military and civilian.

Verification. As Soviet military activities in space expand in coming decades to include testing and deployment of space-based weapons, the United States will seek new capabilities to monitor those activities as it monitors Soviet military activities on earth. New reconnaissance satellites and other kinds of technical collection systems will help. Agreed rules to ease the monitoring task might help even more. These rules could, for example, constrain the time, place, and mode of test; ban methods of concealment and deception; and/or provide for cooperative measures such as data exchanges, prior notifications, and prelaunch inspection of selected payloads. This would require a degree of cooperation greater than was considered seriously during the negotiation of the ABM Treaty, but it is not beyond the range of measures discussed in recent arms control negotiations.

Exotic sensors

Modern sensors serve a wide variety of purposes, such as space exploration, air traffic control, verifying arms control agreements, and gathering intelligence on the characteristics and disposition of military forces and potential targets on the ground, in the air, at sea, and in space. Sensor technology has advanced markedly since the ABM Treaty entered into force. Powerful phased-array radars with advanced signal processing can be deployed relatively rapidly; optical sensors with substantial ABM capability can be installed aboard aircraft or space probes or even aboard the ABM interceptor missiles themselves; and space-based sensors might soon be able to perform all of the functions previously assigned to large ground-based radars. This evolution threatens to undermine the ability of the ABM Treaty regime to meet each of its military objectives: preventing deployment of a militarily significant ballistic missile defense; providing a time buffer against ABM breakout; and guarding against the achievement of significant ABM capability by relabeling dual-use systems.

How might this challenge be met? In particular, how might the ABM Treaty regime be managed to accommodate advances in exotic sensors? Five approaches to this problem have been considered: (1) institute an absolute ban; (2) impose no restraints; (3) constrain testing; (4) limit performance characteristics; and (5) coordinate constraints on sensors with constraints on weapons.

Institute an absolute ban. Under an absolute ban on exotic sensors, neither the United States nor the Soviet Union would be permitted to deploy a nonradar sensor capable of performing the functions of an ABM radar. Yet, some of the capabilities required to perform essential non-ABM functions, such as providing early warning of missile attack and monitoring compliance with arms control agreements, are either identical to or indistinguishable from some of the capabilities required to perform in an ABM role. Thus, an absolute ban on exotic sensors appears impractical.

Impose no restraints. The regime could simply exempt all sensors based on other physical principles (OPP) from the Treaty prohibition on development, testing, and deployment of ABM components that are air-based, sea-based, space-based, and mobile land-based. Thus, exotic sensors, other than fixed land-based ones, would run free. (Large phased-array radars would remain restricted to fixed land basing.) Exotic sensors could perform many important military functions. However, to the extent that such sensors could perform the functions of ABM radars, the absence of constraints on them would drastically reduce the time buffer against ABM breakout and therefore would undermine a principal objective of the ABM Treaty regime. A more moderate approach would exempt only passive sensors from the treaty constraints.

Constrain testing. If the focus were on testing constraints, an exotic sensor would be considered an ABM component if and only if it were of a type that had been tested in an ABM mode. The ensuing challenge would be to define "tested in an ABM mode" in a manner that would serve the objectives of the ABM Treaty regime. In the case of long-range passive sensors, the challenge of verifying a ban on such tests would be extraordinarily difficult, perhaps impossible, to meet.

Limit performance characteristics. Threshold limits might be placed on the performance characteristics of exotic sensors. For airborne optical sensors, for example, the number of aircraft and the size of telescope aperture might be limited. Space-based optical sensors might be constrained by limiting the number of satellites and the size of primary mirror. Verification of these constraints could be facilitated by cooperative measures similar to these considered in the context of space-based weapons.

Coordinate constraints on sensors and weapons. The ABM Treaty imposes stricter constraints on space-based ABM weapons than on the ground-based ones. For this reason, it may be argued, those sensors that could perform an ABM role only if used in combination with space-based weapons need not be limited as strictly as those sensors that could be used with ground-based weapons. According to this logic, satellite-borne infrared sensors for early warning of missile attack, which could in principle be used in conjunction with space-based weapons to intercept ballistic missiles in the early phases of flight, need not be limited as strictly as airborne optical sensors that could in principle work with ground-based weapons to conduct midcourse or terminal intercepts. Devising effective technical constraints on non-ABM sensors is difficult. At a minimum, the regime should prohibit their testing in an ABM mode, should limit their numbers to no more than required for their recognized non-ABM functions, and should provide for inspections and other cooperative measures to facilitate verification.

INSTITUTIONAL AND PROCEDURAL ISSUES

Verification of the ABM Treaty is to be accomplished by NTM. Included in the agreement are obligations ''not to interfere with the national technical means of verification of the other Party'' and ''not to use deliberate concealment measures which impede verification by national technical means.'' There are no provisions for on-site inspection.

A Standing Consultative Commission (SCC) is established as a forum in which the two sides can consider questions concerning compliance, possible amendments, and proposals for ''further measures aimed at limiting strategic arms.'' The role of the SCC has varied in importance over the years since its establishment.

The ABM Treaty is of ''unlimited duration.'' It remains in force unless and until one or both parties take positive action to terminate it. Either party can withdraw upon six months' notice ''if it decides that extraordinary events related to the subject matter of this Treaty have jeopardized its supreme interests.''

The institutional and procedural issues associated with the current ABM Treaty regime are most acute in five areas: (1) verification; (2) dealing with alleged violations; (3) the relationship with strategic arms control; (4) the Strategic Defense Initiative; and (5) U.S.-Soviet relations.

Verification

Although NTM has been adequate thus far to monitor Soviet compliance and (in the case of the Krasnoyarsk radar) noncompliance with the ABM Treaty, NTM alone probably will not provide the verification capabilities required to maintain the Treaty through the end of the century. NTM will, however, remain the mainstay of the verification system.

Thus far, NTM has focused primarily on activities related to land-based ABM components. But the emergence of technologies suitable for space-based ABM sensors and weapons imposes new verification requirements. For example, determining whether a laser in space is capable of destroying a ballistic missile or its elements in flight, or only of antisatellite attack, is equivalent to determining whether a laser is prohibited or permitted under the terms of the ABM Treaty. Accomplishing new tasks of this kind will require expansion and improvement of the United States's NTM assets and its capabilities for analyzing the data collected by them.

Arms control agreements reached after the ABM Treaty, especially the INF Treaty, establish important precedents for cooperative verification measures extending beyond NTM. Comprehensive data exchanges could provide information relevant to determining, for example, whether a space-based laser could destroy a ballistic missile, or whether a ground-based radar under test at an ABM test range should be considered fixed or mobile, or whether a particular large phased-array radar is better suited to tracking objects in space or to early warning of ballistic missile attack. On-site inspections could provide unique opportunities to resolve compliance issues that NTM alone cannot settle. This benefit of on-site inspection, however, must be weighed against the countervailing cost of compromising military secrecy by permitting inspections of sensitive facilities. Prior notification of planned ABM-related tests would permit more effective use of NTM in acquiring the information needed to assure compliance. Cooperative measures such as these can be designed to function synergistically with NTM, yielding an overall verification capability greater than the sum of the capabilities provided by its contributing elements.

Dealing with alleged violations

For the most part, compliance issues under the ABM Treaty, as well as other arms control treaties, involve disputes over the interpretation of language or evidence rather than deliberate efforts to violate its terms. The ABM Treaty establishes the Standing Consultative Committee as a specialized institution for resolving such disputes. The SCC has had considerable success in resolving issues of interpretation so as to meet U.S. concerns, notably in the continuing elaboration of agreed statements and understandings covering testing of SAM components in an ABM mode. On other issues, however, such as the Soviet radar at Krasnoyarsk, the SCC has failed to achieve a satisfactory resolution.

Presumptively, questions of interpretation, clarification, and adaptation of treaty norms should be raised in the first instance in the SCC, where they can be handled at a relatively low level of political exposure, making it more likely that the questions can be resolved on their merits. Some modest steps could be taken to improve the SCC's performance, such as strengthening the obligation of the parties to provide data on issues under consultation.

However, the SCC was not designed as an accusatory or adjudicative institution, and it should not be expected to perform these functions. Formal charges of treaty violation should ordinarily be made and resolved through other, more political channels.

Issues of interpretation and compliance are an inherent feature of any legal regime. A continuing process of negotiation, through the SCC and, if necessary, other channels, must be available to deal with them as an inevitable concomitant of living under the Treaty.

Strategic arms control

The preamble of the ABM Treaty maintains that effective ABM limitations "would be a substantial factor in curbing the race in strategic offensive arms" and "would contribute to the creation of more favorable conditions for further negotiations on limiting strategic arms.'' Indeed, the head of the U.S. delegation stated in 1972 that failure to achieve more complete strategic offensive arms limitations could jeopardize U.S. supreme interests, which in turn would be a basis for withdrawal from the ABM Treaty. Although the SALT I Interim Agreement and the unratified SALT II Treaty have imposed some constraints on U.S. and Soviet strategic offensive programs, the combined number of nuclear warheads deployed on the strategic missiles of the two sides has more than doubled since the ABM Treaty entered into force. Moreover, the U.S. government has accused the Soviet Union of several violations of arms control accords. The publicly available evidence is stronger in some cases than in others; however, virtually everyone agrees that the Soviet radar under construction at Krasnoyarsk is a clear violation of the ABM Treaty. In light of the linkage between offensive and defensive forces, political support for the ABM Treaty regime cannot be sustained indefinitely without progress on limiting and reducing strategic offensive arms.

Strategic Defense Initiative

Clearly the ABM Treaty and President Reagan's version of SDI cannot coexist indefinitely. As long as the United States adheres to the agreement in anything like its current form, the obstacles to achieving the long-term deployment objectives of SDI are insurmountable. Amendment or withdrawal would be necessary even to meet some of the shorter-term goals. A decision either to abrogate the Treaty or to redirect the SDI probably would have to be made within five or ten years. Among the planned tests that could force such a decision are those of the Space Surveillance and Tracking System (SSTS), a space-based interceptor missile, and a space-based laser.

U.S.-Soviet relations

Despite the lack of progress in curbing the competition in strategic offensive arms, and the pressures on the ABM Treaty brought to bear by SDI, the generally positive trends in U.S.-Soviet relations may be sufficient to overcome the obstacles to managing the ABM Treaty regime successfully. The verification measures incorporated in the INF Treaty are far more extensive and intrusive than those in the ABM Treaty and provide a valuable precedent for future negotiations. Discussions in START of substantial and significant reductions of offensive arms, though not yet fruitful, also indicate that both parties are prepared to consider arms control agreements that go beyond codifying each side's defense plans. In recent years, more frequent and higher-level contacts between government officials—civilian and military—have occurred. The U.S.-Soviet competition continues, but the possibilities for cooperation to constrain that competition seem more promising than before.

Approaches

Given the many issues to be addressed in the continuing process of formulating, interpreting, implementing, modifying, and otherwise managing the ABM Treaty regime, and the variety of ways in which each of these issues could be resolved, the number of conceivable outcomes borders on the astronomical. One could hardly begin to define all possible outcomes of interest, let alone identify the one that is to be preferred.

It is useful, however, to outline alternative approaches to resolving the many distinct, but inherently related, ABM Treaty regime issues to be addressed over time. Three approaches are offered here: (1) maintaining the current regime; (2) moving toward a more restrictive regime; and (3) moving toward a more permissive regime. Each approach is intended to be consistent with the fundamental military, economic, and political objectives of the ABM Treaty. The choice among them would depend upon many factors, including how closely and how quickly the United States wishes to approach a meaningful defense against ballistic missiles; the extent to which it wishes to avoid interference by the ABM Treaty regime with other military missions, such as gathering intelligence from outer space, destroying the adversary's satellites in orbit, or actively defending U.S. satellites; the perceived value of formal agreements restricting Soviet ABM (and ABM-related) activities; the implications for other arms control agreements and for U.S.-Soviet relations; and so on.

The three generic approaches are described below. The specific steps listed under each approach are intended to be illustrative rather than prescriptive, and the lists themselves are intended to be suggestive rather than exhaustive.

MAINTAINING THE CURRENT REGIME

This first approach to managing the ABM Treaty regime seeks to adapt to technological and political change in ways that appear to be most in accord with the stated intentions of the United States and the Soviet Union during the two decades since the ABM Treaty negotiations began and with their relevant practices over that period. Attempts would be made to confirm points of implicit agreement and to clarify ambiguities that have arisen. Taking some or all of the following steps would be consistent with the Current Regime approach:

Ground-based systems

- Jointly (i.e., with the Soviet Union) clarify the distinction between fixed and mobile land-based ABM components.
- Jointly clarify the distinction between ABM radars, early-warning radars, and large phased-array radars for space tracking and for verification.
- Implement a robust penetration aids program.

- Agree to confine ground-based ASAT tests to agreed ASAT test ranges; limit the brightness of ASAT lasers to inhibit their ABM potential; and restrict testing with mirror relays to single-bounce scenarios with lofted mirrors against orbiting targets.
- Jointly establish an upper limit on the burnout velocity of SAM interceptors to inhibit their ABM potential.

Space-based weapons

- Jointly confirm that the ABM Treaty prohibits testing a weapon (whether traditional or based on other physical principles) in stable orbit against a strategic ballistic missile or its components in flight or against a target that simulates a strategic ballistic missile.
- Jointly determine whether lofted mode tests are to be permitted or prohibited.
- Jointly establish threshold limits on selected technical characteristics of individual test weapons (e.g., space-based lasers) and of deployed ASAT and air defense systems to inhibit their ABM potential.

Exotic sensors

- Jointly clarify the criteria by which an exotic sensor or collection of sensors is to be judged capable of substituting for an ABM radar.
- Relate constraints on exotic sensors to constraints on ABM weapons (e.g., permissive constraints on boost-phase sensors, such as the U.S. Boost Surveillance and Tracking System [BSTS], would be acceptable provided that restrictive limits are applied to space-based ABM weapons that could be used in conjunction with such sensors; whereas restrictive constraints on midcourse sensors, such as the U.S. Space Surveillance and Tracking System [SSTS], are required to preclude rapid breakout using fully developed and tested ground-based interceptor missiles).

MOVING TOWARD A MORE RESTRICTIVE REGIME

The second approach to managing the ABM Treaty regime seeks to adapt in ways that resolve ambiguities and uncertainties in favor of greater restrictiveness. Taking some or all of the following steps would be consistent with the Restrictive Regime approach:

Ground-based systems

- Ban all ABM development, testing, and deployment.
- Ban all testing and deployment of ground-based ASATs.
- Jointly establish severe limits on the performance characteristics of air defense systems.

Space-based weapons

In addition to taking the steps for space-based weapons outlined above for the Current Regime, take some or all of the following steps:

- Prohibit denial of telemetry, including encryption, and other specified means of interference with NTM during tests, and require that any permitted tests of space weapons (other than ABM weapons, which would remain banned) be conducted only in association with agreed ABM and offensive missile test ranges.
- Ban lofted tests of space weapons.
- Ban ASAT tests against all targets.
- Ban nuclear reactors in space.
- Jointly establish limits on spacelift capacity.
- Require advanced notice and prelaunch payload inspection of all space weapon tests.

Exotic sensors

- Jointly establish limits on the number of airborne optical sensor aircraft and on telescope aperture area.
- Jointly establish limits on the number of satellites bearing large optical sensors and on the primary mirror area.
- Ban nuclear reactors in space.
- Prohibit denial of telemetry, including encryption, and other specified means of interfering with NTM during tests.
- Permit prelaunch inspection of selected sensors.

MOVING TOWARD A MORE PERMISSIVE REGIME

The third approach to managing the ABM Treaty regime seeks primarily to relax the constraints on space-based ABM systems and thereby to redress the double standard under which the Treaty restricts space-based ABM systems far more severely than fixed land-based ABM systems. It might also relax some of the restrictions on land-based systems. Taking some or all of the following steps would be consistent with the Permissive Regime approach:

Ground-based systems

- Implement a robust penetration aids program to compensate for any relaxation of the constraints on ground-based ABM systems.
- Develop and test functional prototype terminal-defense systems comparable in performance to current Soviet ABM systems.

- Permit development and testing of mobile land-based ABM systems and components.
- Permit expanded deployment of land-based ABM systems to provide local defense of retaliatory forces and/or to provide area defense against small attacks or accidental launches.

Space-based weapons

- Jointly establish an agreed orbiting test range (AOTR) for each side within which full-up ABM tests and development of space-based ABM weapons would be permitted.
- Jointly establish limits on the number of sensor-carrying spacecraft that are capable of ABM search, acquisition, tracking, discrimination, or weapon-pointing functions, or that participate in AOTR testing.
- Agree to permit no more than one device of each type (e.g., space-based interceptor, mirror, chemical laser, etc.) in the AOTR at any time.
- Jointly establish threshold limits on key technical characteristics of devices in the AOTR.
- Prohibit interference with monitoring of activities in the AOTR by NTM.
- Ban ABM-capable weapons outside the AOTR, and impose severe limits on the technical characteristics of non-ABM weapons and testing practices of the AOTR.

Exotic sensors

- Exempt from ABM Treaty constraints all sensors based on ''other physical principles'' (i.e., all sensors other than radars), or somewhat less permissively, jointly confirm that such exotic sensors would be considered as ABM components if and only if they were of types tested in an ABM mode. The less permissive choice would call for clarification of the conditions under which an exotic sensor would be considered to have been tested in an ABM mode.
- Implement a robust program of offensive countermeasures to the potential ABM capabilities afforded by the additional Soviet sensors allowed under the more permissive regime.

Concluding Observations

To manage the ABM Treaty regime effectively, we must know what we're trying to do. Each of the three approaches presented here—(1) maintaining the current regime; (2) moving toward a more restrictive regime; and (3) moving toward a more permissive regime—can be implemented in ways that further the objectives of the ABM Treaty. But the choice among alternative approaches is not inconsequential.

Each side would prefer to apply permissive rules to its own programs and restrictive rules to the programs of the other side. To be mutually acceptable, however, the terms of the treaty regime must be the same for both sides.

The attractiveness of a relatively restrictive approach lies in the more severe constraints it would impose on Soviet ABM and ABM-related activities. The attendant disadvantage of the restrictive approach is that it would further inhibit U.S. ABM programs and might also interfere with U.S. efforts in important areas such as intelligence gathering, air defense, and ASAT. Conversely, a more permissive approach is attractive for the flexibility it would permit U.S. ABM and ABM-related programs and unattractive for the relaxation of constraints on corresponding Soviet activities. Trade-offs are unavoidable.

A single coherent approach to all aspects of the ABM Treaty regime has much to recommend it, but such consistency is not essential. For example, in light of the diverse and important military requirements for space-based sensors, and the difficulty of differentiating between sensors that are and are not capable of performing vital ABM functions, a reasonable case can be made for adopting a relatively permissive approach to dealing with space-based sensors. If such a permissive approach were taken, however, the time buffer to deployment of a widespread ABM system would be reduced to the time required for deployment of weapons capable of damaging or destroying strategic ballistic missiles or their reentry vehicles. Accordingly, preservation of an adequate buffer might require adopting a relatively restrictive approach to all ABM weapons that might be used in conjunction with space-based sensors.

Another interesting example arises from consideration of a ground-based ABM system intended to defend against a small attack of the kind that might be launched by accident. To permit deployment (and perhaps even development and testing) of a system designed to defend the entire nation against accidental launches of land-based and sea-based strategic ballistic missiles would require a permissive approach to ground-based ABM systems. Taking such an approach would provide increased incentives for imposing stricter constraints on dual-use ground-based technologies (such as those that might be employed for air defense and ASAT purposes) and for implementation of a robust penetration aids program.

As important as the choice of an approach (or of a mixed strategy of approaches) is the very fact that a choice has been made. The selected strategy should provide guidance not only to those who manage the ABM Treaty regime, but also to those who formulate and implement the nation's defense policies. Adapting the regime to technological and political change will require continuous adjustment of the defense programs of the United States and Soviet Union, as well as continuous adjustment of disputes between the two parties.

Fortunately, the current ABM Treaty regime is remarkably adaptable to change. No fundamental revisions are required to meet anticipated technological or political developments. Moreover, substantial movement toward a more restrictive or a more permissive regime could be accommodated within the existing framework and in a manner consistent with the stated objectives of the United States and the Soviet Union. If both parties wish to maintain an effective ABM Treaty regime for the foreseeable future, by working together they can achieve this joint objective.

Notes

1. This summary chapter draws heavily from preceding chapters in this book. I am indebted to all of the contributing authors for permitting me to borrow from their work so freely and without attribution.

2. The Soviet's large phased-array radar partially constructed at Krasnoyarsk is not within the authorized ABM deployment or testing area, nor is it on the periphery of the Soviet Union, nor is it oriented appropriately for space tracking or use as national technical means. Accordingly it constitutes a violation of the ABM Treaty.

3. The Reagan administration maintained that, under its "broad" interpretation of the Treaty, these constraints on development and testing apply only to ABM components of the kinds existing in 1972 (namely ABM interceptor missiles, associated launchers, and ABM radars) and not to components based on other physical principles; however, the U.S. government has consistently acted in accordance with the traditional interpretation of the Treaty, under which the restriction on development and testing applied to all ABM systems and components regardless of the technologies employed.

APPENDIX A:

THE ABM TREATY OF 1972*

TREATY BETWEEN THE UNITED STATES OF AMERICA AND THE UNION OF SOVIET SOCIALIST REPUBLICS ON THE LIMITATION OF ANTI-BALLISTIC MISSILE SYSTEMS

Signed at Moscow May 26, 1972
Ratification advised by U.S. Senate August 3, 1972
Ratified by U.S. President September 30, 1972
Proclaimed by U.S. President October 3, 1972
Instruments of ratification exchanged October 3, 1972
Entered into force October 3, 1972

The United States of America and the Union of Soviet Socialist Republics, hereinafter referred to as the Parties,

Proceeding from the premise that nuclear war would have devastating consequences for all mankind,

Considering that effective measures to limit anti-ballistic missile systems would be a substantial factor in curbing the race in strategic offensive arms and would lead to a decrease in the risk of outbreak of war involving nuclear weapons,

Proceeding from the premise that the limitation of anti-ballistic missile systems, as well as certain agreed measures with respect to the limitation of strategic offensive arms, would contribute to the creation of more favorable conditions for further negotiations on limiting strategic arms,

Mindful of their obligations under Article VI of the Treaty on the Non-Proliferation of Nuclear Weapons,

Declaring their intention to achieve at the earliest possible date the cessation of the nuclear arms race and take effective measures toward reductions in strategic arms, nuclear disarmament, and general and complete disarmament,

Desiring to contribute to the relaxation of international tension and the strengthening of trust between States,

* Source: U.S. Arms Control and Disarmament Agency, *Arms Control and Disarmament Agreements: Texts and Histories of Negotiations,* 1982 ed. (Government Printing Office, 1982), pp. 139–47, 162–63.

Have agreed as follows:

ARTICLE I

1. Each party undertakes to limit anti-ballistic missile (ABM) systems and to adopt other measures in accordance with the provisions of this Treaty.

2. Each Party undertakes not to deploy ABM systems for a defense of the territory of its country and not to provide a base for such a defense, and not to deploy ABM systems for defense of an individual region except as provided for in Article III of this Treaty.

ARTICLE II

1. For the purpose of this Treaty an ABM system is a system to counter strategic ballistic missiles or their elements in flight trajectory, currently consisting of:

(a) ABM interceptor missiles, which are interceptor missiles constructed and deployed for an ABM role, or of a type tested in an ABM mode:

(b) ABM launchers, which are launchers constructed and deployed for launching ABM interceptor missiles; and

(c) ABM radars, which are radars constructed and deployed for an ABM role, or of a type tested in an ABM mode.

2. The ABM system components listed in paragraph 1 of this Article include those which are:

(a) operational;

(b) under construction;

(c) undergoing testing;

(d) undergoing overhaul, repair or conversion; or

(e) mothballed.

ARTICLE III

Each Party undertakes not to deploy ABM systems or their components except that:

(a) within one ABM system deployment area having a radius of one hundred and fifty kilometers and centered on the Party's national capital, a Party may deploy: (1) no more than one hundred ABM launchers and no more than one hundred ABM interceptor missiles at launch sites, and (2) ABM radars within no more than six ABM radar complexes, the area of each complex being circular and having a diameter of no more than three kilometers; and

(b) within one ABM system deployment area having a radius of one hundred and fifty kilometers and containing ICBM silo launchers, a Party may deploy: (1) no more than one hundred ABM launchers and no more than one hundred ABM interceptor missiles at launch sites, (2) two large phased-array ABM radars comparable in potential to corresponding ABM radars operational or under construction on the date of signature of the Treaty in an ABM system deployment area containing ICBM silo launchers, and (3) no more than eighteen ABM radars each having a potential less than the potential of the smaller of the above-mentioned two large phased-array ABM radars.

ARTICLE IV

The limitations provided for in Article III shall not apply to ABM systems or their components used for development or testing, and located within current or additionally agreed test ranges. Each Party may have no more than a total of fifteen ABM launchers at test ranges.

ARTICLE V

1. Each Party undertakes not to develop, test, or deploy ABM systems or components which are sea-based, air-based, space-based, or mobile land-based.

2. Each Party undertakes not to develop, test, or deploy ABM launchers for launching more than one ABM interceptor missile at a time from each launcher, not to modify deployed launchers to provide them with such a capability, not to develop, test, or deploy automatic or semi-automatic or other similar systems for rapid reload of ABM launchers.

ARTICLE VI

To enhance assurance of the effectiveness of the limitations on ABM systems and their components provided by the Treaty, each Party undertakes:

(a) not to give missiles, launchers, or radars, other than ABM interceptor missiles, ABM launchers, or ABM radars, capabilities to counter strategic ballistic missiles or their elements in flight trajectory, and not to test them in an ABM mode; and

(b) not to deploy in the future radars for early warning of strategic ballistic missile attack except at locations along the periphery of its national territory and oriented outward.

ARTICLE VII

Subject to the provisions of this Treaty, modernization and replacement of ABM systems or their components may be carried out.

ARTICLE VIII

ABM systems or their components in excess of the numbers or outside the areas specified in this Treaty, as well as ABM systems or their components prohibited by this Treaty, shall be destroyed or dismantled under agreed procedures within the shortest possible agreed period of time.

ARTICLE IX

To assure the viability and effectiveness of this Treaty, each Party undertakes not to transfer to other States, and not to deploy outside its national territory, ABM systems or their components limited by this Treaty.

ARTICLE X

Each Party undertakes not to assume any international obligations which would conflict with this Treaty.

ARTICLE XI

The Parties undertake to continue active negotiations for limitations on strategic offensive arms.

ARTICLE XII

1. For the purpose of providing assurance of compliance with the provisions of this Treaty, each Party shall use national technical means of verification at its disposal in a manner consistent with generally recognized principles of international law.

2. Each Party undertakes not to interfere with the national technical means of verification of the other Party operating in accordance with paragraph 1 of this Article.

3. Each Party undertakes not to use deliberate concealment measures which impede verification by national means of compliance with the provisions of this Treaty. This obligation shall not require changes in current construction, assembly, conversion, or overhaul practices.

ARTICLE XIII

1. To promote the objectives and implementation of the provisions of this Treaty, the Parties shall establish promptly a Standing Consultative Commission, within the framework of which they will:

(a) consider questions concerning compliance with the obligations assumed and related situations which may be considered ambiguous;

(b) provide on a voluntary basis such information as either Party considers necessary to assure confidence in compliance with the obligations assumed;

(c) consider questions involving unintended interference with national technical means of verification;

(d) consider possible changes in the strategic situation which have a bearing on the provisions of this Treaty;

(e) agree upon procedures and dates for destruction or dismantling of ABM systems or their components in cases provided for by the provisions of this Treaty;

(f) consider, as appropriate, possible proposals for further increasing the viability of this Treaty; including proposals for amendments in accordance with the provisions of this Treaty;

(g) consider, as appropriate, proposals for further measures aimed at limiting strategic arms.

2. The Parties through consultation shall establish, and may amend as appropriate, Regulations for the Standing Consultative Commission governing procedures, composition and other relevant matters.

ARTICLE XIV

1. Each Party may propose amendments to this Treaty. Agreed amendments shall enter into force in accordance with the procedures governing the entry into force of this Treaty.

2. Five years after entry into force of this Treaty, and at five-year intervals thereafter, the Parties shall together conduct a review of this Treaty.

ARTICLE XV

1. This Treaty shall be of unlimited duration.

2. Each Party shall, in exercising its national sovereignty, have the right to withdraw from this Treaty if it decides that extraordinary events related to the subject matter of this Treaty have jeopardized its supreme interests. It shall give notice of its decision to the other Party six months prior to withdrawal from the Treaty. Such notice shall include a statement of the extraordinary events the notifying Party regards as having jeopardized its supreme interests.

ARTICLE XVI

1. This Treaty shall be subject to ratification in accordance with the constitutional procedures of each Party. The Treaty shall enter into force on the day of the exchange of instruments of ratification.

2. This Treaty shall be registered pursuant to Article 102 of the Charter of the United Nations.

DONE at Moscow on May 26, 1972, in two copies, each in the English and Russian languages, both texts being equally authentic.

FOR THE UNITED STATES
OF AMERICA

RICHARD NIXON

President of the United
States of America

FOR THE UNION OF SOVIET
SOCIALIST REPUBLICS

L. I. BREZHNEV

General Secretary of the Central
Committee of the CPSU

AGREED STATEMENTS, COMMON UNDERSTANDINGS, AND UNILATERAL STATEMENTS REGARDING THE TREATY BETWEEN THE UNITED STATES OF AMERICA AND THE UNION OF SOVIET SOCIALIST REPUBLICS ON THE LIMITATION OF ANTI-BALLISTIC MISSILES

1. Agreed Statements

The document set forth below was agreed upon and initialed by the Heads of the Delegations on May 26, 1972 (letter designations added);

AGREED STATEMENTS REGARDING THE TREATY BETWEEN THE UNITED STATES OF AMERICA AND THE UNION OF SOVIET SOCIALIST REPUBLICS ON THE LIMITATION OF ANTI-BALLISTIC MISSILE SYSTEMS

[A]

The Parties understand that, in addition to the ABM radars which may be deployed in accordance with subparagraph (a) of Article III of the Treaty, those non-phased-array ABM radars operational on the date of signature of the Treaty within the ABM system deployment area for defense of the national capital may be retained.

[B]

The Parties understand that the potential (the product of mean emitted power in watts and antenna area in square meters) of the smaller of the two large phased-array ABM radars referred to in subparagraph (b) of Article III of the Treaty is considered for purposes of the Treaty to be three million.

[C]

The Parties understand that the center of the ABM system deployment area centered on the national capital and the center of the ABM system deployment area containing ICBM silo launchers for each Party shall be separated by no less than thirteen hundred kilometers.

[D]

In order to insure fulfillment of the obligation not to deploy ABM systems and their components except as provided in Article III of the Treaty, the Parties agree that in the event ABM systems based on other physical principles and including components capable of substituting for ABM interceptor missiles, ABM launchers, or ABM radars are created in the future, specific limitations on such systems and their components would be subject to discussion in accordance with Article XIII and agreement in accordance with Article XIV of the Treaty.

[E]

The Parties understand that Article V of the Treaty includes obligations not to develop, test or deploy ABM interceptor missiles for the delivery by each ABM interceptor missile of more than one independently guided warhead.

[F]

The Parties agree not to deploy phased-array radars having a potential (the product of mean emitted power in watts and antenna area in square meters) exceeding three million, except as provided for in Articles III, IV and VI of the Treaty, or except for the purposes of tracking objects in outer space or for use as national technical means of verification.

[G]

The Parties understand that Article IX of the Treaty includes the obligation of the US and the USSR not to provide to other States technical descriptions or blue prints specially worked out for the construction of ABM systems and their components limited by the Treaty.

2. Common Understandings

Common understandings of the Parties on the following matters was reached during the negotiations:

A. LOCATION OF ICBM DEFENSES

The U.S. Delegation made the following statement on May 26, 1972:

Article III of the ABM Treaty provides for each side one ABM system deployment area centered on its national capital and one ABM system deployment area containing ICBM silo launchers. The two sides have registered agreement on the following statement: ''The Parties understand that the center of the ABM system deployment area centered on the national capital and the center of the ABM system deployment area containing ICBM silo launchers for each Party shall be separated by no less than thirteen hundred kilometers.'' In this connection, the U.S. side notes that its ABM system deployment area for defense of ICBM silo launchers, located west of the Mississippi River, will be centered in the Grand Forks ICBM silo launcher deployment area. (See Agreed Statement [C].)

B. ABM TEST RANGES

The U.S. Delegation made the following statement on April 26, 1972:

Article IV of the ABM Treaty provides that ''the limitations provided for in Article III shall not apply to ABM systems or their components used for development or testing, and located within current or additionally agreed test ranges.'' We believe it would be useful to assure that there is no misunderstanding as to current ABM test ranges. It is our understanding that ABM test ranges encompass the area within which ABM components are located for test purposes. The current U.S. ABM test ranges are at White Sands, New Mexico, and at Kwajalein Atoll, and the current Soviet ABM test range is Sary Shagan in Kazakhstan. We consider that non-phased array radars of types used for range safety or instrumentation purposes may be located outside of ABM test ranges. We interpret the reference in Article IV to ''additionally agreed test ranges'' to mean that ABM components will not be located at any other test ranges without prior agreement between our Governments that there will be such additional ABM test ranges.

On May 5, 1972, the Soviet Delegation stated that there was a common understanding on what ABM test ranges were, that the use of the types of non-ABM radars for range safety or instrumentation was not limited under the Treaty, that the reference in Article IV to ''additionally agreed'' test ranges was sufficiently clear, and that national means permitted identifying current test ranges.

C. MOBILE ABM SYSTEMS

On January 29, 1972, the U.S. Delegation made the following statement:

Article V(1) of the Joint Draft Text of the ABM Treaty includes an undertaking not to develop, test, or deploy mobile land-based ABM systems and their components. On May 5, 1971, the U.S. side indicated that, in its view, a prohibition on deployment of mobile ABM systems and components would rule out the deployment of ABM launchers and radars which were not permanent fixed types. At that time, we asked for the Soviet view of this interpretation. Does the Soviet side agree with the U.S. side's interpretation put forward on May 5, 1971?

On April 13, 1972, the Soviet Delegation said there is a general common understanding on this matter.

D. STANDING CONSULTATIVE COMMISSION

Ambassador Smith made the following statement on May 22, 1972:

The United States proposes that the sides agree that, with regard to initial implementation of the ABM Treaty's Article XIII on the Standing Consultative Commission (SCC) and of the consultation Articles to the Interim Agreement on offensive arms and the Accidents Agreement,[1] agreement establishing the SCC will be worked out early in the follow-on SALT negotiations; until that is completed, the following arrangements will prevail: when SALT is in session, any consultation desired by either side under these Articles can be carried out by the two SALT Delegations; when SALT is not in session, *ad hoc* arrangements for any desired consultations under these Articles may be made through diplomatic channels.

Minister Semenov replied that, on an *ad referendum* basis, he could agree that the U.S. statement corresponded to the Soviet understanding.

E. STANDSTILL

On May 6, 1972, Minister Semenov made the following statement:

In an effort to accommodate the wishes of the U.S. side, the Soviet Delegation is prepared to proceed on the basis that the two sides will in fact observe the obligations of both the Interim Agreement and the ABM Treaty beginning from the date of signature of these two documents.

In reply, the U.S. Delegation made the following statement on May 20, 1972:

The U.S. agrees in principle with the Soviet statement made on May 6 concerning observance of obligations beginning from date of signature but we would like to make clear our understanding that this means that, pending ratification and acceptance, neither side would take any action prohibited by the agreements after they had entered into force. This understanding would continue to apply in the absence of notification by either signatory of its intention not to proceed with ratification or approval.

The Soviet Delegation indicated agreement with the U.S. statement.

3. Unilateral Statements

The following noteworthy unilateral statements were made during the negotiations by the United States Delegation:

[1] See Article 7 of Agreement to Reduce the Risk of Outbreak of Nuclear War Between the United States of America and the Union of Soviet Socialist Republics, signed Sept. 30, 1971.

A. WITHDRAWAL FROM THE ABM TREATY

On May 9, 1972, Ambassador Smith made the following statement:

The U.S. Delegation has stressed the importance the U.S. Government attaches to achieving agreement on more complete limitations on strategic offensive arms, following agreement on an ABM Treaty and on an Interim Agreement on certain measures with respect to the limitation of strategic offensive arms. The U.S. Delegation believes that an objective of the follow-on negotiations should be to constrain and reduce on a long-term basis threats to the survivability of our respective strategic retaliatory forces. The USSR Delegation has also indicated that the objectives of SALT would remain unfulfilled without the achievement of an agreement providing for more complete limitations on strategic offensive arms. Both sides recognize that the initial agreements would be steps toward the achievement of more complete limitations on strategic arms. If an agreement providing for more complete strategic offensive arms limitations were not achieved within five years, U.S. supreme interests could be jeopardized. Should that occur, it would constitute a basis for withdrawal for the ABM Treaty. The U.S. does not wish to see such a situation occur, nor do we believe that the USSR does. It is because we wish to prevent such a situation that we emphasize the importance the U.S. Government attaches to achievement of more complete limitations on strategic offensive arms. The U.S. Executive will inform the Congress, in connection with Congressional consideration of the ABM Treaty and the Interim Agreement, of this statement of the U.S. position.

B. TESTED IN ABM MODE

On April 7, 1972, the U.S. Delegation made the following statement:

Article II of the Joint Text Draft uses the term "tested in an ABM mode," in defining ABM components, and Article VI includes certain obligations concerning such testing. We believe that the sides should have a common understanding of this phrase. First, we would note that the testing provisions of the ABM Treaty are intended to apply to testing which occurs after the date of signature of the Treaty, and not to any testing which may have occurred in the past. Next, we would amplify the remarks we have made on this subject during the previous Helsinki phase by setting forth the objectives which govern the U.S. view on the subject, namely, while prohibiting testing of non-ABM components for ABM purposes: not to prevent testing of ABM components, and not to prevent testing of non-ABM components for non-ABM purposes. To clarify our interpretation of "tested in an ABM mode," we note that we would consider a launcher, missile or radar to be "tested in an ABM mode" if, for example, any of the following events occur: (1) a launcher is used to launch an ABM interceptor missile, (2) an interceptor missile is flight tested against a target vehicle which has a flight trajectory with characteristics of a strategic ballistic missile flight trajectory, or is flight tested in conjunction with the test of an ABM interceptor missile or an ABM radar at the same test range, or is flight tested to an altitude inconsistent with interception of targets against which air defenses are deployed, (3) a radar makes measurements on a cooperative target vehicle of the kind referred to in item (2) above during the reentry portion of its trajectory or makes measurements in conjunction with the test of an ABM interceptor missile or an ABM radar at the same test range. Radars used for purposes such as range safety or instrumentation would be exempt from application of these criteria.

C. NO-TRANSFER ARTICLE OF ABM TREATY

On April 18, 1972, the U.S. Delegation made the following statement:

In regard to this Article [IX], I have a brief and I believe self-explanatory statement to make. The U.S. side wishes to make clear that the provisions of this Article do not set a precedent for whatever provision may be considered for a Treaty on Limiting Strategic Offensive Arms. The question of transfer of strategic offensive arms is a far more complex issue, which may require a different solution.

D. NO INCREASE IN DEFENSE OF EARLY WARNING RADARS

On July 28, 1970, the U.S. Delegation made the following statement:

Since Hen House radars [Soviet ballistic missile early warning radars] can detect and track ballistic missile warheads at great distances, they have a significant ABM potential. Accordingly, the U.S. would regard any increase in the defenses of such radars by surface-to-air missiles as inconsistent with an agreement.

APPENDIX B:
THE 1974 PROTOCOL

PROTOCOL TO THE TREATY BETWEEN THE UNITED STATES OF AMERICA AND THE UNION OF SOVIET SOCIALIST REPUBLICS ON THE LIMITATION OF ANTI-BALLISTIC MISSILE SYSTEMS

Signed at Moscow July 3, 1974
Ratification advised by U.S. Senate November 10, 1975
Ratified by U.S. President March 19, 1976
Instruments of ratification exchanged May 24, 1976
Proclaimed by U.S. President July 6, 1976
Entered into force May 24, 1976

The United States of America and the Union of Soviet Socialist Republics, hereinafter referred to as the Parties,

Proceeding from the Basic Principles of Relations between the United States of America and the Union of Soviet Socialist Republics signed on May 29, 1972,

Desiring to further the objectives of the Treaty between the United States of America and the Union of Soviet Socialist Republics on the Limitation of Anti-Ballistic Missile Systems signed on May 26, 1972, hereinafter referred to as the Treaty,

Reaffirming their conviction that the adoption of further measures for the limitation of strategic arms would contribute to strengthening international peace and security,

Proceeding from the premise that further limitation of anti-ballistic missile systems will create more favorable conditions for the completion of work on a permanent agreement on more complete measures for the limitation of strategic offensive arms,

Have agreed as follows:

ARTICLE I

1. Each Party shall be limited at any one time to a single area out of the two provided in Article III of the Treaty for deployment of anti-ballistic missile (ABM) systems or their components and accordingly shall not exercise its right to deploy an ABM system or its components in the second of the two ABM system deployment areas permitted by Article III of the Treaty, except as an exchange of one permitted area for the other in accordance with Article II of this Protocol.

2. Accordingly, except as permitted by Article II of this Protocol: the United States of America shall not deploy an ABM system or its components in the area centered on its capital, as permitted by Article III(a) of the Treaty, and the Soviet Union shall not deploy an ABM system or its components in the deployment area of intercontinental ballistic missile (ICBM) silo launchers as permitted by Article III(b) of the Treaty.

ARTICLE II

1. Each Party shall have the right to dismantle or destroy its ABM system and the components thereof in the area where they are presently deployed and to deploy an ABM system or its components in the alternative area permitted by Article III of the Treaty, provided that prior to initiation of construction, notification is given in accord with the procedure agreed to in the Standing Consultative Commission, during the year beginning October 3, 1977 and ending October 2, 1978, or during any year which commences at five year intervals thereafter, those being the years for periodic review of the Treaty, as provided in Article XIV of the Treaty. This right may be exercised only once.

2. Accordingly, in the event of such notice, the United States would have the right to dismantle or destroy the ABM system and its components in the deployment area of ICBM silo launchers and to deploy an ABM system or its components in an area centered on its capital, as permitted by Article III(a) of the Treaty, and the Soviet Union would have the right to dismantle or destroy the ABM system and its components in the area centered on its capital and to deploy an ABM system or its components in an area containing ICBM silo launchers, as permitted by Article III(b) of the Treaty.

3. Dismantling or destruction and deployment of ABM systems or their components and the notification thereof shall be carried out in accordance with Article VIII of the ABM Treaty and procedures agreed to in the Standing Consultative Commission.

ARTICLE III

The rights and obligations established by the Treaty remain in force and shall be complied with by the Parties except to the extent modified by this Protocol. In particular, the deployment of an ABM system or its components within the area selected shall remain limited by the levels and other requirements established by the Treaty.

ARTICLE IV

This Protocol shall be subject to ratification in accordance with the constitutional procedures of each Party. It shall enter into force on the day of the exchange of instruments of ratification and shall thereafter be considered an integral part of the Treaty.

DONE at Moscow on July 3, 1974, in duplicate, in the English and Russian languages, both texts being equally authentic.

For the United States of America:

RICHARD NIXON

President of the United States of America

For the Union of Soviet Socialist Republics:

L. I. BREZHNEV

General Secretary of the Central Committee of the CPSU

LIST OF ACRONYMS

ABM   Antiballistic missile
ABMT   Anti-Ballistic Missile Treaty
ACDA   Arms Control and Disarmament Agency
ALCM   Air-launched cruise missile
ALPS   Accidental Launch Protection System
AOA   Airborne Optical Adjunct
AOTR   Agreed orbital test range
APS   American Physical Society
ASAT   Antisatellite (weapon)
ATBM   Antitactical ballistic missile

BMD   Ballistic missile defense
BMEWS   Ballistic missile early warning system
BSTS   Boost Surveillance and Tracking System

CWDD   Continuous wave deuterium demonstrator

DEW   Directed-energy weapon
DSAT   Defense against antisatellite weapons
DSP   Defense Support Program

ERIS   Exoatmospheric Reentry Vehicle Interceptor System

FEL   Free-electron laser
FOC   Full operational capability
FPA   Focal plane array

GBR   Ground-based radar
GEO   Geosynchronous equatorial orbit
GLCM   Ground-launched cruise missile
GSTS   Ground Surveillance and Tracking System
GTA   Ground test accelerator

HEDI   High Endoatmospheric Defense Interceptor

ICBM   Intercontinental ballistic missile
INF   Intermediate-range nuclear forces

IOC   Initial operational capability
IR   Infrared

JCS   Joint Chiefs of Staff

LADAR   Space-based laser radar
LASER   Light amplification by the stimulation of electromagnetic radiation
LEO   Low earth orbit
LoADS   Low-altitude Defense System
LODE   Large optics demonstration experiment
LPAR   Large-perimeter acquisition radar
LST   Large space telescope
LTBT   Limited Test Ban Treaty
LWIR   Long-wavelength infrared radar (band)

MAD   Mutually assured destruction
MIRV   Multiple independently targetable reentry vehicle
MWIR   Midwavelength infrared radar (band)

NATO   North Atlantic Treaty Organization
NCA   National Command Authority (Defense)
NPB   Neutral particle beam
NRRC   Nuclear Risk Reduction Center
NTM   National technical means (of verification)

OSI   On-site inspection
OSIA   On-Site Inspection Agency
OT&E   Operational test and evaluation
OTH   Over-the-horizon (radar)

PBV   Postboost vehicle
PBW   Particle-beam weapon

R&D   Research and development
RDT&E   Research, development, testing, and evaluation
RV   Reentry vehicle

SALT   Strategic Arms Limitation Talks
SAM   Surface-to-air missile
SBI   Space-based interceptor
SCC   Standing Consultative Commission
SDI   Strategic Defense Initiative
SDIO   Strategic Defense Initiative Organization
SLBM   Submarine-launched ballistic missile
SLCM   Sea-launched cruise missile
SNDV   Strategic nuclear delivery vehicle
SPS   Solar-powered system
SRAM   Short-range attack missile

SSI   Suspect site inspection
SSTS   Space Surveillance and Tracking System
START   Strategic Arms Reduction Talks
SWIR   Shortwavelength infrared radar (band)

TBM   Tactical ballistic missile
TIR   Terminal Imaging Radar

VLBI   Very-long-baseline interferometry

GLOSSARY

ACCIDENT MEASURES AGREEMENT   Agreement signed between the United States and the Soviet Union in 1971 as a confidence-building measure to reduce the risk of nuclear war.

ACCIDENTAL LAUNCH PROTECTION SYSTEM (ALPS)   An ABM system designed to protect against the accidental or unauthorized launch of a few missiles. The United States has considered the possibility of pursuing ALPS in place of the more costly and technologically questionable "foolproof" SDI, but no concrete decision has yet been reached. The debate concerns in part the number of ALPS sites needed to protect the continental United States. Anything more than one site would require an amendment to or a renegotiation of the 1972 ABM Treaty.

AGREED ORBITAL TEST RANGE (AOTR)   Proposed but as of yet not completely defined concept in which full-up testing of space-based ABMs would be allowed. Mutually agreed rules would be needed to define its location and scope, what types of testing could be done, and what kinds of tests could be done only on the range and not elsewhere in space.

AIRBORNE OPTICAL ADJUNCT (AOA)   A long-wavelength infrared radar (LWIR) sensor carried on an aircraft for high-altitude operations. As of the end of the Reagan administration, the AOA was seen as a major test program to resolve many of the passive sensor issues related to all midcourse sensor systems, including the ability to detect and track incoming targets, to discriminate warheads from decoys, and to transfer data to a battle management system.

ANTIBALLISTIC MISSILE (ABM)   A defensive missile designed to intercept and destroy a strategic offensive missile or its reentry vehicle(s). Current ABM systems typically consist of (1) short- or long-range interceptor missiles, (2) launchers for the interceptor missiles (either in above-ground cannisters or in below-ground silos), (3) radars for identifying and tracking targets and then guiding the interceptors to them, and (4) support equipment. The United States and USSR are both restricted to one ABM site by the 1972 ABM Treaty and its 1974 Protocol. The term is also used interchangeably with *ballistic missile defense (BMD)*.

255

ANTI-BALLISTIC MISSILE TREATY [ABMT]   Treaty signed by the United States and the Soviet Union in 1972 as part of SALT I that restricted each side to two ABM sites (subsequently reduced to one site in the ABM Treaty's 1974 Protocol). In addition, the Treaty limited each side to 100 interceptors and 100 launchers at each site and created the Standing Consultative Commission (SCC). The agreement is of unlimited duration and is subject to review every five years. Technological advances in both traditional ABM systems and other more advanced or "exotic" ones threaten to undermine the original intent of the treaty regime in the future. (See Appendix.)

ANTISATELLITE (ASAT) WEAPON   A weapon designed to destroy satellites.

ANTITACTICAL BALLISTIC MISSILE (ATBM)   These defenses are designed primarily to destroy tactical ballistic missiles, which fall into two groups, *short-range ballistic missiles* (*SRBM*) with a range of less than 500 kilometers (km) and *medium-range ballistic missiles* (*MRBM*) with a range of less than 2,000 km. The ABM Treaty does not expressly prohibit the upgrading of surface-to-air (SAM) antitactical ballistic missiles, as opposed to strategic ballistic missiles. Currently, SAM upgrading has reached such an advanced level that some new SAM developments can have direct application to *ballistic missile defense* (BMD) technology and as such increase the possibility of ABM breakout. See *Surface-to-Air Missile* (*SAM*).

ARMS CONTROL AND DISARMAMENT AGENCY (ACDA)   Created in 1961 by the Arms Control and Disarmament Act, it is the principal agency of the U.S. government responsible for arms control policy.

BALLISTIC MISSILE DEFENSE (BMD)   A term that is interchangeable with antiballistic missile defense. See *Antiballistic Missile* (*ABM*).

BALLISTIC MISSILE EARLY-WARNING SYSTEM (BMEWS)   The U.S. radar system used for detection and early warning of attack by enemy intercontinental weapons. Operational since 1962, BMEWS consists of large phased-array radars at three sites: Thule, Greenland; Fylingdales Moor, England; and Clear, Alaska. The radars in Greenland and England were recently modernized. For a description of the Soviet early-warning network, see *Hen House Radar*.

BALLOON-ENCLOSED RVs   Antisimulation decoy technique in which reentry vehicles are placed inside of balloon decoys to disguise the RVs as decoys. In this case, empty balloons become "replica decoys" (objects that appear the same as reentry vehicles) rather than "traffic decoys" (objects that are meant merely to keep the sensor system busy).

BOOST PHASE   The initial stage of a missile launch, during which time the missile is being powered by its engines. This stage usually lasts from two to five minutes. Destruction of a missile in this stage reduces the size of the attacking forces to be engaged later, because all the incoming missiles warheads and decoys are destroyed.

BOOST SURVEILLANCE AND TRACKING SYSTEM (BSTS)   Proposed geostationary orbit satellite sensor system for early warning and tracking of Soviet ballistic missiles either as a replacement for the *Defense Support Program* early-warning satellite system or as part of a ballistic missile defense system.

BUS   See *Postboost Vehicle* (*PBV*).

CHAFF   Strips of metal foil dispersed around incoming warheads that reflect multiple signals to confuse radar. See *Penetration Aids*.

CONTINUOUS-WAVE (CW) LASER   Any laser whose energy is either contained in pulses of energy lasting on the order of seconds or made up of many repetitively emitted smaller pulses, the aggregate of which lasts on the order of seconds.

CRUISE MISSILE   An unmanned missile propelled by an air-breathing engine that operates within the earth's atmosphere and maintains thrust throughout its flight. Current U.S. systems are considered to be more technologically advanced, of smaller size, and equipped with better guidance systems than Soviet missiles. Cruise missiles may be launched from land (*GLCM,* or *ground-launched cruise missile*), sea (*SLCM,* or *sea-launched cruise missile*), and air (*ALCM,* or *air-launched cruise missile*).

DECOY   A device or technique employed by the offense to hide reentry vehicles in order to prevent discrimination sensors from distinguishing threatening from nonthreatening objects.

DEFENSE SUPPORT PROGRAM (DSP)   A currently active satellite system based in geostationary orbit to provide early warning of ballistic missile attack.

DIRECT-ASCENT ROCKET   Antisatellite missile that travels directly toward its intended target without first going into a stable orbit around the earth.

DIRECTED-ENERGY WEAPON (DEW)   A weapon that destroys its targets by delivering energy to them at or near the speed of light. Examples include chemical lasers, excimer and free-electron lasers, nuclear-bomb-powered x-ray lasers, neutral and charged-particle beams, and microwave weapons. DEWs can be either ground- or space-based, and their potential strategic missions include defense against or destruction of aircraft, missile warheads, and satellites.

EXOATMOSPHERIC REENTRY VEHICLE INTERCEPTOR SYSTEM (ERIS)   A U.S. long-range interceptor designed to attack warheads outside the atmosphere. ERIS is a candidate for use in a U.S. *Accidental Launch Protective System* (*ALPS*) and a near-term SDI deployment.

EXOTIC TECHNOLOGIES   Those technologies that are based on "other physical principles" (a phrase that comes from Agreed Statement D of the 1972 ABM Treaty) than those that underlie the operation of ABM interceptor missiles, their associated launchers, or ABM radar. Within the present technological context, exotic technologies include lasers, particle beams, electromagnetic rail-guns, and infrared sensors. The ABM Treaty, as "traditionally" interpreted, holds that the development and testing of exotic ABM systems and components are permitted only if such systems and components are fixed and land based. The Reagan administration's "broad" interpretation of the ABM Treaty (October 1985) permits the development and testing (but not deployment) of exotic ABM systems and components regardless of their basing mode.

FLAT TWIN AND PAWN SHOP   Soviet engagement and guidance radars that feature a modular construction that reportedly can be assembled and disassembled rapidly. In the future, such modular features would greatly reduce the lead time necessary for ABM deployment, thereby making early detection all the more important.

FOCAL-PLANE ARRAY   A collection of detectors in an optical sensor located in the plane where the light is focused.

FREE-ELECTRON LASER (FEL)   This device, which is part of SDI's *directed-energy weapon* technology program, incorporates a beam of very fast moving electrons bent by magnets to interact with an externally generated laser beam, greatly amplifying the emitted laser energy.

FULL OPERATIONAL CAPABILITY (FOC)   A term applied when an entire new weapon system has passed all tests and is ready for active combat, usually three to four years after production begins.

FULL-UP ABM TEST   A weapon in stable orbit intercepts a strategic ballistic missile in boost or postboost phase, permitting a test of a space-based ABM in what is clearly an ABM mode, and is therefore not permitted by the 1972 ABM Treaty.

GALOSH   The Soviet ABM system deployed near Moscow as allowed by the ABM Treaty. Construction of the Moscow system first began in the early 1960s. The Galosh missile (the interceptor used with the Moscow ABM system) was first displayed in 1964. The system was fully operational by the early 1970s. Currently the Soviets are modernizing the system as permitted by the ABM Treaty, and they plan to deploy Galosh SH-04 missiles with the capability to intercept incoming missiles outside the atmosphere.

GAZELLE HIGH-ACCELERATION MISSILES   Silo-based missiles designed to intercept incoming missiles at shorter ranges. These missiles are to be deployed by the Soviet Union as part of an extensive modernization program of its Moscow ABM system begun in 1978, as permitted by the ABM Treaty.

GEOSYNCHRONOUS EQUATORIAL ORBIT (GEO)   An orbit about 36,000 kilometers from the surface of the earth. In such an orbit, the speed of the satellite is the same as the speed of the earth's rotation so that the satellite remains fixed over one point on earth.

GIGAHERTZ   Unit of frequency measurement: one thousand million cycles per second.

GROUND SURVEILLANCE AND TRACKING SYSTEM (GSTS)   A ground-based rocket-launched LWIR sensor for tracking reentry vehicles and decoys starting in the midcourse phase of their ballistic trajectory. A possible component in a future ballistic missile defense system.

GROUND-BASED ABM SYSTEM   A system in which the rockets or lasers that actually intercept missiles or reentry vehicles are on the ground when the attack begins.

HEN HOUSE RADAR   Soviet early-warning and tracking, phased-array radars around the periphery of the Soviet Union. For a description of U.S. early-warning systems, see *Ballistic Missile Early Warning Systems* (*BMEWS*).

HIGH ENDOATMOSPHERIC DEFENSE INTERCEPTOR (HEDI)   Short-range interceptor designed to attack missiles in the upper reaches of the atmosphere. HEDI is a candidate for use in a U.S. *Accidental Launch Protection System* (*ALPS*) and a near-term SDI deployment.

HOMING SENSOR   Sensor carried aboard an interceptor missile for guidance in the missile's last phase of flight to the target.

''HOT'' INTERCEPTOR   Interceptor of exceptional acceleration and speed.

INFRARED (IR) SENSOR   Sensor that detects optical radiation with wavelengths between about 0.8 and 50 microns (one micron equals one millionth of a meter). Ballistic missiles can be readily detected during the boost phase when their hot rocket exhaust emits copious amounts of infrared energy. Warm reentry vehicles can be detected against the background of cold space in midcourse.

INITIAL OPERATIONAL CAPABILITY (IOC)   A term applied when the first weapon of a series is deployed and ready for use.

INTERCEPTOR   In the context of the ABM Treaty, an interceptor missile is deployed to counter strategic ballistic missiles or their elements in flight trajectory. In the context of antisatellite weapons, it is the term used for the warhead and maneuvering, and homing, apparatus.

INTERCEPTOR FLY-OUT   A term that refers to the portion of an interceptor missile's flight from launch to near interception. The interceptor fly-out capability is determined primarily by its boost acceleration and its burnout velocity. Short-range interceptions emphasize acceleration more than burnout velocity while longer-range interceptions stress burnout velocity over acceleration.

INTERCONTINENTAL BALLISTIC MISSILE (ICBM)   A fixed or mobile land-based rocket-propelled missile capable of delivering a warhead to intercontinental ranges (defined in SALT II as 5,500 kilometers or 3,000 nautical miles). An ICBM consists of a rocket booster, one or more reentry vehicles, RV-associated objects (decoys, chaff, and penetration aids), and in the case of MIRVed missiles, a *postboost vehicle* (*PBV*), or "bus."

INTERMEDIATE-NUCLEAR FORCES (INF) TREATY   Agreement signed between the United States and the Soviet Union in May 1988 that bans all land-based missiles with ranges between 500 and 5,500 kilometers. It is the first treaty signed by the two nations to date to eliminate an entire class of weapons and the first to make extensive use of on-site inspections as a means of verifying compliance with the Treaty.

JAMMER   A transmitter of radio waves designed to interfere with communications or other electromagnetic waves essential to the operation of an aircraft, missile, or sensor. See *Decoy* and *Penetration Aids*.

JOULE   A unit of energy in the metric system. A 60-watt electric bulb consumes 60 joules of energy every second.

KILOJOULE   One thousand joules.

KINETIC ENERGY WEAPON   A weapon that uses high-speed, aimed projectiles to destroy its target.

KRASNOYARSK   The site, in central Siberia, of a controversial Soviet phased-array radar. The United States first discovered the radar in 1983 and has maintained that it is in violation of the 1972 ABM Treaty because of its potential for ballistic missile detection and tracking and because of its location some 740 miles from the nearest Soviet border. As such the United States has demanded that the radar be torn down. According to Articles III and IV of the Treaty and the 1974 Protocol, ABM radars are permitted only at one agreed location. Article VI states that the radars must be deployed "along the periphery" of the national territory and "oriented outward." The Soviets have stated that the radar is for space-tracking and NTM, which, according to Agreed Statement F of the Treaty, are permissible exceptions. The Soviets have not resumed the radar's construction, which was halted in 1985, and most recently have offered to turn the radar over to the Soviet Academy of Sciences for use as an international space research center. Currently, the issue remains unresolved.

LADDER-DOWN TACTIC   An offensive countermeasure employed to mask the approach of oncoming reentry vehicles (RVs). A number of RVs are programmed to approach the target in rapid succession. The first RV is detonated outside the range of defense to produce a fireball that masks the approach of the next RVs so that they cannot be intercepted.

LIGHT AMPLIFICATION BY THE STIMULATION OF ELECTROMAGNETIC RADIATION (LASER)   A light source that produces a highly parallel, and therefore intense, beam of radiation of a single wavelength by a quantum mechanical process.

LIMITED TEST BAN TREATY (LTBT)   Treaty signed between the United States and the Soviet Union in 1963 that bans nuclear weapon tests in the atmosphere, in outer space, and under water.

LOFTED TEST   A test in which a weapon is lofted into space for a few minutes on a suborbital trajectory during which time the weapon attacks a ballistic missile or other target.

LONG-WAVELENGTH INFRARED RADAR (LWIR) BAND   Optical radiation with wavelengths between about 8 and 14 microns (one micron equals one millionth of a meter).

LOW-ALTITUDE DEFENSIVE SYSTEM (LoADS)   U.S. Army endoatmospheric defensive system designed in the late 1970s to protect MX missile silos. It was to be used with the *multiple protective shelters* (*MPS*) basing mode for the MX.

LOW EARTH ORBIT (LEO)   An orbit around the earth of altitude less than several hundred kilometers.

MEGAJOULES   One million joules.

MIDWAVELENGTH INFRARED (MWIR) BAND   Optical radiation with wavelengths between about 3 and 8 microns (1 micron equals one millionth of a meter).

MULTIPLE INDEPENDENTLY TARGETABLE REENTRY VEHICLE (MIRV)   Multiple reentry vehicles carried as part of the payload of a ballistic missile. Each warhead then can be directed to a separate target within a particular range. MIRVed missiles employ a warhead dispensing mechanism called a *postboost vehicle* (*PBV*) to target and release the warheads. The PBV maneuvers in space to achieve successive positions and velocities from which to release warheads in turn directed to specific targets.

MUTUALLY ASSURED DESTRUCTION (MAD)   A term that describes the strategic nuclear deterrent policy of the United States since about 1963. Theoretically, because both the United States and the Soviet Union know that each side possesses the capability to assure the other's complete destruction, both sides are deterred from launching a nuclear attack. The policy has often been criticized as immoral for its targeting of people rather than solely targeting military installations. The United States has stated that it has revised its policy options so that now more emphasis is placed on military and industrial targets. However, as many of these targets are located near heavily populated centers, the effect would appear to be the same.

NATIONAL TECHNICAL MEANS (NTM)   First made explicit in SALT I, NTM is the means used to monitor compliance with treaty provisions that are under the national control of individual signatories to an arms control agreement. NTM can include photo-reconnaissance satellites, aircraft-based systems (such as radars and optical systems), as well as sea- and ground-based systems (such as radars and antenna for collecting signals).

NIKE-X, NIKE-ZEUS, NIKE-AJAX, AND NIKE HERCULES   Early U.S. ballistic missile defensive systems developed by the Army in the 1950s and 1960s.

NUCLEAR RISK REDUCTION CENTER (NRRC) AGREEMENT   Agreement signed by U.S. Secretary of State George Shultz and Soviet Foreign Minister Eduard Schevardnadze in September 1987 that established centers in Washington, D.C., and Moscow to reduce the risk of nuclear war started by accident, miscalculation, or misunderstanding. The centers communicate by government-to-government exchange on fascimile machines similar to those used in the modernized hotline. The centers monitor compliance with the INF Treaty, serve as transmission points for notifications and information exchanges under the 1971 Accident Measures Agreement and the 1972 Incidents at Sea Agreement, and exchange prior notification of nuclear tests and ballistic-missile test launches.

ON-SITE INSPECTION (OSI)   The monitoring of compliance by using inspectors or sensors from one country to examine the other party's installations and/or activities. The INF Treaty was the first to make extensive use of OSI for verification purposes, in large measure due to the willingness of General Secretary Mikhail Gorbachev to cooperate in an area in which earlier Soviet leaders have refused.

ON-SITE INSPECTION AGENCY (OSIA)   Agency charged with the responsibility of conducting and coordinating OSI in the United States and the Soviet Union.

OPERATIONAL TEST AND EVALUATION (OT&E)   After a system is produced, it is subjected to OT&E, or intensive, personnel-conducted tests to make sure that the system performs as it should.

OPTICAL "CORNER REFLECTORS"   Small, reflective cubes that can be used to send light to "blind," or alter, a radar's reception.

OVER-THE-HORIZON RADAR-BACKSCATTER (OTH-B)   A radar capable of tracking air-breathing targets beyond the line-of-sight (over-the-horizon) because its high-frequency energy is reflected by the earth's ionosphere. Both the Soviet Union and United States deploy radars of this type.

PARTICLE ACCELERATOR   Sometimes called an "atom smasher," a particle accelerator generates intense beams of high-energy subatomic particles. See *Particle-Beam Weapon.*

PARTICLE-BEAM WEAPON (PBW)   Weapon that delivers intense beams of subatomic particles and damages its target by overheating it, detonating high explosives in it, melting the target's nuclear material, or injuring its electronics.

PATRIOT   See *SAM-D.*

PAVE PAW   Phased-array radars currently operational at four sites around the continental United States, primarily for early warning of submarine-launched ballistic missile attack.

PENETRATION AIDS (PENAIDS)   Devices employed by ICBMs, SLBMs, and penetrating bombers to neutralize defenses. Both missiles and bombers employ penaids such as decoys, chaff, and electronic countermeasures to mislead or confuse enemy radars.

PERIGEE   The point in an orbit nearest to the earth.

PHASED-ARRAY RADAR   A type of radar whose beams of energy are steered electronically rather than mechanically.

PIXELS   Common abbreviation for the *picture or resolution elements* that make up a digital image.

POSTBOOST VEHICLE (PBV)   Also called a *bus,* it is the final stage of a multiple reentry vehicle missile payload. The PBV, or bus, carries the reentry vehicles (warheads and perhaps decoys) and consists of a guidance package, fuel, and thrust devices. The thrusters enable the PBV to maneuver in space. As it maneuvers, the PBV sequentially launches the reentry vehicles toward different targets.

PUSHKINO   Large, four-sided Soviet radar constructed as part of the modernization of the Moscow ABM system.

REENTRY VEHICLE (RV)   The portion of a ballistic missile that carries the nuclear warhead. It is called an RV because it reenters the Earth's atmosphere in the terminal phase of the missile's flight.

RELABELING   A term that refers to the possibility that ABM technologies can be developed under the guise of serving a non-ABM function, such as ASAT and air defense.

SAFEGUARD   ABM program presented by President Richard Nixon in March 1969 to replace the earlier, and never completed, Sentinel system. Phase one of Safeguard was oriented toward a defense of ICBM sites and was to be followed by phase two, a territorial defense of twelve sites around the country. One Safeguard site was built at Grand Forks, North Dakota, but was later deactivated. Another site was to be located at Malmstrom Air Force Base in Montana but was abandoned before construction got under way.

SAM-D   U.S. antitactical ballistic missile under development during the negotiations of the ABM Treaty in the early 1970s that was designed to intercept short-range Soviet ballistic missiles. Now called *Patriot*. See *Antitactical Ballistic Missile (ATBM)*.

SEARCH AND ACQUISITION SENSOR   A sensor that maintains a constant watch over large regions of space to detect and to localize objects of interest. A search sensor may also provide precise tracking and identification information, or those functions may be performed by other sensors more appropriate to the mission. Sensors of this type, including BSTS, SSTS, and DSP, play the prominent role in ABM systems by performing a variety of essential functions from providing the first detection of an attack to determining the trajectories of ballistic missile boosters, reentry vehicles, and associated objects.

SEMISYNCHRONOUS   An orbit about 20,000 kilometers from the earth's surface in which satellites travel at twice the rotation rate of the earth.

SENTINEL   The first U.S. ABM system, proposed by President Lyndon Johnson in September 1967. It was conceived as a defense against a light attack by China and was to consist of fourteen ABM sites that would protect twenty-five cities around the country.

SENTRY   A traditional terminal defense system oriented toward low-altitude defense of ICBMs studied by the United States in the late 1970s and early 1980s.

SHORTWAVELENGTH INFRARED RADAR (SWIR) BAND   Optical radiation with wavelengths between 0.8 microns and 3.0 microns (a micron equals one millionth of a meter).

SHORT-RANGE ATTACK MISSILE (SRAM)   A rocket-propelled, nuclear-armed missile launched by a penetrating American bomber. It has a range of approximately 200 kilometers at "high altitude," a maximum speed typically around Mach 3.5, and is capable of flying a semi-ballistic trajectory after release from the bomber. The ABM Treaty does not constrain defenses against SRAMs, although questions of overlap with some short-range ballistic missiles are likely to increase with the SRAM-II now under development.

SHROUD   A loose metal covering to protect ballistic missiles from destruction by directed-energy weapons.

SL-X-17, ENERGIYA   Soviet heavy-lift launch vehicle that might be used to deploy a breakout ABM system.

SPACE SURVEILLANCE AND TRACKING SYSTEM (SSTS)   A system of sensor satellites designed to track space objects by their long-wavelength infrared emissions. In an ABM mode, such a satellite system would track reentry vehicles and decoys in the midcourse phase of their trajectory.

SPACE-BASED LASER RADAR (LADAR) A laser based in space, of lower power than a laser ABM weapon, that in principle can be used for detection, tracking, discrimination, and fire control. Its relatively narrow beam means that it is primarily useful for precision tracking and discrimination.

STANDING CONSULTATIVE COMMISSION (SCC) Consultative body established by the SALT I Treaty to address questions of compliance with the Treaty.

STERADIAN A unit for measuring cone size.

STRATEGIC ARMS LIMITATION TALKS (SALT) I First set of negotiations between the United States and Soviet Union to limit the number of strategic nuclear weapons. It produced two major agreements that were ratified by the United States in 1972, the ABM Treaty (a permanent agreement subject to five-year reviews by the United States and Soviet Union) and the Interim Agreement (of five-year duration) that limited offensive arms. See *Anti-Ballistic Missile (ABM) Treaty.*

STRATEGIC ARMS LIMITATION TALKS (SALT) II This Treaty, which was signed in 1979 and was to last through 1985, set limits on the number of U.S. and Soviet strategic offensive nuclear missiles, warheads, launchers, and delivery vehicles and constrained deployment of new strategic offensive arms for both sides. The SALT II agreement was signed by President James Carter and General Secretary Leonid Brezhnev in Vienna, Austria, on June 18, 1979, but was withdrawn by President Carter from Senate consideration. Although the Senate never ratified the Treaty, both the United States and the Soviet Union have adhered to most of its terms.

STRATEGIC ARMS REDUCTION TALKS (START) Bilateral negotiations between the United States and the Soviet Union seeking substantial reductions, as opposed to limitations, in the strategic arsenals of both sides. These talks, which superseded SALT, were initiated by President Ronald Reagan in May 1982. The treaty currently under discussion would limit countable strategic nuclear weapons to 6,000 and launchers to 1,600 per side, with a separate limit of 4,900 ballistic missile warheads, or an overall reduction of approximately one third. Currently the talks are stalled by several key obstacles including SLCM verification, SDI, and the Krasnoyarsk Radar.

STRATEGIC DEFENSE INITIATIVE (SDI) A U.S. research program begun in 1983 to determine if a countrywide population defense against strategic ballistic missiles using novel space-based components was possible.

STRATEGIC DEFENSE INITIATIVE ORGANIZATION (SDIO) The organization responsible for overseeing the Strategic Defense Initiative program initiated by the United States in March 1983.

SUBMARINE-LAUNCHED BALLISTIC MISSILE (SLBM) A ballistic missile carried by and launched from a submarine. U.S. SLBMs include *Poseidon* and *Trident.* Major Soviet SLBMs include the *SS-N-6, SS-N-8, SS-N-18, SS-N-20,* and the *SS-N-23.*

SURFACE-TO-AIR MISSILE (SAM) Ground- or ship-launched air defense missile with ranges up to hundreds of kilometers. See *Antitactical Ballistic Missile (ATBM).*

SUSPECT SITE INSPECTION (SSI) An inspection of a location in which activity banned by a treaty or other agreement is suspected. Such inspections are similar to those conducted at declared facilities.

TELEMETRY ENCRYPTION The process of encoding or scrambling the information a missile sends back to earth during test flight. The unratified SALT II Treaty forbids encryption that interferes with the monitoring of Treaty compliance by national technical means.

TERMINAL IMAGING RADAR (TIR)   Tracking radar currently being developed as part of the SDI system.

TERMINAL PHASE   The last phase of a ballistic missile's flight when reentry vehicles pass through the atmosphere.

TRAJECTORY   The path followed by a ballistic missile during its flight. It is conventionally divided into four phases: boost, postboost, midcourse, and terminal, or reentry.

ULTRAVIOLET EXCIMER LASER   A type of laser in which the material stimulated to produce laser light is made of molecules consisting of two atoms, such as xenon chloride and krypton fluoride, that typically emit ultraviolet radiation (wavelengths between about 1 and 300 billionths of a meter).

VERY-LONG-BASELINE INTERFEROMETRY (VLBI)   Telescope that yields high-resolution pictures of the universe. This technology presents no conflict with the ABM Treaty.

SUGGESTED READING

Books

Aspen Strategy Group. *On the Defensive? The Future of SDI*. Joseph S. Nye and James A. Schear, eds. Lanham, MD: University Press of America, 1988.

Carter, Ashton B. *Strategic Defense Testing and the ABM Treaty*. Scientific American, in press (April 1989).

———— and Schwartz, David N., eds. *Ballistic Missile Defense*. Washington, D.C.: The Brookings Institution, 1984.

Central Intelligence Agency. *Soviet Military Power*. Washington, D.C.: U.S. Government Printing Office, 1988.

Duffy, Gloria, ed. *Compliance and the Future of Arms Control*. Stanford University: Center for International Security and Arms Control, 1988.

Durch, William J. *The ABM Treaty and Western Security*. Cambridge, MA: Ballinger Publishing Co., 1988.

Garthoff, Raymond L. *Policy versus the Law: The Reinterpretation of the ABM Treaty*. Washington, D.C.: The Brookings Institution, 1987.

Graybeal, Sidney N. *SDI and the ABM Treaty*. Washington, D.C.: American Association for the Advancement of Science, 1986.

Kirk, Elizabeth J. *Technology, Security and Arms Control for the 1990s*. Washington, D.C.: American Association for the Advancement of Science, 1988.

Kozlova, Alla. "Debates on the Problems of Compliance with Treaties" in *Disarmament and Security 1987 Yearbook*, (English version). Moscow: Novosti Press Agency Publishing House, 1988.

Krepon, Michael and Umberger, Mary. *Verification and Compliance: A Problem-Solving Approach*. London: Macmillan Press, 1988.

Lin, Herbert. *New Weapons Technologies and the ABM Treaty*. McLean, VA: Pergamon-Brassey's, 1988.

Long, F.A.; Hafner, Donald; and Boutwell, Jeffrey A., eds. *Weapons in Space*. New York: Norton Publishing Co., 1986.

———— "Weapons in Space." *Daedulus*. Cambridge, MA: American Academy of Arts and Sciences, 1985.

Longstreth, Thomas K.; Pike, John E.; and Rhinelander, John B. *A Report on the Impact of U.S. and Soviet Ballistic Missile Defense Programs on the ABM Treaty*. Washington, D.C.: The National Campaign to Save the ABM Treaty, March 1985.

National Campaign to Save the ABM Treaty. *Briefing Book on the ABM Treaty and Related Issues*. Washington, D.C.: The National Campaign to Save the ABM Treaty, 1988.

Scribner, Richard A.; Ralson, Theodore J.; and Metz, William D. *The Verification Challenge: Problems and Promise of Strategic Nuclear Arms Control Verification.* Boston, MA: Birkhäuser, 1985.

Smith, Gerard. *Doubletalk.* New York: Doubleday and Co., 1980.

Stutzel, Walter; Asani, B.J.; and Cowen, R., eds. *The ABM Treaty: To Defend or Not to Defend?* Oxford University Press: SIPRI, 1987.

U.S. Congress, Office of Technology Assessment. *Anti-Satellite Weapons, Countermeasures and Arms Control.* Washington, D.C. U.S. Government Printing Office, September 1985.

————. *Ballistic Missile Defense Technologies.* Washington, D.C.: U.S. Government Printing Office, September 1985.

————. *Directed Energy Missile Defense in Space—A Background Paper.* Washington, D.C.: U.S. Government Printing Office, April 1984.

————. *SDI Technology Survivability and Software.* Washington, D.C.: U.S. Government Printing Office, May 1988.

House, U.S. Foreign Affairs Committee. Hearings before the Subcommittee on Arms Control, International Security, and Science on the Interpretation of the ABM Treaty. 99th Cong., 1st sess., 1985.

Velikhov, Y.; Sagdeev, R.; and Kokoshin, A., eds. *Weapons in Space: The Dilemma of Security.* Moscow: Mir Publishers, 1986.

Warner III, Edward L. and Ochmanek, David A. *Next Moves: An Arms Control Agenda for the 1990s.* New York: Council on Foreign Relations, 1989.

Wilrich, Mason and Rhinelander, John B., eds. *SALT: The Moscow Agreements and Beyond.* New York: The Free Press, 1974.

Articles

Brown, Harold. "Is SDI Technologically Feasible?" *Foreign Affairs* 64, no. 3 (Winter 1985).

Bunn, Matthew. "ABM Treaty Compliance: Star Wars Tests on Shaky Ground." *Arms Control Today* 18, no. 3 (April 1988).

Chayes, Abram and Chayes, Antonia H. "Testing and Development of Exotic Systems under the ABM Treaty The Great Reinterpretation Caper." *Harvard Law Review* 99 (1986): 1956.

Earle II, Ralphe and Rhinelander, John B. "The Krasnoyarsk Radar: A 'Material Breach'?" *Arms Control Today* 18, no. 7 (September 1988).

"Report to the American Physical Society of the Study Group on Science and Technology of Directed Energy Weapons." *Reviews of Modern Physics.* 59, no. 3, pt. 11 (July 1987).

Weinberger, C. W. "Why the ABM Treaty Should be Scrapped." *Wall Street Journal,* editorial page, October 12, 1988, and reply by Gerard C. Smith of November 29, 1988.

Trimble, Phillip. "Beyond Verification: The Next Steps in Arms Control." *Harvard Law Review* 102 (1989): 885.

ABOUT THE EDITORS
AND CONTRIBUTORS

ANTONIA HANDLER CHAYES   is currently Chairman of the Board of Endispute, Inc. During the Carter administration, she served first as Assistant Secretary of the Air Force for Manpower, Reserve Affairs, and Installations and later as Under Secretary of the Air Force where she provided overall program and budgetary supervision with special oversight responsibility for selected programs such as MX missile development, base closures, the Israeli air bases, and international base rights. Ms. Chayes graduated from Radcliffe College, attended Yale Law School, and received her J.D. from George Washington University. She is the author of numerous articles and papers on U.S. national security issues and coauthor of *Testing and Development of "Exotic" Systems under the ABM Treaty: The Great Reinterpretation Caper*. She teaches at the Georgetown University School of Law and at Harvard University's John F. Kennedy School of Government and is on the board of the United Technologies Corporation. Ms. Chayes is a member of the Council on Foreign Relations and the Aspen Strategy Group.

PAUL DOTY   is professor of public policy at Harvard. After four decades in the departments of chemistry and biochemistry, Doty founded and directed Harvard's Center for Science and International Affairs. His research now lies mostly in the area of conventional arms control. He has also served on the President's Scientific Advisory Committee, the General Advisory Committee on Arms Control, and other advisory assignments in the U.S. government. He has organized and lead many Soviet-American and European-American conferences on security policy and arms control such as the Dartmouth Conference, the Committee on International Security and Arms Control of the National Academy of Sciences, and Aspen Strategy Group. Doty is coauthor of *Living with Nuclear Weapons*, founder of the journal *International Security*, and chairman of the Committee on International Security Studies of the American Academy of Arts and Sciences.

ALBERT CARNESALE   is Lucius N. Littauer Professor of public policy and administration and academic dean at Harvard's John F. Kennedy School of Government. His teaching and research focus on American foreign policy and international security with emphasis on policies and issues associated with nuclear weapons. He holds a Ph.D. in nuclear engineering, served on the U.S. delegation to SALT I, is a consultant to several government agencies, and testifies often before congressional committees. Widely published, Carnesale is coauthor and coeditor of *Fateful Visions: Avoiding Nuclear Catastrophe, Superpower Arms Control: Setting the Record Straight, Hawks, Doves, and Owls: An Agenda for Avoiding Nuclear War*, and *Living with Nuclear Weapons*.

ASHTON B. CARTER   is professor of public policy at Harvard's John F. Kennedy School of Government, where he is also Acting Director of the Center for Science and International Affairs and is affiliated with the program on science, technology, and public policy. He received a B.A. in physics from Yale and a Ph.D. in theoretical physics from Oxford, where he was a Rhodes Scholar. He has done theoretical physics research at Rockefeller University and worked at the congressional Office of Technology Assessment (OTA), the Office of the Secretary of Defense, and Massachusetts Institute of Technology. In the Pentagon's systems analysis branch, his responsibilities included command, control, communications, and intelligence; ballistic missile defense; MX missile basing; and various space activities. In addition to his scientific publications and government studies, he coedited and coauthored *Ballistic Missile Defense* and *Managing Nuclear Operations* for the Brookings Institution and wrote OTA's *Directed Energy Missile Defense in Space.* Carter is a member of the Council on Foreign Relations, the American Physical Society, the International Institute for Strategic Studies, and the American Association for the Advancement of Science.

ABRAM CHAYES   is Felix Frankfurter Professor of Law at the Harvard Law School, where he teaches international law. During the Kennedy administration, he served as The Legal Adviser to the Department of State. From 1978 to 1980, he was Chairman of the IAEA International Fuel Cycle Evaluation. In 1969 he coedited *ABM: An Evaluation of the Decision to Deploy an Anti-Ballistic Missile System,* one of the first in-depth studies of ballistic missile defense. He has written extensively on arms control and on the ABM Treaty, frequently with his wife Antonia Handler Chayes. He is a member of the American Academy of Arts and Sciences, a director of the World Peace Foundation, and Vice President of the Albert Einstein Peace Prize Foundation.

RALPH EARLE II,   a graduate of Harvard College and Harvard Law School, is currently practicing law in Washington, D.C., and is the Chairman of the National Board of Advisors for the Lawyers Alliance for Nuclear Arms Control. From 1980 to 1981, Ambassador Earle was Director of the U.S. Arms Control and Disarmament Agency (ACDA). From 1973 to 1980, he was involved in the SALT II Treaty negotiations, first as ACDA representative and later (1978–1980) as chief negotiator. He also served as a consultant on SALT to the U.S. Secretary of Defense, the Defense Adviser at the U.S. Mission to NATO, and the Principal Deputy Assistant Secretary of Defense for International Security Affairs. He is the author of numerous articles on U.S.-Soviet relations and U.S. national security policy and travels regularly to speak to universities and civic groups. Ambassador Earle is a member of the Council on Foreign Relations, the International Institute for Strategic Studies, the American Law Institute, and the Council of American Ambassadors.

BARRY E. FRIDLING   is a member of the research staff of the Science and Technology Division, Institute for Defense Analyses, where he works on signal and information processing, ballistic missile defense, and antisubmarine warfare. He has held the positions of Social Science Research-Council MacArthur Foundation Fellow in International Peace and Security, research fellow in the Center for Science and International Affairs at the John F. Kennedy School of Government, Harvard University, and guest arms control intern at Lawrence Livermore National Laboratory. Dr. Fridling received a Ph.D. in theoretical physics from Brown University where he worked on quantum field theory and strings.

RICHARD L. GARWIN is IBM Fellow and science adviser to the director of research of IBM. An experimental physicist who has worked in particle physics, condensed matter physics, and on the detection of gravitational radiation, he is also a practitioner of technology with 35 U.S. patents on inventions dealing with computers, communications, energy storage, and transmission. At IBM, he has been the Director of applied research and a member of the Corporate Technical Committee. Distinct from his work at IBM, since 1950 Garwin has been a consultant to the U.S. government and its contractors in nuclear weapons, military technology and arms control. He was a member of the President's Science Advisory Committee under Presidents Kennedy, Johnson, and Nixon and a member of the Defense Science Board. Garwin is a member of many societies including the National Academy of Engineering, National Academy of Sciences, and a Senior Member of the Institute for Electrical and Electronics Engineers (IEEE).

SHERRI WASSERMAN GOODMAN is a professional staff member with the Senate Armed Services Committee. She is a member of the Massachusetts bar, has served as a consultant to the Rand Corporation, and has worked for Science Applications, Inc. She received her J.D. cum laude from the Harvard Law School, a master's in public policy from Harvard's John F. Kennedy School of Government, and her B.A. summa cum laude from Amherst College. Her publications include *The Neutron Bomb Controversy: A Study in Alliance Politics* and "Legal Dilemmas in the Weapons Acquisition Process: The Role of Contract in the Procurement of the SSN-688 Attack Submarine" in the *Yale Law and Policy Review*. She is a term member of the Council on Foreign Relations and a member of the International Institute for Strategic Studies (IISS).

SIDNEY N. GRAYBEAL, Senior Vice President for Policy and Planning at System Planning Corporation, has had a career in U.S. governmental service spanning twenty-nine years. Between 1976 and 1979, he was Director of the Office of Strategic Research of the Central Intelligence Agency. He also served in CIA between 1950 and 1964, starting as a guided-missile intelligence analyst and becoming chief of the Guided Missile and Space Division. During his twelve years in the Arms Control and Disarmament Agency, he served as Alternate Executive Officer of the U.S. SALT Delegation throughout SALT I, was appointed a delegate to SALT II, and then served as the first U.S. Commissioner of the Standing Consultative Commission, the body responsible for implementing the SALT I agreements. He has also received the President's Award for Distinguished Federal Civilian Service. Mr. Graybeal, who received his baccalaureate and master's degrees from the University of Maryland, has written and spoken about arms control, intelligence, verification, and other policy issues in various fora.

THEODORE JARVIS, JR. is Director for strategic studies for the MITRE Corporation. From 1975 to 1985, he was responsible for MITRE's planning of the Air Force portion of the World Wide Military Command and Control System (WWMCCS). Earlier projects involved command and control systems for Air Force and Navy strategic forces with emphasis on the support of strategic force operations in a nuclear environment. In the WWMCCS area, he was involved in the development of command and control for MX, GLCM, and the small ICBM; improvement of attack warning and assessment; and application of rule-based systems to the strategic planning process. Among other recent activities, he was responsible for the Battle Management and Command, Control, and Communications part of the Pilot Architecture Study, which aimed at producing an early

270 About the Editors & Contributors

standard architecture for the Strategic Defense Initiative. Jarvis earned his bachelor's and master's degrees in physics from Columbia University.

THOMAS H. JOHNSON is professor of applied physics and Director of the Science Research Laboratory at the U.S. Military Academy at West Point. He has published research in computational fluid dynamics, plasma physics, and laser physics and has worked in various aspects of ABM research since 1966. Dr. Johnson has served in the Air Force Weapons Laboratory, Lawrence Livermore National Laboratory, and the Defense Nuclear Agency. He was also special assistant to the Undersecretary of Energy and later to the Science Adviser to the President. He was a member of the American Physical Society Study of Directed Energy Weapons. His poems and essays have appeared in *The New Republic, Harvard, The American Scholar, The Southern Review, Foreign Affairs,* and many other journals.

GENERAL ROBERT T. MARSH retired from the U.S. Air Force in 1984. He enlisted in the Army Air Corp in 1943 and graduated from the U.S. Military Academy in 1949 and the University of Michigan (MS Aero Eng & MS Inst Eng) in 1956. His military assignments were mostly in the fields of research, development, and acquisition and culminated in command of the Electronic System Division and later of the Air Force Systems Command. Currently a consultant, Gen. Marsh serves as a trustee of the MITRE Corporation and on the Boards of Visitors of the Carnegie-Mellon Software Engineering Institute and the Air Force Institute of Technology.

PATRICIA BLISS MCFATE, Senior Scientist at System Planning Corporation, has served as President of The American-Scandinavian Foundation, Deputy Chairman of the National Endowment for the Humanities, Vice Provost of the University of Pennsylvania, and professor in the School of Engineering and Applied Science at the University of Pennsylvania. She is a Fellow of the New York Academy of Science and a member of the AAAS Committee on Science, Arms Control, and National Security. She received her baccalaureate degree from Michigan State University, her master's and doctorate degrees from Northwestern University; she has taken her post-graduate training from the University of Illinois and Columbia University. She has written extensively in the fields of international studies, science policy, and verification and compliance issues.

JOHN E. PIKE is Associate Director for Space Policy at the Federation of American Scientists in Washington, D.C.

JOHN B. RHINELANDER is a partner in the Washington, D.C., law firm of Shaw, Pittman, Potts & Trowbridge, a member of the Board of Directors of the Arms Control Association, and a lecturer at the University of Virginia Law School on nuclear weapons and arms control. He served as deputy legal adviser in the Department of State from 1969 to 1971 and a legal adviser to the U.S. SALT I delegation when the ABM Treaty was negotiated. He previously was a law clerk to Justice John M. Harlan, served as special assistant to the Secretary of the Navy, and chief counsel and deputy director of the Office of Foreign Direct investments. He subsequently served as general counsel of HEW and under secretary of HUD. He is the coeditor of *SALT—The Moscow Agreements and Beyond* and the author of a chapter on arms control in the nuclear age in a casebook on *Law and National Security* (forthcoming 1989). He is a member of the Council on

Foreign Relations, the International Institute for Strategic Studies (IISS), and the Hudson Institute. He is a graduate of Yale and the University of Virginia Law School.

JOHN C. TOOMAY is a consultant for government and industry and Vice Chairman of the Board of Toomay-Mathis Associates. Mr. Toomay retired from the U.S. Air Force in 1979 as a major general. Most of his military career was spent in research, development, and engineering. His responsibilities included numerous ground-based radar programs and the technology program for advanced ballistic reentry systems. Since retirement, Mr. Toomay has participated in numerous DOD studies, including the Defense Systems Technologies (''Star Wars'') Study, of which he was a Deputy Director. He is currently a member of the Air Force Scientific Advisory Board and the Defense Nuclear Agency Scientific Advisory Group on Effects. Mr. Toomay has a bachelor's degree in electrical engineering and a master's of science degree in business administration. He is the author of a book on radar and a number of other papers and articles. He is a member of Tau Beta Pi, the Air Force Association, the American Institute of Aeronautics and Astronautics (AIAA), the Association of the U.S. Army, the U.S. Naval Institute, and a senior member of the Institute for Electrical and Electronics Engineers (IEEE).

INDEX

ABM. *See under* Antiballistic missile

ABMT. *See* Anti-Ballistic Missile Treaty

Accidental Launch Protection System (ALPS), 38, 39, 55, 117–118, 137

Accident Measures Agreement, 191

ACDA. *See* Arms Control and Disarmament Agency

Active optics, 120

Active sensors, 157, 158, 162–163, 171

Adjunct
    Airborne Optical, 56, 89, 161, 168, 224
    definition of, 46, 56
    LADAR as an, 100

Advanced Launch System, 144

Aerosol clouds, 157

Afghanistan, 31

Agnew, Spiro, 29

Agreed orbital test range (AOTR), 13, 193
    activities on the, 149–150
    activities outside the, 150
    location and scope of the, 148

Air-based systems
    prohibitions of, 47
    testing and development of, 3

Airborne Optical Adjunct (AOA), 56, 89, 161, 168, 224

Air defense
    ABM capability of deployed, 84–85, 222–223
    breakout and, 85–86
    current and future technologies, 82
    detection, tracking, and interception of RVs, 83–84, 108nn.3, 5
    effects of R&D on buffer time, 85–86
    SCC and testing of, 207
    space-based infrared sensors and, 82, 85–86

test, 136

Air-launched cruise missiles (ALCMs), 184, 185

ALPS. *See* Accidental Launch Protection System

American Physical Society, 32, 95, 121, 160, 161, 162

Angola, 31

Antiballistic missile (ABM)
    funding by Congress for Safeguard, 30
    funding by Congress for Sentinel, 28–29

Antiballistic missile capability
    air defense and, 84–85, 222–223
    ASAT and, 90–94, 188, 222–223
    ATBM and, 87, 188, 222–223
    DSAT and, 90, 94–95, 222–223
    interceptor missiles and, 90–91, 222–223
    mirror relays and, 139–141, 152n.12
    SBIs and, 20, 138–139, 152nn.4, 8
    SBLs and, 139–141, 152n.12
    sensors and, 155, 165–166
    SLBMs and, 21
    space-based weapons and, 227

Antiballistic missile system
    definition of, 45
    transfer of, 50
    when do non-ABM systems acquire capabilities of, 60–62

Anti-Ballistic Missile Treaty (ABMT)
    ambiguities in, 53, 146–150, 222
    background of, 2–3
    compliance and, 9
    counting rules used for, 199–200
    defensive concepts versus offensive deployments, 24–25
    draftsmanship and dispute settlement, 199–201, 215n.8

273